# Economics and Institutions

*A Manifesto for a Modern
Institutional Economics*

GEOFFREY M. HODGSON

Polity Press

First published 1988 by Polity Press
in association with Basil Blackwell
Reprinted 1989
Editorial Office:
Polity Press, Dales Brewery, Gwydir Street, Cambridge CB1 2LJ, UK
Basil Blackwell Ltd, 108 Cowley Road, Oxford OX4 1JF, UK

**British Library Cataloguing in Publication Data**

Hodgson, Geoffrey M.
    Economics and institutions : a manifesto
for a modern institutional economics.
1. Social institutions — Economic aspects
I. Title
306      HM131
ISBN 0-7456-0276-2

Typeset by Opus, Oxford
Printed in Great Britain by Billing & Sons Ltd Worcester

# Contents

*Preface*                                                              ix
*Acknowledgements*                                                     xvii

### PART ONE – PRELUDE                                                  1

1  *Introduction and Outline*                                      3
  1.1  The trajectory of critical development            4
    The current theoretical background              4
    Problems of information                         5
  1.2  Some observations                                 7
    Subjectivism and institutionalism               7
    Process and system                              8
    Determinism, purposefulness and choice          10
  1.3  A systems view                                    12
    The endogeneity of preferences and technology   13
    The systems view briefly explored               18
    Economics and the systems view                  19
  1.4  Scope and outline                                 21
    The fate of institutional economics             21
    Outline of this work                            24

2  *On Methodology and Assumptions*                                27
  2.1  The methodological defence of neoclassical theory 28
    Friedman's methodology                          29
    The methodology in practice                     30
    Criticisms of Friedman                          32
    The instrumentalist interpretation              33
  2.2  Empiricism and beyond                             35
    A critique of positivism and empiricism         35
    The falsificationism of Sir Karl Popper         37

# Contents

A critique of Popper's methodology      39

2.3 The fate of methodology      42

Prediction and other obsessions      42

The limits of prescriptive methodology      43

The remaining scope for appraisal      44

The residual function of evidence      47

2.4 Appendix: Friedman and the maximization hypothesis      48

PART TWO – A FAREWELL TO 'ECONOMIC MAN'      51

3 *Behind Methodological Individualism*      53

3.1 What is methodological individualism?      55

Debating methodological individualism      55

Purposeful human action      56

Causality and purpose      59

Psychological explanations of purpose      60

3.2 Critique and implications      62

Spontaneity and absentee explanation      63

The problem of infinite regress      64

Wholes and parts      66

Concluding remarks      71

4 *The Maximization Hypothesis*      73

4.1 The utility of criticizing the maximization hypothesis      74

Revealed preference and beyond      74

The 'evolutionary' argument      76

Other theoretical critiques of maximization      78

Empirical critiques of maximization      83

Evaluations of the criticisms      86

4.2 Problems with the means–ends framework      93

Ends and means      93

Adaptive ends      95

5 *The Rationalist Conception of Action*      98

5.1 Initial criticisms      101

Early critiques      101

Reason and discourse      102

A possible rationalist response      103

5.2 Cognition and the hierarchy of mind      106

Unconscious processes      106

Cognitive theory      107

Multiple levels of consciousness      109

Too little information and too much      111

# Contents

| | | |
|---|---|---|
| 5.3 | Concluding remarks | 114 |
| | The rationalist dilemma | 114 |
| | Conclusion | 115 |

**6** *Action and Institutions* 117
6.1 The impact of cognitive theory 118
Cognition, culture and society 118
Cognitive theory and subjectivism 121
6.2 The significance of institutions 123
Action and institutions 123
Habits 124
Routinization and institutions 130
Routines, institutions and information 131
Orthodoxy and institutions 134
Game theory and institutions 134
Spontaneous order 137
6.3 Some conclusions 138
The potential for cumulative instability 138
The evolutionary character of institutional economics 140

## PART THREE – ELEMENTS OF AN INSTITUTIONAL ECONOMICS 145

**7** *Contracts and Property Rights* 147
7.1 The concepts of exchange and property 148
Defining exchange 148
Exchange and institutions 149
Individualistic conceptions of property and law 151
Williamson's treatment of exchange 154
7.2 Critique of the utilitarian calculus 156
Durkheim and the impossibility of pure contract 157
Some special cases of impure contract 160
The centrality of impure contract 162
General remarks on trust 166
7.3 The impurity principle and the fate of capitalism 167
Impurity and Cartesian thinking 168
Contractual impurities: Schumpeter and Marx 169

**8** *Markets as Institutions* 172
8.1 Defining the market 172
The elusive definition 172
Markets and institutions 173
Types of market institution 176

## Contents

Markets and exchange — 177
Some immediate theoretical consequences — 177
8.2 Why do markets exist? — 179
Transaction costs — 180
On the limits to the growth of the market — 181
8.3 Markets, prices and norms — 182
The establishment of norms — 184
The classical tradition — 186
8.4 The impossibility of perfect competition — 187
The function of conventions — 188
The game-theoretic analysis of markets — 191

9 *Firms and Markets* — 195
9.1 Neoclassical perspectives on the firm — 196
Alchian and Demsetz: the firm as a market — 196
Why do firms exist? — 199
Transaction costs and lack of information — 201
9.2 Notes towards an alternative perspective — 203
Uncertainty and transaction costs — 203
Uncertainty, institutions and the firm — 205
The comparative efficiency of the firm — 208
Innovation and transaction costs — 212
Efficiency, technology and power — 213

10 *Expectations and the Limits to Keynes* — 217
10.1 Expectations in the *General Theory* — 218
Long-term expectations — 218
Keynes' policy conclusions — 220
10.2 Some limitations of the theory — 221
The expecting agent — 222
Firms and financiers — 223
Keynes' rationalist conception of action — 226
Government action — 228
10.3 Austrian and rational expectations alternatives — 230
The endogeneity of expectations — 230
The rational expectations hypothesis — 231
The Austrian theory of expectations — 236
10.4 Lessons for post-Keynesian economics — 239
The imperfectionist interpretation — 240
Conclusion — 241

11 *Direction and Policy Implications* — 242
11.1 Needs and welfare — 243

## Contents

|  |  |  |
|---|---|---|
|  | A road to serfdom? | 243 |
|  | Needs and economic analysis | 245 |
|  | Theories of needs | 247 |
| 11.2 | Systems, impurity and dominance | 252 |
|  | Economic systems as diversified pluralities | 254 |
|  | The principles of impurity and dominance | 256 |
|  | Cybernetics and the impurity principle | 257 |
|  | Illustrations of the impurity principle | 258 |
|  | Extending the impurity principle | 261 |
| 11.3 | Guidelines for economic organization | 262 |
|  | The firm as a system | 262 |
|  | The conditions for innovation | 267 |
|  | Institutional intervention | 269 |

| | |
|---|---|
| *Notes* | 275 |
| *Bibliography* | 306 |
| *Index of Names* | 347 |
| *Index of Subjects* | 356 |

*To Meghnad Desai, Edward Nell and Ian Steedman*
*in gratitude and appreciation*

# Preface

Despite an explosion of publishing activity since the Second World War, economic theory remains in a sorry state. The principal indictment against it is the failure of mainstream theory to provide convincing explanations of many economic phenomena, and to generate policy prescriptions which manifestly can solve outstanding economic problems.

Consider, for example, the theoretical explanation of the relative decline of the British economy. There is little consensus on this issue and many accounts are simply unconvincing. One of the most prominent explanations at present is that the level of wage settlements has exceeded the rate of growth of productivity, leading to excessive costs and a poor competitive position in the world economy.

However, this theory has to be buttressed with further explanations as to why supposedly rational workers would disregard their own long-term interests in a healthy economy and keep their wages 'too high'. Is this in turn due the 'coercive' unions, or to 'rigidities' in the labour market, or 'high' unemployment benefit? Notably, these additional explanations are either unsubstantiated or, if they are, the phenomena involved are often not peculiar to Britain. Thus these auxiliary hypotheses remain controversial and generally unconvincing as part of an explanation of Britain's relative decline.

Orthodox theory is equally at a loss to give a convincing explanation of the remarkable dynamism of the West German or Japanese economies, or the stagnation of productivity growth after reaching a high absolute level in the USA. Notably, all these countries have higher average wage levels than Britain, and this again questions the common presumption that wages are at the root of the problem. As to alternative explanations within orthodoxy the picture is discouraging. For instance, the coeditors of the influential *Brookings Papers in Economic Activity*, when addressing the issue of the stagnation in US productivity growth, concluded: 'Despite numerous studies of the slowdown its causes have remained largely a mystery. In the most comprehensive study to date, Edward Denison examined 17 alternative hypotheses and concluded that alone or in combination they could explain no more than a fraction of the slowdown' (Brainard and Perry, 1981, p. vii). This negligible success in explaining a basic problem, in the common postwar heartland of both world capitalism and economic orthodoxy, is a sad reflection on the subject as a whole.

Incidentally, when faced with theoretical problems such as this, orthodoxy immediately looks at explanations on the market side of the problem, concerning wages and costs, and often ignores the organization of production and the skills and practices of work. If, however, we take a different view then it can be seen that if the organization of production was improved to lead to higher productivity then higher output and higher wages could be compatible. On this basis it could be argued that there is a positive rather than a negative correlation between wages and output. In contrast, orthodoxy persists in its one-sided view and assumes that the firm is a black box which responds directly to changes in costs and the pressures of the market. Orthodoxy is not only unconvincing, it is blinkered as well.[1]

Inspecting the academic journals we are confronted with a great volume of complex formal theorizing and econometric technique. Yet the policies that economists have managed to derive from their theoretical armoury are typically simplistic and dominated above all by the political ideology that has been prevalent in the past. Either wittingly or unwittingly, this is adopted by most economists at the outset. Despite the high degree of formal sophistication, the ideological cart is often still in front of the theoretical horse.

For example, in the debates over public *versus* private ownership and planning *versus* markets, the economic theory usually serves as little more than a thin packaging for a very conventional ideological position of the Left, Centre or Right. The theoretical packaging serves largely to provide a covering of legitimacy, and as an enticement for the influential consumer of the economic advice. Politicians in or out of power are thus able to reinforce their prejudices and cloak them in some academic garb.

Economists can never free themselves entirely from ideology, nor indeed is it desirable that they should attempt to do so. But it is not a satisfactory states of affairs where science is dragged along by the political fashion of the moment; and it is even less acceptable when the ideologies are so crude and well worn. Many such ideologies have already been criticized with destructive effect on their central ideas, but these criticisms are happily ignored by many within the profession.

Alongside the crudely ideological employment of economic theory there is a continuing tendency to devote insufficient academic resources to the development of new solutions to obvious economic problems, despite the failure of the preceding economic policies to succeed. Thus, for example, unemployment is still alarmingly high in many Western countries, poverty still remains significant even in advanced industrial nations such as Britain and the US and relentless blows of famine strike the underdeveloped world. Yet these problems are not the main preoccupations of the majority of economists.

In contrast, mainstream economic theory often serves mainly as an aesthetic game for the theorist, with the prize of academic advancement for those who become adept in developing its skills and who can produce articles for the journals in their frequently stultifying format and style. A piece of work has a greater chance of publication and of becoming 'reputable' if it is infused with mathematical formalism and obscurantist terminology than if it directly and openly addresses the urgent problems of the day.

As an example, consider the following unwitting self-condemnation from Paul Samuelson (1962, p. 1), Nobel Prizewinner in economics and undoubtedly one of the foremost theorists of the postwar period:

> My own scholarship has covered . . . questions like welfare economics and factor–price equalization; turnpike theorems and osculating envelopes; non-substitutability relations in Minkowski–Ricardo–Leontief–Metzler matrices of the Mosak–Hicks type; or balanced budget multipliers under conditions of balanced uncertainty in locally impacted topological spaces and molar equivalences.

This, it appears, is the apogee of formalism for economic science. At the lower levels, students are initiated into this formalism in progressive but somewhat repetitive stages. The whole process has the aura of a protracted initiation ceremony, where future priests overcome their inclination to get involved in the grubby complexities of the outside world. As Neil Kay (1984, p. 188) puts it: 'the individual intent on pursuing a career as economist has to be bright enough to understand the abstract ramifications of neoclassical theory and dumb enough to have faith in them.'

Whilst some have been content with the theoretical ivory tower, others have been all too keen to use their economic theory as a weapon in an ideological crusade. For instance, with the ascendancy of the New Right in 1970s and 1980s, economic theory, even or especially of the most abstract kind, has frequently been employed as an academic legitimization for cuts in public expenditure and for an extension of private ownership and market competition.

It is a savage irony of our times that research into theoretical economics has become one of the many victims of this rightist creed. These ideas would not as easily have become implanted in high public places if they had not been backed by the 'pure theory' of researching economists: those from Adam Smith to Milton Friedman who have proposed a widespread extension of market relations and private enterprise, and urged a minimization of public funding upon which research is partially dependent. New Right thinking has been furthered considerably by the work of many others in publicly funded academic institutions. It has thus begun to saw off the very bough upon which it sits. In this manner, it could be said, such ideas represent a kind of professional suicide.

This is especially the case with the rational expectations hypothesis where it is actually assumed that everyone is basically aware of the underlying economic model. By implication, according to this theory, the economist has little else to offer because everyone is assumed to know in outline how the economy works. Yet economists have been all too eager to rush over this particular cliff, and a few uncritical and esoteric publications on the rational expectations model are currently the best ticket for promotion to an economics chair. Of course, every economist has a right to his or her beliefs (especially if these coincide with the chosen line of research) but there is no such right to carry millions of non-economists into the mire of poverty and destitution as a consequence of ideas which are formally 'interesting' but practically disastrous when applied to policy. The state of economic theory today would be farcical if it were not so tragic.

This state of affairs will not change quickly or easily, nor by the further scribblings of economic theorists alone. But nevertheless there is a duty for all economists to survey the imperfect state of their discipline, stand back for a while from the academic game, and address some of the core theoretical problems which are normally, and conveniently, ignored.

Answers to these problems are not easy to find, and this book does not claim to provide them. It is, however, an attempt to examine the fundamental assumptions of economic theory with a view to making a contribution to the construction of an alternative. A central argument is that conventional theory is guided by an outdated and theoretically unacceptable view of the individual which has been inherited from the classic liberalism of the nineteenth century.

A major theme of this book is the influence of institutions, social practices and history on our ideas, perceptions and actions. It would be inconsistent, therefore, to suggest that this or any other work is entirely original. It is necessary to acknowledge the effect of those very social and cultural forces in the process of its creation.

The reader will be able to trace the influence of several schools of economic thought on the present work. The first is the Post–Keynesian, including such figures as Joan Robinson and George Shackle, and particularly the works of John Maynard Keynes himself. The second is the Institutionalist School, overshadowed by Thorstein Veblen but including other more neglected figures such as Karl Polanyi. The third is the work of Marx, who, despite the efforts of Joan Robinson and others, is still vastly underrated as an economist.

There are also additional important influences, such as the Behaviouralist School, led by Herbert Simon, and an assortment of maverick figures, such as Frank Knight and Joseph Schumpeter. Whilst differences with the theory and policy standpoints of these economists remain, their effect on the ideas presented here should not be denied. This book is unashamedly eclectic in its attempt to incorporate valuable ideas that have been offered by other theorists, including both criticisms of neoclassical theory and elements of a constructive alternative.

There is a second reason why it would be a mistake to judge the present work on the grounds of originality. Whilst its central arguments are a marked departure from orthodoxy in economic theory, it draws on a variety of theoretical traditions elsewhere, namely within sociology, political science, anthropology, psychology and philosophy. On several key points there amounts to a consensus or near-consensus within these alternative disciplines, and notably this is often markedly dissonant from mainstream economic theory.

For example, apart from a few exceptions, the international consensus view within sociology, anthropology, political science and psychology seems to be that agents are not 'rational' in the way that neoclassical economists presume. The orthodox 'economic' canons of rationality are thus widely rejected elsewhere.

A great number of economists, however, remain cheerfully blinkered about their subject. The compartmentalization of the social sciences is reinforced by an attitude where economists can claim that they can have disregard for the contributions of other social sciences to the understanding of economic phenomena. An interview with Robert Hall of the Hoover Institute in the *Wall Street Journal* captured this insular outlook with the observation that the interviewee 'reflects the attitudes of his colleagues in saying he stops reading whenever he sees the word "sociological" in an economics paper'.[2]

One thrust of the argument in the book is not to claim a 'new' refutation of the assumptions of orthodox economics, but to show the poverty of its theoretical presumptions when compared with relevant work elsewhere. This gambit is not as simple as it may seem at first sight, partly because it is impossible to survey the entire field of social science, and partly because there is still fierce controversy within these other disciplines, despite the consensus on other important points.

It should not be suggested, however, that what is involved here is an assault upon or rejection of economics *per se*. The object of the attack is the prevailing orthodoxy, not economics as such. There is a prominent tendency within the economics profession to regard unorthodox approaches or schools of thought as beyond the realm of economics itself. This anti-pluralism or, more strongly, intellectual fascism, is not worthy of a subject which, for good or ill, claims great 'liberal' connections. Another aim of this work is to draw upon a wide range of literature in an attempt to establish the legitimacy of an alternative approach.

The precise definition and demarcation of the territory known as 'neoclassical economics' is, of course, problematic. Nevertheless, at the core of the body of theory usually titled thus is a set of ideas concerning rationality, knowledge, the economic process and the human agent.[3] Neoclassical theory involves:

1   rational, maximizing behaviour by all economic agents, whereby they are assumed to optimize according to preferences which are exogenously given;
2   the absence of chronic information problems, such as radical uncertainty concerning the future, widespread ignorance of the structures and parameters in a complex world, and divergences in individual cognitions of common phenomena; and
3   a theoretical focus on movements towards or attained equilibrium states of rest, rather than on the continuous processes of transformation through historical time.

Within many of the top-ranking economics journals there has been an increasing flow of criticisms of neoclassical theory in the last 20 years. However, given the protocols of publication in these journals, these criticisms are often narrow in scope and formalistic in manner. Whilst many versions of neoclassical theory might prove vulnerable to a great number of criticisms of this type, it becomes necessary to provide a more comprehensive theoretical and conceptual framework if an alternative is eventually to be built.

This present work is a contribution to the project of developing economics along radically different lines. It cannot claim to provide a complete alternative. Given the task at hand this is unlikely to be accomplished by a single author, and even less likely in a single work. This book should be regarded as a signpost for a direction worth taking, not as a complete route map to, nor a survey of, the promised land.

Whilst neoclassical theory has come under increasing attack, it has in response widened and deepened its compass, to span a number of new issues, and in some respects its character has changed. Many of the past attacks on neoclassical theory purported to be devastatingly destructive, but the upshot was that orthodoxy adapted only slightly and went on much as before. These events should suggest that the defects of the neoclassical paradigm are more fundamental than many of the former critiques seemed to imply.

For instance, Piero Sraffa's (1960) work and the capital theory debates of the 1960s were successful in uncovering fatal logical inconsistencies in the neoclassical aggregate production function.[4] However, orthodoxy has either ignored these problems or shifted its emphasis onto the disaggregated versions of the theory. The remarkable survival of neoclassical theory after this destructive attack suggests that its 'hard-core' ideas were to be found elsewhere. They were not in its heroic acts of aggregation.

One outstanding theoretical issue is, therefore, to examine critically the deepest foundations of neoclassical orthodoxy. Notably, however, with a few important exceptions, these fundamental issues have not yet been addressed with sufficient attention by rival schools of thought. Indeed, there has been an understandable, but ultimately self-defeating, tendency by critics of orthodoxy to develop alternative formal models which differ from mainstream constructions in some (important) respects but still share the same core assumptions.

In this manner Keynes' economics were devalued, and their radical break from orthodoxy obscured, by the 'Keynesian' tradition of formalistic modelling in the two decades after the Second World War. It was the minority voices of Joan Robinson, Paul Davidson and a few others who kept the radical message of Keynes alive.

More recently, extensive formalistic developments have taken place within Marxism, using game theory and other mathematical tools.[5] This literature is not without value. Indeed, its analytical rigour is refreshing when compared with the scriptural dogmatism of the Marxian fundamentalists. But it incorporates core assumptions concerning rationality, knowledge and equilibrium which are essentially indistinguishable from neoclassical orthodoxy. Remove the dressing of radical language and we are presented with yet another version of mainstream theory, with its rationalistic and individualistic bias and its mechanistic model of the economic process. Contrary to many of my colleagues, I do not regard this development as wholly positive, nor one which can rescue Marxism from its own theoretical difficulties. On the contrary it is a sign of the decay of its inner core after its brief but much wasted heyday in the 1960s and 1970s. In particular, it is another formalistic diversion from the formidable practical problems of the real world, and a retreat into a scholasticism which seems to be sterile in policy terms.

In part it was disenchantment with the developments outlined above, in both neoclassical economics and some formalistic versions of 'Keynesian' and 'Marxian' theory, that led me to write the present study. After spending much of my academic youth on the diversionary delights of Post-Sraffian value theory, I became persuaded that time was too precious to be thus occupied for an entire career.

A central question, ignored by radical value theorists and many other critics of orthodoxy, is the nature of the human agent and the scope for rationality. Clearly, several versions of 'Keynesian' and 'Marxian' theory are happy to share orthodox axioms in this regard, and to perceive their differences with mainstream theory in terms of other assumptions, some of them quite superficial. But most crucially, the radical alternatives to neoclassical orthodoxy cannot continue to avoid the construction of an alternative theory of human agency, related to the economic context of social relation and institutions. If this work succeeds simply in establishing the urgency of this task then in my view it has not failed.

It would be too irksome to burden the reader with an account of how the present study relates to my own preceding work. It should simply be mentioned that research in the early stages of the production of this book led me to accept a more positive view of the value of psychology for economic analysis. Some lingering preconceptions that psychology was necessarily tied to an individualistic or crudely naturalistic outlook were removed. This change is partially a paradigm shift: not merely the discovery of unknown and valuable material. Indeed, there is a concern in the present work to relate the study of social and economic institutions to their natural and biological environment rather than to adopt the 'closed system' view of society or economy that is found in many versions in the social sciences.

This may contrast with my own preceding practice to some degree, but I shall leave it to the reader and critic to sort further through this dirty linen, if they are so inclined. My final word, before sentence is passed, is that as a theorist I would far rather be moving and developing roughly in the right direction, than being consistently and inflexibly wrong.

Bardon Mill, Northumberland

# Acknowledgements

Work on this book was commenced in earnest in October 1984 with the benefits of a one-year Hallsworth Research Fellowship in Political Economy at the University of Manchester. The author wishes to express his gratitude to this institution, to the administrators of the Hallsworth Fellowship and to the Faculty of Economic and Social Studies and its members.

In addition he would like to express his gratitude to Newcastle upon Tyne Polytechnic for its continuing encouragement of both theoretical and applied research in the social sciences with a funding for research from central government that is much inferior to that of the average British university, and in an overall national climate where such activities are not given the prestige or priority they deserve.

Warm thanks are due to the many people who have read or heard parts of this work in draft and have responded with criticism or encouragement. In this regard, and at the unavoidable risk of making an incomplete list, the author is greatly indebted to Dick Bailey, Roy Boyne, Mark Casson, Meghnad Desai, Sheila Dow, Peter Earl, Dan Edwards, Tony Giddens, Francis Green, Geoff Harcourt, Barry Hindess, Richard Langlois, Tony Lawson, John Pheby, Malcolm Sawyer, Harinder Singh, Ian Steedman, Jim Tomlinson, Arthur Walker and Grahame Wright. Thanks are also due to many other friends and professional colleagues for ideas and stimulating discussions.

An earlier draft of chapter 3 appeared in the September 1986 issue of the *Cambridge Journal of Economics*, and chapter 5 and part of chapter 6 emanate from an article in the *Journal of Economic Issues* in December 1985. The author is grateful to the editors of these journals and to the Association for Evolutionary Economics for permission to use this material. In addition, chapter 10 uses material from an article which appeared in *Keynes's Economics: Methodological Issues* (Croom

Helm, 1985) edited by Tony Lawson and Hashem Pesaran. Permission in this case has also been gratefully received.

Finally, continuing gratitude is due to Vinny for enduring some of the creation pangs of the fourth and longest book since we were married, and to Sarah and James for likewise accepting a domestic inhabitant with limited tolerance and with his mind on other things, and for agreeing that the computer cannot always be used for games and colourful patterns and has sometimes to be used for word-processing.

PART ONE

# Prelude

# 1

# Introduction and Outline

Neo-classical theory is a story for the faithful. Those of us outside the flock in our unguarded moments tend to regard it in much the same way as Bertrand Russell saw theology . . . Time and effort spent on fine points of neo-classical theory appears to heretics and the Damned as a shocking waste of scarce intellectual resources.

Edward J. Nell (1972, p. 447)

This book is born out of the conviction that some of the basic concepts of mainstream economic theory require critical and urgent re-examination. This is not simply because one may be hostile to the prominent policy conclusions. More fundamentally it is because mainstream economics is unacceptable in terms of its theoretical assumptions and the scope and direction of its formal argument.

The main problem is the dominant neoclassical tradition, dating from William Jevons, Alfred Marshall and Leon Walras, and taking a number of modern forms, including monetarism and the 'rational expectations' school. In addition, some criticisms are directed at the important, and until recently neglected, Austrian School, including Carl Menger, Ludwig von Mises and Friedrich Hayek. Whilst some of the criticisms strike with equal force at both targets, in many respects there are important theoretical differences between neoclassical economics and the Austrian School, and these have to be dealt with in an appropriate manner.[1]

This chapter commences with an examination of some recent critical developments in economic theory, showing that they share some common themes in their criticisms of orthodoxy and in their attempts to construct an alternative. However, it is argued here that progress in economic theory cannot proceed simply by an extrapolation of these developments, and must make some additional and fundamental changes in its presuppositions and outlook. These are sketched out in the third section of this chapter, before moving on to an outline of the book as a whole.

## 1.1 THE TRAJECTORY OF CRITICAL DEVELOPMENT

### *The current theoretical background*

In recent years a number of forceful criticisms of neoclassical theory have appeared, even in top-rank economic journals such as the *American Economic Review* and the *Economic Journal*. Yet, as Mark Twain once remarked of himself, announcements of the demise of the neoclassical paradigm are an exaggeration. Despite intense criticism, the dominant approach to economic theorizing displays a resilience that has defied all the heralds of a Kuhnian scientific revolution. Further-more, these criticisms are as yet confined to the avant-garde of theoretical enquiry and it will take some time for the debate to percolate through to the great number of practising economists.

However, whilst it is a mistake to underrate the durability of neoclassical theory, it would also be wrong to make the reverse error and assume that no progressive change in economic thought is possible. Arguably, the central neoclassical constructs of individual choice and maximizing rationality, along with the continuing assumption of the tractability of information problems, have been much affected by some recent developments in economic theorizing. Furthermore, we are now presented with an array of alternatives, ranging from modified versions of neoclassicism to more radical critiques, and including Austrian, Keynesian, Marxian, behaviouralist and a variety of other approaches.

In particular, there are signs that instead of merely proposing an alternative formalistic framework, there is increasing attention to the theoretical foundations. Examine, for example, some of the recent applications of game theory to economics (e.g. Schotter, 1981), plus related work on the theory of norms and conventions (e.g. Heiner, 1983; Sudgen, 1986), plus the development of a 'new institutional' economics (e.g. Williamson, 1975, 1985), plus the re-emergence of the 'evolutionary' approach to the theory of the firm (Nelson and Winter, 1982) and finally a host of works on problems concerning information and uncertainty (e.g. Kregel, 1976; Lawson, 1985; Loasby, 1976; Shackle, 1972; Simon 1957a). A diverse set of approaches is involved here, and there are some important conflicts involved between them. Nevertheless, despite differences in the attitudes to, and distances from, mainstream economic theory, a number of common themes have emerged.[2]

First, the assumption of maximizing rationality with known or estimable alternatives is increasingly being attacked for being too narrow and simplistic. These criticisms range from the slight, such as the difficulty of obtaining information regarding the relevant costs (as in the work of Oliver Williamson), to the more radical, concerning even deeper problems of information and knowledge and the nature of rationality itself.

Second, to varying degrees there has been increasing uneasiness with neoclassical conceptions of time and equilibrium, whilst shifting instead towards a view of economic phenomena as being largely dependent upon the result of learning by economic agents who are moving irreversibily through time. Increasingly, economic phenomena are being seen as both evolutionary and dynamic, rather than equilibriating in the neoclassical sense.

Third, there is a growing recognition of the conceptual significance and practical importance of institutions in economic life, but with varying outcomes in policy terms. Nevertheless, a view is emerging that economic coordination cannot ever be merely a matter of price signalling in markets, but is necessarily supported by a wide range of other economic and social institutions.[3] The latter, despite some old-fashioned neoclassical protestations, are being seen as an important and legitimate topic for economic enquiry.

## *Problems of information*

The above three themes are linked and share some common fundamentals. Above all, all three involve questions of information and knowledge. It is of great significance that a number of influential economists have rejected the traditional assumptions of perfect knowledge and have criticized the preceding tendency to assume information problems away.

This theoretical development has sufficient mass and momentum that it is unlikely to be readily or easily diverted from the attention of economic theorists. Once Pandora's box is opened the demons are unlikely to desist. As Herbert Simon (1976, p. 148) has remarked with some optimism for the heretic: 'As economics becomes more and more involved in the study of uncertainty, more and more concerned with the complex actuality of business decision-making, the shift in programme will become inevitable.'

But it would be a mistake to see an appraisal of the information problem as a single, uncomplicated issue. If it were so then orthodox economics could be reformed simply by appending developments in the area of the 'economics of information' and much of the remaining theory could be left intact.

What should not be taken for granted is the essential nature of either sense data, information or knowledge. Economists often pay lip service to 'information problems' but treat information as if it were a fluid to be passed into and out of the head of each individual. This is a recognition of the importance of information in the economic process, but it is a mistaken and misleading treatment of information itself, which is bound to lead to error and confusion.

The first points that have to be borne in mind are the vital distinctions between sense data, information and knowledge. Sense data consists/of the vast jumble of aural, visual or other signals that reach the brain. We have no other contact with the outside world and our fellow humans other than through this sense data. Whilst sense data is necessary to provide us with information, it is by no means sufficient, and the two are not the same. To derive information it is necessary to impose a conceptual framework on the jumble of neurological stimulii, involving implicit or explicit assumptions or theories which cannot themselves be derived from sense data alone. In other words, there has to be a process of cognition of the sense data, to select from and convert it into a form that is in some sense meaningful and has informational content for the agent.

In addition, as is elaborated below, there are further distinctions to be made, such as between information and varieties of knowledge. Information that may be 'understood' in one way can have a different significance in a different context, or when the theoretical or conceptual framework is changed. There is also the question of 'tacit knowledge', such as that relating to acquired skills, which cannot be readily codified in the form of information that can be passed on to others.

These cognitive and epistemological considerations are familiar to generations of psychologists, philosophers and social scientists. But their profound implications are not always taken on board. For this reason there is some repetition and elaboration of these points in this book. Consideration of them is especially important for economics, because whilst it has begun to address problems of information and knowledge with some seriousness in recent years, discussion of the cognitive and epistemological questions is still relatively underdeveloped and confined to a few economic theorists.

For example, many economic theorists who have addressed informational problems in their work have failed to make any distinction between sense data and information, or recognized the epistemological consequences of cognitive theory. Thus, despite the positive features of recent developments, in important respects many of them are fundamentally and seriously flawed.

It is to be hoped, therefore, that the remarkable progress made by economists in recent years will be followed by a deeper appraisal of these issues. The fact that there has been some hesitation in moving further in this direction may be due, in part, to the challenge to orthodoxy that they present. However, given the momentum that has been built up, progress in economic science is not served by a hesitation due to conservative reasons.

## 1.2 SOME OBSERVATIONS

### *Subjectivism and institutionalism*

Notably, the increasing interest by economists in problems of information and knowledge is in part the result of the persuasive endeavours of the Austrian School. While correctly bringing these issues to the fore, and with a critical effect on much of conventional theory, the Austrian School have insisted on the subjective character of knowledge and expectations, and used such arguments to support ultra-individualistic policy conclusions.

It shall be proposed in this work, however, that this line of argument, whilst moving initially in the right direction, takes an unacceptably subjectivist turn. Whilst it can be accepted that information and knowledge have important subjective and individual features, the concepts and theories that are used in their acquisition are not, and cannot be, purely subjective, as if they resulted from an isolated individual. Given that no information or knowledge is concept- or theory-free, none is purely subjective in its essence.

The point that is argued here is that the cognitive processes are essentially social as well: they involve the use of social language and concepts, and reflect ideas and practices which relate to a social culture. We are all individuals, and the totality of our knowledge and experience is unique, but the mechanisms of our perception and acquisition of knowledge are unavoidably social and unavoidably reflect social culture and practices.

Thus whilst applauding the Austrian emphasis on information problems, and their recognition that information and knowledge cannot be readily and totally transferred from one individual to another, it is necessary to differ from the ultra-subjectivism of their theoretical interpretation and thereby some of the policy conclusions.

The line of argument here leads us directly to the institutionalist character of this work. Information problems lead to questions concerning the nature of information and knowledge and the social processes involved in their acquisition. From developments in cognitive psychology, anthropology and sociology it is evident that these processes are closely related to the norms, conventions and routines of social culture and institutions. Interpretations of sense data are individual but at the same time deeply social, in that they are framed by, and reliant upon, the norms and practices of social life. For this reason the stress on matters of information and knowledge should not lead to a subjectivist outlook, but directly to the study of the cognitive and practical functions of institutions.

As an example, consider how economic agents learn from experience and attempt to reduce their mistakes. This, of course, has become a highly fashionable topic for both mainstream and avant-garde economic theory. Contrary to some of the crude theoretical presentations of this process (e.g. in the rational expectations hypothesis), learning is not simply the acquisition of raw information as it is signalled by economic indicators in the real world. Any such data has to be interpreted before agents can learn. The interpretative framework, and indeed the individual's 'model' of the economy that may be used to evaluate the data and make estimates of the future, is not 'learnt' from the sense data alone. Thus any model of the learning process is inadequate if it takes agents as responding in a straightfoward, automatic and uniform manner to given economic indicators, as if no differing or concept-specific individual processes of cognition were involved.

In short, once questions of information and knowledge are brought to the fore, consideration of the cognitive processes is unavoidable. Whilst cognitive theory complicates matters to a great degree, it is still possible to generalize in economic theory. This is partly because of the close relationship that has been established by psychologists, anthropologists and sociologists between social culture and institutions on the one hand, and cognitive activity and development on the other.

It is because they fail to consider this relationship that the ultra-subjectivist developments in modern economic theory offer a blind alley. It is suggested in this work that this failure is not an accident, but relates closely to an individualistic ideology which eschews questions as to how individual cognitions and preferences develop.

## Process and system

More detailed considerations of the processes of learning and action have further fundamental implications. Just as 'information' is not like an undifferentiated fluid entering the brain, the processes relating cerebral activity and action are varied and complex, and do not occur on one level.

This may seem to be a fairly obvious point but it has deep implications which are rarely taken on board. Even those economists who place great emphasis on the processes of learning in the theory of economic activity most often assume high standards of rationality and high levels of computational ability for the individual. It is assumed that the large quantity of complex sense data received by the individual can be processed in such a manner that no significant parts are ignored, and they all play a role in the calculations of purpose or preference by the agent.

In part it is a habitual response by mainstream economic theorists, who, having being taught that a key feature of economic life is that all commodities are scarce, regard information to be generally scarce as well. Accepting, however, that crucial information is usually scarce, the problem is more complex because sense data itself is not in shortage but in over-abundance. The brain faces the difficulty not only of ignorance in regard to some pertinent facts, but also of dealing with an overwhelming wealth of other signals which are being received all the time.

The view taken in this work is that such arguments lead to the view that the cognitive and cerebral processes are best regarded as a complex and multi-tiered system, and that actions themselves take place in regard to different levels of thought. Thus, as a simple case, there is a distinction between actions which are the result of extensive deliberation and computation by the agent, and those, on the other hand, which are habitual or even reflexive.

This is a step further than regarding rationality as 'bounded' as a result of the complexities of information and the limited computational capacity of the human brain, as in some of the works of Herbert Simon and his interpreters. Cognitive and other cerebral processes are so complex that they are not simply 'bounded' or limited, they also have to take place on different levels. Consequently, we cannot be comprehensively rational or deliberative even concerning the data which *can*, in some sense, be handled by the brain.

As the reader will have realized, this line of argument leads to an extension of the attack on rationality in economic theory, both in the sense of maximizing or optimizing behaviour and in the sense that all actions are presumed to result from rational calculation.[4]

But the consequences of this argument, elaborated in further chapters below, are not purely destructive. There is an important link with other writers such as Anthony Giddens, Michael Oakshott, Michael Polanyi and Thorstein Veblen who have emphasized the function of the habitual, and only partially deliberative, actions in retaining knowledge and skills and promulgating them through society. 'Practical knowledge' and 'practical consciousness' are embedded in economic life. Through structured action in a social context they function as a kind of transmission belt for much of society's productive expertise and technique.

Once again the relevance of the study of social institutions is underlined. Precisely because such actions are not fully flexible and deliberative, and are habitual in the context of a given structure, it is important to examine social institutions to see how habits and routines are formed. The study of institutions offers a means of examining the basis of routinized action from the viewpoint of the system as a whole.

The connection between social institutions and individual ideas was suggested by Veblen (1919, p. 239) when he saw institutions as 'settled habits of thought common to the generality of men'. This quotation gives evidence also of Veblen's stress on the importance of habitual action in economic life. With hindsight we can define a social institution in fuller terms. It is here defined as a social organization which, through the operation of tradition, custom or legal constraint, tends to create durable and routinized patterns of behaviour. It is this very durability and routinization, in a highly complex and sometimes volatile world, which makes social science with any practical application possible at all.

## Determinism, purposefulness and choice

However, as emphasized below, this emphasis on the cultural and institutional conditions of human action does not necessarily lead to a rigid or deterministic outlook. The view is taken that whilst social institutions are important in the processes of cognition and learning, in the formation of preferences and generally in the motivation of action, human activity is not completely or mechanistically determined by its institutional integument.

Indeed, it is precisely because a multi-dimensional or mult-tiered view is taken here of human thought processes that there is more scope to rebut a deterministic or mechanistic view. It is the orthodox, rigid models of preference and action, without true uncertainty and the above-discussed problems of information, which in fact deny real choice. As Brian Loasby (1976, p. 5) and others[5] have argued: 'If knowledge is perfect and the logic of choice complete and compelling then choice disappears; nothing is left but stimulus and response. If choice is real, the future cannot be certain; if the future is certain, there can be no choice.'

Even with the relaxation of the assumption of perfect knowledge in recent neoclassical models, it is not clear that choice is fully reinstated. Even the probabilistic calculus of risk which often accompanies neoclassical theory today[6] still implies a Bayesian (or other similar) determination of choice. A model which includes a random element does not necessarily admit true sovereignty or spontaneity for the individual concerned. Action enslaved by the dice of the cosmos may not be quite as rigidly determined, but it is no more spontaneous or free.

Two systems theorists, Russell Ackoff and Fred Emery (1972), have elaborated a relevant distinction between purposeful and goal-directed behaviour. The difference lies in the set of possible responses to the structural environment faced by the individual. Simpler goal-seeking devices (such as a thermostat) respond in a single and predetermined manner to changes in their enviornment. The most sophisticated type of goal-seeking behaviour is that of a computer or machine that can 'learn' from its mistakes in pursuing goals, and thus can respond in different ways to the same repeated problem. However, in both these cases, the goals are still themselves determined or fixed. The purposeful agent is essentially different in that it can change its goals, and furthermore it may actually do this without any stimulus from outside. Human beings are regarded as purposeful systems of this type. The capacity to change both behaviour and goals without external stimulus means that humans have a *will*, and that some of our choices are real ones.

Clearly, much of orthodox economic theory does not include purposeful behaviour in this sense, and its models are of goal-seeking behaviour of the simplest type. Behaviour is regarded as a determinate function of external inputs to given preferences. In recent years there have been more sophisticated developments with models where a kind of learning is involved. But, for the reasons given above, the agent is still not endowed with choice. It is only the Austrian School who have put forward a view of the agent where both purposes and actions are not determined by the external environment and where real choice is involved.

However, as is argued below, the Austrian theorists go too far in the opposite direction. They seem to argue either that action bears no significant influence of the environment, or that it is beyond the scope of economic theory to enquire as to how purposes and actions may be determined. It will be suggested that the first view is simply untenable and that the second is blinkered.

Consequently, the Austrian approach, despite its important insights concerning purposefulness and choice, is not followed here. In effect, because of these assumptions, Austrian theory is incapable of building any model of the economy which can generate detailed predictions concerning the future. Contrary to many neoclassical theorists, prediction is not all-important. But to ignore it entirely seems to emasculate the science.

The view taken here is that there are external influences moulding the purposes and actions of individuals, but that action is not entirely determined by them. The environment is important but it does not completely determine either what the individual aims to do or what he or she may achieve. There are actions which may be uncaused, but at the same time there are patterns of behaviour that may relate to the cultural or institutional environment within which the person acts. Action, in short, is partially determined, and partially indeterminate: partly predictable but partly unforeseeable, even in terms of the calculus of probability or risk. Human actions can be both routinized and conservative, and display flights of imagination or eccentricity which are beyond rational anticipation and bring the greatest surprise.

Notably, it is this measure or unpredictability which makes the economic future uncertain, in the most radical sense. Because the economy is made up of human beings whose behaviour is partially indeterminate, the future can never be fully anticipated or known. We may be able to make useful and meaningful predictions concerning some events but we can never be certain that they will be true. It may be possible to calculate and assign probabilities to future outcomes but these will always be tentative at most, and futile at the least, because the future is essentially indeterminate and unknown. The partial indeterminacy of human behaviour is one major reason for this fact.

Thus whilst there are some predictabilities and regularities in human behaviour, they are never determinate in a rigid or mechanical sense. Social reality displays a degree of pattern and order, and is subject to uncertainty and potential volatility, at the same time.


## 1.3    A Systems View

The above criticisms of even some of the positive developments in economic theory should suggest that it is not acceptable simply to extrapolate from the course of development of economic theory as we find it in the recent past. Theoretical progress rarely follows a straight line and the correct course will not necessarily proceed exactly in the contemporary direction of the current avant-garde. Understandably, recent developments combine positive and negative features, and it is necessary to direct attention at both.

The author may suffer from an inbuilt sectarianism in criticizing some of the more innovative and avant-garde theorists of the present day, some of which are much closer to the position taken in the present work than their orthodox rivals, but it is hoped that the reader and the criticized theorists may take a more generous view and regard these criticisms as a modest attempt to keep the momentum of positive developments in economic theory on what are perceived as the right tracks.

## The endogeneity of preferences and technology

It is possible, however, to focus on one issue above all others as the hallmark of the divergent approach adopted here. It is the Rubicon that divides an institutionalist or evolutionary approach from theoretical orthodoxy and even some of its critics. In neoclassical theory both the tastes and preferences of individuals, and the technological possibilities and constraints that impinge upon the economy, are regarded as exogenous or given, i.e. outside the system. Neither the Austrian School, nor many behaviouralist economists, nor even some Keynesians, diverge significantly from orthodoxy on this point. This work belongs to a different type principally because this characteristic approach is not followed.

Orthodox economics confines its theoretical analysis to the exchange or allocation of resources, and the decision-making thereby involved, neglecting both the moulding of individual preferences by social and economic circumstances and also the continuous transformation of productive technology through time. We may summarize the orthodox approach diagrammatically as in figure 1.1.

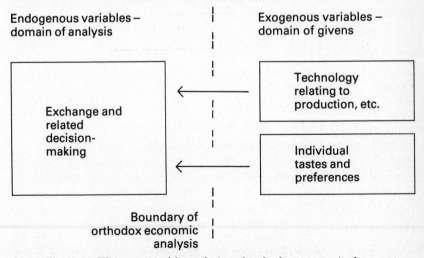

Fig. 1.1  *The scope and boundaries of orthodox economic theory*

Thus, despite all its emphasis on individualism and its subjectivist outlook, orthodox theory puts the formation and moulding of individual tastes and preferences beyond the scope of its analysis. In some cases, as in the work of Gary Becker (1976) and others, this is achieved by making the further restrictive assumption that preferences do not in fact alter over time. They are thus not only outside the economic system but given sanctity and permanence as well. In other accounts, such as in the work of Friedrich Hayek (1948, p. 67), the task of explaining the springs of conscious action is a matter for 'psychology but not for economics . . . or any other social science'. Whilst the analyses here are different they have a common effect: to exclude such matters entirely from the domain of economic enquiry.

A consequence of this insular attitude is to disregard the impact of advances in psychology and other social sciences in the understanding of the processes and structures governing human action. Particularly, as noted above, the link between the cognitive processes and the formation of goals and expectations, on the one hand, and the social and cultural environment, on the other, is downplayed or ignored. Notably, both the pure and applied research that has been done by several scholars on the relationship between psychology and economics is largely dismissed by the orthodox theorist.

When it comes to the determination and transformation of technology, orthodox economics is blind, usually taking technology as given and asocial, as if it had nothing to do with the system of industrial relations and the method of organization of work within the firm. Technology is treated as a natural fact – beyond the scope of any social science.

As an example, orthodox economist Ivor Pearce (1977, p. 27) has approvingly described the production function of neoclassical theory as being determined by the 'laws of physics'. This, of course, ignores the fact that production is an organized social activity, involving relations between persons themselves as well as between persons and nature. However, he is in august company. In the last century John Stuart Mill (1871, Bk 2, ch. 1, p. 199) wrote that the

> laws and conditions of the production of wealth partake of the character of physical truths. There is nothing optional or arbitrary in them. Whatever mankind produce, must be produced in the modes, and under the conditions, imposed by the constitution of external things, and by the inherent properties of their own bodily and mental structure.

Thus Mill, like most neoclassical economists to this day, sees production and technology as given and asocial: determined by supposedly fixed physical (and perhaps physiological) laws, and unaffected by the social relations and institutions of production in the real world, with all their manifest variety and change.

At any given stage of technological development a variety of methods of organizing production are both possible and obvious even to the casual observer. The workforce will have varied skills and capacities to learn, and there will also be cultural variations and differences relating to trade unions and labour practices. There is no physical or technological law which says that production has to be organized in just one way. And insofar as there is variety in these institutions and relations of production there will be a variety of costs, and levels of productivity. Economists are in error if they assume that production is simply determined by technology or the laws of physics.

One consequence of the mistaken, neoclassical view of production is that in over 100 years orthodox theory has failed to make any significant advance in the understanding of long-run technological progress and transformation. Thus, for instance, it is still standard practice in both microeconomic and macroeconomic models to simply assume a figure for the rate of growth of productivity over time. Thus a crucial economic variable is simply plucked, as it were, from the air. Furthermore, to this day neoclassical theory has not provided any rationale for its 'well-behaved' aggregate production function, despite the devastating Sraffian critique of the 1960s and early 1970s. The explanation of technology and production has remained a mystery, and orthodoxy still devotes insignificant intellectual resources to research in this sphere. This is no accident, of course, as these phenomena are wrongly regarded as exogenous to the economy at the outset.

In contrast to the orthodox view, the approach here is to regard both technology and individual tastes and preferences as, at least in the long run, part of the economic system and thus phenomena which have to be explained by economists. This contrasting view is shown in figure 1.2.

Note that, unlike orthodoxy, the institutionalist approach includes both technology and individual tastes and preferences as part of the economic system to be examined. Furthermore, the term 'socio-economic system' is used to emphasize the fact that the economy is inseparable from a host of social and political institutions in society at large.

In some very limited respects this broadening of the domain of economic enquiry reflects some pronounced developments in postwar economic orthodoxy. Thus, for example, Anthony Downs (1957) has broadened the orthodox marginalist analysis to cover the political sphere, and he has been followed in this territory by a burgeoning literature of 'public choice' economics in a neoclassical mould. Second, Gary Becker is famous for his extension of neoclassical theory to cover

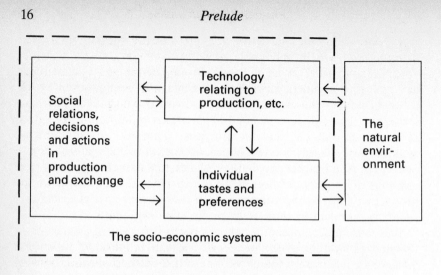

Fig. 1.2　*The projected domain of institutional economic theory*

the home and family in a number of well-known publications. And third, Robert Lucas (1972) and the rational expectations theorists have revolutionized neoclassical theory by making expectations endogenous. In a sense, therefore, we may take encouragement from these three developments as they are clear evidence of a pronounced tendency, in a fashion, to widen the analytical compass of the subject.

Notably and typically, however, these developments within the neoclassical school abruptly stop short at the boundaries of the terrain mentioned above. There is no attempt nor inclination to bring the determination of technology into the system, and a principled reluctance to consider the factors moulding or affecting the tastes and preferences of the individual. Whilst a few of the orthodox signposts are roughly in the right direction, the crossing of this boundary would require a shift of imagination, paradigm and underlying ideology of earthquake proportions.

The main reason for this is that orthodox economic theory is wedded to the classic liberal ideology where the individual is regarded as an autonomous and elemental unit. In adopting a systems view we are in a sense repeating the age-old counter-proposition that the behaviour of individuals is in part formed by their social and general environment. It is an old idea, but central to all the radical counter-attacks to individualism and liberalism through the centuries. Note, however, that we do not have to make the obverse error, frequently committed in the past, that the social environment explains all. We may deny that the individuals are completely autonomous and free, but we do not then have to place them in deterministic chains.

Indeed, as established above, it is neoclassical theory that takes a deterministic view by making the individual a prisoner, not of the social environment, but of his or her immanent and often invariable preferences and beliefs. These determine behaviour on highly mechanical lines.

In the case of this work, however, the broadening of the scope of economic enquiry does not mean a widening of a mechanistic or deterministic model. For instance, apart from the question of the endogeneity of tastes and technique, the emphasis here on problems of information and uncertainty is coupled with that of indeterminacy: there are niches for uncaused causes. In addition the model of maximizing 'rational' behaviour is rejected. Whilst the theoretical system is here widened, it is changed fundamentally in its character as well.

It is reasonable to describe the approach here as 'holistic' in that it embraces questions of the determination and evolution of tastes and preferences. However, the word has led to much confusion, both by supporters and opponents of a holistic approach. Thus, for example, in reacting against some versions of holism, one individualistic critic describes it as 'the doctrine that we should somehow study wholes *directly* without considering the workings of parts in a meaningful way' (Langlois, 1983a, p. 584). However, this is not what many systems theorists mean by holism. In the present work it is used in a sense that is different from the latter definition, as a loose imperative that social and economic theory should be broadened to embrace all relevant variables and elements. It is not some kind of theoretical short cut towards the understanding of systemic parts without considering their own properties and relations.

One important consequence of the systems view adopted here is that it is possible to focus on the processes of transformation of both individual tastes and productive technology through time. By bringing these into the system their evolution and change become legitimate and major topics of enquiry. By contrast, in the orthodox schema, we are guided towards equilibrium conditions that arise from optimizing with given tastes and techniques.

Nevertheless, the adoption of a wider or more holistic view does not on its own prevent an equilibrium approach. It would be possible simply to broaden the compass of the equilibrium framework, and incorporate tastes and techniques in the same manner. However, an emphasis on the ecological dimension and the dynamic interaction between the social and natural environment is a useful antidote against retaining an equilibrium outlook in a widened scheme. The rejection of the maximizing hypothesis is also relevant here. The systems view that is taken in the present work is essentially an evolutionary one, emphasizing ongoing processes and dynamic transformation.

*The systems view briefly explored*

Note, therefore, that the socio-economic system is here regarded as an 'open' rather than a 'closed' system in the sense originally defined by Ludwig von Bertalanffy (1950). A closed system will reach some kind of steady state because, by definition, it has no connection with or influence from an external environment. An open system may or may not reach an equilibrium or steady state, depending on whether or not its environment itself is unchanging. Normally, systems theorists make the reasonable assumption that the environment is variable and does not reach its own equilibrium.

Neoclassical theory effectively adopts an open-system model of the economy, but assumes that its 'environment' consists of given, static functions governing individual preferences and productive technique. Consequently, the model can reach a state of equilibrium. But this is both unrealistic and unacceptable. Not only do real-world 'environmental' conditions change, including both the natural environment and the other elements which are exogenous to neoclassical theory, but also, as noted above, the theory is incapable of directing attention at the processes of economic transformation.

It is thus a serious mistake to suggest that neoclassical theory is the expression of a systems view in the economic sphere. This error has been made by some neoclassical economics, such as E. Roy Weintraub (1979, pp. 71–2), and by Robert Lilienfeld (1978) (a critic of systems theory). Notably, both these authors focus on neoclassical general equilibrium theory as a culmination of systems theory in economic science. Admittedly, general equilibrium theory does take a view of the economic system where numerous functions determining both individual preferences and productive activities interact with each other. But also, general equilibrium theory regards the economy basically as a system of exchange, governing the allocation of resources between autonomous agents. Production is an exogenous 'black box', with processes governing individual tastes and preferences as a theoretical void. At most, general equilibrium theory is an expression of a systems approach only in a very limited and inadequate sense.

However, it should be made clear that systems theory is not a miracle cure for a bedraggled science. When systems theory became more and more fashionable in the 1950s and 1960s exaggerated claims for its potency were made with great frequency. In retrospect, the gains that have been made have been much more modest, and the overblown claims have led to much disappointment. Indeed, it may be preferable that the term 'systems *theory*' were dropped, so as to avoid building up any more false hopes, or giving the further impression that it is a theoretical panacea.

In addition, there are many different approaches in the application of systems ideas, and the usual crop of disputes amongst system thinkers. Fortunately, we do not have to engage in these controversies here. What is being suggested is, broadly and simply, a view of the economy that is system-wide in that it embraces both tastes and technology, and in that it is an open system with respect to the natural world. It is this basic systems perspective that is important in differentiating this work from orthodox economic theory.

The criticism of orthodox economics from a systems perspective has been put eloquently by the physicist Fritjof Capra (1982, pp. 194–5):

> Present-day economics is characterized by the fragmentary and reductionist approach that typifies most social sciences. Economists generally fail to recognize that the economy is merely one aspect of a whole ecological and social fabric; a living system composed of human beings in continual interaction with one another and with their natural resources, most of which are, in turn, living organisms. The basic error of the social sciences is to divide this fabric in fragments, assumed to be independent and to be dealt with in separate academic departments.

The earlier discussion above should suggest that a systems view does offer something for economics. Furthermore, some of the general theoretical results developed by systems thinkers do have some application in this subject area.[7]

### Economics and the systems view

By way of illustration the influence of a systems view can be traced in the history of economic thought. Adam Smith, for example, developed an idea of an economic system in which the processes of production were endogenous. He placed production at the centre of his *Wealth of Nations* with his dynamic theory of the division of labour. For Smith the technology was not taken as given, but regarded as under continuous transformation partly as a result of changes in economic conditions.

Karl Marx followed this lead in his first volume of *Capital*. He covered much new ground with his examination of the processes of production, considering changes such as in the length of the working day and in the intensification of labour, and the dynamic transformation of technology under the capitalist system. Marx is also responsible for a sustained challenge to some of the individualistic assumptions behind orthodox economic thought, by repeatedly emphasizing the social nature of individuality. Thus, for instance, he wrote that '*man* is no abstract being encamped outside the world. Man is *the world of man*, the state, society' (Marx and Engels, 1975, p. 175). Whilst Marx wrote long before the rise of a modern systems view, as an economist his work reflects systems ideas to an extent rarely matched in other economists.

Whilst remaining a critic of some aspects of Marxian theory, Thorstein Veblen was to some extent influenced by Marx. In addition he reacted strongly against neoclassical theory as it was developing around the turn of the century. In his criticisms he put great stress both on the processes of economic evolution and technological transformation, and the manner in which individual action is moulded by circumstances. He saw the individual's conduct as being influenced by relations of an institutional nature: 'The wants and desires, the end and the aim, the ways and the means, the amplitude and drift of the individual's conduct are functions of an institutional variable that is of a highly complex and wholly unstable character' (Veblen, 1909, p. 245).

A remarkably explicit statement in a similar general vein comes from Frank Knight (1924, pp. 262–3):

> Wants are usually treated as *the* fundamental data, the ultimate driving force in economic activity, and in a short-run view of problems this is scientifically legitimate. But in the long-run it is just as clear that wants are dependent variables, that they are largely caused and formed by economic activity. The case is somewhat like that of a river and its channel; for the time being the channel locates the river, but in the long run it is the other way.

Knight is an unusual but apposite economist because he was influenced by both the institutionalists and the Austrian School. Furthermore, as James Buchanan (1968, p. 426) puts it, Knight is 'that rare theorist who is also an institutionalist, an institutionalist who is not a data collector'. On the whole, however, the American institutional economists did tend to neglect matters of theory after some notable contributions by Thorstein Veblen, John Commons and others. The systems view is sustained, not in crisp theoretical statements but in the continuing insistence, with plentiful topical illustrations, of the malleability of tastes and the interaction between technology and the economy. Some of the supreme contributions of this genre come, of course, from the pen of John K. Galbraith.

Gunnar Myrdal, an important dissident economist, and a Nobel Prizewinner, has explicitly propounded a systems view. He has argued that in 'regard to practically every economic problem, scientific study must concern the entire social system, including, besides the so-called economic factors, everything else of importance for what comes to happen in the economic field' (Myrdal, 1976, p. 82). The work of Nicholas Georgescu-Reogen (1954, 1971) is notable in that he has probed the boundaries of orthodox theory in two directions, both in regard to consumer theory and the theory of production, thus breaking down the traditionally narrow range of thought. Another prominent economist influenced by a wider view is Kenneth Boulding (1985). Given the number of other economists expressing related ideas[8] the popularity of systems thinking in economics seems to be on the increase.

More specifically there are a number of economists, mainly from the Marxian and Sraffian theoretical traditions, who have stressed the non-autonomy and adaptability of preferences, and explicitly or by implication the social character of individuality itself.[9] Others have insisted on the need to examine further the processes of technological change.

It should also be noted that the systems perspective outlined above directs attention to the interface between the socio-economic systems and the natural environment. A further positive sign is the recent emergence, in embryonic form, of a heterodox economics which places such matters to the forefront, inspired, in the main, by Fritz Schumacher's (1973) classic work.[10]

Thus it seems that the systems approach has already started to make a serious impact, both in explicit and implicit forms. This is at least one optimistic sign of progress in economic science. To make serious further advances, however, the Rubicon has to be crossed, to join others that are already encamped on the opposite bank, and the terrain of classical liberalism has to be abandoned.

### 1.4 SCOPE AND OUTLINE

It is hoped that the preceding sections of this chapter account for some aspects of the argument and other features of this book. What should be clear is that before institutional economic theory can proceed apace a great deal of the undergrowth has to be cleared.

This is so for a number of reasons. First there is the critical attack that has to be mounted on the negative aspects of orthodox economic theory. Second there is the need to develop a dialogue with avant-garde theory. Third, however, is a need to regain a momentum within institutionalist theory itself, as its own progress has not been uninterrupted.

### *The fate of institutional economics*

To elaborate the third point, it should be remembered that in the interwar period institutionalism was actually the dominant school of economic thought in the US. It lost ground to neoclassical formalism partly because it neglected its own task of underlying theoretical development.

It is not difficult to see how institutionalism became bogged down. After establishing the importance of institutions, routines and habits, it underlined the value of largely descriptive work on the nature and function of politico-economic institutions. Whilst this was of value it became the predominant and almost exclusive practice for institutionalist writers. The institutionalists became data-gatherers *par excellence*.

The error here was largely methodological and epistemological, and committed by many institutionalists with the exception of Veblen himself and a few others. It was a crucial mistake simply to clamour for descriptive 'realism', by gathering more and more data, or by painting a more and more detailed picture of particular economic institutions. This is because we cannot ever gain a more accurate or adequate understanding of economic reality exclusively by observation and the gathering of data. Contrary to the empiricist view (and as is emphasized in the next chapter), science cannot progress without a theoretical framework, and no observation of reality is free of theories or concepts.

Thus, whilst positivism and empiricism remained the dominant implicit and explicit philosophy for Anglo-American theory, the theoretical development of institutionalism became frozen. It reached a plateau in the US, and in Britain it never became established. In some quarters institutionalism became synonymous with a naive descriptive approach, by both practitioner and critic alike.

Notably, some institutionalists continue to criticize the competing neoclassical theory with the understandable but largely ineffective claim that the latter is 'unrealistic'. A similar accusation is repeated today by many Post-Keynesian economists. It is argued by many institutionalists and Post-Keynesians that, by contrast, their theories are based on 'facts'.

The problems with this position are discussed in the next chapter. As many defenders of neoclassical theory have pointed out, no scientific theory can ever be fully realistic. Some simplifying assumptions must be made. It should be added, furthermore, that 'facts' do not speak for themselves, and, to repeat, they are infused with the concepts and theories of the observer.

This does not, of course, mean that the neoclassical assumptions are valid. The argument here is that neoclassical theory cannot be refuted or dislodged simply by pointing at 'facts' or the 'real world'. Neoclassical theorists have their own reasons for their fundamental assumptions, and a different line of attack is required to dislodge them. The official methodology of neoclassical economists is not acceptable, but neither is the view that assumptions can or should be 'realistic' in some empiricist sense.

Notably, and unlike many of his later followers, Veblen did not concentrate simply on the charge of 'unrealism' when attacking neoclassical theory. As Thomas Sowell (1967) has argued, Veblen (1919, p. 221) accepted that to be 'serviceable' a hypothesis need 'not be true to life'. He understood that 'economic man' and similar conceptions were 'not intended as a competent expression of fact' but represented an 'expedient of abstract reasoning' (p. 142).

Veblen's crucial argument against neoclassical theory was not that it was unrealistic but that it was inadequate for the theoretical purpose at hand. His intention was to analyse the process of change and transformation in the modern economy. Neoclassical theory was inadequate in this respect because it indicated 'the conditions of survival to which any innovation is subject, supposing the innovation to have taken place, not the conditions of variational growth' (Veblen, 1919, pp. 176–7). But what Veblen was seeking was precisely a theory as to why such innovations take place, not a theory which muses over equilibrium conditions after technological possibilities are established. 'The question', he wrote, 'is not how things stabilize themselves in a "static state", but how they endlessly grow and change' (Veblen, 1954, p. 8).

This feature of Veblen's methodology is an important one, but it was not fully developed nor consistently applied. His followers, with greater empiricist leanings than he, left it behind. It is not for the first time that the disciples of a great thinker took away a mere fraction of their leader's ideas into the later world.

Since the Second World War, neoclassical theory has been in the ascendant throughout the Western world. However, institutional economics has survived, largely in the US, and in the last decade or so it has shown strong signs of theoretical development.

The revival of institutional economics should not neglect the theoretical task, nor fall once again into the empiricist trap. There are a number of reasons why it is possible, even likely, that the same type of errors will not be repeated again.

The first is the movement of neoclassical theory itself, ironically, in a vaguely institutionalist direction, with developments such as the 'new institutional economics' of Oliver Williamson and others, and the growth of the Property Rights School. This movement has a strong theoretical bias (even at the cost of ignoring much of the empirical evidence that does not square with their results), and thus a critical examination of this trend from a more radical, non-neoclassical, institutionalism cannot avoid the theoretical issues that are involved.

Second, there have been important theoretical developments from other traditions, particularly the Post-Keynesian and the Marxian, which should be taken into account. Indeed, what is required is less a development of institutionalist theory itself but a synthesis of some of the elements of institutionalist, Marxian and Post-Keynesian analysis. Despite its advances, institutional economics in the past was not able to provide a theoretical system approaching the calibre of that of Karl Marx or John Maynard Keynes. New developments might usefully incorporate some of Marx's ideas on, for instance, the nature of economic systems and the theory of production, as well the work of Keynes and some of the Post-Keynesians in the area of, for instance, uncertainty and monetary theory.

Consequently, the adoption of the 'institutionalism' label for this work is not straightforward. Contrary to many institutionalist writers, the epistemological position here is strongly anti-empiricist. In addition, the author is more strongly influenced by Keynes and Marx than by Veblen. However, the label has a forceful appeal because, unlike the 'Keynesian' and 'Marxian' labels it can span a wider and more comprehensive theoretical terrain. Furthermore, it has the advantage that the analysis is not personalized, and the temptation to tedious textual exegesis from the works of a single Great Master is removed.

In addition, both 'Keynesian' and 'Marxian' theory carry with them a baggage of inadequate or erroneous theorizing which has proved difficult to shed. It will be a long time, for instance, before Keynesian theory overcomes its still-widespread interpretation in terms of models of the IS–LM type. The relative obscurity of the 'institutionalist' label has advantages in this respect, particularly in the British context. One of the mildly amusing advantages of describing oneself as an institutionalist in Britain is that your colleagues are unlikely to have much of a preconceived idea of what the label means, and a more substantive discourse may ensue. However, as always, crossing the Atlantic will bring different problems.

## Outline of this work

It should now be clear why the second chapter of this work is on methodological issues. In addition to the clarification of the relationship with earlier institutionalism, the more important task is to rebut the traditional methodological defence of the assumptions of neoclassical theory. It shall be argued that not only does this defence fail, but that the route is open for the scientific development of economic theory along different lines.

Part two is devoted to a critique of 'rational economic man'. Whilst there are some constructive arguments involved in these chapters, the main task is to dispose of the fundamental assumptions concerning human agency in the orthodox theory. To this end the matter is approached from four aspects in turn.

The first, in chapter 3, is a critique of the 'methodological individualism' which informs Austrian and much neoclassical theory. It is argued that the underlying problem with this stance is its failure to examine the processes that influence individual tastes and preferences. But the argument here does not go to the opposite extreme and assert a crude primacy of society or institutions over the individual.

Chapter 4 is devoted to a discussion of criticisms of the neoclassical assumption that economic agents are continuously maximizing or optimizing. A number of other critics have attacked the maximization hypothesis and their views are evaluated. Many of these criticisms focus on the problems concerning maximizing rationality with large amounts of information in a complex environment, and in general they are upheld. In addition, the growing experimental evidence from psychologists which weighs against the maximization hypothesis is discussed. Finally, there is a fundamental criticism of the utilitarian foundations of the maximization hypothesis in which ends are completely separated from means.

Chapter 5 covers a different aspect of rationality in both neoclassical and Austrian theory. It is the idea that action is dominated by rational deliberation and calculation. There is a philosophical critique of this notion, as well as a critique which draws on material elsewhere, particularly from cognitive psychology. The argument here is for the notion of different levels of consciousness or deliberation. Indeed, it is argued that without such an idea, any emphasis on purposive action is devoid of meaning.

The focus of chapter 6 is on the nature and function of habits, routines and institutions. Not only is orthodoxy criticized for either eschewing or downgrading the role of habits and routines in economic life, but some constructive notes are made as to how such concepts should play a central part.

Whilst part two is devoted to a critique of orthodox ideas concerning human action and agency, part three is concerned with specific social institutions, such as the market and the capitalist firm. However, it is far beyond the scope of this work to build a complete theory in this area. What is offered are a number of notes and observations, with the hope that they may contribute to future theoretical work.

Chapter 7 concentrates on some categories which are elemental to a capitalist system, namely contracts, exchange and property rights. The influence of classic conceptions of these categories, and classic liberal views of the state, is identified and criticized. Drawing on some aspects of the work of the sociologist Emile Durkheim, an alternative to a liberal-utilitarian framework is suggested, in which concepts such as routine and trust have a central significance.

The analysis moves on in chapter 8 to discuss the market. In emphasizing the point that the market is itself a social institution it is argued that orthodox theory often mistakenly treats it as if it were a natural state of affairs, consisting merely of the sum total of individual exchanges. The discussion leads on to discuss the function of rigidities and norms in market systems, and again counters the orthodox view where such inflexibilities are regarded in a negative light, largely as restrictions upon the operation of a mythical 'pure' market.

Chapter 9 is devoted to a discussion of the capitalist firm in the context of its market environment. Clearly, the subject area here is so wide and complex that only a few notes can be offered. Nevertheless, some doubts are expressed on the possibility of explaining the nature and existence of the firm largely or wholly in terms of the vague but fashionable idea of 'transaction costs'. Some suggestions as to an alternative line of argument are put forward.

The discussion shifts from what is traditionally described as micro-economics to the macroeconomic sphere in chapter 10. The main object of discussion is the formation and function of expectations of the future in the economic system, concentrating particularly on the work of Keynes but also directing some criticisms against the rational expectations and Austrian schools.

The final chapter is largely devoted to policy matters. An attempt is made to draw together some of the threads of the preceding argument and to suggest some of the policy implications of the analysis. The stance throughout the work that the tastes and preferences of the individual are not to be regarded as given or exogenous has clear implications for the economics of needs and welfare. The chapter commences with a discussion of this issue, drawing on some recent work in the area. The chapter moves on to consider implications regarding economic organization, both at the level of the firm and the economy as a whole.

Critiques of orthodox economic theory are often rebutted because they have little or nothing to offer in its place. It is a bit much to expect, however, that a single work can demolish the edifice and build a complete alternative structure. The burden of argument here is that the accumulating criticisms of the mainstream approach now press with so much weight that they cannot continue to be ignored. Second, there are now so many tools and materials available for the building of an alternative that the rebuttal cannot serve as an excuse. If we search for an alternative to neoclassical theory we may find that in substance it already exists. The main problem is to convince those that still insist on viewing reality through neoclassical spectacles that it might be worthwhile to ponder the world a while with them removed.

# 2

# On Methodology and Assumptions

Neoclassical theory has made economics the preeminent social science by providing it a disciplined, logical analytical framework. To abandon neoclassical theory is to abandon economics as a science.

Douglass C. North (1978, p. 974)

The retention of the neoclassical core and the continued insistence on its mastery as the prerequisite for being considered competent in the field means . . . economics can never hope to become a science. Economics as a discipline therefore has a choice: It can retain the neoclassical core of its theory or, alternatively, it can one day become a science. It cannot have it both ways.

Alfred S. Eichner (1983a, p. 518)

The two quotations above, one from a well-known neoclassical economic historian and the other from a leading member of the Post-Keynesian school, illuminate a stark methodological rift that divides economists today. According to the first quotation, neoclassical theory, through its logic and rigour, has become part of the enduring foundation of economic science. According to the second author, neoclassical theory 'has not been validated empirically' (Eichner, 1983a, p. 510). In consequence it is not acceptable as a basis for the development of economics as a science and it must be replaced by something else. Clearly, here are two views of the scientific status of neoclassical economics which are diametrically opposed.

With controversy within the profession being at this pitch it is difficult to avoid some of the underlying questions of methodology. In any case it would not be easy to embark on a critique of neoclassical theory, let alone a discussion of viable alternatives, without some preliminary remarks in this area. Although methodological statements appear elsewhere in this work it would be useful to outline some of the key issues at this stage.

The context of the argument is as follows. In the past, institutionalist and other criticisms of neoclassical theory have been deflected by assertions of its scientific character. This assertion is on the basis of methodological arguments put forward by Milton Friedman or Fritz Machlup, or on the claim that neoclassical economics is founded on a Popperian methodology. It shall be demonstrated, however, that these methodological positions do not stand up to modern scrutiny, based on recent developments in the philosophy of science. Whilst this methodological critique does not on its own devastate neoclassical assumptions and models, it does demonstrate that the bases for past claims that neoclassical theory is scientific are ill-founded.

Furthermore, there is a growing, if not dominant, view amongst philosophers of science that the search for a single, prescriptive methodology is likely to fail. This opens up a more open and pluralistic methodological perspective. Consequently, the methodological route is open for the creation of an alternative to neoclassical orthodoxy.

## 2.1 THE METHODOLOGICAL DEFENCE OF NEOCLASSICAL THEORY

However, before an alternative route is taken it is necessary to deal with the neoclassical defences. In the many months of writing and rewriting, an imaginary neoclassical critic watched this book as it was created. He – his manner was undeniably male – noted the repeated and perhaps tedious appeals of the author for insights and evidence from both other disciplines and within economics to be taken into account. The critic was not impressed by the arguments, nor by the abundant quotations of material from fringe economics, psychology, sociology, politics and anthropology. There were many shakings of his imaginary head, and sighs of disapproval, leading the writer to wonder why the critic stayed so long. Despite his nagging protestations I was impressed by his patience and wondered if his less imaginary counterparts would stay for a fraction of the time. But what impressed me even more was that his response rested on the arguments found in a single, classical essay, which has been by far the most powerful weapon in defence of the neoclassical citadel.

Milton Friedman's formidable (1953) methodological defence of neoclassical theory is so widely invoked in orthodox circles that it is unavoidable as a focus for any methodological discussion in economics. For those that believe that assumptions in economic theory can be straightforwardly tested or validated empirically, it contains an answer that cannot easily be disregarded. Moreover, the central ideas in this article have been widely accepted, even by economists who would not accept many of Friedman's economic theories and policy recommendations. We thus commence with an assessment of this rampart for neoclassical theory, and survey its strengths and weaknesses.

Consistent with some faults which have been found by other critics of Friedman's essay, it is argued here that Friedman's criteria for the adoption of a theory are both theoretically incoherent and have not, in fact, been adopted by neoclassical theorists in practice. Neither are attempts to restate Friedman's argument in Popperian terms any more successful: one reason being due to serious flaws that have been discovered in Sir Karl Popper's methodology. First, however, we start with a summary of Friedman's methodological position.

## Friedman's methodology

Friedman commences his famous essay by invoking the distinction between positive and normative science outlined by John Neville Keynes (1891). He states his belief that a positive agreement amongst economists on the effects of policy proposals would help to clarify debate and even work towards the establishment of a wider, normative consensus.

In a crucial passage Friedman asserts that the 'ultimate goal of a positive science is the development of a "theory" or "hypothesis" that yields valid and meaningful (i.e. not truistic) predictions about phenomena not yet observed' (1953, p. 7). Following this, Friedman proposes a number of criteria for the acceptability of a theory. Naturally, logical completeness and consistency are important. But supreme emphasis is put on the proposition that 'the only relevant test of the *validity* of a hypothesis is comparison of its predictions with experience' (pp. 8–9).

Additionally, since a finite amount of evidence can never, by Friedman's argument, reject all conceivable rival theories except one and thus select a single theory, a further criterion is required. Although this 'must to some extent be arbitrary . . . there is general agreement that relevant considerations are suggested by the criteria "simplicity" and "fruitfulness", themselves notions which defy completely objective specification' (p. 10).

Friedman argues that a 'hypothesis is important if it "explains" much by little, that is, if it abstracts the common and crucial elements from the mass of complex and detailed circumstances surrounding the phenomena to be explained and permits valid prediction on the basis of them alone' (p. 14). Further, it is not actually possible to test a theory by the 'realism' of its assumptions: 'the relevant question to ask about the "assumptions" of a theory is not whether they are descriptively "realistic", for they never are, but whether they are sufficiently good approximations for the purpose in hand. And this question can be answered only by seeing whether the theory works, which means whether it yields sufficiently accurate predictions' (p. 15).

Friedman then moves on to apply these arguments against the anti-neoclassical critics, and in defence of neoclassical assumptions such as the hypothesis of maximization. In some respects his arguments are similar to those of Fritz Machlup (1955, 1972) who has repeatedly argued that not all assumptions of a theory can be tested empirically and that fundamental assumptions such as rationality and the maximization hypothesis are not vulnerable to an attack which is supposedly based on empirical evidence.

Neoclassical theorists have repeated these arguments to great effect within the profession, especially in rebutting the view that a good or valid theory must have realistic assumptions. It is frequently pointed out that all theories have assumptions which involve simplification or abstraction. Thus, for example, in most forms of macroeconomic modelling (including neoclassical, Keynesian and Marxian) simplification is achieved by heroic aggregation which reduces the number of commodities in the economy from many millions to dozens or less. Theory can never precisely mirror reality in all its complexity.

Since 1953 this argument has been repeated countless times to protect the fundamental assumptions of neoclassical theory from attack. In particular it is an often-repeated rebuttal to those who challenge the assumption that agents act as if they were maximizing their expected utility. Other examples are legion: the still frequent assumption of perfect competition, the related assumption of perfect knowledge, the assumption of U-shaped long run average cost curves, the assumption of a 'well behaved' production function, and so on. All these are frequently justified on the grounds that, as in other theories, they are bound to be approximations and not fully realistic, but nevertheless they are useful and scientifically valid because they yield 'correct predictions'.

## The methodology in practice

Despite the ritual citation of Friedman's article, it is arguable whether the 'correct predictions' methodology has actually been carried out in practice. To take a single example at this stage: the consumption function. Francis Green (1979, 1984) has shown conclusively that the two theories that are favoured by neoclassical economists, namely the life-cycle hypothesis and Friedman's own permanent-income hypothesis, have never yet had their superiority over alternative theories demonstrated by any evidence. He argues that preceding ideas such as the relative income theory and the habit persistence theory (both of which, incidentally, have an institutionalist flavour) were relegated to virtual oblivion not because they failed to predict accurately but because they did not fit in with neoclassical preconceptions. In addition, Green suggests that ideological factors have been involved in the ascendancy of the neoclassical theories.

If economists had actually lived according to the predictionist creed it is arguable that the subject would have developed in a very different way since the 1950s. Given that 'success' in making 'correct' predictions is being judged in relation to other, contending, theories then there would have been many more attempts to examine hypotheses along with, and on the same terms as, their rivals. To be convincing, any claim of good performance according to the 'correct predictions' criterion has to show that its rivals are wanting. Instead, the norm in the literature is simply to show that the chosen hypothesis is adequate according to the currently accepted statistical tests. But even an $R^2$ of 98 per cent may be not good enough if there is a rival which scores 99. Yet the normal practice is to ignore the obvious fact that in a developing science practical success in 'making correct predictions' is a relative matter, and to proceed by simply disregarding the actual or potential competition.

To foreshadow some further arguments below, even if attempts have been made to live by Friedman's words, on reflection a statistical comparison of relative or absolute performance in terms of 'correct predictions' rarely, if ever, brings about a clear and decisive verdict. There are usually a variety of data sets, of variable quality, and the testing of the hypothesis involves a number of auxiliary hypotheses which make discriminating judgement more difficult. It is arguable that Friedman's method has not been implemented, and even if an attempt was made it would not work satisfactorily.

It would be impossible to attempt a survey of the attempts of all the upholders of Friedman's 1953 article to apply the criterion of 'correct predictions' in their evaluations of economic theories. But later in this work a number of cases are cited of an apparent shortfall between neoclassical theory and predictive performance.

Clearly, however, this is not the crucial issue. If neoclassical economists were to admit that they had not been very diligent in applying Friedman's methodology then a response would be to declare good intentions to enforce it in future. The failure of application is illustrative, but it is a methodological critique which must take priority. To this we now turn.

*Critos*

## Critics of Friedman

Naturally, such a prominent methodological argument with strong implications for economists has attracted a great deal of critical attention.[1] A number of important criticisms should be noted. First, Ernest Nagel (1963) shows that Friedman uses the terms 'realistic' and 'unrealistic' ambiguously. If an assumption is 'realistic' does that mean that it is simply testable, or largely confirmed by the evidence, or that it is true? Thus different supporters and critics of Friedman have used his 'unrealism' argument in varied and confusing ways, and in part the confusion is due to Friedman himself.

Second, an allied line of argument is developed by Alan Musgrave (1981) who argues concisely but effectively that Friedman fails to distinguish between different types of assumption at the basis of a theory. In particular, *negligibility* assumptions state that some factor has a negligible effect upon the phenomenon under investigation. For example, air friction may be assumed to be negligible in a theory relating to mechanical motion. *Domain* assumptions are different in that they specify the domain of applicability of a theory, without necessarily suggesting that the assumption is realistic or unrealistic. Thus a theory based on the assumption that an economy is closed may not involve the idea that the adjustment required to the theory is negligible if it were applied to an open economy, but, instead, that the theory applies to closed economies as a particular domain of application. Still different are *heuristic* assumptions which are not made for either of the above reasons but to develop a theory by 'successive approximation' in that simplifying assumptions are made at the early stages of presentation of a theory, to be dropped or modified later.

From this standpoint Musgrave (pp. 379–80) is able to criticize Friedman effectively for his statements that 'the more significant the theory, the more unrealistic the assumptions . . . To be important . . . a hypothesis must be descriptively false in its assumptions . . . the relevant question to ask about the "assumptions" of a theory is not whether they are descriptively "realistic", for they never are' (Friedman, 1953, pp. 14–15). Musgrave suggests that in these passages Friedman has negligibility assumptions in mind, and argues that it is an error to regard them as necessarily 'descriptively false'. Negligibility assumptions do not necessarily involve a description of reality that is false or inaccurate. Instead they involve a proposal that such-and-such a factor is negligible and thereby 'irrelevant for the phenomena to be explained'. Thus in much modelling in mechanics the assumption that air resistance is negligible can thus be a true statement about reality. A formal model which assumes that this resistance is zero will not, of course, be 'true' in the sense that it corresponds precisely with reality. But it could still be descriptively valid, because, by virtue of this very assumption and others which demarcate between what is and is not negligible, it is attempting to explain the phenomena under investigation.

### The instrumentalist interpretation

Nevertheless, it is possible to revise Friedman's argument so that it is invulnerable to many of these criticisms. This is done by re-interpreting his proposed methodology as a variety of instrumentalism. Such a viewpoint is suggested by Lawrence Boland (1979a) and approved, apparently, by Friedman himself (see Boland, 1982, p. 171; Caldwell, 1982, p. 178).

The instrumentalist position is that theories are best regarded as *nothing more* than instruments. Consequently, the idea of the truth or falsity of a theory is both irrelevant and meaningless. A theory is a tool, and it is judged on some instrumental criterion of its effectivity. Furthermore, despite Friedman's own phraseology in his 1953 article, neither the realism nor unrealism of a theory or its assumptions is important. From a strict instrumentalist point of view the unrealism of an assumption neither adds to nor detracts from the stature of a theory. It simply matters whether or not the theory is useful according to some instrumental criterion. In Friedman's presentation a theory is applauded according to whether or not it makes 'correct predictions'. It is possible to rewrite Friedman in these terms, and, as Boland suggests, to thus devise an artful strategem for the defence of his methodology.

According to this reasoning the acceptability of Friedman's methodology rests upon an assessment of instrumentalism. Boland rashly proposes that 'no one has been able to criticize or refute instrumentalism' (1979a, p. 521). Nevertheless, Bruce Caldwell (1980b) and others have put forward several substantive points against this very approach. Before some of these are mentioned it should first be pointed out, as Alan Coddington (1979) suggests, that there are different varieties of instrumentalism.[2] In Friedman's version the utility of a theory is judged by its ability to make 'correct predictions'. Coddington dubs this 'predictionism'. But non-predictionist versions of instrumentalism are possible; a theory could be judged by its usefulness as a tool for business practitioners, or by its capacity to sustain a particular political ideology.[3]

Whilst there is no decisive 'proof' of the inferiority of instrumentalism, and equally no independent logical demonstration of its superiority, criticism is still possible, based on an examination of the implications of taking such a view.

The first point deserving emphasis is the implicit dismissal of the goal of truth by the instrumentalists. If truth is an objective, be it distant or close, then instrumentalism does not serve to bring us closer to it. As D. Bear and Daniel Orr (1967) show, false assumptions can lead to true or predictively adequate consequences. So if theories are to be true as well as yielding correct predictions, then prediction must be supplemented by other (non-instrumentalist) criteria of theory appraisal.

If explanation is also a virtue of scientific enquiry then predictionist instrumentalism is again a diversion. Careful modelling and assessment of proposed causal linkages gives way to bland statistical correlation in a competition for predictive adequacy. In addition, Karl Popper (1965, pp. 113–14) points out that acceptance of instrumentalism rules out the possibility of falsification in science. Within strict instrumentalism a theory is neither true nor false; in its terms a theory can be found adequate or inadequate, but never rejected by disconfirmation.

However, the non-falsifiability of theories could be interpreted as a positive virtue, because if theories are never to be weeded out then we can allow a hundred wild and varied flowers to bloom. However, Friedman's own presentation of instrumentalism is far from being tolerant or pluralistic in this sense. Evidently, his marketplace libertarianism does not extend from his politics to his scientific methodology.

It should be emphasized, as Caldwell (1980b, p. 369) points out, that philosophers of science 'since the 1940s have been unanimous in their rejection of the notion that the only goal of science is prediction. Even such positivist philosophers as Carl Hempel have claimed that explanation, not prediction, is the goal of science'. Above all, it is Friedman's rejection of the explanatory function of economic theory in particular and science in general that has provoked much understandable hostility from critics.

Finally, on a less conventional tack, it has to be stated that Friedman's predictive instrumentalism does unjustifiably take the concepts of 'prediction', 'observation' and 'experience' for granted. Although Friedman clearly and correctly rejects a naive empiricism where theories mirror facts, his argument does rest on a version of empiricist epistemology. For his methodology to be sustained, the 'predictions' of a theory have to be appraised objectively, and independently of any other theory, hypothesis or conceptual framework. Otherwise his argument would go round in circles: theories are validated by the predictions, but predictions depend upon this or other theories, which in turn are validated by predictions, and so on.

To make sense of Friedman's methodology it has to be assumed that at some stage 'predictions', 'observations' and 'experience' are independent of the theoretical or conceptual framework of the researcher. If the supreme test of a theory is its capacity to yield 'correct predictions' then some observations used to test the theory have to be regarded as objective tests, and should not be moulded or rigged by any other theory. If any observation was theory-bound then we would require a further, atheoretical observation to give the theory binding the former prediction the Friedman test. For Friedman's methodology to work, sooner or later we require a set of observations free of any theory at all. Thus the testing of a theory by its predictions unavoidably involves the adoption of an empiricist epistemology.[4]

2.2   EMPIRICISM AND BEYOND

*A critique of positivism and empiricism*

Empiricism, which includes positivism as a large subset, has been criticized extensively for centuries.[5] It boils down to the view that sense data, or 'experience', are the ultimate source of all knowledge. The key criticism of empiricist epistemology worthy of emphasis here (and elsewhere in this book) is that no observation can be independent of the conceptual framework, language and theoretical system of the observer. Consequently, no 'objective' facts can be known untainted by the preconceptions of the investigator. All facts are expressed in some form of language, and an aconceptual or atheoretical language is impossible.

The criticism should not be confused with a denial of the existence of real world, outside our heads, nor with a statement to the effect that all knowledge is 'subjective'. Whilst many critics of empiricism have adopted such views, they do not necessarily follow from the key criticism stated above, nor are they adopted by the present author. Furthermore, as is argued below, a rejection of empiric*ism* does not necessarily imply a suggestion that empiric*al* work in science has no value. It can be noted here that an anti-empiricism, combined with the denial of the complete subjectivity of knowledge, and coupled with an acceptance that in the development of science data-gathering and analysis can have a positive weight, are all methodological features of this present work.

None of these positions is inconsistent with the rejection of empiricism. To repeat: as observers of the social or natural world, there are no 'facts' which are perceived independently of our theories or concepts. Any observation requires both selection and interpretation. Empirical work involves the search for and selection of data from a mass of information which cannot all be addressed by the theory. What ususally confronts the scientist is a choice of phenomena, and a decision that some data must be rejected. Furthermore, the questions that are asked and the interpretations placed upon the analysis are all inevitably coloured by the preconceptions, past experiences and anticipations of the observer. 'Neutral' and 'objective' empirical work, where the facts 'speak for themselves', and experience and empirical evidence are the unbiased tutors of scientific advance, is an impossible dream.

In rejecting the idea of a readily discernible set of objective, hard facts, 'out there', we should not fall into the opposite error of assuming that knowledge is entirely a matter inside the individual's head. Evidence, whilst being unavoidably selected and moulded by the observer, is not purely subjective. 'Facts' cannot be ascertained independently of theories or concepts of the researcher, but that does not mean that their substance is entirely reducible to theories or concepts, or that facts or theories are purely subjective in character.

By its nature, explicit knowledge is communicable and thereby expressed in the form of a (social) language. Thus any unit of such knowledge is further structured by the mode of expression of the particular language that is used, and this structuring is a product of social relationships and processes. To some extent the socially imprinted language affects the theories that are developed. Furthermore, as a number of philosophers of science from varying points of view have emphasized,[6] science is a social activity and its development involves the social generation, scrutinization and acceptance or rejection of theories, procedures and norms. Consequently, science can never be 'neutral' in the sense that it is entirely free of the biases and preoccupations of society and the scientific community.

We can never prove that a world exists outside our heads but that does not mean that it is legitimate or desirable to assume otherwise. The standpoint here is that there is a real world beyond ourselves, and beyond our narrow perceptions of it, which, to some extent can be perceived and appraised; notwithstanding the entirely valid proposition that there is no perception or appraisal independent of the preconceptions of the subject. In short, perception, whilst unavoidably theory-bound, has a real object. In this manner it is possible to ally an anti-empiricism with a realist philosophy of science.[7]

The main arguments against an empiricist position are widely known and may be familiar to a number of practising researchers. However, they are not given sufficiently serious attention or weight. They are like a nagging, intractable problem which would sabotage the slow 'progress' of day-to-day activity if it was to be discussed too seriously or too often. This case of cognitive dissonance for the empirical researcher is as serious as it is for parents trying to rear young children in the era of nuclear weapons: most of us are aware of the dangers and awesome possibilities, but it is difficult to function in everyday life by giving them the prominence they perhaps deserve. For many people the dissonance is overcome by acting as if the problem did not exist.

Perhaps some researchers manage to live with the philosophical critique of empiricism by accepting in principle that there is no observation that is free from theoretical or conceptual framing, but assuming that it can be progressively minimized by careful statistical work and reasoned interpretation of the data. However, this idea of theory as a 'successive approximation' to empirical reality has to be treated with some care. The problem is that there is no purely empirical criterion with which we can judge if an embellishment to a theory makes it 'closer' to reality or not. One consequence of the rejection of empiricism is that there is no objective, atheoretical yardstick with which the 'distance' of a theoretical model from the real world can be measured.[8]

All that can be conceded is that 'better approximation' may be apparent within the terms and assumptions of the theoretical paradigm itself. Without a yardstick of success, 'successive approximation' can only be the goal of 'normal science' (see Kuhn, 1962) where there is a consensus in the scientific community and a shared set of approaches and conventions. It may be a worthy goal of theoretical development to create such a consensus, or to replace an older one by a different approach, but there is no prescription to be found in methodology to lend any given paradigm automatic support.

## The falsificationism of Sir Karl Popper

The arguments in the preceding section are not original and they are found, in various forms, in the writings of a number of philosophers. In particular, there is a repeated attack on empiricism in the works of Karl Popper. He has always denied the possibility of an atheoretical language of observation. Furthermore, his contribution is notable for its eloquent and developed attack on positivism, and on the associated idea that through observation it is possible to 'verify' an assumption or a theory.

A discussion of Popper is important because, contrary to his apparent anti-empiricism, his work in fact offers a refuge for some defenders of neoclassical theory, and it is possible to amend slightly Friedman's 1953 essay so that it complies with a version of Popper. Indeed, according to Lawrence Boland (1982, p. 171) 'Friedman claims to be closely allied to Popper's views'. In concurrence with this, Mark Blaug (1978, p. 714) writes that 'Friedman is simply Popper-with-a-twist applied to economics'[9] What then, in brief, is the substance of Popper's contribution?

In his formative years, Popper was deeply affected by his observation of Marxism, Freudianism and other sets of ideas which purported to be scientific. They seemed to make statements about the world which were not capable of refutation. In contrast, he was impressed in his studies by the development and eventual acceptance of Einstein's theory of relativity, which allegedly depended on the results of a number of 'crucial experiments'.[10]

Popper's writings on methodology involve a direct attack on positivism in general, and in particular the sophisticated version developed by the Vienna School in the 1920s and 1930s. As Popper rightly points out, despite its best efforts positivism is still defeated by the problem of induction: there is no amount of empirical evidence which can prove the truth of an universal statement. This is because it is always possible that further evidence will appear to disconfirm such a proposition; we can never be sure that the universal statement will not eventually be refuted by some as yet unknown piece of evidence. Consequently, as far as universal statements go, no amount of empirical evidence can provide a confirmation of their truth. On this basis Popper finds that all varieties of positivism (including logical positivism) are fundamentally flawed.

Popper's 'solution' to the problem of induction is to shift the focus from whether or not they are true to whether or not they are false: from the process of verification to that of refutation. Notably these two processes are not symmetrical. He argues that whilst no limited amount of empirical evidence can verify a universal statement, a finite amount of evidence can show that such a statement is false. No finite amount of evidence can prove that 'all swans are white', but the single observation of a black swan will refute that proposition. In short, according to Popper, it is by falsification rather than verification that the growth of knowledge proceeds.

Furthermore, the scientific character of a theory or proposition is not to be judged by the amount of empirical evidence upon which it apparently rests, or which can be quoted to give it 'verification'. The hallmark of a scientific theory, according to Popper, is its potential falsifiability. The progress of science depends on bold, non-tautological conjectures, with high information content, which are testable in the sense that they can conceivably be shown to be wrong. In contrast, a non-scientific or 'metaphysical' theory is one with which all such evidence can be conveniently explained away. Popper places the theories of Freud and Marx in the latter category.

True Popperian defenders of neoclassical theory do not argue that its assumptions have been verified by correct predictions. Instead, they assert that the predictions of neoclassical theory are both testable and have, in fact, turned out to be correct. This has given neoclassicism the highest possible Popperian status of a theory that is both scientific and non-falsified. Thus, despite Popper's attack on positivism and empiricism, in effect the neoclassical Popperian ends up using the same criterion of 'correct predictions' to give neoclassical theory a positive appraisal.[11] Once again, attention is diverted from the question of the 'realism of assumptions', this time to the issue of falsification of the hypotheses in question. The main difference between Friedman (1953) and Friedman-rewritten-in-Popperian-terms is that in the latter 'correct predictions' do not confirm a theory, they simply fail to falsify it. In practice, as this case illustrates, Popper's attack on positivism is much less revolutionary than it would appear at first sight.

## A critique of Popper's methodology

Whilst Popper has put a great deal of effort into developing and refining this methodology, it has continually faced a couple of related and nagging problems. If Popper's falsificationism is to be interpreted crudely then if just one empirical observation were to counter a hypothesis then the latter would have to be discarded. If the theory proposes that $X$ will happen and we observe that it does not, then the theory is falsified and has to be rejected. However, it would be difficult for any science to proceed on such strict criteria and it is hard to see how knowledge could grow if every negative observation were given this weight. Such a 'naive falsificationism' can be detected in Popper's earlier works, but it is later rejected as he has reached a 'sophisticated' falsificationism in his more mature writings.[12]

'Sophisticated' falsificationism does not treat hypotheses as isolated constructs; instead they are treated as parts of larger, dynamic, theoretical systems which are evolving through time. Theoretical propositions do not stand alone; they depend in turn upon other assumptions, and are links in chains of a logical argument. In form and substance the theoretical system changes as new arguments and assumptions appear. However, whilst it allows us to take a more sophisticated view of theoretical discourse and development, the rejection of naive falsificationism leaves open the question as to when falsifying evidence shall, and shall not, be allowed to demolish a theory.

To this first nagging problem Popperians have failed to provide an adequate solution.

The point that hypotheses do not stand alone relates to the so-called Duhem–Quine thesis, named after the French physicist Pierre Duhem and the American philosopher Willard van Orman Quine.[13] This thesis states that it not possible to falsify single hypotheses because it is invariably conjunctions of hypoheses which are being tested. In these circumstances it is difficult to falsify theories according to Popperian criteria. According to the Duhem–Quine thesis we can never be sure that the main hypothesis has been put open to falsification on its own, and that other auxiliary hypotheses are not involved.

An example which illustrates the problem of the conjointness of hypotheses in economics is provided by Rod Cross (1982b). The hypothesis of a stable demand for money has always to be tested jointly with a large number of other hypotheses; such as the hypotheses in defining the relevant explanatory variables, hypotheses involved in their measurement, hypotheses from the type of economic theory that is utilized, hypotheses regarding the time lags in the demand for money function, hypotheses underlying the *ceteris paribis* clause, hypotheses regarding the statistical methods involved and the degree of tolerable error, and so on, *ad nauseam*. The key proposition is never open to falsification on its own.

In short, therefore, no science has proceeded, and cannot in principle proceed, in strict Popperian terms. There are ostensibly insurmountable difficulties with both 'naive' and 'sophisticated' falsificationism. In the event of any falsifying observation it is not clear whether it is the main hypothesis or its auxiliaries that are falsified.

Apart from the Duhem–Quine thesis there is another line of argument, developed forcefully in a work by Barry Hindess (1977c), which is fatal for the Popperian methodology. The argument shows that despite Popper's attack on positivism, there is a residual empiricism in his methodology in the notion that a theory is to be tested against the facts of observation.

This verdict may be surprising, in view of Popper's rejection of the positivist idea that a theory can be verified by the facts, and his denial of the existence or possibility of an atheoretical observation language. He takes the view that the distinction of Rudolf Carnap and other positivists between theoretical and observation languages is untenable. Popper insists that all statements of observation are always interpretations and that 'they are interpretations in the light of theory' (Popper, 1959, p. 107n.).

However, this recognition that all observation is theory-bound does not save Popper's methodology. On the contrary its incoherence is underlined. The problem with Popper's position is that he still retains the decisive criterion that a theory is to be tested against the facts of observation. But, as Hindess (p. 165) argues, if there is no possibility of an atheoretical language of observation – a point accepted by Popper – then 'the doctrine of the testing of a theory against the facts has no rational foundation'. Popper's position is incoherent because he accepts completely that all facts and observations are coloured by theoretical preconception, but on the other hand the idea of decisive empirical tests of potential falsification is the centrepiece of his methodology. Yet it is impossible for a theory to be falsified 'by the facts', as facts themselves are always tied to a theoretical discourse.[14]

In some ways this argument is similar to the one based upon the Duhem–Quine thesis, once it is accepted that all observations involve theories, conceptual frameworks or hypotheses. Thus any observation which, according to Popper, could conceivably 'falsify' a theory cannot be made independently of a number of auxiliary hypotheses, some of which are related in particular to the act of observation. If we thus establish the statement that at least one auxiliary hypothesis is involved in any observation, then Hindess' argument against Popper fits very well with the more general problem of the Duhem–Quine thesis discussed above.

As an example, consider the various, contesting theories of inflation which propose that the overall price level is determined by the quantity of money, or the wage level, or whatever. Presumably, according to Popper, a theory in this group would be falsified if there were no series of observations with any lagged or unlagged correlation between the independent variables and the price level. However, any such observations would depend upon a whole series of presumptions and theories surrounding the very concepts and measurement of the 'price level', the 'money supply' or the 'wage level' or whatever. Indeed,there has always been controversy over such measures. And in each case some theoretical formulation is involved, not least in the specification of the methods of measurement. Thus it is not at all clear how any such theory of inflation could be decisively falsified by any series of observations.

For these reasons, a decisive empirical shoot-out where one set of econometricians supporting one theory concedes victory to another on the basis of 'the evidence' is an extremely rare event. If it were to occur it would more likely to be because one side lost faith or nerve; it cannot be because evidence showed without further ado that a theory was incontrovertibly false.

In sum, Popper's critique of logical positivism does not mark a revolution leading to the foundation of a secure, post-positivist methodology of science. The reason being that he ultimately fails to shed the empiricist idea of the testing of a theory against the facts, thus a residual empiricism remains. Instead of a revolution in methodology, Popper's work is one of the last chapters in the philosophy of science in the positivist era, it is not the first part of something new.


## 2.3   THE FATE OF METHODOLOGY


*Prediction and other obsessions*

The precepts of the official methodology of economics have been identified and criticised in an article by Donald McCloskey (1983), describing them as 'modernist'. They include the following:

- Prediction is the goal of science.
- Only the predictions or observable implications of a theory matter to its truth.
- Observability entails objective, reproducible experiments.
- A theory is proved false if and only if one of its experimental implications proves false.
- Kelvin's Dictum: 'When you cannot express it in numbers, your knowledge is of a meagre and unsatisfactory kind.'[15]
- It is the business of methodology to demarcate scientific reasoning from the non-scientific, and positive judgements from the normative.
- The adoption of Hume's Fork: worthwhile discourse has either to contain 'abstract reasoning concerning quantity or number' or 'experimental reasoning concerning matter of fact and existence'. If not 'commit it then to the flames, for it can contain nothing but sophistry and illusion'.
- Scientists have nothing to say as scientists about values, whether of morality or art.

McCloskey's judgement on the current status of these propositions should disturb any practising advocate of any version of Friedman's methodology: 'Few in philosophy now believe as many as half of these propositions. A substantial, respectable, and growing minority believes in none of them. But the large majority of economists believe them all' (McCloskey, 1983, p. 485).

Making use of developments in modern philosophy, McCloskey then proceeds to develop a strong critique of these modernist precepts. Much of this critique is based on problems of internal inconsistency. For example, the hostility of modernists to 'metaphysical' statements has to be cast into the flames for it itself is metaphysical. Indeed, the criterion that theories have to be judged primarily by the predictions is, itself, metaphysical, and suffers likewise under the modernist doctrine of Hume's fork.[16]

The dethronement of prediction is surely to be applauded. Whilst it is sometimes possible to hazard an informed guess concerning the future, it should be pointed out that, in social science, predictive accuracy is partly a matter of luck or chance and can never be founded solely on a deterministic model. Part of the problem is that social systems depend upon knowledge and we cannot predict what future knowledge will be. Furthermore, predictions of the future are often confounded by the familiar phenomenon of the self-fulfilling prophecy, and other problems related to the fact that the observer is part of the system being observed. For instance, if an acknowledged authority predicts that the dollar will fall in value, this statement may itself help to lower its parity. Notably, the impossibility of assured prediction is not confined to economics. A similar problem is found in quantum physics with the Heisenberg uncertainty principle.[17]

## The limits of prescriptive methodology

More generally, there are problems with all universal, prescriptive methodologies. Explicit in the main tradition of methodological writing, from Hume to Popper, is a quest for an epistemology to help generate sound, scientific knowledge and a set of methodological criteria to judge one theory against the next. But, as Hindess (1977c) argues with great effect, this whole project is doomed. Overtly or covertly, all such procedures eventually rely on an empiricist theory of knowledge where at some stage 'facts' are used to test a theory in some way. Prescriptive methodology has either to adopt the unacceptable proposition that an atheoretical language of observation is possible, or by rejecting this idea it becomes internally incoherent in that it nevertheless attempts to test a theory against the facts.

The general idea that science should be ruthlessly scrutinized according to a universal methodological protocol is unacceptable. As Bruce Caldwell concludes after a scrupulous tour through economic methodology: 'The most significant contribution of the growth of knowledge philosophers was the demonstration that the quest for a single, universal, prescriptive scientific methodology is quixotic . . . no universally applicable, logically compelling method of theory appraisal exists' (Caldwell, 1982, pp. 244–5).

This judgement goes against the grain for many economists, even some of those that are highly proficient in the area of methodology. As an example, the clear and well-written essay on methodology by Mark Blaug (1980) proceeds to judge the corpus of economic theory against a single set of criteria – mainly Popperian but with a dash of Lakatos. The procedure is simply to judge the major features of modern economic theory according to several dubious epistemological and methodological precepts.

The conclusion is seemingly unavoidable: there is no way in which a rational or coherent prescriptive methodology for economics can be discovered, and the search for a universally valid or even optimal methodology is futile. With the benefit of hindsight after an unsuccessful, intense, and century-long search for the methodological Holy Grail, it is reasonable to conclude that there is no possibility of an extra-theoretical court of appeal to judge theories.

## *The remaining scope for appraisal*

At this stage in the argument one may decide to abandon the methodological defence of neoclassical theory. After all, if theories cannot effectively be judged by a universal, methodological protocol, it could be argued that orthodox economics should continue as before because it is seemingly invulnerable to any methodological onslaught. Perhaps 'anything goes', and economists should continue to do what economists continue to do.[18]

Indeed, in existing circumstances the adoption of a 'free-market' methodology of 'anything goes' would be an improvement on the methodological dogmatism which condemns unorthodox schools of thought within economics as unscientific. Debate and development within economics would be much improved if neoclassical orthodoxy did not dismiss entirely its Keynesian, institutionalist or Marxian rivals on the grounds that they do not conform to the methodological prescriptions of Karl Popper or Milton Friedman in his 1953 essay. Likewise, if neoclassical orthodoxy is to be dismissed, it would be unwarranted to do so simply on the basis that it does not conform to a particular methodological precept.

To recapitulate, the argument so far in this chapter is that the application of single, prescriptive methodology to economics is unacceptable and, indeed, methodologically unsound. Note, however, that this methodological position has itself been established through a methodological discourse. Thus there is a further role for methodology that still remains after the search for a universal, optimal methodology is abandoned. Such analysis involves a 'rational reconstruction of the methodological content both of the writings of economic methodologists and of the various research programmes within the discipline' (Caldwell, 1982, p. 245). The methodologist can then attempt a critical assessment of the methodological content involved in the rational reconstruction, involving an examination of the underlying assumptions, and an exposition of the 'hidden agenda' behind a research programme.

As Caldwell (1982), Hindess (1977c) and others have argued, there is another way in which the application of methodology can be effective. That is the stratagem of criticism of a discourse from within. For the purpose of such criticism the basic objectives and boundaries of a discourse are taken as given. One of the key methods is then to show that in these terms key theories are imperfectly or incompletely established. Thus, for example, Stanley Wong's (1978) critique of Paul Samuelson's theory of revealed preference proceeds by reporting that the research programme attempted to resolve three mutually inconsistent problems, and was unable to resolve any of them with success. 'Internal' methodological criticism of this type avoids the pitfalls of dogmatic, methodological universalism, on the one hand, and anarchic, methodological nihilism, on the other.

Whilst one may concede the powerful potential and importance of 'internal' methodological criticism, does this mean that no methodological criticism is possible between paradigm and paradigm? It can be argued quite briefly that it is unreasonable to exclude this possibility. The reason is quite simply that it is impossible to draw clear, fixed boundaries between schools of thought within a science, or even between one science and its academic cousin. No school, no science is a seamless whole. Each is in a process of metamorphosis and change. Each has a history and a genealogy involving other sciences and schools.

Schools of thought do not develop in isolation. Sometimes one grows by the profound mutation of another, as Marx's economics developed out of, and by criticism of, the classical economics of Smith and Ricardo. On other occasions a more extreme reaction was involved, rejecting the bulk of the presuppositions of the earlier school. In this way the Austrian School developed in reaction to German historicism, and the Institutionalist School was founded in dissent over the teachings of American neoclassical theorists. In still other cases, such as the development of neoclassical economics in the 1870s after the breakup of the Classical School, there are significant elements of both continuity and discontinuity with the past.

Furthermore, even when rival schools of thought clash in seemingly diametric opposition, it is often the case that hidden and common underlying assumptions are involved. Thus, for example, many rival models of the UK or US economies (including those that have justifiably or unjustifiably attracted labels such as 'monetarist' or 'Keynesian') embody a number of questionable common assumptions such as: (most) markets clear, there is a downward-sloping demand curve for labour, capital is homogeneous, or productivity, tastes and preferences are exogenously determined. These linkages give a common platform for controversy that spans the rival approaches, and furthermore allow criticism of the common assumptions from a quite different viewpoint.

It is also a general rule that no school of economics is internally homogeneous. There are profound differences between the works of Smith and Ricardo in the Classical School, between the neoclassical theory of Walras and that of Marshall, just as there are important differences between the 'orthodox' works of Kenneth Arrow, Milton Friedman, Robert Lucas and Paul Samuelson today. Given that there will always be controversy and differences of viewpoint within as well as between schools of economic thought, does this mean that 'internal' criticism must be confined to a sub-school, rather than a school?

Any idea that methodological criticism *always* has to be internal in character ends up in absurdity because of the difficulty of defining and policing the boundaries between the internal and external theoretical domains.

The progress of scientific theory is one of continuous but uneven development. Science exists within a social and political environment which is always changing, and from which different pressures are being brought to bear. Language and culture are changing too, so the very media of expression of the science will mutate over time. It is at least highly unlikely that a clean, hard-edged, theoretically consistent and complete scientific system will ever appear.

Indeed, following the proof of the mathematician Kurt Gödel it is reasonable to presume that a consistent and complete theoretical system is impossible, not because of the evolutionary nature of knowledge, but on the logical impossibility of establishing such an outcome. Using the case of the arithmetic of the integers, Gödel shocked the protagonists of axiomatic thinking:

> He presented mathematicians with the astounding and melancholy conclusion that the axiomatic method has certain inherent limitations, which rule out the possibility that even the ordinary arithmetic of the integers can ever be fully axiomatized. What is more, he proved that it is impossible to establish the internal logical consistency of a very large class of deductive systems . . . In the light of these conclusions, no final systematization of many important areas of mathematics is attainable, and no absolutely impeccable guarantee can be given that many significant branches of mathematical thought are entirely free from internal contradiction.
>
> (Nagel and Newman, 1959, p.6)

Given that consistency and completeness can never be fully achieved 'in the ordinary arithmetic of the integers', formal reasoning in economics is even less likely to attain this result. There is always likely to be a large number of true and important theorems that cannot be formally proved, and the economist, even at the most fundamental level of theoretical discourse, will always be forced to make implicit or explicit assumptions which are not substantiated by formal reasoning. Consequently, such factors as insight and intuition are indispensible to even the most formalistic presentations in economic science.

### The residual importance of evidence

In rejecting the empiricist notion of given and atheoretical evidence 'out there' which can be used either to 'verify' or 'falsify' or 'appraise' a theory, this does not mean that evidence has no weight or function in the progress of science. First of all it is necessary to think of evidence in a different manner, not as something given, but something which is partially *generated* by the theories and concepts at hand. The rejection of empiricism does not mean that evidence has no importance for science, nor that empirical work is of no significance or value. It means, however, that the facts do not 'speak for themselves'.

There is an important example of the role of evidence in regard to the assessment of the neoclassical maximization hypothesis. It is argued below (pp. 89–93), and in conflict with some arguments to the contrary, that experimental and other evidence does give weight to the criticisms of this core idea. Some additional considerations regarding the residual importance of evidence are raised briefly here.

A research programme based on a particular theoretical system or paradigm generates its 'own facts' which are nevertheless gathered through, and coloured by, the concepts and theories involved. These facts may be perfectly intelligible in terms of the theoretical presuppositions or, on the other hand, they may create problems or anomalies for the reigning paradigm. Thus, for example, in the late 1960s there was a flurry of debate and theoretical innovation in mainstream economics when the Phillips Curve was defied by the simultaneous existence of high inflation and high unemployment. This contrary evidence was not used to 'falsify' the theory, indeed the dominant response was simply to change the analysis into an 'expectations-augmented' Phillips Curve through the addition of one extra variable. Evidence is never decisive or entirely compelling, but it can, and often does, have an effect.

Thus an 'internal' critique of a theory might consider how well it has dealt with the problems or anomalies that are created by its 'own facts'. Moreover, there are important cases where alternative research programmes share a number of common facts and theoretical ideas, as exemplified by the debate between the monetarist doctrine and the

Hicks–Samuelson version of Keynesianism in the 1960s and 1970s. Consequently, comparative evaluation of different theories is sometimes possible when they share some commonly appraised 'facts'. In these circumstances at least, 'external' critiques may carry some force.

Consequently, we are not forced into a relativist or subjectivist position concerning theories and facts. Theories are always unfolding and developing (albeit at very different rates), and partially incomplete, and thus are likely to refer to changing and overlapping sets of knowledge. There is no such thing as a fixed and complete theoretical system, with its own exclusive facts, hermetically sealed from the rest of the scientific world. Whilst some theoretical systems are notoriously insular and blinkered, ultimately none is an island. It is this very interconnectedness of the scientific process that means that a relativist view is misconceived.

Conversely, for reasons already explored, there is no possibility of a single, absolute theory, nor a purely absolutist conception of knowledge or facts. Absolute truth is a chimera, and there is no royal road to science. Further, science itself is not fixed or absolute. As Larry Laudan (1977) has argued, it is better regarded as a process, successively uncovering and attempting to solve problems and anomalies. And, as Thomas Kuhn (1962) and others insist, this process is not independent of the social system within which scientists work, the prevailing ideologies, and the internal sociological dynamics of the scientific community.

2.4  APPENDIX: FRIEDMAN AND THE MAXIMIZATION HYPOTHESIS

We now turn to some aspects Milton Friedman's 1953 essay. As we have seen, Friedman's general argument is that a theory is validated (or, alternatively, non-falsified) by its capacity to yield 'correct predictions'. But in the 1953 article itself there is a jumble about what this means. We are told that assumptions do not have to be, or ideally should not be, realistic; what matters is the predictive performance of the theory based upon them. However, given that the simplest of theoretical systems is in fact a tangled web of conjoint hypotheses and assumptions, it is not always entirely clear what is an assumption and what is a theory.

A particularly important case is the maximization hypothesis. Is it a basic assumption upon which is built the theory of consumer behaviour and the theory of the firm, or is it a general theory about human action which is based on other, more fundamental, assumptions? It is not clear whether it is a theory to be confirmed (non-falsified) by 'correct predictions', or a basic assumption which is to be defiantly 'unrealistic' and which is only 'tested' indirectly in terms of the predictive performance of the theoretical system to which it contributes.

The strange answer implied by Friedman is that such a proposition is both a derived theory *and* a basic assumption at the same time. In fact he uses the word 'hypothesis' ambiguously, both as a constructed hypothesis and as a fundamental axiom, to obscure the distinction between the two.

Friedman introduces the hypothesis of maximization with the 'unrealistic' assumption of leaves 'deliberately' seeking to maximize the amount of light each receives (1953, p. 19). The word 'deliberately' is analytically unimportant, because the essence of the assumption is that the leaves are maximizing their sunlight, whether deliberately or not. The word, however, has a double rhetorical function. First it makes the hypothesis sound 'unrealistic', as it implies that each leaf has a conscious brain. And second it underlines the status of the maximization hypothesis as an assumption, and not a theory, in this case.

The theory, derived from the assumption of sunlight maximization, is that leaves will be placed in certain patterns relative to each other, they will face towards the sun, be more plentiful on the sunward side of the tree, and so on. The theory is 'presumably valid' because its predictions are sufficiently accurate. Likewise, in moving from the arboreal to the pecuniary world we have a 'hypothesis', i.e. a theory, of the maximization of returns. This theory is 'justified by evidence' (p. 22). But this evidence is 'of a very different character' (p. 22). In fact it is not evidence in the positivist sense, it is another theory – the familiar idea of 'natural selection' and the survival of the (maximizing) fittest. Presumably the only 'evidence' which could falsify this proposition is that no firms existed at all. It is theory, not evidence, which suggests that (most) firms that happen to survive must be maximizers.

Seemingly aware of the problem in his argument, Friedman shifts the status of the maximization 'hypothesis' in the very next paragraph. He writes: 'An even more important body of evidence for the maximization hypothesis is experience from countless applications of the hypothesis to specific problems and the repeated failure of its implications to be contradicted' (p. 22). Not only do we have an implicit shift from positivism to Popper, in the use of the concept of falsification rather than the principle of confirmation used earlier, but also the maximization 'hypothesis' is now not only a theory to be tested by evidence, but an assumption from which further (undetailed) theoretical 'implications' can be derived. This shift in meaning, from theory to assumption, is confirmed later when we are asked to 'assume' that 'entrepreneurs seek to maximize their returns' (p. 27).

Following the (p. 22) fanfare for an 'even more important body of evidence', by which to grant scientific esteem to the maximization hypothesis by the non-falsification of the somehow-derived 'predic-tions', we have a passage of immense vacuousness. We are told that 'this evidence is extremely hard to document' and it 'is scattered in numerous memorandums (sic), articles and monographs' (pp. 22–3). However, we are given no reference to any one of them. Quickly grabbing for a figleaf, the argument is then immediately switched to mid-paragraph. It is now the 'failure of any coherent, self-consistent alternative to be developed and be widely accepted' that is testimony to the worth of the maximization idea. Thus, by sleight of hand, we have the 'evidence' that the majority of economists continue to believe in a hypothesis being used as a reason for its acceptability. Here we are simply asked to accept the maximization hypothesis on the grounds that it is accepted by others.

The article has proved to be devastatingly persuasive, both in the methodological prescription that prediction is the measure of any theory, and in the particular view that neoclassical economists do not have to be concerned about evidence of the 'unrealism' of the maximization hypothesis. Yet it fails in the case of this most crucial of hypotheses to place its predictive money according to the dictates of its methodological mouth. Furthermore, it appears that Friedman is not clear here as to what is being tested and what is not.

The scandal of this affair is not principally Firedman's article itself, for it ranks very highly as an attempt by an economist to come to grips with methodology. The scandal is that the majority of the profession, even including those that are critical of monetarism or other aspects of Friedman's economics, have swallowed its argument sustaining the maximization hypothesis so uncritically and for so long, and continue to cite the 1953 article with blanket approval.

PART TWO

# A Farewell to 'Economic Man'

# 3

# Behind Methodological Individualism

The unit is not an individual but a social individual, one who has a place in the social order . . . To understand the individual we must study him in his group setting; to understand the group we must study the individuals whose interrelated actions constitute it.

Solomon Asch (1952, p. 257)

Methodological individualism has become a more fashionable slogan for economists in recent years. In specific terms we are being urged to accept a doctrine within which all explanations of social phenomena have to be couched in terms of statements about individuals. However, the term has a wide and sometimes ambiguous usage and is being employed as a packaging for all kinds of methodological and theoretical prescriptions. For example, it has been regarded as a commandment that thou shalt, where possible, place macroeconomic statements on firm microeconomic foundations (e.g. Blaug, 1980), or an injunction against (reckless) aggregation, particularly in regard to welfare criteria or social welfare functions (e.g. Kirzner, 1981; Littlechild, 1978), or as an inspiration for recent theoretical developments in economics with pro-market policy conclusions (e.g. Furubotn and Pejovich 1974).

One of the further problems in discussing this topic is that often the term 'methodological individualism' carries an ideological charge. Indeed, by both advocates and opponents it is too frequently confused with individualism of a political variety. However, the connection between political and methodological individualism is merely assumed by these supporters or critics, or supported by cursory argument. It is never demonstrated with any rigour.

Although there is a lack of uniformity in the use of the label, it is argued here that the key element in the classic statements of methodological individualism is a refusal to examine the institutional or other forces which are involved in the moulding of individual preferences and purposes. We are thus confronted with a remarkable optimism about the possibility of explanation of social phenomena in terms of individuals, but an extreme reluctance to give even partial explanations of individual behaviour in social or even psychological terms. This refusal is both dogmatic and, as is argued below, unacceptable on analytical grounds.

Of course, most theorists would accept that external factors are important in the explanation of human action. The difference is that in the case of the methodological individualist the effect of the external world is given limited scope. The individual is taken as given, facing the world outside and reacting to it through the perception of its constraints and opportunities. So far so good, but the methodological individualist does not go further and consider the effect of culture, social psychology, etc., on the process and framework of perception itself. Furthermore, perception is not all. Individual purposes themselves bear the imprint of the external world.

The methodological individualists' reduction of explanation and thereby causality solely to individuals has a further implication: the explanation of social phenomena proceeds, even by a circuitous route, irreversably from (individual) parts to (social) wholes. By jettisoning as outside the domain of economic inquiry any analysis of the formation and moulding of individual purposes it becomes possible to assert a so-called 'compositive method' in the analysis of social phenomena.

In contemporary economic theory this tendency is expressed in a number of ways. In some cases any change in the tastes of the individual is deemed to result from the individual and not elsewhere. In others the moulding of individual preferences is denied by the suggestion that they do not in fact change through time. The individual utility function is regarded as both immutable and beyond 'dispute'. Thus in the works of Gary Becker (e.g. 1976) and his followers it is asserted or implied that all apparent changes in tastes and goals are based on a single and fundamental utility function. Individual purposes or preferences are the bedrock, and the economic edifice has to be built upwards from these allegedly firm, if not sacred, foundations. As George Stigler and Gary Becker (1977) boldly assert: *'De gustibus non est disputandum.'*

A second set of examples relate to the widely adopted project to rebuild macroeconomic theory upon some version of neoclassical, microeconomic foundations. In neoclassical theory it is assumed that the functions governing individual preferences and productive technology are formed exogenously or given. Consequently a number of feedback influences on the nature and constitution of these functions are excluded from the project. The influence of the whole upon the parts is simply as a constraint upon or an input to a pre-given function, not a change in the function itself. The result is effectively an aggregation of wholes from parts, and a dissolution of the macro into the micro, in which the former becomes merely a summation of the latter. The micro affects the macro, but not vice versa, because such crucial feedback mechanisms are ruled out.

It is an objective of this chapter to challenge these developments, not in all cases directly, but via a critique of the doctrine of methodological individualism. The links between the above developments in economics and the latter methodology are discussed further below. This critique does not involve a rejection of all its insights or contained propositions, but it does reach a conclusion that the established version of methodological individualism is seriously flawed.

This chapter commences with a discussion of the development of the doctrine and the past controversies surrounding it. Following this, the crucial feature of the key statements of methodological individualism is identified as its statement of the primacy of individual purposefulness, and its failure or refusal to give an adequate account of the formation of purpose itself.

The chapter proceeds with this theme, by exploring the possible reasons for this failure or refusal and criticizing them one by one. It is then argued that the methodological individualist has no satisfactory line of retreat by admitting some degree of social or institutional influence in the formation or moulding of individual purposes. This retreat, as is explained below, is blocked by the problem of infinite regress. The chapter concludes with a discussion of some of the remaining issues surrounding the doctrine and some of the important implications for economic theory.

### 3.1 What is Methodological Individualism?

*Debating methodological individualism*

Methodological individualism has a long history, but it is in the works of the utilitarians and liberals of the late eighteenth and early nineteenth century that it begins to permeate social science. Precursors are found, for example, in the works of Jeremy Bentham and other liberal thinkers of the eighteenth and nineteenth centuries. John Stuart Mill wrote: 'the Laws of the phenomena of society are, and can be, nothing but the actions and passions of human beings', namely 'the laws of individual human nature.' Mill continues: 'Men are not when brought together, converted into another kind of substance, with different properties' (Mill, 1875, Vol. 2, p. 469).

Apparently[1] the term 'methodological individualism' was invented by Joseph Schumpeter in 1908. A better-known announcement of the term is that of Ludwig von Mises, who was one of the first to highlight the underlying issues in a general treatise on economics. We shall rely here principally on von Mises' precise and definitive statement. According to him, the principle of methodological individualism involves the recognition that 'all actions are performed by individuals' and 'a social collective has no existence and reality outside of the individual members' actions' (von Mises, 1949, p. 42).

It should not be overlooked that von Mises, as well as bringing explicit discussion of this principle into economics, also recognizes (albeit dismissively) some of the opposing views. Von Mises is evidently aware of the counter-arguments that the individual is an 'empty abstraction'; that persons are always members of a social whole; that we are products of social evolution; and that reason and language, upon which thought and action depend, are manifestly social phenomena. Von Mises goes so far as to accept that 'in the sphere of human action social entities have real existence. Nobody ventures to deny that nations, states, municipalities, parties, religious communities, are real factors determining the course of human events' (pp. 41–2). Since some economic individualists already acknowledge these counter-arguments, the debate will not be served simply by their reassertion, without deeper enquiry into the issues involved.

There has been a more searching inquiry but it took place within sociology of the 1950s and 1960s and was largely ignored by economists.[2] In any case the outcome was not entirely clear and much confusion still remains.

The work of Steven Lukes (1968, 1971, 1973) is valuable for helping to sort out the myriad of often conflicting propositions which are involved. He pointed out that methodological individualism should be distinguished from 'truistic social atomism', i.e. truisms such as 'society consists of individuals', or 'institutions consist of people plus rules and roles'. Methodological individualism, although often confused with truistic social atomism, means much more. It proposes an *explanation* of social phenomena in individual terms (Lukes, 1968).

## Purposeful human action

Von Mises (1949, p. 11) asserts clearly and forcefully that the analysis of economic and social phenomena requires the premise that human action is purposeful and goal-directed. Such notions of consciousness and purpose cannot be verified empirically, but in that respect they are not unique. All sciences have concepts at their 'hard core' which are not open to testing or falsification, but which help to define the character of the science. To put it a different way, we are asked to proceed from the initial level of abstraction of the purposeful human agent.

However, stress on this principle is not confined to liberals or New Right individualists. In a famous passage in the first volume of *Capital*, where he begins to analyse the process of production, Karl Marx wrote: 'what distinguishes the worst architect from the best of bees is that the architect builds the cell in his mind before he constructs it in wax' (1976, p. 284). In the ensuing description of the labour process Marx goes on to refer to work as 'purposeful activity' and he emphasizes the point repeatedly. In this way, Marx distinguishes the active element (labour) from the passive (capital goods) in the process of production, and it is not difficult to see how radical conclusions can be drawn from such an analysis (Hodgson, 1982a–c). However, for Marx the active human will is not operative in this sphere only. In exchange, the juridical contract 'is a relation between two wills' (p. 178).[3]

Turning to the members of the Institutionalist School, they too have an explicit notion of purposeful, individual human action. John Commons, in particular, argues that the 'science of the human will' acting in both 'individuals and all collective organizations is the 'twentieth century foundation' of economic science (Commons, 1950, p. 36). Although the argument is not applied so consistently or forcefully it is there too in the work of other institutionalists such as Thorstein Veblen and Wesley Mitchell.

Perhaps curiously, in view of its frequent association with an individualistic perspective, it is more difficult to find explicit statements of individual human purposefulness in the works of the Neoclassical School. This is partly because the individual is viewed as merely reacting in a programmed and optimizing fashion to the economic environment. Once preferences are given, choice is then predetermined. The individual is placed in a mechanical world in which particles respond directly to a combination of diverse forces. Strikingly, Vilfredo Pareto wrote: 'The individual can disappear, provided he leaves us this photograph of his tastes' (1971, p. 120). In such a mechanistic view, questions of will or purpose fade into the background. But for all that they are not necessarily excluded. For instances, Leon Walras, the most formalistic of the founders of neoclassical theory, wrote in his *Elements of Pure Economics* that: 'Man is a creature endowed with reason and freedom, and possessed of a capacity for initiative and progess' (Walras, 1954, p. 55). Indeed, for Walras and many other writers, it is the 'exercise of the human will' (p. 61) which distinguishes the social from the natural world.

The principle of the purposeful individual has no direct empirical verification, but it does itself have some basis in real-world institutions. For, without such clear evidence, in practice the principle must be *assumed* by the members of a market system working with individual property rights. The core of the legal system in a market-dominated society is contract law. For this system to operate it must typically be able to attribute consciousness and purposefulness to the parties in any contract. The notions of intent and responsibility are crucial, as they often are in criminal law. It could be argued that the modern legal system has provided the 'material foundation' for the assumption of the purposeful individual.

However, the necessity to attribute individual intent is by no means universal in law. The twentieth-century legal system admits the possibility of actions which are not fully planned or purposive. For example, consideration is made for acts of blind rage, of 'diminished responsibility', and of the physical and mental state of mind of the accused. There is the crime of manslaughter and 'strict liability' laws where intent is expressedly ignored. Even in the area of contract law, as well as elsewhere, a party can be sued for negligence not due to intent. In a world of contracts and markets it is no accident that the principle of the purposeful individual should have wide currency in both popular and philosophical thought, but it should not be overlooked that it is strongly qualified or even excluded in a number of areas within the modern legal system, even in relation to contract law itself.[4]

It is argued here that it would be a mistake to follow the Austrian School and raise the principle of individual purposefulness to the status of a universal principle governing all human action. In their work there is no adequate differentiation between actions which are carefully planned and others, such as habits, etc. The intransigence of von Mises and his followers on these points follows from the simple dogma that 'economics is the science of purposeful action' and its automatic consequence that everything else has to be ruled out of court.

The attribution of purposefulness to important human actions is in contradistinction to the idea that intent can be attributed to collectives, such as institutions or social groups. With good reason, some of the advocates of methodological individualism make this point. By explicitly or implicitly attributing intent, collectives are misleadingly treated as if they were individuals. Often this does involve an unsatisfactory explanatory short cut. But it can amount to little more than a convenient linguistic shorthand, and would seem legitimate when members of collectives are unanimous or near-unanimous in their purpose and there are clear mechanisms for reaching a collective decision (e.g. 'it was a foremost aim of the Thatcher government to bring down inflation').

Nevertheless, serious problems can arise when general explanations of large-scale phenomena are posed in such terms.

For example, the severe limitations of the assumption that complex ruling groups are motivated in some sort of collective and deliberate manner are explored in the context of international relations by Graham Allison (1969, 1971) and John Steinbruner (1974). Typically, in most neoclassical textbooks the large firm is unrealistically treated as if it had a single and simple objective, i.e. profit or utility maximization. Another example is the misuse of the concept of social class in some Marxian writing, where classes have purposes and strategems of their own: an especially grave error in the absence of any mechanisms for individuals to reach such a collective decision.[5]

It may be argued, however, that in cases where such mechanisms exist there are grounds for ascribing 'purposefulness' to collectives or groups, and thus its connection with individuals is over-restrictive. In response it should be insisted that individual purposefulness is not the same thing as group or collective 'purposefulness' and in any case a distinction between these two should be made. The argument thus revolves around the definitions of words. At least for the purposes of this critique of methodological individualism it is important to accept a definition of 'purposefulness' related fundamentally to individuals and to accept some common ground with the individualists on that point.

## Causality and Purpose

Clearly, the principle of the purposeful individual is not sufficient to define the doctrine of methodological individualism, although it makes a strong appearance in most statements of the creed. What in addition appears to be central is the idea that individual purpose is a *sufficient* cause of all social action.

Some members of the Austrian School make this explicit. Israel Kirzner seems to have such an idea in mind when he writes of the economy as a 'subtle social process set in motion by interacting, purposeful human individuals' (Kirzner, 1982, p. 1). As often, Ludwig von Mises is clear and to the point: 'As an a priori category the principle of action is on a par with the principle of causality' (von Mises, 1960, p. 14).

However, this is actually an idea of considerable antiquity. It is what Sir John Hicks (1979) recently dubbed the 'Old Causality', i.e. causation stemming from the decisions of an agent. With this notion a version of methodological individualism appears to be established in the following way: by the assertion of the individual character of purpose, by the implicit or explicit assumption that purpose is the source of all action in society, and by the consequent reduction of the explanation of basic cause to purpose itself. It is possible, of course, for this argument to be tautological, as indeed it is in von Mises' hands; to flow simply from the definitions of action as purposeful human behaviour, and of cause as purpose itself. The quarrel then would be whether or not these definitions of cause or action are adequate, or can capture the essence of the concepts as they are used today. It is argued below that these uses of the term are indeed both arbitrary and over-restrictive.

In the variety of methodological individualism espoused by von Mises and others, individual and purposeful action is the steam driving the socio-economic engine. Institutions and collectives in themselves are not purposeful, except as the aggregate of the various purposes of the members, furthermore, according to this view, individual action alone is regarded as the prime explanation or cause. Von Mises goes so far as to recognize, for example, the importance of the ideas that circulate in society and are passed from generation to generation, and their effect on human behaviour. But then, as if to clinch the argument, he asserts that 'thinking is always a manifestation of individuals' (1949, p. 178).

The main problem with this type of argument is not to do with what it says but what it does not say. Whilst purposeful individuals may act and cause events, we are left asking: what causes the purposes to arise in the first place? More often than not there is no clear answer to this question, and the writings of methoodological individualists are marked by an extreme reluctance to give it any further discussion within the discourse of social science.

## Psychological explanations of purpose

When pressed, methodological individualists often gesture towards a psychological explanation of purpose, but they do this, however, as a means of excluding the matter from economics. Von Mises, for example, wrote of 'the psychological events which result in action' (1949, pp. 11–12). But it is significant that, for von Mises amongst others, possible social or socio-psychological explanations of 'psycho-logical events which result in action' are not mentioned in his work. Furthermore, von Mises asserts that the science of human action is not concerned with the internal psychological processes which result, or can result, in action, but with action as such.

Hayek makes an identical point on several occasions, 'It is a mistake' he writes in one place, for social scientists to believe that their aim is to explain conscious action. 'This, if it can be done at all, is a different task, the task of psychology' (Hayek, 1952a, p. 39). Hayek, an acknowledged expert in theoretical neuro-psychology (Hayek, 1952b), goes a step further by expressly excluding social factors: 'If conscious action can be "explained", this is a task for psychology but not for economics . . . or any other social science' (1948, p. 67). It is indeed very strange that Hayek can write in both fields without attempting to build bridges between the two.

This invocation of psychology here seems to divert any explanation of individual purpose from any area of social science, psychology being regarded as excluded from this terrain. Ostensibly, by putting the explanation of conscious action out of bounds in this manner, the apparent purpose of methodological individualism is served. We cut short any explanation of individual purpose in economic or any other social-scientific terms.

However, this device does not work as designed. Modern psychology has a strong social psychological element, and furthermore one which could be used to counter a methodological individualist position.[6] In addition, as Paul Hirst and Penny Woolley argue with great eloquence, it would be wrong to conceive of sciences such as psychology and even biology as essentially asocial: 'it is not necessary in order to analyse the effectiveness of social relations . . . that they be rigidly differentiated from biological or psychological phenomena' (Hirst and Woolley, 1982, p. 24).

The assumption that the explanation of purpose and conscious action is mainly or wholly a matter for psychology (perhaps with the assistance of physics, biology, etc.) but not for social science, has been defined elsewhere as psychologism (Agassi, 1960, 1975; Morgenbesser, 1967a; Popper, 1945). Clearly, at least one of Hayek's statements fits this description.

There are good grounds to be wary of any approach which attempts to explain human behaviour in terms which relate exclusively to psychology, particularly a psychology of an individualistic or crudely naturalistic kind. More generally, the deficiencies of psychology as an exclusive source of explanation are largely to do with the fact that its research programme does not devolve upon historically specific social institutions. Its central object of study is the human psyche, or human behaviour in relation to others in rather general terms. Psychology has a great deal to offer to social science, but it is too narrowly conceived to provide a complete explanation of social phenomena.

Whilst Hayek suggests that a psychologistic type of explanation is the only one that would be appropriate, it should be noted that Karl Popper (1945) retains an adherence to methodological individualism whilst forcefully rejecting psychologism. One of his principal reasons for doing so is to reject explanations of social phenomena in terms of 'human nature', conceived asocially, and to endorse the idea that social institutions and the social environment are part of the explanation of human action. Considering this, Lukes (1968) goes so far as to suggest that Popper, by admitting institutional and other explanations, is not a genuine methodological individualist at all, whilst Mark Blaug (1980, pp. 49–50) finds in Popper a confusion between political and methodological individualism which mars his work. The substance of Popper's version of methodological individualism is put into question.

Indeed, as is argued below, once institutional or other social explanations of purpose are admitted it becomes theoretically arbitrary to plump for the individual as the sole basis of explanation. However, even amongst some writers who accept the significance of institutional influences upon individual purpose formation there is a strong reluctance to remove or qualify the primacy of the 'individualist' label in describing their own doctrine. In particular, Joseph Agassi (1960, 1975) and Lawrence Boland (1982), following Popper, proclaim 'institutional individualism' against the 'psychological individualism' of others. But why is theirs an 'individualist' rather than (say) an 'institutionalist' methodology? Why can't noun and adjective be switched, to give 'individualist institutionalism'? Or why cannot the primacy of the individual be qualified by a label such as 'structured individualism', or whatever? The reason why such alternative labels are not entertained is not entirely clear. For whatever reason, the wide use of the methodological individualism label is evidence of its magnetic attraction to a variety of theorists.

In contrast, the strict Austrian position of von Mises and others avoids such problems by removing the question of the determination or moulding of individual purpose entirely from the scene.

## 3.2 Critique and Implications

Despite the persistent tendency of orthodox economics to regard the preferences and purposes of the individual as either given or exogeneous to the economic system, the case for including institutional and social as well as psychological factors in the determination or moulding of individual purposes is overwhelming. It is important to emphasize that institutions are not simply relevant as barriers or constraints, or even for estimating the likely behaviour of agents. In this sense individuals may *respond* to institutions in pursuit of their goals. But there is an additional sense in which institutions and culture are important: *they play a part in actually influencing and moulding those purposes themselves*. Factors such as institutional structure and routine, and social norms and culture, affect not only our eventual actions but also our views of the world and the purposes to which we aspire.[7]

If social psychology, sociology or other social sciences are to be included in the explanation of individual purpose then it is pertinent to ask why this explanation is not regarded as being within the province of economics or 'the science of human action'. Why stop with individual purpose; why not try to explain that as well?

## Spontaneity and absentee explanation

An argument that explanation has to stop where von Mises and Hayek propose is suggested by Ludwing Lachmann (1969). He makes a distinction between purposes and plans, on the one hand, and motives on the other, implying that motives may be determined by 'psychic processes' (p. 94) but that plans are often spontaneous and thus cannot be a response 'to anything pre-existent' (p. 93). Von Mises (1960, p. 11) comes close to this when he argues that 'the same situation has a different effect on different men' giving scope for notions of 'free will, of the irrationality of what is human, spiritual, or historical, of individuality in history'. Lachmann's distinction does not seem plausible, nor his view that plans are entirely and always uncaused. But the relevant point is that both authors imply that there is a strong spontaneous and indeterminate element in the formation of purposes or plans, and thus they cannot be encompassed by a determinate theory, be it from psychology or from social science.

The acceptance of a degree of spontaneity and indeterminacy in the formation of expectations and plans is indeed desirable in social science. But Lachmann and von Mises imply that this is ground for the exclusion of *any* systematic influence, and thereby refuse to theorize about plans and purposes at all. Thus von Mises jumps to the rash and rather nihilistic conclusion that 'there is no hope of achieving knowledge of a regularity in the phenomena' of behaviour by consideration of 'objectively distinguishable periods or conditions of life' (1960, p. 11). However, work in the social sciences does indeed suggest that social institutions and conditions of life do have a significant effect on human behaviour, and this can be accepted whilst giving simultaneous emphasis to the spontaneous and indeterminate elements, and without relapsing into a variety of determinism. A measure of indeterminacy need not, and should not, exclude social and institutional factors within the theory of human action.

An alternative reason for neglecting explanations of purpose is also implied in the work of the Austrian School. In its more dogmatic version it is based on the assertion that economics is about human action, not the 'events which result in action' (von Mises, 1949, p. 12). This defensive response simply rules the area of enquiry as beyond bounds without any further justification or reason. The less dogmatic version, conveyed by some Austrian sympathizers, is that the Austrian research programme is just a particular method which takes purposes and goals as given and is concerned to examine their systemic results. In this milder version no claim is made for this project to represent the totality of all economic or social science. Consequently, it cannot deride those who regard the explanation of the formation of purposes and goals as having some significance.

### The problem of infinite regress

If there are determinate influences on individuals and their goals then it would be wrong to exclude them from 'the science of human action'. In turn, the response may be that such an investigation would be in terms of other purposeful individuals. Be that as it may, it is no reason for not attempting to explain individual purpose, *even if* we anticipate a further individualist result.

But where would the analysis stop? The purposes of an individual could be partially explained by relevant institutions, the social culture, etc. These, in turn, would then be explained in terms of other individuals. But their purposes and actions could then be partly explained by cultural and social factors, and so on, indefinitely.

This can be represented diagrammatically as in figure 3.1, where P represents the purposeful action of an individual, I represents institutions and culture, and O represents any plausible other elements, if they were to exist, such as a degree of randomness in the formation of purposes. Alternatively, O could be simply taken to indicate that the P and I factors are not sufficient to explain a purposeful action, and thus that to some degree this action is indeterminate. The explanatory links are indicated by arrows.

We are involved in an apparently infinite regress; similar to the puzzle of 'which came first, the chicken or the egg?'. Such an analysis can never be completed, and it will go on without end. It is simply arbitrary to plump for one rather than the other; to say that is is, 'all reducible to individuals' just as much as to say it is 'all social or institutional'. As Robert Nozick remarks: 'In this apparent chicken and egg situation, why aren't we equally methodological institutionalists?' (1977, p. 359). The obvious suggestion is that a synthesis of explanations, involving both individual agency and social structure, is requried.

A neoclassical theorist may argue that social and institutional factors could be embedded within a theoretical model in the tastes and

Key:
P — purposeful action of an individual
I — institutions and culture
O — other factors

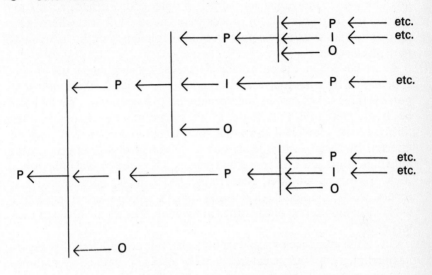

Fig. 3.1  *The infinite regress of explanatory terms*

preferences of individual agents at a given time. The model would then proceed to explain human behaviour on the basis of those individuals. But if social influences are (partially) formative at one point, why can they not change or mould preference functions at other times as well?[9]

In terms of figure 3.1 it can be noted that whilst there is no symmetry between the explanatory terms P and I, it is possible to 'reduce' all explanations to individuals (by stopping every time a P term is reached) as it is to 'reduce' all explanations to institutions (by stopping every time an I term is reached). In other words we can move back, hypothetically through time, distilling out P causes at every stage, and reducing non-P elements to their P components until the residue is insignificant; likewise we can operate a similar procedure, but distilling out the I elements at every stage. Because both procedures are possible neither individuals nor institutions have 'first-cause' primacy over the other.

The riposte of the methodological individualist that all social phenomena can be traced back to and explained in terms of individuals commits the same kind of theoretical error as the advocate of the labour theory of value who argues that the production of all commodities can ultimately be traced back to labour, and that is sufficient to justify the theory.[10] Both are arbitrary. Both subsume the other factors which are involved in the production of labour or the influencing of individuals, content to stop short when labour or the individual is reached. Within methodological individualism there is no place for further explanation beyond the individual, or for processes of causal feedback, where other parts or wholes constitute a portion of the explanation of the 'individual' parts themselves.

As we have seen, the only plausible excuse for stopping at the level of explanation of the individual would be to suggest that individual purposefulness was *entirely* indeterminate or spontaneous. Whilst it can be freely admitted that there is an indeterminate element in the formation of individual purposes, the acceptance that it is *partially* affected by social factors leads one to investigate their effects on the individual and their own respective origins. Once the partial influence of social factors is admitted then to ignore them is, paradoxically, to renege on the methodological individualist's promise and to neglect to explain them in terms of the other individuals that are involved in their make-up.

Given the influence of social institutions, it is argued here that we are justified in giving such structures some analytical prominence combined with the notion of the agency of the individual. The aim should be to avoid the pitfalls of voluntaristic individualism on the one hand, and structural determinism on the other. There is no single or clearly marked route to success, but it is a direction worth taking neverthel-ess.[11]

This should not be a revolutionary move, but it may be in practice because the influence of social institutions on individual goals and choices is almost entirely excluded by mainstream economic theory. As Frank Knight put it, orthodox microeconomic theory 'takes all economic individuals at *data*, not subject to "influence", and assumes that they view each other in the same way' (Knight, 1935, pp. 282–3). Typically, in neoclassical theory wants and preferences are simply taken as given. This does not only give neoclassical theory a propensity for unnecessarily rigid assumptions about the individual, but it reinforces the essentially static and timeless character of that theory where there is no momentum of development or change from the past nor spontaneous aspiration towards the future.

## Wholes and parts

The inclusion of social structures and institutions in the moulding of human action, appearing both as partial explanations and things to be explained, would be inconsistent with the work of methodological individualists such as Hayek who believe that whilst 'the method of the natural sciences is . . . analytic, the method of the social sciences is better described as compositive or synthetic. It is the so-called wholes . . . which we build up or reconstruct from the known properties of the elements' (Hayek, 1952a, p. 39).

It may be that what Hayek describes as the 'compositive' or 'synthetic' method is part of the hidden agenda of some versions of methodological individualism. It involves an insistence that explanations of social wholes have to be built up conceptually from their individual parts. However, this methodological imperative is rarely expressed with rigour and in detail. Neither is the use of the term consistent within the Austrian School. In contrast to Hayek's statement that it is '*the* method of the social sciences' (emphasis added), Lachmann (1969, pp. 94–5) uses the term in a different sense, placing the 'compositive method' alongside an additional 'obverse' scheme which is allegedly analytic rather than synthetic. A measure of further clarification is required from those that make use of this term.

Nevertheless, despite some degree of ambiguity, here we shall accept a definition of the 'compositive method' in the following form. As Hayek says, it is a method of theory-building which starts from given elements, and builds up a picture of institutions and social wholes. In mainstream economics the basic elements are sometimes taken as households plus firms, but now increasingly these too in turn are built up of their constitutive individual parts.

The structure of explanation is pyramidical. Each element rests on elements below it. Once a part is composed of elements below it in the hierarchy, their character does not change when structures are built up with these consituent elements. Investigation proceeds in one direction only; the macro is explained by the micro, the parts explain the wholes. As the Austrian School insist, the starting point of the anlaysis must be the human individual. Here it all begins and beneath it no further analysis is invoked.

Clearly, a methodology of this type extends much further than the Austrian School, to include the representative neoclassical economist as well. Within mainstream economics it is the norm to build up a picture of, say, aggregate demand, simply from the aggregate of individual consumer preferences, or more generally to assume that individual optimizing behaviour can be readily aggregated up to the economic system as a whole. Even the adoption of interdependent utility functions does not break this mould, as the functions themselves are still given at the outset, and they are not themselves continuously moulded by social circumstances. The problem, still, is that the underlying preference function is 'immanently conceived'.

That the adoption of a 'compositive' method is much more wide-spread than in the work of Hayek and the Austrian School is shown by the preoccupation of mainstream economists with the attempt to construct macroeconomics on microeconomic 'foundations'. Indeed, it is suggested that macroeconomics should be dissolved entirely into microeconomic theory, so that it becomes merely a resultant of the latter. It is an intention of the present work to challenge this research programme. Some of the major arguments to be presented here could be roughly characterized as urging a commensurate priority to the placing of *micro*economics on adequate *macro* foundations, including a consideration of social institutions and culture.[12]

The current mainstream preoccupation with the explanation of wholes in terms of their constituent parts is not without its positive features. For too long economists have considered households or firms simply as unitary elements, making decisions as if they were single actors, and disregarding the real individuals involved, such as the workers in the firm or women in the household. At the level of abstraction of the theory of the firm or the household it is a positive step to attempt to explain their nature and dynamics partly in terms of the structured groups and individuals within them. This breaks the widespread habit of treating these institutions as if they were purposeful units in themselves.

However, this does not imply support for the compositive method as defined above. The latter suggests, for example, that the demand function of a household can be explained simply in terms of the purposes or preferences of, say, husband, wife and children, and the goals of a firm in terms of those of the relevant individuals concerned. What is left out of this approach is the continuous influence of social institutions, such as the family or the firm itself, and social culture and roles, on the preferences and purposes of the individuals involved. Whilst the aims and character of individuals help to explain the behaviour of social structures, also roles, culture and institutions have a partial effect on the goals and behaviour of individuals. This is not a deterministic view because it is not being suggested that individual behaviour is *completely* determined in this way.

The methodological individualist claim to be able to explain these social and institutional influences once more by reference to individuals is illegitimate; since to the problem of infinite regress is now added the difficulty that to do this would be to break from the strict hierarchical order of the 'compositive method'. It would involve a jump from the level of the individual to the level of the institution or structure, and then back to other constituent individuals. Once we admit the possibility of explaining an individual element in terms of factors of an equal or higher order in the hierarchy then the spell of the compositive method is broken. It becomes no longer possible to work exclusively in its terms.

Against the 'compositive method' it is not sufficient to warn of the 'fallacy of composition', in which the system as a whole is regarded as a mere aggregation of its individual elements, and simply assert that the 'whole is more than the sum of the parts'. The latter point is accepted by many methodological individualists including Hayek (1967, pp. 70–1) himself. The real issue is whether or not the parts function merely because of their inherent qualities, after taking in inputs (information, etc.) from outside, or whether there is a more complex web of determination where parts are partially constituted in their relations with the whole.

In more general terms the non-synthetic character of a systemic whole is stressed by systems theorists (see Emery, 1981). One early example is the work of Andras Angyal (1941), who argued that wholes cannot be compared to additive aggregates at all; in the formation of wholes something different from a summation of parts takes place. In summations the parts function because of their inherent qualities. On the other hand, when a number of parts constitute a whole, the parts do not enter into such a connexion by means of their inherent qualities, but by means of their position and function in the system. 'The formation of wholes is therefore not additional to the aggregation of parts, but something of an entirely different order' (Angyal, 1941, p. 256).

In defending methodological individualism from attack Richard Langlois (1983b, p. 632) asserts that it is 'not a debate about whether properties of the whole can be deduced solely from properties of the parts; rather it is a debate about *what shall be considered the parts*'. For the methodological individualist, he writes, 'the only acceptable parts are the knowledge, expectations, intentions, and actions of human beings.' Langlois is right with the former point: the bone of contention is in the latter. The individual 'parts', precisely because they relate closely to and are affected by the whole, cannot be taken as given.

What is all the more strange is Langlois' (1983a, p. 586) assertion that the best forms of systems theory are best understood as 'intelligent methodological individualism'. On the contrary, the least mechanistic and most innovative of the systems theorists have broken from such a view, whilst retaining meaningful notions of individual consciousness and agency in social science. Despite positive aspects of the work of Hayek and others in the development of a systems view of society, such works are limited by their treatment of the irreducibility of the individual 'parts', and are blinkered to many of the challenges of a systems view.

A point made by Arthur Koestler (1967) is relevant here. He writes that wholes and parts in an *absolute sense do not exist anywhere*, either in the domain of living organisms or of social organizations. What we find are intermediary structures on a series of levels in an ascending order of complexity: sub-wholes which display, according to the way you look at them, some of the characteristics commonly attributed to wholes and some of the characteristics commonly attributed to parts. (p. 65)

As a result, Koestler rejects the view that the individual is an 'indivisible, self-contained unit' (p. 86).

This issue has emerged elsewhere. For instance, Kenneth Arrow (1968) argues that explanations of all economic phenomena have to be reduced to individuals, regarding this as a salutary 'rejection of the organism approach to social problems' (p. 641). In a work on the modern corporation very much inspired by systems theory, Neil Kay responds to Arrow with an argument that is similar to Koestler's. 'The individual', he writes, 'is a holistic concept no less and no more than the concept of the corporation' (Kay, 1979, p.211). Consequently, and contrary to what is implied by Arrow and others, the individualistic line of argument does not find a completely defined behavioural unit when it reaches the individual.

Clearly, however, it would be a dangerous mistake to deny any special place to individuals in a hierarchical and holistic scheme. The theoretical and policy danger would be to somehow dissolve the characteristics and rights of individuals in a wide-angle view of the multi-levelled hierarchy. But this is not a picture that we are forced to endorse. The recognition of a multi-levelled hierarchy where individuals are wholes as well as parts, does not mean that individuals are denied a special place in the analysis, nor that they are denied their rights.

After all, many different kinds of analysis can have dangerous policy consequences if they are mishandled. Such distortions and misconceptions have often proved persuasive in resisting new theories in the past. For instance, some theologians argued against Copernicus and Galileo on the grounds that if the Earth was not at the centre of the universe then the dignity and special place of humanity would be undermined. Others attacked Darwin on the grounds that his theory meant that in essence humans were little more than apes. But today many people would freely deny the geocentricity of the universe and endorse Darwinian evolution whilst proclaiming simultaneously, and quite rightly, that human beings have special characteristics and rights.

Likewise, any danger that may exist in the extension or misinterpretation of a systems view does not mean that the systems approach should itself be rejected. Such a danger, furthermore, offers no justification for the pronouncement of the analytical irreducibility or indivisibility of the individual. The perceived possibility of one serious error does not justify another.

The point, to repeat, is that the individual part cannot be taken as given. As Anthony Giddens states: 'What the "individual" is cannot be taken as obvious' (1984, p. 220). Our very individuality and capacity to be free is formed by our socio-economic environment. The basic element in society is not the abstract individual, but the social individual, one who is both constructive within and constructed through society. We should thus avoid, in Patrick Burman's words, 'a sterile polarity between the individual and the social' (1979, pp. 374–5). Emphases on the primacy of 'the individual' and of 'society' are both false.

### Concluding remarks

The research programme of methodological individualism can proceed only on the basis of a rigid and dogmatic compartmentalization of study. The global effects of human purpose are regarded as all-important, but the study of the formation of purposes themselves is dismissed as if it were secondary or even beyond the legitimate boundaries of social science itself. One of the thematic arguments in this book is that there are good reasons to be wary of taking individuals and their preferences as the starting point of analysis both in economics and more generally in social science.

To repeat, the position taken here is not that the plans and purposes of an individual are determined *entirely* by his or her socio-economic environment. Neither is the methodological individualists' proposition that all social phenomena are explicable in terms of individuals to be replaced by an insistence that the spurs to action can be explained in their entirety in terms of collectives or wholes.

What is argued is that the socio-economic and institutional environment has a significant effect on the kind of information we receive, our cognition of it, or preferences, and thereby much of our behaviour. Once this point is admitted, as several adherents to methodological individualism have done in the past, the doctrine is then open to critique, as a result of its theoretically arbitrary adoption of the 'individualism' label and its inbuilt problem of infinite regress.

But it should not be suggested that the concerns of the methodological individualists are entirely without substance. As Anthony Giddens (1984) argues, there is an inherent duality between 'agency' and 'structure' in society. The fact that this controversy is very much alive is evidence of the inherent tension of duality between these terms. Thus one cannot but agree with Bruce Caldwell (1984a, p. 377) in his statement that such ideas deserve 'a fair hearing from the economics profession'. But this would be helped if there were greater clarity in the burgeoning statements for methodological individualism, and less of a reckless association between it and varieties of individualism of a political kind.[13]

Despite the impression given by many adherents of methodological individualism, it is quite legitimate to deny that only purposes or actions of individuals are explanatory, whilst at the same time we retain a respect for other people and a belief in 'valuing their autonomy, their privacy and their self-development' (Lukes, 1973, p. 148). These beliefs are not undermined by a conviction that whilst people are, on the one hand, purposeful and have real choices, they are, on the other, moulded by their cultural and institutional environment.

Indeed, if we were to believe that action was entirely the result of constrained but otherwise free individual choices, then we may be quickly drawn to the conclusion that a great number of people are stupid, irrational, evil or insane. On the contrary, the institutionalist view leads us to emphasize that much of this behaviour is moulded by factors outside the individual concerned, and it leads to a greater respect for that person in his or her predicament, as well as a more fruitful and less simplistic explanation of those actions themselves.

Critics of some of the propositions associated with methodological individualism are by no means forced down a slippery slope to totalitarianism. A position which inflates the causal role of the individual while pushing into the background the extent to which he or she is socially formed has no exlusive claim to political virtue, nor to theoretical integrity.

# 4

# The Maximization Hypothesis

Few textbooks contain a direct portrait of rational economic man . . . He lurks in the assumptions leading an enlightened existence between input and output, stimulus and response. He is neither tall nor short, fat nor thin, married nor single. There is no telling whether he loves his dog, beats his wife or prefers pushpin to poetry. We do not know what he wants. But we do know that, whatever it is, he will maximize ruthlessly to get it.

Martin Hollis and Edward Nell (1975, pp. 53–4)

The concept of rationality is indeed very special, in at least the sense of its pride of place in orthodox theory. But economists are much more cavalier in their use of the term 'rational' than their colleagues in other social sciences, often alleging that any statement of non-rational behaviour is derogatory of fellow humanity or absurd. However, a brief excursion into the literature of other social sciences, particularly sociology and anthropology, will reveal complex and unresolved problems surrounding the term.[1] Matters would be improved considerably if economists were to relate to this literature and take more frequent excursions across the often artificial boundaries between the social sciences.

However, that may be to expect too much. In terms of the analysis of scientific methodology of Imre Lakatos (1970), assumptions of rationality in one form or another are part of the 'hard core' of mainstream economics. Typically, such 'hard core' assumptions are often unquestioned, and rarely, if ever, proposed for empirical testing. Instead, they tend to serve as shibboleths and are very difficult to dislodge.

This is especially true in the case of modern neoclassical economics, for here economics is defined by its fundamental assumptions and method, and not by its devotion to the economy as the object of analysis. Strangely, the theoretical apparatus and method define the subject, not what it may purport to study. 'Rationality' is one of its basic assumptions, placing itself in a position of dogmatic invulnerability: protected not merely by apparent horror for the alternatives, but by the denial of full status as an economist to all those that dare to question it. Indeed, in economic circles to question the idea that human agents are rational is to risk disapprobation, exile or worse. An economist who raises such questions is likely to be met by the accusation that he or she is abandoning 'economics' itself.

But even the most dogmatic neoclassical theorist should accept, on reflection, that this cannot be the case. There is a tradition of heretics stretching back to Thorstein Veblen and before, and culminating in at least one Nobel Prizewinner in economics, who have questioned or even rejected the neoclassical presupposition of maximizing rationality. Furthermore, they have questioned the artificial duality which prescribed that if people are not seen as 'rational' then they must automatically be regarded as 'irrational' or even insane.

After briefly outlining some of the relevant developments in neoclassical theory, this chapter moves on to discuss the much-invoked 'evolutionary' defence of the idea of maximizing rationality. After concluding that the defence is insufficient, the main section proceeds to evaluate past criticisms of the maximization idea. Despite a gallant attempt by an economic methodologist to rebut these criticisms, it is argued that they are nevertheless explosive in their force. The final section of the chapter considers some fundamental problems with the utilitarian framework within which this notion of rationality is situated.

## 4.1   THE UTILITY OF CRITICIZING THE MAXIMIZATION HYPOTHESIS

The idea of 'rational economic man' has dominated neoclassical economic theory since its inception.[2] There have been adaptations of definition, but central to them has always been the idea that agents are maximizing something, usually called 'utility'. Lionel Robbins, in his famous *Essay on the Nature and Significance of Economic Science* (1937) argued that this principle is equivalent to one of having consistent orders of preference. Most neoclassical theorists proceed on this basis, assuming a weak preference ordering which is transitive and irreflexive.

### Revealed preference and beyond

Paul Samuelson (1938) claimed to show how preferences can be 'revealed' from observation of the choices of a consumer. It was thus claimed that demand theory was liberated from the restrictions of subjective introspection imposed by former presentations. Samuelson argued that neoclassical theory had become 'scientific'; consumer behaviour was to be explained simply by observation of consumer behaviour. As Ian Little (1949, p. 90) remarked, as a result of this work 'a theory of consumers' demand can be based solely on consistent behaviour'. Furthermore, it appeared to many economists that neoclassical demand theory became open to falsification. One way that such a refutation could occur would be through the observation of intransitive preferences. The unlikely observation of such inconsistency would refute the theory.

There are many problems with this position, which has nevertheless remained the convention for some time. The first is the claim that intransitive preference orderings have actually been observed, or could be expected, in practice.[3] It has been shown that such phenomena can be explained theoretically by models in which products do not have one, but many, attributes (Georgescu-Roegen, 1954; Tversky, 1969). On these grounds, inconsistent or intransitive preference orderings should be common and 'rational economic man' may even be the exception rather than the rule.

A second criticism is discussed in more detail below. It is the often-raised point about the extreme and unacceptable assumption of perfect knowledge in neoclassical choice theory. For example, Peter Earl (1983) notes an estimate that there are at least 10,000 different products in the average supermarket, and the consumer cannot be expected to make a global and consistent choice over this number of products. It would be impossible to know and assess the relevant characteristics of each and every one.

A third problem arises from the fact that we cannot simultaneously 'reveal' all preferences. Given that observed choices are separated over time, we can never be sure that two 'revealed choices' emanate from the same preference function, and thus in turn 'reveal' a 'preference'. It could be that the preference function has changed. There is no way of knowing. Once we take account of time, the operational meaningfulness, as well as the falsifiability, of the theory are brought into question. Revealed preference experiments, which take place through time, can never be used to falsify the consistency assumptions.[4]

Significantly, however, avant-garde neoclassical theory shows signs of adaptation in the face of at least one of the above problems. Whilst the literature still contains abundant references to 'rationality' and 'rational behaviour', indicating that a hard-core notion still remains, some writers have changed the list of fundamental axioms. In particular there is discussion of a consumer theory without the assumption of transitivity (Chipman 1971; Sonnenschein, 1971). These works include a demonstration that 'the properties of consumer behaviour that are necessary to prove the existence, optimality, and unbiasedness of competitive equilibrium depend only on the fact that consumers are maximising. It follows that the transitivity axiom is both an unneccesary and limiting assumption in the theory of consumers' behaviour for competitive equilibrium analysis' (Sonnenschein, 1971, pp. 220–1). A 'rational' choice is now regarded as one in which a person selects an element of an attainable set to which no other element is preferred.[5] This formulation allows for the possibility that the person may be indifferent between a number of 'best' elements.

If the notion of rationality is used in a sense that is equivalent to consistency then there is a slight but meaningful distinction between the ideas of rational and maximizing behaviour. But once the axiom of consistency was undermined it became even less easy to sustain. Indeed, it could be argued quite plausibly that maximization was the essential idea behind rational economic man all along. In recent years, more attention has been devoted to applying the neoclassical analysis to a world where time, risk and imperfect information are real. But the notion of maximization still remains, perhaps in a modified form. Agents are seen to be maximizing expected utility, and are able to adjust their behaviour, according to some Bayesian process, on the basis of new information. Whatever the changes and elaborations of the theory, economic man remains essentially the maximizer and optimizer of old.

## The 'evolutionary' argument

One of the persistent arguments in favour of maximization, as articulated by Armen Alchian (1950) and Milton Friedman (1953), is that maximizing behaviour is likely to be prominent just as 'fit' species are likely to survive and multiply in the natural world. More specifically, Friedman argues that the firms that maximize their expected returns, or act as if they were so maximizing, will survive and prosper, whereas the remainder will decline or go bust. Thus, through a process of 'natural selection', firms that behave as if they were maximizing will predominate. It is through this theoretical and 'evolutionary' argument that the assumption of maximizing behaviour for the firm is seen to be justified.

The strong point in this argument is that it leaves on one side the questions as to whether or not the firm is deliberately maximizing, or actually making calculations according to a maximization formula, or actually trying to search for an optimal strategy. The Alchian–Friedman argument bypasses all these issues. Maximizing behaviour is not necessarily purposeful or goal-seeking. Firms tend to maximize because those are the firms that are more likely to survive. In this respect, it is argued, the processes as to how a firm may have actually maximized are irrelevant.

Superficially this argument is persuasive, but on close inspection there are problems. The first element to be questioned is the immediate assumption by neoclassical theorists that the maximizing of 'expected returns' is in fact the criterion which corresponds to survival and evolutionary predominance. Furthermore, what does this assumption actually mean in substance?

On reflection it does not tell us very much. Strictly, it does not imply that the firm will behave with an eye on immediate pecuniary gain. As Robert Axelrod (1980a, 1980b, 1981, 1984) has shown in a theoretical study, given minimal preconditions cooperative behaviour is likely to evolve. It is well known that there are many examples of cooperation or 'altruism' in the animal world. Even in the business world it is common for a firm to give part of its profits to charity or to help another firm in trouble. Arguably the firm is doing this so as to increase the chances of reciprocal help, or customer loyalty, if it ever finds itself in trouble in the future. Clearly it could be argued that a firm could be doing this to increase its 'expected returns'. Consequently this maximization idea implies a whole range of plausible business behaviour and does not generate a clear and specific 'prediction' of what the firm will do.[6] Similarly, the survival criterion in the animal world can imply an infinite number of possible types of behaviour. It could be that, when pressed, the neoclassical proposition that 'existing firms maximize' turns into little more than the tautology that 'existing firms survive'.

Even more seriously, as Sidney Winter (1964) has demonstrated, there are fundamental problems with the use of an evolutionary model in the economic context. In the animal world, according to modern Darwinian theory, a species may become more 'efficient' through mutation. Its characteristics and behaviour are all encoded in its genes. The process of reproduction ensures that the offspring carry similar genetic information and are thus similarly programmed and will tend to act in a similarly efficient way. The crucial point, Winter emphasizes, is that no similar mechanism is specified in the neoclassical theory.

Assume that a firm just happens to be maximizing, for whatever reason. For it to survive it must *continue* to maximize. It must contain a mechanism for preserving this behaviour and transmitting it from one period to the next. In addition, to account for a large population of maximizing firms, there must be a mechanism through which maximizing behaviour is passed on to other, either new or existing, firms. No such mechanisms are specified.

The mechanism proposed by Richard Nelson and Sidney Winter (1982) is that the firm contains habits and routines which act as 'genes'. The implication of their argument is that the firm progresses through its structured routines, and it is not actually optimizing in a neoclassical sense. In chapter 6 the significance of habits or routinized behaviour is examined at length, suggesting a very different approach from that offered by neoclassical theory.

Given these arguments, the only resort left for the neoclassical theorist would seem to be to resurrect the earlier notion that maximizing is deliberative, conscious behaviour. To be a strategy that is sustained through time, and passed on to others, it must be a strategy that is being consciously pursued, and is capable of being codified and learned by others. Consequently, the criticisms that are associated with this conception of maximization as conscious and calculating cannot be disregarded. They are examined in the next section.

Incidentally, if we shift attention from the firm to the consumer, 'natural selection' arguments for maximization without rational calculation carry even less weight. Whilst there is the spur of competition and the punishment of bankruptcy in the business world, there is no similar 'weeding-out' mechanism in the case of the consumer, unless we resort to the tautological formulation that identifies optimization with simply being alive.

Whilst there is competition of a kind between consumers, it is expressed in the vagaries of fashion and conspicuous consumption, and 'failure' in this case does not mean the removal of the consumer from the scene. Consumer maximization could be simply supported with the argument that people will tend to prefer more to less. However, as we shall see below, there are severe difficulties as to the assessment of what is 'more', especially in situations of uncertainty or risk, and in decision-making through time.

## Other theoretical critiques of maximization

Criticisms of the maximization hypothesis emanate from small but diverse groups of economists, outside the mainstream of modern economic thought. First, there are arguments that maximizing behaviour is not possible. For example, George Shackle (1955, 1972) has developed a critique based on ideas from both Friedrich Hayek and John Maynard Keynes. His work emphasizes the immense problems of gathering and processing sufficient information, and of the uncertainty involved in making any real choice. Related points are made by Kenneth Boulding (1956) who argues that maximizing behaviour unrealistically proposes that agents are not only conscious of the alternatives that lie before them and what will follow from their actions, but that they also know the complete set of their preferences. In addition, they are capable of calculating the probability of outcomes in order to maximize the expected value of their acts, 'a feat of mathematical agility which would take centuries of experience and enormous electronic calculators to perfect' (p. 84).

Notably, Harvey Leibenstein (1976, 1979) also denies that all economic agents maximize. His argument is that firms will not reach the norms of attainment that are specified by neoclassical theory because of '$X$-inefficiency'. In practice, he argues, firms do not maximize profits (nor minimize costs). Whilst the $X$-inefficiency argument may be a convenient illustrative device it remains tied to the neoclassical framework. $X$-inefficiency itself is defined in terms of neoclassical norms. Leibenstein argues that neoclassical theorists are wrong because they fail to acknowledge the existence of such inefficiency, but he then seems to draw the conclusion that policies must be so designed that it is minimized and that reality then conforms to the neoclassical model. However, in a world of uncertainty and ignorance some slack capacity is necessary to deal with contingencies. A firm that rid itself of slack would be inflexible and less likely to survive. Furthermore, and as Leibenstein (1983, p. 841) himself has admitted, as yet there is no finished theoretical foundation for this central idea in his writings. Neither have his works yet generated an experimental research programme to compare with that of Herbert Simon and the behaviouralists, to whom we shall now turn.

From the outset, Herbert Simon's behavioural research programme has emphasized the weight of uncertainty and incompleteness of knowledge that bears upon decision-making, and, by comparison with the task of maximizing on the neoclassical model, the limited computational capacity of the human brain.[7] A key feature of Simon's work is that he rejects the global maximization hypothesis but retains a qualified and explicit notion of 'bounded' rationality. Thus, for example, agents may not be able to gather and process all the information for reaching global maximization decisions, but they can make a 'rational' decision within a small set of possibilities. Consequently, it is suggested by Simon (1957a, b, 1959, 1979) and Richard Cyert and James March (1963) that firms and consumers are not maximizing, but 'satisficing' (i.e. simply trying to attain acceptable minima), given the impossibility of dealing substantively with all the information required to attain a maximum.

However, there is a means by which the satisficing concept can be easily digested by neoclassical theorists. Using the overworked concept of 'transaction costs', some people interpret the Simon–Cyert–March view as the proposition that it would be 'too costly' to collect all the necessary information to determine the overall maximum. According to this interpretation, 'satisficing' is essentially cost-minimizing behaviour. This, of course, is just the dual of the standard assumption of maximization. Thus, with the aid of a few new theoretical devices, the 'satisficing' proposition is reduced by some economists to merely another version of the neoclassical maximization hypothesis. It is thus gobbled up as a 'special case' of generalized neoclassical theory and rendered harmless to orthodoxy.

But this would not do full justice to the force and impact of the behaviouralist argument. First, as Herbert Simon (1962, 1976), Janos Kornai (1971) and others have emphasized, the notions of equilibrium and global rationality in neoclassical economics are intimately connected. Neoclassical maxima are attained through global calculation, whereas bounded rationality is associated with procedural revisions as information becomes available or is assessed. Thus to 'attack the concept of unbounded rationality is to attack the value of neo-classical equilibrium analysis' (Tisdall, 1976, p. 208).

In addition there would seem to be a problem with the attempted translation of 'satisficing' into a special case of maximizing behaviour. For this to work the agent must attribute a perceived value to the 'cost' of obtaining further information whilst optimizing. But how is this value determined? How is it known that the marginal cost of obtaining further information exceeds the marginal benefit from its possession? It is in the nature of information that we are ignorant of its content before we possess it (see Arrow, 1962). So how can decisions about gathering further information be costed?

This decision cannot be made on the basis of any substantial and objective calculation of the costs because that would assume that the information search had already proceeded in earnest. Consequently, the evaluation must be largely on the basis of a subjective whim or guess, or it must rely crucially on the established routines and the assessment and experience of other economic agents. In the former case the door is opened to an Austrian variety of subjectivism. In contrast, in the latter case, by admitting an important role for convention and routine, a move is made away from pure subjectivism and towards a more 'institutionalist' understanding of economic phenomena. The neoclassical attempt to subsume 'satisficing' seems to create a dilemma for orthodoxy of this type.

Neoclassical rebuttals of the criticisms of their maximization hypothesis most often suggest that problems to do with information are exclusively to do with its scarcity, and not with the agent's problem of coping with or understanding the data in a finite period of time. The 'scarcity' concept has pride of place in the orthodox paradigm, and there is a common tendency to regard information as a single, undifferentiated 'substance', with its own 'market' which would logically be either clearing or in shortage or in excess supply. Yet information is by its nature heterogeneous and complex, and the problem is not always of not having information but of knowing how to deal with it. Problems of this type lead some theorists to write of information overload as well as shortage.

Criticisms of the maximization hypothesis from Boulding and Simon in particular have always stressed both the shortage of certain types of specific information, and the limited capacity of the human brain to deal with the large amount of data presented to it. Consequently, rationality is not simply 'bounded' in the sense that there is too little information upon which reason can be based, but also that there is too much information to compute or assess.

This theme is developed in later chapters of this work. But it is not a new idea, even within economics. Roy Radner's important (1968) article on competitive equilibrium under uncertainty addressed the theory of competitive markets of Kenneth Arrow and Gerard Debreu in which it is assumed or implied that a market exists for the exchange of every possible commodity on every possible date in every possible state of nature. Thus if there are a thousand commodities, a thousand 'dates', and a thousand 'states', then there will have to be a billion different markets. One of Radner's arguments is that in practice the number of markets has to be reduced. One mechanism is the introduction of money, but strictly this cannot be included in an Arrow-Debreu world. He argues that 'a demand for liquidity arises from *computational limitations*, and would be present even in a world of certainty about the environment if that world were sufficiently complicated'. Consequently, 'there is a basic difficulty in incorporating computational limitations in a "classical" equilibrium theory based on optimizing behaviour' (p. 32).

Elsewhere, Jacob Marschak and Roy Radner (1972, p. 315) argue convincingly that the sort of computational and analytical ability involved in the neoclassical picture of economic man is no less than that of a perfect mathematician. Other theorists, perhaps without accepting the full force of the Marschak–Radner argument, have begun to reflect along similar lines. For example in his book on uncertainty John Hey writes that 'the optimization problems that . . . agents are supposed to be solving . . . are so complicated that the economic theorist . . . probably spent several months finding the solution . . . The "as if" methodology is stretched to breaking point . . . Have we not gone wrong somewhere?' (Hey, 1979, p. 232).

More recently, Ronald Heiner (1983, 1985, 1985–6, 1986) has advanced the argument by addressing directly the problem of the full use of available data. Using empirical support from psychology and elsewhere, Heiner argues that normally there is a gap between the 'competence' of an agent and the 'difficulty' in selecting the preferred alternatives. One prominent possibility is that such a 'C–D gap' could result from the burden of excess information placed upon an agent in making a decision.

A good illustration of this is provided by Heiner (1983, pp. 563–4) in his discussion of Rubic's Cube. Apparently, there are over 43 trillion possible initial positions from which to unscramble the cube. However, the data required in any attempt to work out the quickest way of doing this are readily available by observing the scrambled patterns on the faces of the cube. The 'rational maximizer' of neoclassical theory is assumed to be capable of using, and use, all this data in finding the best way of solving the puzzle. He or she is assumed to have a mathematical and computational agility which would lead directly to the solution.

In contrast, cube analysts have developed simple procedures to unscramble the cube (see Heiner, 1983, p. 564 for references). These follow a hierarchical sequence and are largely independent of the initial scrambled position. They are all sub-optimal in that they do not unscramble the cube in the minimum number of moves. But from an operational point of view they are much more useful than trying to compute and execute the 'optimal' solution.

Another example comes from the development of computer algorithms to play chess. The chess board, like Rubic's Cube, readily displays, at no further cost, all the data required for any attempt to find an optimal solution. It is thus described by game theorists as a game with 'perfect information'. Consequently, according to game theory, there is always a strategy which will assure one of the players of a win, or at least of a tie (Trakhtenbrot, 1963, p. 15).

In practical terms, however, due to finite speed and memory, even the modern computer is not always able to give a complete analysis of all the options available and derive the substantively optimal solution. Consequently, computer programmers have followed and extended the decision procedures of the human chess expert. Studies show that expert players compensate for the limited computational ability and capacity of the human brain by searching incompletely through the immense tree of move possibilities, with criteria for selecting a viable move.[8] A skilled human player routinely memorizes a large collection of possible patterns of the pieces, together with procedures for exploiting the relations that appear in these patterns. A computer program for playing chess relies less on pattern recognition, and more on an extended search of the move possibilities according to more rigid decision rules. However, in both cases, players do not 'maximize' by computing the optimal strategy but 'satisfice' by finding one that is 'good enough'.

Rubic's Cube and the chess algorithm provide excellent examples of available data that are imperfectly used. As we shall show in the next chapter, cognitive psychology provides another rich vein of examples, showing that the full use of available data is a rare exception rather than the rule. It is typical of human behaviour, even with sophisticated economic agents with the full use of modern information technology, to systematically ignore both received sense data and even information which, in some sense, is 'understood'.

Case studies in politics and international relations suggest that decisions are not made on the basis of all the accessible information, but in regard to the subset of information which is meaningful or acceptable in relation to existing cognitions and choices.[9] Members of the American military 'knew' of reports of the impending Japanese attack on Pearl Harbour, but, because this information did not square up with the appraisal of the military situation, it was regarded as erroneous and filtered out of reports. A husband may have evidence that suggests that his wife is having an affair, but for peace of mind or marriage the reaction is simply to disregard the information, and to place it, as it were, out of mind.

The problem of the complexity and abundance of sense data, and the limited computational capacity or ability of the human brain to deal with it, is central to the argument in this book. In contrast, in most orthodox accounts of information problems in economics the problem is regarded as one of information scarcity. Furthermore, mainstream neoclassical theory is empiricist, in that it makes no distinctions between sense data, information, and knowledge, and assumes that information or knowledge are provided from experience independently of the beliefs, concepts or theories of the observer. Such empiricism is the obverse of its rationalism, in the sense that it is assumed that rational calculation both dominates human behaviour and is rapidly accomplished without cost. In contrast, information is treated here as complex and non-homogeneous, open to cognitive interpretation, and generally not presented in a form which is amenable to global rational calculation, even if such calculations were possible.

## Empirical critiques of maximization

As behaviouralist and other writers have made clear, there is an impressive body of experimental evidence in psychology to do with choice and decision-making under uncertainty. Some of the results are highly relevant to current economic controversies and appear to undermine models of behaviour based on substantive (or global) rationality. This psychological evidence suggests that people do not use all the evidence that is available to them, that they do not revise their probability estimates by as much as Bayesian expectations theorists assume, and that they use 'rule of thumb' and other measures to deal with risk or uncertainty.[10]

An example of the type of psychological test involved is the event-matching experiment of Feldman (1963) in which a subject is presented with a random sequence of Xs and Os, of which 70 per cent are Xs and 30 per cent are Os. The subject is asked to predict the next symbol, with rewards for each correct prediction. Ostensibly 'rational' behaviour is always to predict X, as this ensures the highest chance of success.

The evidence suggests that subjects are rarely 'rational' in this sense. Simon (1976) was aware of only two people who consistently chose the X option: they were both well-known and expert game theorists upon whom the experiment was once tried. In his experience all other subjects acted as if the sequence was patterned, not random, and tried to guess by extrapolating the pattern. This kind of guessing would be likely to lead to X and O being chosen in proportion to the number of times that they occur in the sequence, i.e. 70 and 30 per cent respectively. As a result the overall prediction accuracy would be 58 per cent, as opposed to 70 per cent under ostensibly 'rational' behaviour. In later experiments it has been shown that subjects act in a similar manner even when they are told that the sequence is random; they act in a non-'rational' manner and try to impose pattern and meaning on the events.

Another example is the phenomenon of preference reversals, as outlined by Sarah Lichtenstein and Paul Slovic (1971, 1973). These can occur when individuals are presented with a choice between two gambles, one featuring a high probability of winning a modest sum of money, and the other featuring a low probability of winning a large monetary amount. Statistically, of course, the two gambles should be compared by working out their expected values, i.e. the probability of winning multiplied by the amount of money to be won. However, even when the expected values of the gambles are identical, the typical finding is that people will tend to choose the former and safer gamble, but when asked to rank the gambles in terms of their value they will assign the larger monetary value to the bet involving the larger amount of money.

Clearly, this behaviour violates conventional preference theory and the idea that people are consistently maximizing in situations of risk.

According to Slovic and Lichtenstein (1983, p. 597) in their review of subsequent experiments and debates, preference reversal 'can be seen not as an isolated phenomenon, but one of a broad class of findings that demonstrate violations of preference models due to the strong dependence of choice and preference upon information processing considerations'.

In a manner characteristic of his own open and enquiring mind, but in variance with many other neoclassical economists, Kenneth Arrow (1982) has provided a number of real-world economic examples which suggest that the psychological experiments are not simply extreme and perverse cases but that they correspond to much more general phenomena. Taking an example from the world of insurance, Arrow quotes a 'striking' real life situation which

> has given grounds for doubt as to the validity of expected utility hypothesis. Since 1969, the United States government has offered flood insurance at rates which are well below their actuarial value. The intention was to relieve the pressure for the government to offer relief when floods occurred. Under the usual hypothesis of risk aversion, any individual should certainly be willing to take a favourable bet, even more because it offsets an otherwise fluctuating income. Yet until the government increased the pressure by various incentives, very few took out this insurance. A careful study by Kunreuther (1978) failed to uncover any reason consistent with the usual explanations of economic rationality. The main distinguishing characteristic of those who took out flood insurance was acquaintance with others who took out insurance. This might be taken as an explanation in terms of information costs, but the information seems so easy to acquire and the stakes so large that the hypothesis hardly seems tenable. (Arrow, 1982, p. 2)

In case such examples are regarded as marginal exceptions to a hypothesis of rationality which may be useful when applied to more central features of economic life, Arrow quotes several studies of securities and futures markets which again contradict the strict assumptions of maximizing rationality in situations of uncertainty or risk. He points to the inconsistency between the rational maximizing model and some common eventualities in financial markets. These include the 'excessive reaction' of securities and futures markets to 'current information', the 'tendency to ignore prior information' that would be used to calculate Bayesian probabilities and the 'insensitivity of judgements to sample size', even by experienced and highly competent practioners. In his view, such phenomena are directly interpretable in the theoretical terms advanced by psychological experimenters (such as Daniel Kahneman, Sarah Lichtenstein, Paul Slovic and Amos Tversky) to explain their results.

Faced with this evidence, Arrow finds the argument unconvincing that a sort of 'natural selection' process will ensure that rational behaviour will eventually thrive. First, not all arbitrage possibilities exist, and second 'if everyone else is "irrational", it by no means follows that one can make money by being rational, at least in the short run' (Arrow, 1982, p. 7). Consequently, in a world where many actors are 'irrational' there is no necessary reason that the 'rational' actors will prosper, survive and grow in numbers relative to the rest.

Arrow concludes with the hope that he has 'made a case for the proposition than an important class of intertemporal markets shows systematic deviations from individual rational behaviour and that these deviations are consonant with evidence from very different sources collected by psychologists' (p. 8). In effect, he is arguing that the neoclassical presuppositions of rationality, upon which his life's work in general equilibrium theory is based, have to be questioned or even abandoned.[11] Statements of such devastating honesty and candour are rare in the history of science.

## Evaluations of the criticisms

We have seen that there are two types of criticism of the neoclassical maximizing hypothesis. The first is the theoretical argument concerned with complexity, knowledge, uncertainty and limited computational capacity. It is a 'possibilities' critique, found in the work of Shackle, Boulding, Simon and others, which aims to show why, given the problems of complexity and information, maximization could not occur even if it was tried. The second is based on experimental work in psychology and evidence from elsewhere. It suggests that maximization is far from being typical, and that 'non-rational' behaviour could even be prevalent in the economic world.

Lawrence Boland (1981) has argued that criticism of the maximization hypothesis is futile. Uncertainty or incomplete knowledge, he points out, do not prevent maximizing behaviour; the reason being that true knowledge is not necessary for successful and determinate decision-making. A consumer, for example, may *think* that he or she has the 'best' commodity bundle, given the constraints, even if this is not the 'best' from that consumer's point of view, and this would still suggest that he or she is maximizing. Maximizing behaviour cannot be ruled out as a logical impossibility even with incomplete knowledge and a high degree of uncertainty.

Boland correctly points out that there is no inductive method which can prove that general empirical statements are true, because there could always be an unobserved case that counters the statement (see also Boland, 1982). Given this general problem of induction, maximization, if it were to occur, must of necessity be with incomplete knowledge. Merely pointing to uncertainty and limited knowledge does not show that agents are not maximizing. Thus Boland concludes that the Shackle–Hayek–Keynes 'possibilities criticism' of the maximization hypothesis 'is a failure' (1981, p. 1032).

Note, however, that Boland's criticism of the 'possibilities' critique considers only that part of it which relates to limited knowledge and uncertainty. The argument based on an overload of data or limited computational capacity is not considered. The case of limited computational capacity undermines (but does not refute) Boland's counter-argument because in this case agents are likely to know that all available data are being utilized and that in consequence they will be aware that in some sense they are not acting in an optimal manner. Widespread self-awareness of non-maximizing behaviour would undermine Boland's counter-argument. The contrary possibility that an agent may still think that he or she is maximizing cannot, of course, be ruled out. But in the light of the above argument the assumption of universal maximization becomes even more questionable. This is illustrated perfectly by the large number of chess players and Rubic's Cube manipulators who know perfectly well that their own efforts are sub-optimal!

The psychological and empirically based criticism is also given short shrift by Boland. He argues that the maximization hypothesis, in spite of all the empirical evidence 'against' it, is non-falsifiable. To argue, for example, that firms do not maximize profits, does not mean that they do not maximize something else. If subjects do not choose X all the time to maximize their rewards in the event-matching experiment discussed above, then that does not necessarily mean that they are irrational. It could be assumed that their objective function included something else (e.g. variety or excitement) as well as the explicit rewards. The neoclassical maximization hypothesis is: 'For all decision makers there is something they maximize.' It is non-falsifiable for the reason that, despite any evidence, there could always be something else that agents were maximizing. Thus Boland concludes that the experimental evidence cannot be used to falsify the neoclassical hypothesis.

However, as Boland makes clear, the hypothesis is not a tautology, because it is conceivably false. All paradigms or research programmes have, in their 'hard core', crucial and non-tautological assumptions. Maximization is characteristic of neoclassical theory. It is, by assumption, considered fundamental. According to Immanuel Kant, Thomas Kuhn (1962), Imre Lakatos (1970) and other philosophers, all sciences have to make use of 'metaphysical' assumptions which are not 'subject to any empirical test' (Kant, 1929, p. 7). For example, the fundamental idea of cause and effect is neither verifiable nor falsifiable in empirical terms, but it is not a tautology. The same could be said of the maximization hypothesis.

Theorists like Fritz Machlup (1972) offer a standard response to the allegation that the maximization hypothesis is metaphysical. Machlup openly admits that it is a 'fiction' and points out that all sciences have propositions of similar status at their core. He quotes John Stuart Mill in his presentation of maximization as a 'fundamental assumption', who cautions that no 'political economist was ever so absurd as to suppose that mankind are really thus constituted' (Mill, 1844, p. 139). Machlup's defence is simply that the fiction is 'useful', and necessary 'for the theoretical system in which it is employed' (p. 114). This argument seems to be circular, in that the hypothesis is one of the basic assumptions of the theoretical system and thus is bound to be 'necessary' for it. Typically, in order to decide what is a 'useful fiction' and what is not, neoclassical theory relies on its 'best predictions' criterion (Friedman, 1953). But far from confirming neoclassical theory on these grounds, the empirical evidence can be regarded as putting many of its fundamental assumptions into doubt.

If fictions and metaphysics are unavoidable does that mean that we are faced with an essentially arbitrary choice; to accept neoclassical theory and its metaphysical foundations, or to reject it and find another approach along with metaphysical baggage of its own? Boland offers no help here. Indeed, the danger in his position is that it seems to offer a Popperian methodological absolutism which dismisses the role of evidence in the choice of theory except in the case where that evidence can be used to refute a falsifiable proposition. Karl Popper's falsificationism can thus be used for a nihilistic rejection of relevant facts. As Bruce Caldwell (1982, p. 128) rightly points out: 'because there are many roads to criticism, an overemphasis on the specific Popperian directives artificially limits the types of critical discourse considered permissible.' He thus rightly suggests that 'Boland's definition of criticism is overly narrow' (Caldwell, 1983, p. 825) and that a wider assessment of theory should be involved.[12]

Indeed, according to the Duhem–Quine thesis (discussed in chapter 2) it would be very difficult to falsify a theory using Popperian methods. According to the Duhem–Quine thesis we can never be sure that a single theory is being appraised in isolation from other auxiliary hypotheses. An observation which appears to falsify the theory can always be explained away by pointing to one of the additional assumptions. Thus an experiment which suggests non-maximizing behaviour in choosing a set of items can always be dismissed by changing the implicit assumptions concerning the composition of the maximand. The maximizer could always be actually maximizing something else.

Boland makes this very point, but does not seem to recognize its generality according to the Duhem–Quine thesis. In this light it is reasonable to ask why such a song and dance should be made about the 'futility of criticizing the neoclassical maximization hypothesis'. On Popperian grounds it could be equally 'futile' to criticize monetarism, general equilibrium theory, IS–LM analysis, Sraffian theory and the economics of Marx or Keynes! Caldwell is thus correct in his suggestion that critical discourse has to be widened from the canons of Popperian methodology if criticism is to be effective at all.

It is worth emphasizing that the actual development of both natural and social science does not strictly conform to the Popperian and falsificationist model. This point has been argued extensively by Lakatos (1970) amongst others. Falsifying evidence has often been ignored away, and other evidence of a more tangential nature has frequently had a more critical impact. Sometimes changes have occurred for reasons not directly to do with the evidence at all.

The consequence of admitting evidence exclusively on falsificationist grounds is that the accumulation of awkward or conflicting evidence does not necessarily have a bearing on the assessment or development of a theory. It is of course true that no finite weight of evidence can prove general statements, nor overcome the problem of induction. And, of course, all facts are theory-bound, coloured by the preconceptions of the observer and do not speak for themselves. But that should not exclude questions of weight of evidence, along with theoretical considerations, in accepting or rejecting a general maximization hypothesis. In rejecting a crude empiricism where it is mistakenly assumed that facts always 'speak for themselves' we should not assume a Popperian view where facts speak decisively but only on rare and special occasions. Facts do not speak without preconceptions and theories, but they can make an impact, even when they do not falsify, which it is foolish to ignore.

In the history of science the weight of evidence is never crucial on its own, but it can play an important role. Evidence does not show directly that a particular theory is valid or invalid, but it may be much more difficult to fit evidence into one theory rather than another. Consider, for example, the historical debates about whether the Earth or the Sun was at the centre of the solar system. The tortuous complications involved in placing the evidence into a Ptolemaic view of an Earth-centred universe were always a great burden for that theory. When the scientific and ideological conditions began to change, in the late sixteenth and early seventeenth centuries, the nagging problem of reconciling the data on planetary orbits with a Ptolemaic view was significant in assisting the ascendancy of the heliocentric idea attributed to Copernicus (see Koestler, 1959). Thus it is possible to recognize the part played by the empirical evidence whilst at the same time accepting that other factors (including developments in technology, religion and theoretical physics) were very important in the move away from the idea that the universe was centred on the Earth.

Imagine instead, for a moment, that we are blessed or cursed with a mediaeval mind, and that we are observing the universe through Ptolemaic eyes. Then the fact that all the stars appear to be moving in tiny, coordinated, annual circles does not actually refute our view that the Earth is at the centre. Indeed, like the neoclassical maximization hypothesis, Ptolemy's proposition that the universe is centred on the Earth is irrefutable. Notably, it was never falsified by evidence on Popperian lines. Neither could it ever be, because as Albert Einstein has pointed out, the basic choice between Ptolemy and Copernicus was between two rival coordinate systems, both of which are essentially arbitrary. Given that there are no absolute grounds to dismiss the choice of any origin or axes for a coordinate system, no conceivable evidence would show that the Earth was not at the centre of the universe. After all, mapmakers do not conclude that their maps are 'wrong' because the points they survey are found to be shifting rapidly due to the rotation of the Earth; instead they adopt an even more 'naive' coordinate system to that of Ptolemy where the earth is stationary, and they may even adopt the convention that Greenwich Observatory lies on one of the axes.

However, coordinate systems are not all equally useful or functional for the stimulation of insight and the development of theory. The progress of cosmology as a science is roughly measured by its capacity to assume a widening perspective in space and time, and as we follow the early cosmologists and move away from the surface of the Earth and consider the solar system as a whole, it is much easier to explain the motion of the planets with a heliocentric coordinate system than from the viewpoint of Ptolemy. Furthermore, once religious or other doctrinal constraints are removed, then on practical grounds (such as advanced navigation) it is much more plausible and convenient to assume that all the stars are not moving in annual circles, and instead their apparent yearly movement is due to the circuit of the Earth around the sun.

Another example of the role of evidence comes from geology. In 1910 Alfred Wegener published the view that the continents on the surface of the Earth had once been together and had gradually drifted apart. He was impressed by the simple observation that the coasts of some continents (such as Africa and South America) seem to fit together readily like pieces in a jigsaw. However, this clear and durable evidence was ignored and his theory of continental drift was ridiculed by the scientific community. However, half a century later, after the gathering of abundant rock-core-sample and rock-magnetism data which were consistent with the theory, opinion rapidly changed. The evidence did not refute the idea that continents were static, neither did it prove that they had moved apart. But the harmony of the data with the idea of drifting continents was so striking that Wegener's theory gained instant credibility. What was previously regarded as implausible or absurd rapidly became the consensus amongst geologists.

Whilst we should not expect a similarly rapid reaction to evidence within economics (partly because ideology plays a much stronger role than in the modern natural sciences) such examples show that the weight of evidence, even if never sufficient and rarely decisive, can be significant in a shift of paradigm or reassessment of a theory.

Theories are often accepted or rejected on operational grounds, and not because one has triumphed over the other in terms of Popperian methodology. In fact, it is just as 'futile' to criticize the neoclassical maximization hypothesis as it is to criticize Ptolemaic astronomy or the proposition of static continents. But in practical terms all three have been superseded. Just as modern navigation tables are not calculated under Ptolemaic assumptions, managers, advertising experts and market researchers generally do not operate under assumptions of consistent preferences or according to the principle of maximization. In fact, they tend to assume that, in part, tastes can be shifted by clever development, marketing and advertising of the product 'image'. The concepts that they find useful are not the ones that are central to the neoclassical theory. Evidence and experience has helped to shift them in a different direction.

The weight-of-evidence argument would appear to reinstate many of the criticisms of the neoclassical model. Whilst, for example, the event-matching experiment does not disprove that agents are maximizing, it is substantial evidence impelling the theorist to begin to consider a world in which they are not. On the contrary, a Popperian absolutism would lead us to entirely disregard such results. Evidence cannot refute the neoclassical maximization hypothesis, but its combined weight can, and does, raise questions about its validity and leads to a search for theoretical alternatives.

We may note here, however, that the evidence is not purely psychological in character. Consider a relevant example from the political sphere. Here neoclassical economist Anthony Downs (1957), closely followed by James Buchanan and Gordon Tullock (1962) have brought the axiom of the rational and maximizing agent into political science. In their theoretical models politicians maximize rewards and spells in power and voters maximize net benefits. But here the neoclassical theory of democracy meets a problem. Given that the vote of a single individual amongst thousands or millions will make the tiniest difference to the outcome, the expected rewards from the outcome of a single vote are likely to be very small indeed. When, in addition, there are tangible travel and other costs to voting, why do 'rational' people vote at all? Thus the neoclassical theory of political behaviour meets a difficulty, sometimes known as 'the paradox of voting', in explaining a basic political act.

Stanley Benn (1976), in his critique of Downs, argues that 'a rational electorate would be expected to register *no* votes, and the system would promptly collapse' (p. 253). Downs recognizes this problem and his defence is to argue that people also have a long-term rational interest in keeping democracy going: so they vote. But this is inconsistent with his preceding argument that a single vote can make little difference with large electorates. As Benn puts it, the voter is 'no more the crucial agent in determining long-run gains than in determining the party that will govern' (p. 253).

The Downs problem does not lead inexorably to the rejection of the hypothesis of maximizing behaviour. The phenomenon of half or three-quarters of the electorate being willing to vote in presidential or general elections does not imply that those individuals are not maximizing. They may be getting oodles of utility simply from the act of placing their vote. We cannot prove that this is not the case, but the Downs problem should impel us to search for an alternative theory. As Brian Barry (1970, p. 23) asserts: 'It may well be that both the costs and . . . benefits of voting are so low that it is simply not worth being "rational" about it. Thus habit, self-expression, duty and other things have plenty of room to make themselves felt.' We may be faced with a choice between theories, some of which are perhaps non-falsifiable in Popperian terms. But that does not mean that we should always be indifferent between them, nor disregard the evidence, however malleable or theory-bound it may be.

There are other good examples from economics where the weight of evidence is significant in assessing the neoclassical maximization hypothesis. In their famous book on the theory of the firm, Richard Cyert and James March (1963, ch. 7) tried to put the 'satisficing' hypothesis to the test by modelling the decision behaviour of a department manager in a retail store. Their model assumed that if sales of an item were more or less at past performance levels then prices would be set as before. If sales slipped below this satisficing level then prices would be adjusted. Cyert and March compared their computer model of this decision procedure with the actual sales decisions of the department manager, and found that it predicted some 85 per cent of the price decisions *exactly*. Whilst this highly impressive evidence does not refute the maximization hypothesis, and nor does it prove the satisficing model to be correct, it must have considerable weight in any relatively open-minded or progressive scientific discourse.

It should be noted, however, that not all the evidence conforms strictly and exclusively to the behaviouralist model. The event-matching experiment described above is a case in point. The 'paradox of voting' is another example. These suggest a deeper explanation than mere satisficing. Whilst the evidence does not necessarily establish the proposed alternative model, it does still carry weight against the neoclassical hypothesis of maximization.

## 4.2 PROBLEMS WITH THE MEANS–ENDS FRAMEWORK

*Ends and means*

Rational economic man has distinct ends, clearly distinguished from means and unaffected by them. In both neoclassical and Austrian theory, the moulding or determination of ends by social or other circumstances is beyond the compass of investigation. In contrast, the means involved to attain given ends are given the utmost attention. Neither type of theorist is concerned with explanations of why, for example, an individual may have a preference for fast cars or expensive clothes; but they are preoccupied with theories which purport to answer questions such as whether the person saves or works harder to gain these objectives. Ends are taken as given, but the choices of means employed to attain such objectives are the subject of some scrutiny. In both cases the determination of ends is exogenous to the theory. The consequence, however, is that the possibility of the ends being altered or affected by the chosen means is ignored. A simple, one-way causality from one to the other is assumed. Thus, in orthodox theory, 'the end justifies the means'.[13]

However, what is highly relevant to institutional economics is the extent to and the manner in which ends and means are entwined. Whilst the distinction between ends and means is often meaningful, a suggestion that they are always rigidly distinct and practically independent is misleading and erroneous. In contrast, critics of 'rational economic man' rightly stress their interdependence. As Mark Lutz and Kenneth Lux put it: 'Means often affect ends, the latter only becoming clear in retrospect. Also, ends may affect means' (Lutz and Lux, 1979,

p. 62). Martin Hollis and Edward Nell make a similarly directed point: 'As many studies show, large corporations rarely decide to expand, diversify or merge, in order to achieve clearly defined ends. The ends are understood and defined only afterwards and by then they have often changed' (Hollis and Nell, 1975, p. 51). Arguably, individuals too may not always rigidly hold to clear or specific ends, and individual ends could also be defined retrospectively.

In a sense it is strange that orthodox economics should differentiate so enthusiastically between ends and means, for the modern economy contains a form in which *in excelsis* means and ends are entwined: money. This substance owes its essential value to its quality as a means (of exchange, store of wealth, etc.), yet, as Georg Simmel points out, in modern society the acquisition of money itself becomes an end: 'The inner polarity of the essence of money lies in its being the absolute means and thereby becoming psychologically the absolute purpose for most people' (Simmel, 1978, p. 232). Thus money, in a capitalist economy, is an extreme and important example of a means becoming an end. However, the inter-penetration of means and ends is not confined to this extreme case.

In the orthodox view, ends and means are structured in a hierarchy, a given end becoming a means to another end. For example, my end to catch the next train to town is merely a means of transportation to work, which, in turn, is a means towards personal remuneration, and so on. In contrast, what is being proposed here is an even deeper inter-relationship in which means can alter ends in the process of achieving them. Furthermore, ends are not always fully formed and clearly articulated, and often their ramifications are too complex to give rise to a fully informed choice of means. Herbert Simon saw the limitations of such a fixed hierarchic arrangement of means and ends: 'Instead of a single branching hierarchy, the structure of conscious motives is usually a tangled web or, more precisely, a disconnected collection of elements only weakly tied together.' He concludes that 'in actual situations a complete separation of means from ends is usually impossible' (Simon, 1957b, pp. 63–5).

The possible interaction between means and ends, and the moulding of wants by activities, have been ignored by mainstream economic theory, where wants are treated as being expressed by fixed functions of utility or preference.[14] In addition, less attention is given to the underlying fixity of the assumptions than to the mathematical and formalistic structure that is built upon them.

*Adaptive ends*

An important discussion of adaptive preferences is by Jon Elster in his appropriately titled *Sour Grapes* (1983a). This work, along with his *Ulysses and the Sirens* (1979), raises questions about the utilitarian means–ends schema that underpins neoclassical theory. The fox, being unable to reach the tempting grapes, declares that they are not ripe. Elster regards this as a preference shift as a consequence of a failed attempt to obtain satisfaction. The shift, in this case, is towards the end-state: the fox would obtain less, or even negative, marginal utility from the consumption of the grapes after the change in preferences than before his failed attempt. The reverse phenomenon Elster describes as 'counter-adaptive preferences', where preferences shift in the opposite direction. There are everyday examples such as 'the grass is always greener on the other side of the fence' and 'forbidden fruit is sweet'.

There are many possible cases from everyday life where preferences could be regarded as changing because of the acquisition of new experiences. A person may prefer to live in the town rather than the country, or to consume lager rather than ale, but on experiencing the other option his or her preferences may change. However, these could all be regarded as cases of a more general phenomenon of preference change through 'learning'. Such behaviour can be fitted into a developed neoclassical framework in which the over-riding preference function relates to an informed choice, and not one based on limited or faulty information.

Elster deals with these phenomena by questioning the notion of 'being informed' in this context. Does the new situation lead to the revelation of 'true' underlying preferences or does it cause a fundamental shift in those preferences themselves? It is arguable that if a person finds that his or her preferences shift towards rural life and real ale then these new preferences are 'informed in the sense of being grounded in experience, not in the sense of being grounded in the meta-preferences of the individual' (1983a, p. 113). And ends that are 'grounded in experience' are clearly interactive with the means employed that give rise to such experiences. However, this argument is not decisive. Too much hinges on the insufficiently elaborated concept of being 'grounded in experience'.[15]

According to cognitive theory, and it is a point widely accepted by philosophers, there is no perception or appraisal of experience which is free of the cognitive framework or conceptual apparatus of the observer. Consequently, if preferences are adaptive then it is the cognition of experience that matters, and ostensibly similar experiences can be perceived in widely differing terms.

A brief discussion of the theory of cognitive dissonance, as proposed and developed by Leon Festinger (1957) and others, is relevant at this point. The theory suggests that when people are faced with a difficult choice between alternative courses of action their cognition of the alternatives alters to render one of them more acceptable, and the choice then seems in prospect or retrospect easier to make. For example, experiments with children faced with a choice between toys of comparative appeal suggest an increase in the relative perceived attractiveness of the chosen toy, after the choice was made.

More than two decades after the theory of cognitive dissonance had become widely utilized in psychology, it was applied to economics by George Akerlof and William Dickens (1982). They propose a model in which people not only have preferences over states of the world, but also beliefs about the state of the world. In addition, people have some control over their belief systems, and they can be selective in their choice of information so as to conform to adopted beliefs. Although Akerlof and Dickens do not make much of the point, this is an important case of people not making full use of the information that is available to them. According to Festinger's theory, they do so to reduce psychological tension or instability. Akerlof and Dickens consider the case of workers in a hazardous industry adjusting to the risks by choosing to believe that the job is really safe, and consequently refraining from using safety equipment when it becomes available, even when it is in their interest to use it.

The authors consider the possibility that workers will have 'rational expectations' and know that their beliefs will change after they enter the hazardous industry. Reasonably, however, they regard the personal awareness of future behaviour and beliefs to be unrealistic. Indeed, precisely because evidence alone cannot be decisive in refuting a theory, there is no necessary reason why people should learn about the validity or invalidity of their belief systems and adjust them progressively towards some 'true' model. Generally, cognitive theory challenges any such necessary progression, and explains why people can remain with a belief system even if others regard it as untenable or absurd.

In the light of this brief discussion of cognitive theory, consider the view that apparent adaptations of preferences are all manifestations of an immutable and enduring set of meta-preferences (as in the work of Gary Becker). If preferences over belief systems are to be included in the model then it would be possible that apparent preferences, according to the current belief system, could remain inconsistent with the over-riding preference function. Furthermore, because crucial information is ignored, there is no necessary process of adjustment towards the over-riding set of meta-preferences. Consequently, apparent preferences and meta-preferences could remain permanently out of line. In this case the very idea of a permanent, underlying preference system is undermined.

The above arguments, once again, are not a decisive refutation of the idea of a stable, over-riding preference function. But they still carry some weight, and they suggest an alternative (and arguably more plausible) way of interpreting economic behaviour. In an alternative conception preferences and ends are not immutable, and they can adapt in response to perceived experience or changes in beliefs. However, such adaptation is not always gradual or progressive, and changes in cognitive framework can lead to a rapid change of apparant preferences or lifestyle. Examples of this come readily to mind, such as the case of women, whose horizons were previously limited to children and the home, becoming interested in feminist ideas, and leading to dramatic alterations to lifestyle and personal aims. It is difficult (but not, of course, impossible) to reconcile such dramatic changes with a single, stable set of meta-preferences.

The explanation of all behaviour in terms of an over-riding preference function which encompasses all possible states of the world, and determines all choices through time, is an extreme and highly questionable position. It is extreme because it is assumed that the preference function is 'immanently conceived' and is subsequently unaffected by the rich experience of life and the development of lifestyles and aspirations. Underneath, the individual remains unmoved, choosing and acting in accordance with the complex machinery of preferences. The alternative proposal that preferences are adaptive and responsive to individual experience is more plausible for that reason.

Nevertheless, there are reasons why neoclassical theory has progressively inclined towards the more extreme and untenable position. The first is partly to do with ideology. If preference functions are regarded as being affected by experience then individual aims and purposes can no longer be regarded as inviolable, and this in turn is a challenge to the classical liberalism and individualism which have traditionally been associated with neoclassical theory. Indeed such a challenge would go against the orthodox article of faith that the individual is the given and irreducible unit of analysis.

The second reason is that if ends are jumbled up with means then it is all the more difficult to follow utilitarian methodology and take a value-free stance. It is no longer possible to adopt the norms of means–ends rationality, and confine value judgements simply to the assessment of ends. If the 'end no longer justifies the means' then a hard-and-fast distinction between positive and normative economics is doomed.

# 5

## The Rationalist Conception of Action

In the social sciences we are suffering from a curious mental derangement. We have become aware that the orthodox doctrines of economics, politics, and law rest upon a tacit assumption that man's behaviour is dominated by rational calculation. We have learned further that this is an assumption contrary to fact. But we find it hard to avoid the old mistake, not to speak of using the new knowledge.

Wesley Mitchell (1918, p. 161)

Dominant within mainstream economic theory is the idea that all action is regulated by rational calculation. Moreover, we are assumed to possess an individual mechanism for assigning values to policy outcomes. This is more or less what has been dubbed 'the rationalist conception of action' by Barry Hindess (1977c) and the 'analytic paradigm' by John Steinbruner (1974). We shall use the former term here. The essential idea that is common to these definitions has been extensively criticized not only by Hindess and Steinbruner but also by a large number of other social theorists.[1]

It may be remarked that neoclassical theory does not imply conscious rational deliberation, and instead that optimizing behaviour is promoted by some Darwinian mechanism of the 'survival of the fittest'. Take Milton Friedman's famous example (1953, p. 21) of the skilled billiard player who does no complex calculations but acts 'as if he knew the complicated mathematical formulas that would give the optimum directions of travel, could estimate accurately by eye the angles, etc., describing the location of the balls, could make lightning calculations from the formulas, and could then make the balls travel in the direction indicated by the formulas'. Friedman justifies the assumption of a lightning, rational calculator not on the grounds that it is realistic but because skilled players would reach 'essentially the same result'.[2]

Friedman then goes on to argue that a skilled businessman would not necessarily know and analyse all the cost and revenue functions for the firm, but a businessman who acted 'as if' such an analysis had been performed would be more likely to survive. As noted in the preceding chapter, this 'natural selection' argument has been criticized with devasting effect by Sidney Winter (1964). To repeat, the main problem with it is that there is no specified mechanism through which such optimal behaviour, if arrived at for some reason, can be sustained and passed on through time, and spread to other agents.

Some notion of rational deliberation is necessary to support the maximization hypothesis, otherwise there would seem to be no explanation as to how it is sustained and how others catch on to the idea. The removal of the element of rational deliberation in the presumption of maximizing behaviour leaves neoclassical theory without any apparent, plausible mechanism for explaining the supposed retention of maximizing behaviour by the firm through time or its transmission from one firm to another. Arguably, the 'evolutionary' argument for maximization is forced to rely upon a rationalist conception of action.

Furthermore, as we have noted in the case of the consumer, 'natural selection' arguments for maximization without rational calculation do not seem to apply because, unlike firms, if people did not maximize they would not necessarily die and disappear from the scene. The question really to be asked is what happens to neoclassical theory when rational deliberation is removed?

If it is proposed that neoclassical agents are not rational deliberators, then they cannot be choosers in the full sense of the word because they are not making choices on the basis of any conscious deliberation and reasoning. Choice, in the fullest sense of the word, is something more than mechanical determination or habit. Thus any denial of the centrality of rational deliberation in neoclassical theory involves the relegation of the concept of choice which has tradtionally been held in great esteem by that school.

In the light of the above arguments we are justified in retaining the view that neoclassical theory has a strong implicit or explicit attachment to the concept of 'economic man' as a *de facto* rational calculator. There may be those that are willing to deny the necessity of such an idea, and remove all pretences that neoclassical theory embraces the notion of choice. In addition, they must either find an alternative mechanism for the transmission of maximizing behaviour by the firm, or abandon the 'evolutionary' argument for the maximization hypothesis. Let these theorists state their position and act upon it; it is to the others that the remarks in this chapter pertain.

Such rational calculation in neoclassical theory embraces all relevant variables. Significantly, it makes little difference to neoclassical theory if the chooser is a human being, a computer or a machine. Generally, the rational calculation is at the same level of 'consciousness', whether this is the consciousness of an aware human being or a programmed computer. The key point is that the calculation embraces all relevant information, involving the maximization of a single-value outcome (e.g. utility or profits).

In contrast, the behaviouralist model (e.g. Simon, 1957a) incorporates a payoff vector rather than a single-value function as in the neoclassical case. Furthermore, each component of the behaviouralist payoff vector is restricted to a limited number of outcomes (e.g. satisfactory/unsatisfactory) rather than a cardinal or ordinal scale. We are assumed to act with given goals in mind but to examine the results of action until an acceptable ('satisficing') combination is reached, rather than to engage in a continuous trade-off as in the neoclassical scheme.

However, the behaviouralist model, like the neoclassical one, still assumes that agents are focusing on a set of policy outcomes and subjecting them to some form of rational calculation. In the behaviouralist schema rationality is 'bounded', but it is still calculating rationality, and it still dominates most human action within the theory. The leading behaviouralist Herbert Simon has developed a forceful critique of the neoclassical conception of rationality, but in some versions the behaviouralist alternative does not stray a great deal from this orthodox model. Actions are still driven by reason, and this reasoning proceeds as conscious, logical deduction from the individual's premises or given knowledge. Behaviour is still governed by intent and rational deliberation, despite the fact that Simon is profoundly aware of the computational limitations of the mind and the complexity of the information involved. Behaviouralism thus offers an incomplete challenge to the rationalist conception, although it marks an important step forward from the neoclassical theory.

Members of the Austrian School do not adopt a determinate model of human behaviour. The process of assessment of policy outcomes is subjective, avowedly complex, and to some extent indeterminate, but it is assumed that action results from reason nevertheless.[3] It is notable, therefore, that whilst challenging the neoclassical paradigm to different degrees, neither behaviouralist nor Austrian theory abandon a rationalist conception of action in general terms.

It should be emphasized that the critique embarked upon here does not involve the suggestion that no actions are motivated or dominated by reason. it simply involves the rejection of the idea that all (relevant) action is dominated primarily by rational calculation. It is argued that there is a large class of actions which are relevant to economics and which arise in a different manner. Consequently, it is necessary to develop a theory of action which does not rely largely or exclusively on rationalist mechanisms and premises.

The arguments for doing so are on methodological, psychological, sociological and other grounds. For those economists who are unfamiliar with such literature it should be pointed out that the argument does not depend on the adoption of an eccentric or factional view. Disputes within these subjects are notorious. But there is almost certainly a majority amongst the contributors to this literature who would not accept the methodology and preconceptions of neoclassical economics in particular, and the rationalist conception of action in general.

### 5.1 INITIAL CRITICISMS

*Early critiques*

It is not popular to do so today, but there are precedents amongst economists for questioning the rationalist conception of action. Thorstein Veblen (1909) developed a critique of the view of human conduct 'as a rational response to the exigencies of the situation in which mankind is placed.' The view of his follower Wesley Mitchell has been noted in the quotation which heads this chapter. However, rejections of the rationalist conception are not confined to the institutionalist school.

Another precedent is found in the work of neoclassical economist and sociologist Vilfredo Pareto. He wrote an entire volume on what he called 'non-logical conduct', this being defined as behaviour where means are not logically related to given ends (Pareto, 1935, vol. 1, p. 77). Pareto's notion of 'logical' actions is more or less equivalent to what is called 'means–ends rationality' in the modern literature. 'Non-logical' conduct includes 'the many human actions, even today among the most civilized peoples, [which] are performed instinctively, mechanically, in pursuance of habit' (p. 83). Despite his belief that the 'actions dealt with in political economy . . . belong in very great part to the class of logical actions' (p. 78), Pareto notes in his *Manual of Political Economy* that in real life non-logical and logical actions 'are almost always mixed together' (1971, p. 30).

Pareto's version of neoclassical theory, unlike the contemporary one, is thus not claimed to have near-universal applicability to social phenomena. His rationalist conception of action is applied to an important but limited class of conduct. In contrast, the tendency in modern neoclassical theory (e.g. Becker, 1976) is to accept fewer and fewer such limitations, and to claim that neoclassical theory (and by implication rationalist conceptions of action) can apply to an extremely wide variety of human acts.

The behaviouralist position is much more cautious. In one of his earlier works Simon took the view that the 'assertion that human beings are always or generally rational . . . has been decisively refuted by modern developments in psychology and sociology' (1957b, pp. 61–2). Simon is one of the very few contemporary economists who have tried to take such developments seriously, even if, despite this remark, behaviouralist models of action involve a limited challenge to the rationalist conception. It would be a great advance for economics if levels of scepticism about rationalist conceptions of action similar to those expressed by Simon, Pareto, Mitchell or Veblen were to be found amongst the majority of the profession. Unfortunately, however, economics is presently moving in discernible annual increments in the opposite direction.

The arguments here against the rationalist conception of action are: first that it is methodologically incoherent; second that it is psychologically crude; and third that it is oblivious to positive developments in other social sciences, particularly sociology and political theory. A prominent theme in some of these arguments concerns the processing of large amounts of complex information in the human mind, and the impossibility of a comprehensive rational calculation with an integrated value outcome.

### Reason and discourse

According to the rationalist conception, action is primarily governed by reason. But rarely is it asked: what of the act of reason itself? If action is purposeful, what of the action of deliberating or reasoning about purpose? Reasoning itself is action, as well as being intimately connected to other forms of practice. But how are we to account for actions in terms of reasons, if reasoning is an act? Reasons, stemming from the act of reasoning, will have to be given reasons in their turn. And these second-order reasons have to be formed by reasons of a third order, and so on. To stop this potentially infinite regress we require a set of reasons themselves unformed by reasoning. Supporters of the rationalist conception of action are thus placed in a dilemma: either to admit the possibility of acts in general not governed by reason, or to suggest that reasoning in particular is non-rational in that it is not guided by reason. Both of these alternatives are strictly inconsistent with the rationalist conception of action.

Hindess (1977a, c) raises the problem of inconsistencies or mistakes within the sphere of reason, and shows that the rationalist conception of action cannot admit the possibility of internal, logical contradiction within discourse. Such a contradiction would conflict with rationalist norms and presuppositions. The 'rationalist conception of the production of discourse cannot be sustained without denying the very possibility of contradiction in discourse . . . If contradiction is possible then discourse cannot be the product of *rationalist* mechanisms' (1977c, pp. 218–19). He shows, furthermore, that the attempt to deal with inconsistency or mistake by presupposing a higher-order decision rule 'which specifies the conditions in which each rule may be called upon to take effect' (1977a, p. 176) does not solve the problem. This super-rule has to exclude inconsistencies or mistakes within itself, or it has to fall outside the rational sphere.

We are thus forced to accept that some acts are not governed by reasons. This judgement should not be confined to discursive acts alone. Indeed non-rationality would be expected to a greater extent with actions not necessarily and intimately connected with the reasoning process. But it is important to note that this problem for the rationalist conception of action arises when it is applied to the level of discourse: the same level as reasoning itself.

The rationalist conception divides social reality into two parts. It postulates 'a realm of ideas (values, representations, meanings), a realm of nature and a mechanism of the realization of ideas in the realm of nature, namely human action' (Hindess, 1977a, p. 162). To avoid self-contradiction the rationalist conception of action cannot itself be applied to the realm of ideas. Paradoxically, the rationalist conception does not apply to its own region of origin; it applies only to action in the natural or material world.

The rationalist conception of action is based on a 'dualistic philosophy' (von Mises, 1957, p. 1) involving a crude, clear and Cartesian boundary between nature and the realm of human thought. But in doing so, however, it lapses into self-contradiction from which there is apparently no escape.

## A possible rationalist response

The rationalist response may be to accept that the rationalist conception of action cannot refer to reason; but to all other acts: 'All action is rational, other than the act of reasoning. The latter is taken as a special case.' Alternatively, words could be redefined so that reasoning is not an act. These responses overcome one of the problems of logical inconsistency in the unqualified rationalist position, and thus may be claimed to keep the idea in dispute intact.

However, this qualified rationalist conception of action is still open to severe criticism. The qualified version still cannot admit the possibility of logical inconsistency in the reasons that are assumed to relate to a set of acts. This is not a trivial matter. Action is sufficiently complex and varied that it would require a large number of inter-connected reasons if it were accounted for in rationalist terms. On reflection, from the known instances where we *do* act for conscious reasons, it is usually the case that our motives are complex and subject to a large number of related inferences or conditions. It is very rare that we simply do $A$ to achieve $B$. It is more often that we do $X$ and $Y$ and $Z$ to achieve $P$ or $Q$, which may lead to $I$ or $J$, or $S$ or $T$, which may lead to other ends, and where there is a complex web of interrelations between many of the variables. It would be heroic to assume that the entire network of reasons were logically consistent and free of intransitivity and contradiction. For us to act in a rationalistic and logically consistent manner not only would we have to be fully aware of our ends and the relevant means, but also we would have to act as a mammoth logical computer, continually checking and monitoring the many and complex reasons for our acts.

As in any real-world organization, decisions to act have to be broken down and considered on a number of discrete levels. For individuals, major strategic decisions (jobs, residence, marriage, children) are taken on a higher level, but necessarily without full consideration of all the detailed implications. Given the complexity involved, it is not feasible to draw out all the logical consequences, even from the limited amount of available information. Lower-level decision-making (what to have for lunch, whether to watch television or go to a restaurant) has a more 'tactical' and non-strategic character. In a complex world, people, like organizations, have to incorporate a degree of hierarchy in their decision-making processes. Given any plausible amount of relevant information, it would be inconceivable that we could consider all the lower-level implications of any higher-level decision. Thus we cannot envisage or obtain a complete and consistent set of reasons to attach to all our acts.

As suggested by the lexicographic model of choice, even the selection of a single product is accomplished after consideration of a number of hierarchically ranked attributes.[4] In purchasing a car we may first decide if it reaches certain minimal criteria of roominess. If so, we may then consider its petrol consumption. If it is satisfactory on that score we may then consider its potential reliability, and so on. This may appear to be a realistic choice procedure but it is not compatible with a complete and consistent preference ordering. In a lexicographic model people do continuously trade-off all the qualities of goods against each other, the gain of one thing compensating for the loss of another. At any given point in time, some qualities are considered and others ignored. If two goods have essentially different characteristics then a compensatory, trade-off relationship between the two is restricted or ruled out. For instance, the consumption of no quantity of diamonds can compensate for the lack of water of a person suffering from thirst.

If we move on from choices between attributes of goods, to choices between goods and between different activities, then the necessity of some hierarchical ranking of the decision-making procedure becomes even more evident. Even if we do attach reasons to all of our acts it is unlikely that in their totality they will form a seamless and consistent whole. Such an outcome is ruled out by the sheer complexitiy of the decision-making process.

However, we could adopt a hierarchic decision-making model (such as a version of lexical choice) without breaking from a modified version of the rationalist conception of action. Even if our reasons are inconsistent when taken as a whole, at a given level of decision-making we may still act for certain (consistent) reasons. Nevertheless, the adoption of a hierarchical model of decision-making may open a Pandora's box. To see this we must ask why a hierarchical approach should be considered in the first place. Initially, one of the most compelling arguments in its favour is to do with the computational limits of the human brain. In a highly complex world we are not able to engage in a complete and continuous trade-off of choices as in the neoclassical model. Even if we had the relevant information we could not carry out a full rational calculation of the likely payoffs from all the options. A hierarchical process of decision-making is ostensibly a means of coping with this complexity by relating different types of decision and action to different levels of deliberation.

But if a problem of complexity is as severe as suggested here, then it is doubtful whether a multi-level hierarchy can overcome the computational limitations of the human mind within the framework of a rationalist conception of action. Even if we could break down decision-making into some structured system the rationalist conception would require that every tier of decision-making were still at some full level of conscious deliberation. We would be liberated from the requirement to render all decisions into a coherent and consistent whole, but we would still be required to carry out and monitor decision-making at all levels in the hierarchy. Even this is an awesome task.

Psychologists argue that mind and body can cope with this problem, but only through the use of unconscious and semi-conscious mental processes. The mental drives of human action are indeed structured in some sort of complex hierarchy, but they cannot all be subject to the fullest level of conscious deliberation. It is to this central and crucial point that we now turn.

5.2   COGNITION AND THE HIERARCHY OF MIND

### Unconscious processes

Neoclassical economics does not make any distinction between actions that do and do not result from full conscious deliberation. All acts are programmed at the same level according to the given functions of preference or utility. The Austrian School makes an equivalent error by assuming that all (relevant) actions result from planning and deliberation at the same level of consciousness. Consequently both schools of thought in economics have an undifferentiated conception of the human psyche. This is appartently uninformed by Sigmund Freud and the many varied developments in psychology since his death.

The behaviouralist approach offers slight but significant improvements in this regard. For example, in his work Simon recognizes the existence and function of unconscious habit in human action (1957b, p. 88). But it is difficult to see how habit, or unconscious actions in general, can play a prominent part in the formal behaviouralist theory that is based on some type of ('bounded') rational decision-making. By definition, habitual action does not imply the current articulation of *any* (maximizing or satisficing) goals. It could be argued that habitual action is simply the repetition of a previous action that was the subject of some (bounded) rational calculation. But to regard them merely as repeats of decisions that were fully rational is partially to degrade the importance and bearing of habits in themselves.[5]

Despite frequent statements of the value and importance of psychology in behaviouralist and Austrian theory, and to some extent in neoclassical economics as well, we find little reference amongst economists to the possibility of unconscious, sub-rational processes.[6] Of course, it was Freud who popularized the concept of the unconscious. But we do not have to tie ourselves to a Freudian theoretical framework to retain this idea. There is reason to be sceptical of much of Freudian theory. But it would be a blinkered mind that entirely dismissed the revolutionary change in the way we see ourselves that is offered by the Freudian analysis. The fundamental idea of there being processes at work in the human mind that are not fully conscious or deliberative has a following that is much wider than those of strictly Freudian persuasion. Indeed, if we exclude the behaviourist and 'experimental' psychologists, who greet concepts like 'consciousness' with extreme disapprobation, then the idea of unconscious or subconscious mental processes has wide allegiance. Outside economics the idea is commonplace.

One reason why economists have failed to embrace this twentieth-century innovation in psychology is not difficult to find. Freud and the Post-Freudians suggest that our actions are not all determined by rational calculation or conscious deliberation. To put it bluntly, this flies in the face of the widespread assumption in economics that we are masters and mistresses of our fate. If we are not sovereign over all our mental processes and actions then how can such an idea as 'consumer sovereignty' over the economy be entertained? How can an agreed contract between two agents be regarded as a fair expression of their needs if it results in part from motives or drives that are not fully conscious? The central idea of the inviolability of individual judgement is placed under threat. Post-Freudian theory undermines some of the main nineteenth-century liberal assumptions with which mainstream economics is often so keen to associate.

Yet the world of advertising has a different view of consumer behaviour which is all too well known. The appeal is not predominantly to reason but to the subtle symbolic significance or 'image' of the product. Sex, glamour, anxiety, escapism and envy are used to full effect. Researches show that people who claim not to be influenced by such advertising techniques are nevertheless affected, and furthermore that they often 'rationalize' their choice after the event (Garfinkel, 1967, pp. 113–14). Other studies have concluded that a substantial proportion of purchases do not involve deliberative decision-making by the consumer, even in the first instance of purchase of a particular product (Olshansky and Granbois, 1979). The analysis of advertising and purchasing has become fertile ground for the Freudian psychologist, the semiologist, the anthropologist and the sociologist of culture. But mainstream economics, with its obsession with rational choice, has very little to offer. Instead, it prefers to believe in an unreal world that conforms to classic liberal theory.

*Cognitive theory*

The significance of the basic idea of unconscious mental processes is especially acute in the area of cognitive psychology. Consider in particular the visual perception of an object, say something moving through the sky. Without plan or intention our eyes pick up sense data, and our mind becomes aware of something which is of different colour from its background, and which is moving and changing its apparent shape. We are at first unaware of what the object is, but we do not necessarily deliberate about its identity as we would with mental process at a higher level.

Usually we recognize the object in a split second, without full conscious deliberation. In this time the brain manages to process the vast quantity of sense data received by the eyes. Although this amount of data, measured in terms of binary 'bits' or whatever, is simply enormous, it is not sufficient to tell us what the object is and what it is doing. The brain has to carry out complicated mental operations to judge the speed, size and form of the object. Without conscious rational calculation it attempts to identify the type of object it has perceived by searching its conceptual memory. Thus we recognize the object as a flying bird. We carry out this sort of mental operation almost continuously, accomplishing highly complicated and largely unconscious processing operations on vast quantities of data.

It is only in exceptional cases that our unconscious mind is unable to reach a firm decision and we have to deliberate about the identity of the object. Even when the sensory data is highly ambiguous, such as in the famous and contrived 'optical illusions', our mind does not always consciously deliberate about whether, for example, the picture is of a single vase or two human faces. As we stare at the image we may simply alternate our perception of it, from one interpretation to another.

Passages like the following are commonplace in cognitive theory:

> The incoming stimulus information confronts us with an infinitely complex universe. Limited to percepts, we would be hopelessly enslaved to the uniqueness of each object, event, or relation. But the chaotic jumble of sensory stimuli is reduced to manageable terms by the formation of *concepts*. By this process our knowledge is transformed from a multiplicity of percepts to a limited number of informational units. We learn to pay attention to some features of an object and to ignore others. Some attributes are abstracted from the total percept and compared with those abstracted from other perceptions. (Spradley, 1972, pp. 9–10)

This echoes the definitive work of Ulric Neisser, *Cognitive Psychology*, and its 'central assertion that seeing, hearing, and remembering are all acts of construction' (1967, p. 10), and that of Jean Piaget who argues that in the end 'the relative adequacy of any perception to any object depends on a constructive process and not on an immediate contact' (1969, p. 365).

Cognitive theory shows that the mind responds to the vast amount of sense data it receives by working to reduce uncertainty at the conceptual level and by giving the 'chaotic jumble' of stimuli some sense and meaning. In general we simulataneously face the problem of having too little information and too much. This apparent paradox arises from us having too much data for the mind to process at one time, and too little of the sort of information that is most important for decision-making. To put it slightly differently, we face the problem of having too much data and too little knowledge.

It would not be possible to process all the given sensory data in a rational, conscious calculation. At least at the cognitive level we do not make the best use of all the available information, neither do we deliberate to any great extent upon it. The crucially relevant step is that we form concepts, based on our past experience, to categorize the sense data and to endow it with meaning. Given these considerations, the orthodox economists' models of rational calculation cannot generally apply. As Steinbruner notes in his discussion of speech perception: 'Here the performance far outstrips what can be done by conscious explicit calculation using even the largest and most sophisticated of computers, and, of course, the process proceeds without awareness or conscious direction' (Steinbruner, 1974, p. 93). Indeed, it is precisely the routinization of the congitive processes and the lack of full awareness that makes such complex 'calculations' possible.[7]

Even in cases where the percepts are relatively uncomplicated, such as our perception of the layout of the chess pieces on a board, or the configuration of Rubic's Cube, it is still not generally possible to calculate rationally all the possibilities and to choose an optimal course of action. As Ronald Heiner (1983) points out, and as discussed in the preceding chapter, there is generally a gap between the difficulty of the decision-making problem and the competence of the individual to solve it. Even in cases where the amount of information is small, it may have complex ramifications and global, rational calculation is still ruled out. Cognitive or framing processes are still involved in the perception and assessment of problems involving relatively little information, and in these cases we still rely on conventions and routines to choose or act.

## Multiple levels of consciousness

One element common to all schools of Post-Freudian psychology is the idea that human consciousness does not operate on a single, and in some sense rational, level. Basically, Freud divides the mind into the conscious and the unconscious. Arthur Koestler and others, however, have proposed a more complex demarcation:

> The Cartesian tradition to identify 'mind' with 'conscious thinking' is deeply engrained in our habits of thought, and makes us constantly forget

the obvious, trivial fact that consciousness is not an all-or-nothing affair but a *matter of degrees*. There is a continuous scale of gradations which extends from the unconsciousness that results from being hit on the head, through the restricted forms of consciousness in dreamless sleep, dreaming, day-dreaming, drowsiness, epileptic automatisms, and so on, up to bright, wide-awake states of arousal. (Koestler, 1967, p. 238)

Koestler, like many others, has been influenced by systems theory, making use of its concept of a structured hierarchy of control mechanisms.[8] It has been usefully applied to the human mind by a number of psychologists and systems theorists.[9] By whatever route, however, the argument for conceiving the mind and consciousness as multiple-levelled and hierarchical is compelling. The argument about whether 'economic man' is entirely rational or non-rational is a false dichotomy. Human agents are both rational and sub-rational at the same time.

At higher levels of consciousness and deliberation we do make a limited number of rational calculations upon which we base plans for future action. But it is a 'common mistake', as John Searle points out, 'to suppose that all intentional actions are the result of some sort of deliberation, that they are a product of a chain of practical reasoning'. For example, deliberation is not always present in the act of everyday conversation. 'In such cases, there is indeed an intention, but it is not an intention formed prior to the performance of the action.' Searle calls this 'intention in action' (Searle, 1984, p. 65). In general, Searle's (1983, 1984) work is distanced from behaviourist and mechanistic conceptions of the mind, and it does not make the error of assuming an undifferentiated level of consciousness and intentionality.

The concept of 'intention in action' is at a level similar or slightly higher than 'practical consciousness' as defined and used extensively by Anthony Giddens: 'Practical consciousness consists of all the things which actors know tacitly about how to "go on" in the contexts of social life without being able to give them direct discursive expression' (1984, p. xxiii). Notably, Giddens is aware of our intellectual debt to Freud but he rejects the psychic divisions of 'id', 'ego' and 'super-ego', and the idea that 'practical consciousness' is protected by a bar of pscyhological repression from reaching the full light of reason. The influence of Freud on Giddens' adoption of a non-unitary concept of consciousness is, however, abundantly clear.

Somewhere below intentions in actions lie habits. These are themselves of different kinds. There is the habitual twitch or nervous response. Other habits cover acts that are complex and were formerly planned, such as the daily habit of driving to work that becomes so deep-rooted that we switch, as it were, to 'autopilot', and think consciously of other things, arriving at our destination being unable to remember any incident on the journey. Below habits could be classified a variety of reflexes, and automatic actions such as breathing.

There is also a category of act which suggests that the hierarchy may not be simple or one-dimensional. It is the case of 'weakness of will' or 'incontinence' in which persons act against their considered or 'rational' judgement. We may act in a particular way whilst knowing that it is not in our best interests. An intemperate outburst, or the one-drink-too-many before driving home, may be familiar examples. Weakness of the will provides a serious philosophical problem for the rationalist conception of action, resulting from the agent's own acceptance of an inconsistency of intention and act. As Donald Davidson (1980, p. 42) concludes after a meticulous discussion of this topic: 'What is special in incontinence is that the actor cannot understand himself.' Habits or reflex actions may be consistent with higher-level intention, but incontinence, by definition, is not.

The structural complexity of the mind is further illustrated with the example of sleep. The complex phenomenon of dreaming shows that different levels of consciousness are possible within sleep itself, while full, wide-awake activity is curtailed. During sleep the majority of reflexes or autonomic actions remain functional. However, our senses may be unconsciously discriminatory in that we may hear a telephone ringing but not our own snoring.

## Too little information and too much

Apart from difficulties with sleep and incontinence, and the above-discussed problem of inconsistency, rational-choice theorists can always claim that each level of consciousness and action can be explained by a single, overall 'rational' mechanism. Habits, for example, can be regarded as repeated acts that are perfectly 'rational', given the lack of information in the hands of the actor that could lead to a change of behaviour. Thus Anthony Downs (1957) suggests that habitual voting for one party, despite some ignorance of its policies, is 'rational' because of the difficulty and 'cost' to the citizen of obtaining the appropriate information to reconsider or adjust voting behaviour. Similarly, Gary Becker (1976) claims that there are stable underlying preferences that encompass not only simultaneous action at all levels but also what appear to be 'changing' preferences through time. There are even highly sophisticated and avant-garde neoclassical models of human behaviour that include decision-making processes at more than one level, but with an over-riding 'rationality' (Thaler and Shefrin, 1981; Winston, 1980), in an attempt to incorporate some form of 'habitual' action.

However, what is common to all these responses is the lack of an explicit differentiation between levels or degrees of consciousness in the decision-making model (even if there may be different levels of decision) and an assumption that there is an underlying, or long-run, stable preference function that governs behaviour overall. As Barry Hindess (1984, p. 270) argues, this type of response 'misses the fundamental point. The objection here is not simply that the rational choice approach neglects important dynamic elements, but also that it treats actors, precisely because they are rational, as characterized by one form of assessment of their ends and conditions of action.' Thus Hindess emphasizes the inevitability of different, socially determined forms of calculation, and focuses on their conditions of existence and effects. But there is also a diversity of levels and forms of calculation and cognition within the human mind, relating to its hierarchical structure. Thus an additional and equally fundamental argument against the idea of a single, underlying preference function is that the computational limitations of the human mind make full conscious deliberation at all levels of decision-making impossible.

Faced with complex and multiple levels of consciousness, and with non-integrated value outcomes, neoclassical proponents of the rationalist conception of action are in some difficulty. It becomes highly implausible to assume that all action is equally rational, at all levels of consciousness and intentionality. With the assumption of global rationality and maximizing behaviour the neoclassical economists do not distinguish between different acts in this way. In the neoclassical scheme all action is at the same level of consciousness – the level of a utility-maximizing machine.

The above argument against global rationality is very close to that of Simon (1955, 1959) in its emphasis on 'bounded rationality', i.e. the limited computational capacity of the human mind. The behaviouralist position is much superior in this regard to that of the neoclassicals. However, as pointed out above, there is no clear and sustained differentiation of substance in behaviouralist works between conscious and unconscious processes. Furthermore, whilst there is a strong and necessary emphasis on the existence of imperfect information and bounded rationality, there can be insufficient recognition that information does not enter raw into the decision-maker's mind. The perceptive, cognitive and conceptual processes are sometimes downgraded or ignored.[10]

Turning to the Austrian School, James Buchanan (1982) has raised objection to the assumption of von Mises and other Austrian economists that all action reflects 'conscious, active, or creative choice' (p. 15). In an earlier article, Robert Nozick asks if conditioned behaviour by humans is 'action' in the Austrian sense, and if so would the same apply to rats and pigeons (1977, p. 364)? The Austrian economist Karen Vaughn (1982) suggests that it would, citing the remarkable experimental work on rats by John Kagel et al. (1981) who have 'revealed' downward-sloping 'demand curves' for food from their behaviour. However, this response violates the rigid methodological dualism of the Austrian School, where the realm of choice and action applies specifically to the human and not to the natural world.

In one of the few passages of Austrian writing to confront some of these questions, Ludwig von Mises writes:

> The vigorous man industrially striving for the improvement of his condition acts neither more nor less than the lethargic man who sluggishly takes things as they come. For to do nothing and to be idle are also action, they too determine the course of events. Wherever the conditions for human interference are present, man acts no matter whether he interferes or refrains from interfering. He who endures what he could change acts no less than he who interferes in order to attain another result. A man who abstains from influencing the operation of physiological and instinctive factors which he could influence also acts. Action is not only doing but no less omitting what possibly could be done. (von Mises, 1949, p. 13)

This argument is extremely weak. Action is here implicitly re-defined as that which 'determines the course of events', in contrast to the spirited definition of action two pages earlier in his work as 'purposeful behaviour'. Admittedly (with the exception of incontinence) we can sometimes purposefully override habitual or autonomic actions. But it is not necessarily purposeful behaviour to fail to attempt to override such acts. A purposeful act to buy (or not to buy) an expensive gift for a companion is not at the same level of purposefulness and rationality as the action of scratching (or even refraining from scratching) one's nose.

If the abstention from action is to be regarded as purposeful in the manner suggested by von Mises then it would imply that we continuously monitor not only our own physiology, but also our entire environment for opportunities to act. A person who is lethargic and fails to react when faced with a £20 note lying in the road is not 'acting' in the same way as one who thinks about it for a while and makes the conscious decision to leave it there. If all forms of real-world inaction are to be regarded as equivalent then this would imply some continuous and omniscient monitoring process governing all potential acts.

Ironically, the reason why this is not feasible derives from the very sort of consideration that the Austrians have quite rightly brought to the fore in a different context: the impossibility of dealing with and processing the vast quantity of information that is involved in the planning of a modern economy (e.g. Hayek, 1935). But a similar point applies to the human mind as well. Both our physiology and our environment are so complex that the human mind cannot commit all the sensory data it receives to the same level of conscious deliberation. The process of concept formation is indispensible precisely because it imposes some sort of order and meaning at some semi-conscious level, so that conscious deliberation can become possible to some higher and more abstract degree. Full conscious deliberation at all levels of mental activity is not possible.

Thus the Austrian standpoint has few advantages over the neoclassical one in this respect. In both cases it is assumed that all action is equally purposive and deliberative. This seems to contradict the Austrian emphasis on the information problem and the degree of complexity in human life. To use a phrase of Friedrich Hayek, just as a central planning agency cannot concentrate *all* the relevant information for national economic planning as if it were 'in a single head', neither can the human mind fully and rationally process all the information relating to individual human action at the highest level of deliberation.

Once again there is considerable support for this type of argument from cognitive psychology. For instance, Joachim Wohlwill (1962) argues that activity at the lower, perceptual level is characterized by the systematic rejection of excess information. In contrast, at higher, cognitive levels there is much less redundancy involved. In logic or mathematics, for example, little or none of the signs and symbols can be ignored. Thus we do not treat all information in the same manner at same levels of thought. At the perceptual level our minds have to simplify and be selective. We cannot monitor all our actions to equal extent as von Mises and others imply.

With the argument cited above, von Mises (1949) has entered the Orwellian world of double-speak. For him, inaction is action. After a dozen pages the content of his *magnum opus* is emptied of the dramatic promise of its title.

### 5.3   CONCLUDING REMARKS

*The rationalist dilemma*

In some respects Friedrich Hayek takes a more sophisticated stand. His critique of behaviourism in *The Sensory Order* (1952b) deals directly with the question of the existence of purposefulness and consciousness in a psychological and neuro-physiological setting. Hayek views the human mind and nervous system as a complex and hierarchic structure, involving both conscious and unconscious mental processes.

It should be noted that in important ways Hayek's work in this area is a deviation from the mainstream Austrian position. The Cartesian, 'methodological dualism' of von Mises is abandoned. In the process, however, key concepts such as purpose and action are degraded of the meaning invested in them elsewhere. For instance, Hayek suggests that machines can be produced to 'show all the characteristics of purposive behaviour'. Although such machines 'are comparatively primitive and restricted in their range of operations compared with the central nervous system' and for this reason 'cannot yet be described as brains', Hayek believes that 'with regard to purposiveness they differ from a brain merely in degree and not in kind' (1952b, p. 126).

Strong arguments against this 'computers can think' type of view are presented in Searle (1983, 1984) and they need not be repeated here. It is sufficient to note that in neoclassical, behavioural and even Austrian theory the notion of purpose and choice ends up losing some of its essential content. Through its determinism, the neoclassical view of the mind excludes real choice. The behaviouralists have been somewhat indiscriminate, seeing 'purposive behavior sequences' (Simon, 1956) in simple cybernetic models of adaptive behaviour. Also, despite intentions, in at least two cases Austrian economists have ended up by degrading the notions of action or purpose. The Austrians draw a boundary between the social and the natural sciences, partly on the basis of the existence of purposeful action in the former and not the latter. When Hayek crosses this boundary from social science into psychology and neuro-physiology, he is thus forced to deny in the latter some of the propositions that elsewhere he lauds as axiomatic to his social science.

It may appear paradoxical, but only by denying that *all* mental processes are at the same level of rationality can we sustain the idea that *some* actions are purposeful and deliberative in character. Just as the solipsist, by asserting that life as a whole is a dream, degrades the concept of the dream itself, those that argue that all action is purposeful and rational end up by emptying those very concepts of much of their content. This, it turns out, is the rationalist dilemma.

## Conclusion

The rationalist conception of action is untenable on several grounds. At the philosophical level it involves a Cartesian division of the world into two, and it cannot explain the act of reason in its own terms without lapsing into self-contradiction. The rationalist conception is incompatible with the type of theoretical outlook which is common in psychology, anthropology and sociology today.

This incompatibility is typically acute in the sphere of cognitive psychology. Some hierarchical structuring of the human mind, at different levels of consciousness, is necessitated by the complexity of cognitive and thought processes and the quantity of sense data and information with which we have to deal. Cognitive theory suggests that for rational thought we are faced with the simultaneous and apparently paradoxical problem of having too little information and too much data.

This imbalance in quantity between data of different degrees of relevance is combined, in practical circumstances, with a time constraint which has important implications for rationality and freedom of choice. We are bombarded with signals from a complex world in which we have limited time and relevant information with which to act. Niklas Luhmann (1979, p. 24) expresses this conflict neatly:

> The world is being dissipated into an uncontrollable complexity; so much so that at any given time people are able to choose freely between very different actions. Nevertheless, I have to act here and now. There is only a brief moment of time in which it is possible for me to see what others do, and consciously adapt myself to it.

Consequently, as Luhmann argues, we have to rely on trust in others, or trust in the fact that the world will continue more or less as before, to provide a basis upon which to act.

In addition it is argued here that the hierarchical manner in which complex data is processed by the human mind has a parallel in the hierarchical organization of action itself. We rely upon routines and habits, which are both forming and formed by social institutions. This next stage in the argument is developed in the next chapter.

# 6

# Action and Institutions

In any society, the pattern of people's lives and their living conditions take the forms which they do, not so much because someone makes a series of decisions to that effect; but in a large part because certain social mechanisms, principles, assumptions – call them what one will – are taken for granted . . . there is power inherent in anonymous social mechanisms and assumptions – in 'social institutions' – not just in individuals or groups . . . Power is to be found more in uneventful routine than in conscious and active exercise of will.

John Westergaard and Henrietta Resler (1976, pp. 142–6)

In his major work *The Economic Approach to Human Behaviour*, Gary Becker suggests that many social scientists hide their own lack of full understanding of neoclassical theory behind an alternative argument. This consists of suggestions that humans, instead of being consistently rational, exhibit 'ignorance and irrationality', where behaviour is allegedly explained by 'custom and tradition, the compliance somehow induced by social norms, or the ego and the id'. These are 'tempting materials', according to Becker, for 'ad hoc and useless explanations of behavior' (1976, p. 13). In this manner all such non-neoclassical explanations of human behaviour are shunned.

It is not clear, however, why neoclassical explanations based on utility maximization and stable preferences are immune from the very same charges. Becker's immanently conceived and permanently stable preferences are somewhat *ad hoc*, and the usefulness and operational value of utility analysis is indeed open to question.

There are very good reasons at least to taste the fruit that Becker would like to forbid. In this chapter we shall fall to this temptation and briefly sketch out some elements of a non-neoclassical explanation of action, emphasizing his rejected terms of ignorance, irrationality, custom and tradition. Far from being *ad hoc*, it will be suggested that such an approach is more plausible and fruitful than neoclassical theory, and that it is worthy of attention, intellectual resources and development.

For instance, one of the significant features of cognitive theory in psychology, sociology and anthropology is that it draws a link between the concepts and framework of cognition and the cultural norms and environment. It is shown below that this literature establishes that the cognition of sense data is typically done in a manner which reflects the cultural and institutional integument. Consequently, a stress on the learning and the acquisition of knowledge has to examine the concept-forming framework of institutions and culture.

In addition, not only is information perceived through a cognitive framework that is affected by culture and institutions, but institutions themselves play an important role as informational guidelines which are essential for action in a complex economic environment which is only partially known and understood. A number of economic theorists have emphasized this point in recent years and their work is surveyed below.

Furthermore, an implication of the hierarchical view of rationality and consciousness that was developed in the preceding chapter is that the important notions of routinization and habit in social and economic life can be accommodated. Both neoclassical and Austrian theory fail to treat these issues in a satisfactory manner, and are thus unable to appreciate the function of habit and routine in enabling individuals to learn and carry out complex actions in an uncertain and complicated world.

The main concern in this chapter is to examine the importance of institutions and routine in economic life. The first section continues the discussion of cognitive theory and relates this to the cognitive functions of routinized, cultural patterns and norms. In the second section the aim is both to establish the significance of both routinized behaviour and institutions, and to criticize some neoclassical and Austrian approaches to these phenomena. The chapter concludes with a discussion of some of the key features of institutional economics that connect to the preceding discussion.

## 6.1   THE IMPACT OF COGNITIVE THEORY

*Cognition, culture and society*

The significance of cognitive theory for the discussion at hand has been noted in the preceding chapter, showing that thought is not all at the same level of rationality or deliberation. In addition, cognitive theory relates to the argument in the present work in an even more important sense. It introduces a social, cultural and institutional dimension that is prominent in the cognitive literature and difficult to avoid. One consequence is that the neoclassical view of the continuously calculating, rational agent is all the more difficult to uphold.

Whilst living and acting in the world we are continuously in receipt of a vast amount of sense data. The attribution of meaning to this apparently chaotic mass of data requires the use of acquired concepts, symbols, rules and signs. Perception is an act of categorization, and in general such categories are *learned*. The categorization process, as Jerome Bruner puts it,

> is the categorization of an object or sensory event in terms of more or less abundant or reliable cues. Representation consists in knowing how to utilize cues with reference to a system of categories. It also depends upon the creation of categories-in-relationship that fit the nature of the world in which the person must live . . .(A)dequate perceptual representation involves the learning of appropriate categories, the learning of cues useful in placing objects appropriately in such systems of categories, and the learning of what objects are likely to occur in the environment. (Bruner, 1973, p. 12)

Whilst cognitive theorists differ in their interpretation of cognitive phenomena[1] and in the significance they attribute to the social dimension in the acquisition of concepts, it is rarely excluded. They are generally agreed that much of our conceptual apparatus is acquired through social interaction with others. There is a widespread acceptance, for example, that our education and socialization in early years helps up to develop our innate perceptual equipment and form a conceptual basis to understand and act in a complex and changing world. In fact, Bruner's work, quoted above, represents one of the more subjectivist theories of perception, contrasted with others, such as Ulric Neisser (1976), who give even greater emphasis to the function of anticipatory perceptual schemata through which new information is continuously processed.

At least for the socialized adult, most concepts and perceptual frames are expressed in terms of a (social) language and they relate to the social world. For this reason cognition has cultural specificity. The acquired conceptual framework reflects our culture and the social norms and rules that we inherit. As Barbara Lloyd asserts: 'individuals growing up in different cultures may well learn different rules for processing information from the world around them' (Lloyd, 1972, p. 16). Just as our knowledge of the world does not spring out alive from the sensory data as it reaches the brain, only through the acquisition of a complex and culturally specific conceptual framework can sense data be understood. The reality, outside our heads, may exist independently of our cognition of it. But the 'reality' we 'see' and 'understand' is partially socially constructed.[2]

The differences in type of cognitive and cultural theory cannot be discussed here, and it is not necessary to do so. There is, however, a wide consensus on some fundamental issues: facts do not speak for themselves; and the acquisition of knowledge about the world is not simply an individual but a social act. This passage is typical:

> Each of us likes to think of himself as being rational and autonomous. Our ideas seem to be peculiarly our own. It is hard for us to realize how little of our information comes from direct experience with the physical environment and, how much comes only indirectly, from other people . . . One's prior beliefs, attitudes, and values form a frame of reference – a kind of cognitive map for interpreting reality that precedes and controls the exchange, of information and influence . . . Since individuals differ considerably in their communication experiences, we can expect that their maps of social reality will also vary greatly. (McLeod and Chaffee, 1972, pp. 50–1)

Despite the increasing interest of economists in issues relating to information, knowledge and uncertainty, the essential difference between sensory data and knowledge has not permeated orthodoxy at all. Apart from the Austrian School, there is rarely any suggestion that the presentation or availability of information does not mean that it will be equally or uniformly perceived. It is widely assumed that all agents learn in similar ways. The issue of cognition is excluded by default or by design.

Remarkably, however, cognitive divergence between economists themselves has become more and more prominent at the policy level. Since the late 1960s the postwar consensus that dominated economic theory and policy has broken down. The polarization and controversy has increased to the extent that the common conceptual ground for the evaluation of policy has become quite narrow. Gone are the days when almost all economists were agreed on the criteria for the evaluation of policies. It is now possible for a group of economists to be presented with the same data concerning the performance of an economy, and to disagree diametrically as to whether the facts indicate a healthy condition. It is a common error to ascribe these differences in evaluation simply to lack of full information or technical knowledge of the 'true' workings of the economy. But in matters as complex as an economic system we have every reason to put cognitive differences to the fore. Disagreements about policy evaluation result partly from differences in conceptual framework, and the related value systems, and no amount of new information will *necessarily* reduce these over time.

## Cognitive theory and subjectivism

One of the few economists to recognize the distinction between sense data and knowledge is Friedrich Hayek. Facts, he argues, are bound by concepts or theories, and agents in a sense 'create' the reality in which they act (Hayek, 1952a). For this and other reasons there is a strong anti-empiricist element to Austrian theory, expressed by Israel Kirzner when he writes of its 'serious reservations about the general validity and importance of a great deal of the empirical work being carried on in the economics profession today' (Kirzner, 1976b, p. 40).

However, the accommodation to cognitive theory by the Austrian economists is partial and one-sided. It is used with positive and convincing effect to demolish empiricism and an over-emphasis on econometric testing. But the idea of agents 'creating' reality is also used for the end of reinforcing the subjectivism of the Austrian paradigm. As Hayek put it in an often-quoted remark: 'every important advance in economic theory during the last hundred years was a further step in the consistent application of subjectivism' (1952a, p. 31).

In some respects all human agents are unique in their cognitive abilities and in the body of concepts they have acquired. Consequently, cognitive theory does show that human knowledge has subjective elements. But if some of the *subject matter* of cognition is subjective, does that mean that the entire *process* of cognition is subjective as well? As one commentator of Hayek has wittily observed: 'If Social Science is subjective because its subject matter is, then by the same argument Ornithology would have to be considered a bird-like science and Archaeology an archaic one' (Rudner, 1954, p. 165). As Stephan Boehm (1982) shows, this ambiguity surrounding the very notion of subjectivism has damaging consequences for Austrian theory as a whole.

Emphatically, cognitive theory does not lead to the exclusion of the social dimension but its reinforcement. We cannot hope to create a conceptual framework capable of handling vast quantities of information on our own. We have to rely on interactions with others to develop our cognitive skills, to form judgements about the world and to acquire guidelines for action. Furthermore, for cognition we rely on a language and linguistic structure which is socially formed. These basic points are uncontroversial, even simplistic, at least for the social psychologist. Consequently, there are no clear boundaries between the sub-disciplines of cognitive and social psychology. Indeed the areas of study overlap and form the further sub-discipline of cognitive social psychology. In defiance of the extreme subjectivism of the Austrians, the social dimension to cognitive theory will not go away.

Consider the experiments in social psychology which reveal the influence of others in the formation of our judgements and acts. For example, Solomon Asch (1952, ch. 16) showed that a single individual will very often alter his or her own explicit judgement when faced with an unanimous but erroneous majority. A group of subjects were asked to identify which of the three lines of clearly different length was equal to a standard line. Unknown to the critical subject, it had been pre-arranged with the remainder of the subjects that they would call out the same wrong answer in some cases. It was found that the critical subject would make an incorrect judgement in order to conform to the majority in as many as one in three cases, despite the fact that the difference in length of the two lines was quite obvious to the observer.

Even more striking are the experiments of Stanley Milgram on obedience and authority. An experiment was set up in which a 'scientist' (suitably clothed in a white coat) asked a member of the public to administer electric shocks to a subject. Milgram found that a majority of ordinary, reasonable adults would administer to another person electric shocks that were apparently painful, dangerous and even fatal, if ordered to do so by the person in apparent authority. In fact, the shocks were not real and the person receiving them was a trained actor, crying out in pain and eventually feigning unconsciousness or death. This challenging experiment indicates how much people will change their behaviour according to the institutional setting. '*There is a propensity for people to accept definitions of action provided by legitimate authority.* That is, although the subject performs the action, he allows authority to define its meaning' (Milgram, 1974, p. 145).

This argument connects with the concept of legitimation which was used with some prominence by Max Weber (1947). This concept suggests, in concurrence with Milgram, that there is a widespread tendency for social actors to believe in, and accept the authority of, that which is deemed a legitimate order. The acceptance of the legitimate authority of the 'scientists' in the Milgram experiments could be seen to arise from their social status, their public esteem, and the high value place on 'science' in modern culture. Another important source of legitimation, as Weber himself pointed out, is the legal system. People tend to have particular 'respect for the law', and the essence of this phenomenon cannot be captured simply by a neoclassical, cost-minimizing, rational choice framework.

There are now a large number of experiments in social psychology which suggest, but not always in such a dramatic fashion as those of

Milgram, social and group influences on behaviour and cognition. These influences achieve even greater recognition when we approach or cross the boundaries with sociology or anthropology. An important illustration is found in anthropological work on the acquisition of linguistic skills and the learning of signs and meanings. As Mary Douglas argues: 'speech is a social phenomenon, and . . . social decisions mark off the boundaries between different provinces of meaning' (1973, p. 13).

One of the few economists to take this point on board is Ian Steedman (1980). In a work tucked away in a relatively obscure journal, convenient for the orthodox to ignore, he writes of the 'intrinsically non-autonomous' character of preferences and beliefs. From the moment we are born we begin to acquire a social language and a shared symbolic order. Individual knowledge is expressed in a social language and passed through a set of socially acquired cognitive filters. We perceive much of the world through language and symbols that have no meaning in an individual sense. Our express aims and purposes, whatever their individual qualities, are formulated in language that is in its essence not individual but social.[3]

## 6.2   THE SIGNIFICANCE OF INSTITUTIONS

### Action and institutions

A point that is stressed in this work is that most significant views on rationality and action outside orthodox economics are incompatible with the unsatisfactory notions that prevail in economics today. This is true for sociology as well as psychology and anthropology. Decades ago Talcott Parsons (1940) made a plea that economists should abandon their narrow and uncomplicated view of human motivation and rationality and pay heed to 'work going on in other fields of the study of human behaviour'. Such a request is worthy of repetition and brief discussion here.

At the outset, Parsons emphasizes that economic activity takes place within an institutional framework. Institutions are not simply organizational structures: 'They are *normative* patterns which define what are felt to be, in the given society, proper, legitimate, or expected modes of action or of social relationship' (p. 190). While veering toward a questionable functionalism in an ensuing passage, with mention of 'the requirements of institutional patterns', Parsons makes points that would be accepted by a wide range of social theorists. 'Institutional patterns depend', he argues, 'on the support of the moral sentiments of the members of society' (p. 192). Concerning the origin of these 'moral sentiments' he writes:

> The prevailing evidence is that the deeper moral sentiments are inculcated in early childhood and are deeply built into the structure of personality itself. They are, in the deeper senses, beyond the range of conscious decision and control, except perhaps in certain critical situations, and even when consciously repudiated, still continue to exert their influence . . . (T)he fact that concretely economic activities take place in a framework of institutional patterns would imply that, typically, such disinterested elements of motivation play a role in the determination of their course. (p. 193)

In discussing the idea of self-interested behaviour, Parsons is keen to show that this too has social and institutional facets: 'it can be seen that a very substantial component of the individual's own self-interest is directly dependent on his enjoying the favourable attitudes of others with whom he comes into contact.' However, for Parsons 'the most crucial point' is that the content, or objectives, of self-interest are themselves socially formed: 'For it is precisely around social institutions that, to a very large extent, the content of self-interest is organised.' It is the organisation of the diverse potentialities of human action into a coherent system that is 'one of the most important functions of institutions' (p. 197).

The pleas of Parsons and other sociologists from a wide range of viewpoints have been ignored. Economists remain with their simplistic and untenable view of human rationality. One of the consequences of the argument in this chapter is that neither the means nor the ends of 'subjective' rationality can be taken for granted. Even at the level of fully deliberative decision-making, institutions and social culture make themselves felt, not merely as constraints, but also in moulding the formation of preferences and enabling the acquisition of knowledge upon which choices are made.

However, it is necessary to examine less deliberative aspects of thought and action to uncover the full complexity and significance of the interplay between institutions and action in society and the economy. We embark upon this discussion with a look at the functions and formation of the important class of actions known as habits.

*Habits*

Given that fully conscious rational deliberation about all aspects of behaviour is impossible because of the amount of information and computational competence involved, human agents have acquired mechanisms for relegating particular ongoing actions from continuous rational assessment. These are commonly known as habits, and their high degree of relevance to our subject was emphasized by Thorstein Veblen in many of his works. Indeed, according to Veblen, institutions themselves were comprised of 'settled habits of thought common to the generality of men' (Veblen, 1919, p. 239).

The significance of habits has also been recognized by other economists such as Frank Knight. He believed that the forces that help to mould human society 'belong to an intermediate category, between instinct and intelligence. They are a matter of custom, tradition, or institutions. Such laws are transmitted in society, and acquired by the individual, through relatively effortless and even unconscious imitation, and conformity with them by any mature individual at any time is a matter of "habit"' (Knight, 1947, p. 224).

George Katona, one of the leading figures in the neglected sub-discipline of psychological economics, has argued that habits play a key part in such economic behaviour. This applied to the study of business, and not simply to the consumer. In Katona's view: 'There is ample evidence that routine behaviour is very frequent in business life' (1951, p. 230). Furthermore: 'To understand business life, both habitual and routine acts and their abandonment through making genuine decisions must be studied. Because of the frequent occurrence of habitual behaviour, business activity cannot be viewed as a process of continuous adaptation to changing conditions' (p. 52).

In contrast, in neither neoclassical nor Austrian theory is there a sufficient appreciation of habits. The Austrians, for example, regard all action, habitual or otherwise, as purposeful. The neoclassical economist holds the view that habits can be represented with a version of the standard preference function. Habits are thus regarded as 'rational' actions that are repeated because the 'cost' of changing them is perceived as too great; or they are seen as the repetition of some preceding rational choice; or as the outcome of a Darwinian process of 'natural selection' which ensures that all repeated acts tend to be optimal and thereby 'rational' simply because the agent repeating them has survived.

Yet all these neoclassical attempts to encompass habits contradict the everyday and commonsense understanding of the word. In general, people do not knowingly perceive or calculate the cost of dropping a habit. Nor do they always acquire habits from conscious and rational choice. And the idea of all persistent habits being 'optimal' contradicts the notion of 'bad habits' that most of us have and would like to lose. Thus a first point to be made against the neoclassical treatment of habits is that they do not match the everyday meaning of the term.

A second point follows from the discussion in the preceding chapter. One of the functions of habits is to deal with the complexity of everyday life; they provide us with a means of retaining a pattern of behaviour without engaging in global rational calculations involving vast amounts of complex information. The processes of action become organized in a hierarchical manner, facilitating monitoring at different levels and rates, and with different degrees of response to incoming information.

Given that habits are repeated acts, the mainstream neoclassical view would instead imply that agents are acting not only on the basis of a full, global calculation of all the costs and benefits involved (or acting 'as if' this is the case) but also that a complex calculation occurs whenever a new piece of information is received. In other words, it is implied that the perpetration of habits involves continuous overall monitoring and calculation to an extent which is impossible given the amount and complexity of the information involved.

A more sophisticated, but infrequently utilized, neoclassical approach is to regard habitual acts as being governed by a secondary function of preferences. This, in turn, is governed by a higher-order, primary preference function, to which habitual preferences gradually adjust towards over time (Thaler and Shefrin, 1981; Winston, 1980). This two-level approach removes the implication that habits require continuous global monitoring to render them consistent with overall preferences, but it still requires an extensive and implausible degree of rational calculation. Lower-level choices over habitual acts are still seen to be made as if with a full calculation of benefits and costs. However, it is in the very nature of habits that they may not be consistent with fully conscious, rational choice. In contrast, all neoclassical attempts to model habits treat them as being ultimately consistent with an over-riding preference function.

To sustain a more adequate notion of habits we have to include levels of action that are not open to full, conscious deliberation, and which do not necessarily all lead to a consistent outcome. In fact, partially deliberative levels of thought are highly relevant to all human activities. In most cases, action springs from both deliberative and non-deliberative sources. Below the level of full deliberation there is what Michael Oakeshott (1962) calls 'practical knowledge' and Anthony Giddens (1984) 'practical consciousness'. Such mental activity helps people to 'go on': to act without giving their choices direct discursive expression. Michael Polanyi (1967) developed an entire theoretical system to explain the relevance of 'tacit knowing' to human action and the acquisition and development of technical habits and skills.[4]

Significantly, Oakeshott (1962, p. 11) argues that rationalism amounts to a denial of the existence of practical knowledge. Likewise, it is suggested here that the presuppositions of neoclassical or much Austrian theory amount to the denial of the existence or theoretical relevance of habits in the analysis of human action.

Indeed, because the concept of habit suggests that some actions flow from full, conscious deliberation, whereas others do not, this must imply some kind of hierarchical division of levels of consciousness in the mind. For reasons already noted we should expect hostility to this idea from both positivists and classical liberals. Positivism fails to find empirical support for the very idea of consciousness; whereas classic liberals eschew the idea that the individual is not fully purposive in his or her actions. In a place where positivism and classic liberalism meet, in neoclassical economic theory, we find a doubled hostility and a categorical rejection of the concept of habit as it is understood in daily life.

We acquire habits in various ways. Sometimes it is through the imitation of others. This does not always result from full, conscious choice, as all animal species are born with some capacity to imitate. The development of the intellectual and practical skills of young children is based largely on imitation, and we retain this faculty in later life, often without conscious thought about what we are doing.

In other cases habits may result from open, conscious choice. Thus after consciously choosing to purchase a car, the result may be its habitual use, normally without much deliberation or comparison of the marginal costs of alternative means of transport. We may initially use the car because we see it as more comfortable, and choose it on that basis, but on later occasions any such rational deliberation does not take place. We simply 'get into the habit' of using the one rather than the other, even if conscious deliberation was crucial at the start.

Whatever their origin, repeated acts tend to congeal into habits, and become removed from the sphere of rational deliberation in the mind. This should not necessarily be regarded as some kind of mental defect. As suggested above, habits, like some other forms of non-deliberative thinking, can have an important positive function. In fact, the capacity to form habits is indispensible for the acquisition of all sorts of practical and intellectual skills. At first, whilst learning a technique, we must concentrate on every detail of what we are doing. It takes us a great deal of time and effort to learn a new language, or to play a musical instrument, or to type, or to become familiar with a new academic discipline. Eventually, however, intellectual and practical habits emerge, and this is the very point at which we regard ourselves as having acquired the skill. When analytical or practical rules are applied without full, conscious reasoning or deliberation then the technique can be said to have been mastered.

However, as Arthur Koestler points out: 'There are two sides to this tendency towards the progressive mechanization of skills' (Koestler, 1967, p. 131). On the positive side, mechanical habits help us to deal with complexity and information overload, by removing several aspects of action from conscious deliberation. Thus when driving fast or in heavy traffic we do not have to concentrate on changing gear or turning the wheel. We do these automatically, enabling the conscious mind to concentrate on potential danger such as by observing the behaviour of other vehicles or the state of the road.

On the negative side, mechanical habits can remove important actions from the due exercise of deliberation and creative skill. This limitation is likely to be more serious with the more complex, higher-level activities. To be able to hit the right key of the typewriter as if by pure reflex is extremely useful; 'but a rigid style composed of clichés and prefabricated turns of phrases, although it enables civil servants to get through a greater volume of correspondence, is certainly a mixed blessing' (Koestler, 1967, p. 132).

At the level of reasoning and scientific discourse there are even greater dangers in the development of rigid habits of mind. The habitual use of particular concepts and modes of thought may mask the hidden assumptions and axioms that are being employed. We may appear to be 'persuaded' by evidence or argument without adequate deliberation on all the aspects of the problem. Scientific researchers may habitually employ categorizations or techniques without questioning whether their use is legitimate. We need to look no further than our own discipline. Concepts such as 'supply', 'demand', 'utility', 'equilibrium', 'competition', 'capital', 'market' and 'rationality' are used with great propensity, without questioning their meaning or the legitimacy of their application in a given context. If economists needed to be convinced of the existence of intellectual habits, then the unquestioning use of such conceptual stereotypes should suffice.

Of course, with the standard neoclassical arguments it is possible to conceptualize action in different terms. No evidence can show that a given act is regulated either by unconscious or conscious thought processes. Thus it cannot be proved that unconscious habits exist. But, to repeat, neither can we prove the reality of the fundamental relation of cause and effect. The argument here is that it is reasonable, given the evidence on human behaviour and our understanding of the workings of the human brain, to assume that habits are real.

Whilst inductive reasoning cannot prove that habits exist, this does not mean that empirical evidence does not have a bearing on the matter. A great deal of data can be marshalled to support the idea of the importance of habits in economic life. Regarding consumer behaviour,

John Maynard Keynes wrote in the *General Theory* that a 'man's habitual standard of life usually has the first claim on his income' (Keynes, 1971b, p. 97). Since then a number of studies offer some support for this proposition.

For instance, a consumer survey by George Katona and Eva Mueller (1954) found that most households did not make most purchases after careful consideration, deliberation or planning, and in general consumer buying was not preceded by an extensive search for consumer information or shopping around. Exceptions included a small number of items, often of a much higher price than average, and special purchases such as presents. Robert Ferber (1955) found that a substantial proportion of consumer-durable purchasing was carried out without advance planning, and a similar result was obtained by Joseph Newman and Richard Staelin (1972) in a study of the buying of cars and major household appliances. Such surveys led Richard Olshansky and Donald Granbois (1979) to conclude that a substantial proportion of purchases do not involve decision-making in a meaningful sense.

James Duesenberry's (1949) now-neglected theory of the consumption function proceeded on the basis that an established level of income, plus the cultural norms faced by the consumer, would help to establish a lifestyle, pattern and level of spending, and this would be affected less dramatically by short-term fluctuations in income. Duesenberry's consumer acts adaptively but also habitually, and does not closely resemble the calculating maximizer of the neoclassical world. Duesenberry himself provided some significant statistical support for his theory.

The famous econometric study of aggregate consumer demand in the US by Hendricks Houthakker and Lester Taylor (1966) finds that the major part of consumer spending is subject to inertia, i.e. primarily dependent on preceding consumption. The relative stability of consumer behaviour has been invoked as an argument for stable preference functions in a neoclassical mould, but the evidence could also be interpreted in a theoretical framework which gave due recognition to habit as a crucial feature of consumer behaviour.

The rational expectations hypothesis proposes that agents make full use of the available information and adjust their actions rapidly as new information is received. On the contrary the received evidence does not seem to lend support to this hypothesis (Lovell, 1986; Pesaran, 1987) and on the contrary it has been argued that instead the evidence may suggest that 'people really do use ad hoc simple expectations rules' (Shiller, 1978, p. 40). Another interpretation of this evidence is that it is explained by habitual behaviour, and that the apparent inertia in the formation of expectations suggests the habit-driven failure of agents to appraise or act upon all the information that is available to them.

There is also evidence to indicate that other habitual practices are significant within the firm. Even if prices and quantities are being altered frequently, there are studies which support the proposition that these adjustments are often the consequence of routinized procedures and practices within the organization.[5]

## Routinization and institutions

As we have seen, neoclassical theory implies that economic behaviour is essentially non-habitual and non-routinized, involving rational calculation and marginal adjustments towards an optimum. In contrast, the view taken here is that the study of habits is important for economics because it relates to the large amount of routinized behaviour in the economy as a whole. This point does not simply apply to consumer behaviour, where the influence of custom and routine may be more readily accepted. Even in the dynamic and competitive economic world of selling and buying, boom and slump, and where prices of some commodities can change from day to day, the prominence and weight of social routine is difficult to overestimate.

For instance, all economic activity takes place within a framework of traditional law, which is perceived not through detailed knowledge of the statutes but through casual observation of its operation, and through which agents are able to judge the viability of contracts, and the likely legal consequences of a range of acts. Business itself is bound by informal customs and rules which have to be acquired by all participants, action in conformity with them sometimes marking acceptance into a business community and serving as a token of trust. These customs and rules can vary from country to country and have sometimes to be learned by a foreign businessman attempting to bring imports to the unfamiliar land.

On a more immediate basis, members of a business community exist and act within a network of contacts and these are often bound by rules or routinized arrangements of a formal or informal nature. It is widely accepted that many, if not all, labour markets are built upon a series of rigidities of contract and behaviour, a great number underlined by tradition and the prevailing social culture. But it is not so universally recognized that such norms and rules may have important and even necessary functions for industrial relations and the labour market. Likewise the rules and routinized arrangements in the business communities of managers, financiers, shareholders and elsewhere may also be positively important for the operation of the system.

The significance of habits within the workplace itself should not be ignored. All work, whether 'skilled' or 'unskilled' by name, involves a degree of practical knowledge, or know-how which is both acquired and routinized over time. Indeed, it could be conjectured that most of the industrial skill of a nation consists of a set of relevant habits, acquired over a long time, widely dispersed through the employable workforce and deeply embedded in its practices. Thorstein Veblen is responsible for drawing our attention to this fact, and for a theory of economic evolution based on the conflicting habits and expectations of the workforce and the business community.[6]

Similar ideas have re-emerged in the impressive work of Richard Nelson and Sidney Winter (1982).[7] Their work is centred on the firm, and this is regarded as having habit and routinized behaviour as an important, although not universal, characteristic. Being concerned to show how complex technological skills are acquired and passed on within the economy, they argue that habits and routines act as repositories of knowledge and skills. In their words, routines are the 'organizational memory' of the firm (p. 99). Consequently, Nelson and Winter do not simply argue that habits and routines are widespread within the organization in addition they have functional characteristics, as proposed in their theory of economic change.

So far we have touched upon the question of the origins and existence of habits and routinized behaviour. Clearly the next step is to consider their functional significance for human action as a whole.[8]

## Routines, institutions and information

Routines are not simply actions that have become congealed; in addition they both enable and mould future action. One feature of their enabling role has been mentioned already; habits and routines may have a positive role since full conscious deliberation over all aspects of behaviour is impossible because of the amount and complexity of information involved. Thus for the individual agent habits and routines have a functional significance in that they reduce the amount of deliberation involved in the complexities of day-to-day behaviour. However, this is only one facet of the general cognitive and informational functions of social institutions and routines.

An important enabling function of institutionalized routines is to do with the information they provide for other agents. This point is of some significance and it will be developed in later parts of this work. This aspect of routinized behaviour has received very little attention from economists, yet arguably it is fundamental to the analysis of all social and economic institutions, including, in particular, markets.

There is an obvious way in which most institutions provide information. All social organizations gather and process some amount of information on a day-to-day basis, and this may be available within or outside the institution. However, the informational function of institutions is much wider and deeper than this. It is not simply the direct use of the information gathered by agents who are a part of the institution. Through their very existence, and the established, visible character of much of the associated behaviour, institutions actually create and in some sense broadcast additional information as well.

Stabilized and routinized behaviour establishes and reproduces a set of rules and norms 'fixed by habit, convention, tacit or legally supported social acceptance or conformity' (Kornai, 1982, p. 79). These are not necessarily inviolable, but the point is that they help agents to estimate the potential actions of others. This point is of considerable importance, but we must turn to the outskirts of mainstream theory to find any serious discussion of the positive coordinating role of routines and norms. One early and neglected statement in this regard, by Frank Knight and Thornton Merriam (1948, p. 60), is as follows:

> One individual can choose or plan intelligently in a group of any size only if all others act 'predictably' and if he predicts correctly. This means, *prima facie*, that the others do not choose rationally but mechanically follow an established and known pattern, or else that the first party has coercive power, through force or deception. (. . .) Without some procedure for co-ordination, any real activity on the part of an individual, any departure from past routine, must disappoint the expectations and upset the plans of others who count on him to act in a way predicted from his past behaviour.

The informational role of routines and institutions has not had much prominence in economics since those lines were written. There are, however, some notable disconnected statements and discussions of varying length on the theme in recent years.[9]

The critical point is that both routines and formal institutions, by establishing more or less fixed patterns of, or boundaries to, or regulations over, or constraints upon, human action, actually supply information to other agents. Such inflexibilities or constraints actually suggest to the individual what other agents might do, and the individual can then act accordingly. Whereas if these rigidities or 'imperfections' did not exist the behaviour of others could change with every perturbation in the economic system, and such frequent adjustments to behaviour might be perceived as random or chaotic.

In other words, institutions and routines, other than acting simply as rigidities and constraints, play an enabling role, by providing more-or-less reliable information regarding the likely actions of others. Thus the habits and routines formed by some individuals enable the conscious decision-making of others. One consequence of this function of institutions is that in a highly complex world, and despite uncertainty, complexity and information overload, regular and predictable behaviour is possible.

It is also possible to see how habits and routines may actually mould action in a fundamental way. Even if we assume that tastes and preferences are given, and do not change, then the informational function of institutions and routines will lead to certain patterns of action, biased by the information that the institutions provide. On the basis of the assumption that agents are 'rational maximisers', Andrew Schotter (1981, 1985) shows that institutions and constraints play such a functional role. Thus, for example, there are fixed rules and times for the opening and closing of markets to coordinate buyers and sellers, and traffic signals and rules of the road exist to coordinate the actions of drivers at junctions.

If we make the less rigid assumption that individual tastes and preferences are malleable and will change or adapt, then the objectives and behaviour of agents can be moulded or reinforced. The existence of rules and institutions could stress some behavioural propensities, as feelings of nationalism can be heightened by ceremonies and symbolic acts. Alternatively, there could be counter-adaptive preferences giving rise to rebellious behaviour where individuals react to norms and traditions in a negative way. Even in this instance, routines or institutions affect human behaviour and cognition. Thus either positively or negatively institutions and routines are likely to affect both preferences and behaviour. There is nothing sinister here: the conclusions are not necessrily deterministic. What is advanced is the idea that routinized behaviour is not neutral in its effects on human preferences and action.

It should be stressed that the information created and distributed by social institutions has a social and not a purely subjective character. It is established by the routinized behaviour of a group of individuals and becomes more significant the more widespread, stable and established such behaviour might be. Its foundation is the social institution, even if the information given may be perceived differently from individual to individual. Consequently, in recognizing the informational function of institutions we are breaking from a purely subjectivist perspective.

This general argument about institutions has been applied by some writers to a set of novel analyses of the function of rigidities and 'imperfections' on the market system. These approaches are radically different from neoclassical and Austrian theory in that institutions are not merely regarded as constraints on 'free' behaviour. In addition, the policy conclusions differ markedly from the fashionable edicts against market restriction and regulation that emanate from a number of influential orthodox economists, including some from the Austrian School. The application of this perspective on institutions to the particular case of the market is a theme of chapter 8.

### Orthodoxy and institutions

It is important to emphasize the departure here from much orthodox theory in its treatment of routinized behaviour and institutions. The former are explained away, and the latter are regarded as tacit or given constraints, under which the rational, calculating individual acts. On the whole, with the exception of some recent and notable developments, they are given a negative evaluation; as limits to or restrictions upon otherwise free behaviour. Some institutions may be regarded as essential to social life, but these are usually regarded as punctuating exceptions. In contrast, it is argued here that an extensive space between institutions is inconceivable. Even if action is free, it is riddled with habit and routine, and permeated with the culture and structure of the system. Institutions are the substance, rather than merely the boundaries, of social life.

One problem with the purely negative view of institutions as constraints, as economists such as William Lazonick (1981) and Lawrence Boland (1979b) suggest, is that it puts to one side the problem of explaining the evolution of institutions themselves, and fails to incorporate the behaviour of those that may act to change institutions and shift constraints, rather than taking them as given. As Scott Moss (1981, 1984) shows, striking and unconventional conclusions, particularly undermining the general applicability of the idea of a long-run equilibrium, can be drawn from a model in which agents do not take constraints as given, and part of their 'rational' behaviour may consist of trying to shift them so as to achieve their ends. Furthermore, the work of Janos Kornai (e.g. 1982) elaborates a useful distinction between 'hard' constraints which are difficult to shift and those which are 'soft'.

In orthodox theory, constraints are viewed simply negatively and as an effect of the past, but in the present the individual is positively 'free' within the limits set by them. Consequently, the orthodox paradigm does not perceive the effect of currently 'free' behaviour as a reproducer of routine, which may become a constraint in the future; and it cannot see institutionalized routine as a positive enabler of 'free' action in the present.

### Game theory and institutions

However, there are recent developments which go some of the way to assuage these criticisms. These developments retain the idea of rational choice, to examine the function of institutions and norms with particular use of the tools of game theory. Thus Edna Ullman-Margalit (1977) examines the emergence of social norms, Andrew Schotter (1981) considers social institutions in general and markets in particular, and Robert Sugden (1986) extends this type of theory to the analysis of rights and welfare. There is a great deal of positive value in these analyses, particularly as an antidote to many of the other treatments of social institutions in mainstream theory.

Nevertheless, there is still a divergence with the type of perspective that is offered in the present work. Two points are worth emphasizing. First, the use of game theory suggests that the individual is developing a strategy where the payoffs for various eventualities are known in advance. In reality, however, the outcomes may not be known, and indeed the number of 'strategic' possibilities is likely to be so vast that not all strategies can be considered and analytical computation of comparative payoffs is not possible. Game theory does not account for the degree of complexity and ignorance in the real world.

Second, it is typical of all these presentations to take the individual, and his or her purposes and interests, as exogenous or given. Sometimes this involves an explicit acknowledgment of a methodological individualist stance. The factors influencing the formation of the individuals purposes and goals are not taken into account. In particular the function of habits, routines and institutions, in moulding the substance as well as the context of purposeful behaviour, is disregarded.

Of course, no example from life can show conclusively that individual preferences and purposes are moulded by the environment. It can be presumed that the subjects of the Milgram experiments are acting as if they are calculating that the best strategy is to respond to authority with deference. In general, wanton disregard for authority in society would be punished, so is this not simply a rational, calculating response?

On the contrary, however, the real impact of the Milgram experiments, as with many other experiments in social psychology, is that they produce behaviour that is so different from what would be expected of average individuals, with threats and punishments that are mild by comparison, that they suggest that the individual is actually being changed by the context of his or her action.

Consider as a second example the situation facing the soldier in battle. Should he go into attack with his comrades and risk death, or desert and risk capture and punishment? It is quite possible to present the options in game-theoretic terms and consider the payoffs of the various eventualities. Ullman-Margalit (1977) considers an example such as this in her book. What this payoff matrix analysis seems to leave out is factors such as training and leadership in the formation of the soldier's own perceptions and preferences, and the blind routinization of many actions before and during battle. The training process is designed to subliminate many actions and responses in a battle situation: to condition the soldier so that they become habits. Furthermore, it is difficult to encompass the function of charismatic leadership in war without accepting that it may actually mould and develop individual motivation (Keegan, 1976). The experience of army discipline and war itself actually changes the person, making him capable of intentions and acts that he would not have entertained before.

Third, the issues here are clearly of importance in considering the inferior payment and status that is afforded to women (or other disadvantaged groups) in society. The argument presented here is not simply that women may face a more limited opportunity set, but that their goals and choices are actually moulded by culture and routine so that many may actually choose to stay in the same positions and occupations, even when choices and incentives are available. A theory that simply takes the motivation and preferences of individuals as given will fail to take this point on board. Women are not simply the willing or unwilling victims of circumstance, they are actors moulded by those circumstances themselves.

Fourth, a prominent example in the discussion of the emergence of behavioural norms is why (nearly all) people drive on the left in Britain and on the right in most other countries (Langlois, 1986c; Sugden, 1986). Clearly the emergence and reproduction of this norm can be explained in terms of the obvious dangers and disadvantages in driving on the 'wrong' side of the road. Likewise, there are similar reasons for the acceptance of priority conventions for traffic at crossroads (Schotter, 1981). Whilst the game-theoretic explanation of these phenomena has a superficial attractiveness, other closely related examples cannot be explained so easily and they result in a challenge to the utilitarian or game-theoretic explanation.

Take, for instance, the introduction of the law making the wearing of seat belts compulsory in Britain in 1983. Contemporary surveys show that a large number of drivers did not wear seat belts before the law was enacted, but afterwards this number was reduced to a tiny minority. What had happened to cause this change in behaviour?

Of course, this switch of behaviour can be explained by reference to the penalties of breaking the law, the disutility of being singled out for the disapproval of others, and so on. There is also the matter of the prominent information campaign on the safety benefits of the seat belt which may have drawn the drivers' attention to the benefits of wearing the seat belts and the 'costs' of doing otherwise.

But are these explanations entirely convincing? After all, the chances of being detected not wearing a seat belt by the police are relatively small. In addition the information campaign was well under way before 1983, thus its independent effects do not seem to have been so great as the enactment of the law.

A more convincing explanation is that the law itself had a powerful legitimizing influence on the drivers. Consequently their goals and preferences actually changed in favour of a safer course of action. The authority of the law had the effect not simply of changing behaviour by the introduction of penalties or the perception of costs and benefits. In addition, it changed those individuals themselves and their goals. The practice of wearing seat belts became embodied in habit and widely rationalized by a widespread belief in their contribution to reducing injury and death.

## Spontaneous order

This line of discussion is relevant to Friedrich Hayek's (1982) concept of 'spontaneous order'. Much of his argument that norms and conventions can arise, as it were, spontaneously, through the interaction of individuals is interesting and instructive. Note, however, that it is one-directional in its scope. An order is defined essentially as a state of affairs in which people can *form correct expectations*' because of the existence of some pattern or regularity in social life, (Hayek, 1982, vol. 1, p. 36). Thus when Hayek writes that 'a spontaneous order results from the individual elements adapting themselves to circumstances' (p. 41) he means that behaviour may adapt given the information and constraints that are presented. The adaptation in behaviour results primarily from a change in information or perception, not from a change in the individual's preferences or constitution.[10]

Hayek's recent work is an advance on much orthodox thinking, in that norms and conventions do not appear mysteriously from outside, and he attempts to explain them in a sophisticated way as the unintended consequences of accumulated individual acts. But, characteristically, he still regards individual purposes and preferences as being exogenous to the system. Thus Hayek does not acknowledge that norms and conventions may actually result in the adaptation of the character and purposes of the individual. Order does not simply affect expectations, it affects individuals themselves.

Similarly, Sugden (1986, p. vii) argues that 'if individuals pursue their own interests in a state of anarchy, order . . . can arise spontaneously'. However, it is not considered that the individual's 'own' interests may themselves be moulded and structured in a social process, and that the order itself may have something to do with what the individuals themselves may take those interests to be.

Notably, therefore, as Anthony Giddens (1982b, p. 8) puts it, *both* human subjects and social institutions are *'constituted in and through recurrent practices'*. Thus, despite their laudable appeals to an evolutionary conception of the emergence of social institutions, Hayek, Sugden and others do not consider the evolution of purposes and preferences themselves. Individuals are regarded as if they are born with a fixed personality; they are not constituted through social processes. The analysis has then to proceed from these given individuals to examine the spontaneous order that may emerge; it does not consider the kind of individual that may emerge from a social order of a given type, and contribute further to the evolution of the social order in the future.

Once the preferences and purposes of the individual are taken as endogenous, then the idea of the 'spontaneous order' can take different forms. A process of cumulative, or circular, causation is possible. There can be a 'virtuous' circle where civilized behaviour is both built up by, and contributes to, cohesive social norms. But also the circle can be 'vicious', in that a shortage of solidarity and trust may accelerate a propensity for individuals to diminish further their tolerance or altruism, thus advancing the process of social decay.

The fact that an order may appear to be spontaneous, and resulting from individuals pursuing their ends, itself gives it no sanctity or moral priority over any other order that may arise. The fact that a given order has emerged and reproduced itself through time indicates that it is moulding and forming individual goals and intentions as much as it is a reflection of them. More than in the limited sense of forming expectations, the order helps to form the individual, just as the acts of the individual help to form the order.

A fully evolutionary view would take into consideration both the emergence, and affect of, the cultural and institutional framework on the purposes and actions of the individual. In this richer sense we are able to appreciate the significance of the past in structuring the present. The present is history: we make and are made by it at the same time.[11]

## 6.3  SOME CONCLUSIONS

*The potential for cumulative instability*

Whilst the continuously calculating, marginally adjusting agent of neoclassical theory is here rejected, placing stress on inertia and habit instead, it should not be forgotten that habits themselves can change. And whilst we carry the burden of the past in the form of the institutions that mould and dominate our lives, institutional economists such as Veblen never overlooked the processes through which institutions and habits may evolve: 'The situation of today shapes the institutions of tomorrow through a selective, coercive process, by acting upon men's habitual view of things, and so altering or fortifying a point of view or a mental attitude handed down from the past' (Veblen, 1899, p. 190).

Furthermore, in stressing the importance and functional character of habits and routine, it should not be overlooked that conscious choices and purposive action are involved as well. Thus the 'selective, coercive process' is not confined to a fixed groove. Institutions change, and even gradual change can eventually put such a strain on a system that there can be outbreaks of conflict or crisis, leading to a change in actions and attitudes. Thus there is always the possibility of the breakdown of regularity: 'there will be moments of crisis situations or structural breaks when existing conventions or social practices are disrupted' (Lawson, 1985, p. 921). In any social system there is an interplay between routinized behaviour and the variable or volatile decisions of other agents.

The interaction between habitual and deliberative action, and the consequent tension between institutional stability and structural breaks should be emphasized. The adoption of an institutionalist view of the formation and development of conduct does not imply an adherence to determinism. It is possible to stress both the weight of routine and habit in the formation of behaviour and the importance of some elements of strategic deliberation and their possibly disruptive effects on stability. Such a tension between regularity and crisis is shown in the following quotation from Veblen:

> Not only is the individual's conduct hedged about and directed by his habitual relations to his fellows in the group, but these relations, being of an institutional character, vary as the institutional scene varies. The wants and desires, the end and the aim, the ways and the means, the amplitude and drift of the individual's conduct are functions of an institutional variable that is of a highly complex and wholly unstable character. (Veblen, 1909, p. 245)

With these ingredients it is possible to envisage processes whereby for long periods the reigning habits of thought and action are cumulatively reinforced. But this very process can lead to sudden and rapid change. The very ossification of society could lead to the decimation of the economic infrastructure from more vigorous competition from outside, or there could be an internal reaction leading to a newly modernized order. Conversely, a recklessly dynamic system may suffer from lack of continuity or skill or outlook, and reach an impasse because in its own breakneck pace its members were left without enduring values or goals.

In Veblen's view the economic system is not a 'self-balancing mechanism' but a 'cumulatively unfolding process'. Economic institutions are complexes of habits, roles and conventional behaviour. However, because of the momentum of technological and social changes in modern industrial society, and the clashing new conceptions and traditions thrown up with each innovation in management and technique, the cumulative character of economic development can mean crisis on occasions rather than continuous, gradual change or advance.

Despite the geographical and intellectual remoteness of Keynes' work from that of the American institutionalists, an impressive juxtaposition of behavioural regularities in accordance with reigning conventions, and possible cumulative instability, is found in a crucial chapter in Keynes' *General Theory* (Keynes, 1971b, ch. 12). Keynes' standpoint is, however, different in key respects and it is discussed in chapter 10.

The upshot is that the institutional perspective adopted here involves a radical break from the type of theorizing based on the concept of equilibrium that has pervaded orthodoxy for more than a century. The ideas of general or partial equilibrium, and theoretical descriptions of equilibriating mechanisms, dominate neoclassical theory. Yet all the past great heretics of economic thought, including Karl Marx, Thorstein Veblen and John Maynard Keynes, have attempted to broaden the scope of economics from an exclusive obsession with equilibrium theorizing. Scepticism over the value of equilibrium theory is a positive feature of the work of the Austrian School, that of George Shackle, of the behaviouralists, and the Post-Keynesians. The tension between stability and breakdown in an evolving institutionalist framework suggests too an abandonment of mechanical equilibrium in similar terms.

## *The evolutionary character of institutional economics*

In shifting the emphasis away from comparative statics and other forms of equilibrium theorizing, to what sort of alternative paradigm can economists appeal? As the American institutionalists and other recent writers such as Nicholas Georgescu-Roegen (1971, 1978) and Richard Nelson and Sidney Winter (1982) have suggested, a fruitful alternative paradigm is likely to take an evolutionary perspective rather than that of mechanical equilibrium.

It may appear, however, that neoclassical theory relies on a persistent biological and Darwinian analogy in its analysis of competition or even individual rationality. For example, since Armen Alchian's classic (1950) article the basis for the supposition that firms are maximizing profits has often been the suggestion that such firms are 'fittest', more likely to survive, and more likely to become typical as less able firms drop out.[12]

However, as Sidney Winter (1964) argues extensively, the appeal to Darwinian notions of evolution is unsuccessful because the mechanisms involved in the sustenance and procreation of such maximizing behaviour are not specified. As yet, no neoclassical theorist has explained satisfactorily how a firm, once it happens to maximize, will continue to do so. The managers of the enterprise may know that such behaviour is optimal in some sense, and pursue it for that reason; but the adoption of maximizing behaviour as such a goal, rather than a result of past evolution and 'natural selection', is inconsistent with any Darwinian presentation. Likewise, neoclassical theory fails to explain, in Darwinian terms, how the characteristics of a 'fit' firm are passed on to other, succeeding, new firms. Consequently, the neoclassical invocation of Darwin fails, because even if maximizing behaviour is adopted there is no Darwinian reason given why it should be generalized throughout the economy as a whole.

One major difference between the Darwinian model of evolution and the economic and social world is that in the former the environment is not regarded as being subject to large and rapid change. The process of 'natural selection' works slowly, over a long period of time, and for species to become established a stable environment is generally necessary so that their distinctive characteristics can show their superiority in the contest. Small variations in the environment may ensure that the more adaptive species prosper, but a big change, such as the proposed meteorite which suddenly altered the Earth's climate and wiped out the highly successful dinosaurs, can entirely disrupt the process of 'natural selection'.

In contrast, the environment faced by the consumer, the firm or the national economy changes rapidly and sometimes suddenly as prices fluctuate, stock markets boom and crash, governments change, wars erupt and natural disasters strike. A smooth, Darwinian process of gradual 'natural selection' of the fittest and most rational consumers, and the most efficient firms and national economies is thus ruled out. Like the dinosaur, the survival of a maximizing person or a productive firm for a forthcoming period of time is subject to a large measure of luck.

As we have seen, in the case of the firm the neoclassical 'natural selection' theory lacks a viable mechanism to transmit the characteristics of surviving firms from one generation to the next. In the natural world, and according to many biologists, such a mechanism is the gene. This contains the hereditary information which is passed on from each organism to its successors. The Neo-Darwinian argument is that particular genes contribute to characteristics and behaviour which are conducive to survival. 'Fit' organisms bestowed with such genes will thus be more likely to pass them on to their progeny. Genes contain the information to form and programme the organism, thus, in a stable environment, genes aiding survival will tend to become more prominent in succeeding generations. Over time, random mutations and Mendelian combinations of parental genes lead to the diversification of species and the possible development of more sophisticated life forms. In contrast, in neoclassical theory, there is no explicit and equivalent mechanism to pass on analogous information from one firm to the next.

However, once we move outside the confines of orthodox economics, and incorporate some of the features of the above discussion of social institutions, we can find mechanisms which play a similar evolutionary role to that of the gene in the natural world. Such mechanisms are organizational structures, habits and routines. Whilst these are malleable and do not mutate in the same way as their analogue in biology, structures and routines have a stable and inert quality and tend to sustain and thus 'pass on' their important characteristics through time.

Furthermore, habits and routines can enable the survival and transmission of behavioural patterns from one institution to another. As an important type of example, the skills learned by a worker in a given firm become partially embedded in his or her habits, and these will survive if the person changes employer, or if they are 'taught', explicitly or by imitation, to a colleague. Thus the habits of employees, both within the particular firm and the social culture, act as carriers of information, 'unteachable knowledge', and skills. Note that we are not talking of evolution here in the biological manner of passing on characteristics from individual to individual. Whilst, of course, individuals are intimately involved, the transmission is not biological but from institution to institution and in that way to individuals.

The idea that routines within the firm act as 'genes' to pass on skills and information is adopted by Nelson and Winter (1982, pp. 134–6) and forms a crucial part of their theoretical model of the modern corporation. However, they do not explore its wider significance for economic theory. From the point of view of an evolutionary economics, routines are crucial throughout the economy and society and not simply to transmit managerial and work skills within the firm.

For instance, the consumption patterns of the individuals within the household are sustained through a set of formed routines. These can be affected by the social culture, and by the characteristics of the individuals concerned. They are passed on through keeping-up-with-the-Jones imitation and the tendency to conform, and by children reared within the family acquiring some of the more enduring habits and routines. It is also possible to detect the widespread influence of routinized behaviour in all established social institutions, including the education system, the scientific community, public services, trade unions, and all aspects of local and national government. In a similar manner routines act as 'genes' within all these institutions.

However, as Nelson and Winter elliptically suggest, there is a further reason why routines do not act as genes in the strict biological sense. Genes contain coded information which is preserved in the DNA and which does not alter significantly through the reproductive lifetime of an individual organism. In biology, as noted above, evolutionary change occurs through random mutations and Mendelian combinations of different sets of parental genes. In contrast, in the social world, habits and routines that are acquired by an individual can change through time. Furthermore, the new characteristics can often be as easily passed on as the older aspects of habitual behaviour. Thus, in contrast to Darwinian biology, the inheritance of *acquired* characteristics is possible.

Thus the true analogue to social and economic evolution in the science of biology is not the work of Charles Darwin but the earlier notion of Jean Baptiste Lamarck. He argued that mutations occur because an organism passes on newly acquired adaptations of behaviour to its offspring through heredity. Lamarckian theory has fallen out of favour in biology because of its failure to explain or find evidence for a mechanism through which acquired characteristics could be passed on to offspring. However, in contrast, in the social world acquired characteristics can be inherited. Thus in some senses Lamarckian theory applies to social and economic evolution. Ironically, only by abandoning neoclassical theory can a tenable evolutionary analogy find in economics a proper place.

In contrast to orthodox Darwinian biology, economic evolution is not always gradualistic, and rapid 'mutations' are possible as rapid transformations in the social, economic and technological culture lead to the rapid acquisitions of new skills and routines. It is in this manner, for example, that many less-developed countries have adopted and sometimes even excelled in the application of modern technology. Furthermore, it is possible that some forms of routine behaviour can be discontinued as confidence in their efficacy or worth is shaken by changes in economic conditions or expectations. Economic evolution does not proceed in classic Darwinian terms, where slow changes occur in generation after generation, and the typical or 'equilibrium' form of an organism changes gradually over time. Instead, as suggested above, it can proceed by succession of periods of stability and crisis, of apparent equilibrium and cumulative instability.

Clearly, such an evolutionary perspective involves a break from the conventional dualism discussed above, in which agents in the present are positive and free, and routines and contraints are simply a negative restriction upon their freedom. In contrast, routines play a positive as well as negative part by passing on skills and other behavioural information from one agent or institution to the next. Furthermore, to repeat, action in the present has the potential function of establishing or reinforcing future routine: thus that which is apparently 'free' may act as a rigidity or constraint in the future; and that which is apparently ossified and inflexible may provide vital behavioural information for the present. One feature of human action is the intended consequence of a purposive act. But also, through the transmission belt of routine, and through the interaction with others in a world which is inherently uncertain, there are crucial unintended consequences as well.[13]

# PART THREE

# Elements of an Institutional Economics

# 7

# Contracts and Property Rights

No social system can work which is based exclusively upon a network of free contracts between (legally) equal contracting parties and in which everyone is supposed to be guided by nothing except his own (short-run) utilitarian ends.

Joseph A. Schumpeter (1976, pp. 423–4)

Until quite recently, and with rare exceptions, orthodox economists took such concepts as exchange, the market and the firm for granted. However, recent analysis of property rights and the structures of production and exchange have changed this to some extent and legitimized the study of institutions within the subject. Nevertheless, most of these developments retain the principal features of neoclassical theory. Economic man now inhabits social institutions but he still calculates and maximizes as best as he can. Furthermore, as is argued in this chapter, concepts such as exchange and property which are elemental to any study of institutions, are still being treated in an unsatisfactory fashion.[1]

Thus it is an aim of this chapter to clarify some terms which are central to economic discourse, and which have fortunately been receiving closer attention by economists in recent years. One of the central questions is the extent to which the concepts of exchange and property have to be defined in relation to the state and law. Behind different views on this question lie different perceptions of the nature and function of the state. Unfortunately, however, even the more innovative work by economists is normally imbued with an unacceptable, classic liberal, position on the state, as has mainstream economics for two centuries.

As well as attitudes to the state the question of exchange raises questions concerning the utilitarian outlook. This, of course, is also central to mainstream economic theory. Some further criticisms of utilitarianism are raised in the second section of this chapter. There is a rich vein of sociological analysis, almost completely ignored by economists, which undermines the utilitarian calculus by showing its limitations even in the price-tagged acts of exchange. The argument points in turn to further issues which are developed in later chapters of the present work.

### 7.1 THE CONCEPTS OF EXCHANGE AND PROPERTY

An emphasis on property rights is not new. As 'property rights' economist Steven Pejovich (1982) argues, one of the earlier theorists to emphasize the function of property relations was Karl Marx. In addition there is a widespread acceptance of the influence of American institutionalists such as John Commons.

### Defining exchange

A key point that has thus re-emerged is that exchange is not simply a two-way transfer of goods, services or money between agents; it involves a transfer of property rights as well. Thus, in the sense that economists use the term, exchange does not occur when, say, a bee gathers nectar from a flower and in that act deposits pollen. Clearly, a two-way transfer of physical substances has taken place, but it is not an act involving the exchange of property rights. The idea that transactions involve property rights as well as goods or services is made particularly clear in the work of Commons (e.g. 1950, pp. 48–9).

However, it should be emphasized that such a conception of exchange has not been universally adopted. For instance, Ludwig von Mises (1949, p. 97) defines exchange as 'an attempt to substitute a more satisfactory state of affairs for a less satisfactory one'. In short, according to von Mises, action is exchange. Not only is any mention of property rights absent here, but also von Mises (pp. 195–7) dwells on the matter of 'autistic exchange' which is said to be performed without reference to other individuals. He cites the example of an isolated hunter 'exchanging' cartridges and leisure for food. Thus exchange becomes a broad and universal category, covering the lonely activities of Robinson Crusoe as well as interpersonal transactions in a social setting, and without any apparent or necessary relation to property in the legal or traditional sense.

This unacceptable concept of 'exchange' is sufficiently broad to cover production as well. The idea of production being an 'exchange with nature'[2] is still prominent in the mainstream neoclassical literature and has yet to be attacked by the 'Property Rights School' with their customary vigour. Yet it is obvious that nature has no property rights to exchange. By suggesting that nature can exchange property with humans, as if she were a purposeful agent, both neoclassical and Austrian economists have devalued the very concept of property rights which has now become so fashionable. They emphasize human 'choice' and 'purposefulness' but then apply it in a context where they are removed of much of their meaning.

An excessively wide concept of exchange is also found in orthodox sociology. In his influential work, Peter Blau (1964) recognizes that exchange involves human agency, but he develops a theory in which an enormous number of 'voluntary' social activities are regarded as acts of exchange. The tribal tribute from the member of the tribe to the chief is 'exchanged' for the benefits of the security and cohesion of the tribal system. The work of the modern housewife is 'exchanged' for a share of the wealth and earnings of the male wage-earner, and so on. This definition of 'exchange' becomes so broad that it loses close resemblance to the specific type of exchange that we find in modern market economies.

In fact, Blau makes an influential distinction between 'social' and 'economic' exchange, defining the latter as being based on a 'formal contract that stipulates the exact quantities to be exchanged' (1964, p. 93). However, this subdivision is unsatisfactory. Arguably, a large number of 'economic' contracts, especially the employment contract, have important informal features, are imperfectly specified, and often cannot stipulate 'the exact quantities' to be exchanged. Blau himself partly recognizes this in a footnote (p. 93), but passes it by, seemingly content to accept that the hiring of workers falls outside his definition of 'economic' exchange, and content to leave the allusion that the labour market is outside 'the economy'.

Blau's 'economic exchange' roughly corresponds to what Herbert Simon (1951) describes as a 'sales contract' but Simon goes on to show that in economic life there are other regular contractual agreements which fall outside this category. Thus Blau's definition of 'economic exchange' corresponds to an excessively narrow class of transactions, whilst 'social exchange' is too broad, and eroded of distinctive meaning. It is an example of undue universalization: taking a category that applies to a particular context and applying it indiscriminately to human affairs through time and space.[3]

## Exchange and institutions

Contrary to the view of some economists discussed below, a system of commodity exchange requires a combination of *both* state and customary institutions. It is argued here that in any developed system of commodity exchange there must be a legal system enscribing and protecting rights to individual or corporate property. There must be a body of contract law with criteria for distinguishing between voluntary and involuntary transfers of goods and services, and courts to adjudicate in such matters. In addition, however, the evolution of law is not simply a matter of legislative construction; a great deal of law grows out of custom and precedent. Property and contract law are not exceptions. Consequently, the existence of property and exchange is tied up with a number of legal and other institutions.

The intentional and voluntary aspects of exchange are given prominence within contract law. However, as noted in chapter 3, whilst the concept of intent remains central, the law recognizes the context and complexity of human judgement and thus qualifies it at the same time. It would be an extreme position to accept the literal word of consent or agreement, and to ascribe full, rational intent to all acts. At the other extreme, expressed intent would be disregarded and humans would be deemed to have no responsibility for what they say or do. The legal system has to continuously steer a course between such extremes.

Economics must attempt to follow some kind of course between these extremes as well. Whilst it would be a mistake to regard all exchanges as if they resulted from comprehensive rational deliberation, the intentional aspect of the contract should generally remain predominant. Despite qualification and amendment, intention and consent still remain central to the law, and it relies on the objective test of agreement and assent in many instances. For example, the distinctions between love-making and rape, and gift-giving and theft, rest above all on the matter of the explicit denial or otherwise of consent.

Economists have often broken this rule by suggesting the existence of 'implicit contracts', especially in relation to employment. A widely quoted argument is the supposed existence of an 'insurance' agreement between employer and employee to deal with the contingency of economic recession. It is presumed that there is an implicit contract which provides wages which correspond to the average of fluctuations in the value of the workers' marginal output over the trade cycle. Wages thus become unresponsive to short-term changes in economic conditions. This argument is then used to explain the manifest downward rigidity of money wages: a theoretical problem which has perplexed non-institutional economists for generations.[4]

However, whilst the law sometimes finds 'implied terms' in a contract that have not been stated by any of the parties involved, there is also a vigilant attempt to keep such factors in proportion and retain the notions of conscious, explicit intent or agreement at the centre of much of the law. The idea of an implicit contract should not be dismissed from either law or economics, but it must be used with much more care than is suggested by the past and recent practice of many economists.

Notably, during the American Civil War, the Reverend Samuel Seabury (1861) argued that there was an implicit contract between master and slave which devolved 'on the one party the duty of care and protection, and on the other party the duty of service' (p. 139). This was seen as 'a contract for life, which neither master nor slave can, as a general rule, escape' (p. 155). Consequently, a slave attempting to escape would be in breach of his or her implicit contract. On this basis Seabury proceeded to argue that slavery was legally and morally justified. The true moral of the story is that an unacceptable interpretation may result if the notion of explicit agreement between the parties is abandoned. A reckless search for an 'implicit contract' is likely to lead to its 'discovery' in the form of an apologia for the *status quo*.

In many cases it is very difficult to ascertain intention or consent after the event. To do this in social life we rely on accepted signals and signs: the word 'yes', the nod of the head. Significantly, these signs are embedded in customs and rules, and depend upon their context. Thus the presentation of the goods at the supermarket checkout is the accepted signal of 'intention to purchase' at the displayed prices; the nod of the head at auction is a signal that the person is willing to buy at one increment higher than the last stated price. Notions such as intention and consent are problematic, but in modern society there is a complex system of institutionalized signs and rules to ascertain whether or not they exist. Intention and consent are in this sense institutionalized in symbol and routine.

## Individualistic conceptions of property and law

Whilst the concept of property rights is now given much more attention within economic theory, in many respects these developments have not gone far enough. Consider first the key statements of the Property Rights School, such as those collected together in the volume edited by Eirik Furubotn and Steven Pejovich (1974), and including milestones such as the articles by Ronald Coase (1960), Harold Demsetz (1967) and Armen Alchian and Harold Demsetz (1972).

Their argument is broadly that externalities, such as pollution and traffic noise, are best not dealt with through government intervention as many economists have argued in the past. Instead a solution is found by developing and enforcing a system of defined individual 'property rights'. Those inconvenienced by polluted air or traffic noise would sue those responsible for the inconvenience.

The crucial step in this argument is simply the establishment of a system of individual benefits and disbenefits. As Harold Demsetz (1967, p. 348) states: 'a primary function of property rights is that of guiding incentives to achieve a greater internalization of externalities.' Essentially, this is the application of the well-worn, classic liberal dogma that 'the individual is the best judge of his own welfare' to instances of externality, such as pollution, thus removing one of the remaining welfare arguments for state intervention.[5] To the Property Rights School the 'structure of property rights' refers primarily to a set of incentives and disincentives for individual action, but not essentially to the institution of property itself.

By providing individual incentives and disincentives in the form of so-called 'property rights' in areas hitherto uncovered it is imagined that the scope for government intervention would be reduced and individuals would be more free to assess benefits and disbenefits on their own and act accordingly. However what the proposal reduces with one hand it increases with another. By extending the domain of formal property and ownership the state remains involved, but in a different way, through the extension and enlargement of litigational activity.

However, it is not in the tradition of either classical liberalism or orthodox economics to see extensions of formally defined property rights as involving increasing state intervention in civil society. Instead, classic liberal theory saw property as some kind of natural right to goods or services, or even, in some reified manner, as those goods themselves.[6] The 'property rights' theorists have corrected these latter errors but they continue in the same liberal tradition. They fail to see that the extension of 'well-defined property rights' does not provide a means of reducing the role of the state, but on the contrary by extending formal property relations the state becomes ever-more deeply involved in the daily intercourse of social life.

The manner of this penetration by the state is different from the type of intervention that the 'property rights theorists' wish explicitly to avoid. In place of measures such as strict laws against pollution, everyone becomes involved in a tangled and inescapable web of ceaseless potential or actual litigation and recourse to law.

The popular myth that the extension of formal property rights and commodity exchange necessarily involves a withdrawal of the state from social life is effectively rebutted by Karl Polanyi. In his classic discussion of the growth of market relations in Britain in the eighteenth and nineteenth centuries, he observes:

> The road to the free market was opened and kept open by an enormous increase in continuous, centrally organised and controlled interventionism . . . (The) introduction of free markets, far from doing away with

the need for control, regulation, and intervention, enormously increased their range. Administrators had to be constantly on the watch to ensure the free working of the system. Thus even those who wished most ardently to free the state from all unnecessary duties, and whose whole philosophy demanded the restriction of state activities, could not but entrust the self-same state with new powers, organs, and instruments required for the establishment of *laissez-faire.* (Polanyi, 1944, pp. 140–1)

In the classic liberal tradition, the property-rights theorists envisage a hermetic division between politics and economics, and between the state and civil society. The state is seen as basically a guardian of private interests, to intervene and adjudicate only when necessary. It stands over civil society but it does not intermingle with it. Civil society is regarded as being essentially separate from the state: as the summation of atomistic and rational individuals trading and accumulating their property.

In part the error is to erect a rigid dichotomy between the state and nexus of individual interests. In any real-world capitalist system the state and civil society each have a distinct identity, but that does not mean that they are divided by a Chinese Wall. The two spheres have both a measure of autonomy and a degree of mutual inter-penetration. It is a mistake to see civil society as either entirely subject to, or entirely separate from, the state.[7] The structural relationship is more complex, as Alfred Stepan (1978, p. xii) neatly elaborates:

The state must be considered as more than the 'government'. It is the continuous administrative, legal, bureaucratic and coercive systems that attempt not only to structure relationships *between* civil society and public authority in a polity but also to structure many crucial relationships within civil society as well.

The failure to see the structuring function of the state is exhibited in the tendency of the Property Rights School to reduce the concept of property to a relation between an individual and a good, whereas through its institutional connection with social customs and the state, it is simultaneously a relationship between persons as well as things.[8] This stripping of the social and institutional aspect of the property concept enables the school to mistakenly treat 'property rights' largely or wholly as a set of incentives and disincentives for the owner: as simply an amended Benthamite calculus of pleasure and pain.

If the Property Rights School were openly to recognize and accept the legal and statutory aspect of property rights then they would face a problem. Their propensity to find market-based and private-property solutions to every economic problem could not apply to the institutions which themselves help to generate those property rights. The state itself cannot be regulated or rendered efficient by an extension of property rights in the very institution which produces those rights. A logical tangle is created by the remedy. It is no accident, that property is defined by the property rights theorists in a manner that has little or nothing to do with the state.

Thus, despite their forceful attempts to recognize the wider context of economic activity, the Property Rights School have not overcome most of the deficiencies of preceding orthodox theory. As Hans Nutzinger (1982, p. 188) concludes: 'Property rights economics is too important to be left to the property rights economists.'

However, an adequate conception of property is not achieved by merely bringing in the state as a *deus ex machina* to define and sustain the idea of ownership. Essentially, this is the solution of Thomas Hobbes in his *Leviathan*, where the sovereign, standing above and apart from society, is seen to enforce order and prevent its degeneration into chaos. There is a common thread between the Hobbesian view and later developments in liberal theory because both involve the same rigid dichotomy between civil society and the state.

### Williamson's treatment of exchange

Marc Galanter (1981) identifies a tendency towards 'centralism' in some versions of legal theory, where disputes are regarded as being normally resolved by reference to the legal apparatus of the state. In reaction against this 'centralism', Oliver Williamson (1986a, pp. 186–7) argues that it can sustain a harmful over-compartmentalization within social science. Thus, neoclassical economists have traditionally avoided any study of the legal context of contract and exchange. 'A division of effort thus arises whereby economists are pre-occupied with the economic benefits that accrue to specialization and exchange, while legal specialists focus on the technicalities of contract law' (Williamson, 1983, p. 520).

However, Williamson's attempt to rectify a deficiency of mainstream economic theory is unsatisfactory. In rejecting the 'legal-centralism' view, and by suggesting that contractual commitments can be sustained and supported entirely by arrangments between individual agents, he throws out the baby with the bathwater.

Of course, most contractual disputes are resolved without direct recourse to the courts; but this does not mean that the state has no place in the everyday process of contract. After all, the mere possibility of access to the courts is sufficient for the legal system to bear upon contractual agreements. It is not necessary that people actually appear in court for the state to have such a function. Whilst both formal and informal norms and rules play an important part in a system of exchange, in a modern society these rules are buttressed and sometimes created by law and the state (Collins, 1986). In fact, as is argued below, Williamson fails to make the observation that most arrangements are made without full recourse to legal formalities the meaning and significance it deserves.

Williamson's main alternative theoretical construction, to fill the vacuum thus created by the dismissal of the state from the analysis, is the idea of 'hostages' to support exchange. A 'hostage' refers to a class of arrangements where, for example, both parties to an agreement are committed to specific and non-salvageable costs. The effect is to tighten the bond between the two parties and to minimize the chance of default before the contract is completed. In addition, other arrangements are mentioned, such as an agreed arbitration procedure, which aid contracting without recourse to a formal legal apparatus. Thus, in Williamson's view, a system of exchange and contract is possible and sustainable without the state.[9]

The positive part of Williamson's argument is his rejection of an excessive legal formalism where it is assumed that exchange arrangements are continuously expressed in formal legal terms and processed no more than one step away from the courts. In effect, Williamson is rebutting the view that civil society is completely penetrated by the state. Although fault can be found with his general argument this particular conclusion can be endorsed.

However, in line with liberal precedents, Williamson is proposing the theoretical possibility of a 'state of nature' from which the sovereignty of the state is entirely removed. His opposition to 'legal centralism' bends the stick to the opposite and equally unacceptable extreme.[10]

Williamson's analysis thus follows Bernard Mandeville's *Fable of the Bees*, by proposing that social order and cohesion is possible on the basis of entirely self-seeking individuals. Indeed, Williamson's models of contracting behaviour all involve an especially self-interested version of neoclassical economic man: one who is not altruistic but 'opportunistic'. Opportunism is defined as a variety of self-interest seeking that is pursued 'with guile' and 'even among the less opportunistic, most have their price' (Williamson, 1979, p. 234n.). This concept of 'opportunism' is regarded by its author as being central to his transaction costs analysis (pp. 233–4).[11]

In developing models of contract and exchange which result simply from the operation of self-seeking calculation, Williamson follows the Property Rights School in failing to recognize that the basis of everyday contract is necessarily a combination of both the laws that are passed by government, and also centuries of accumulated custom and tradition.

The legitimating function of the legal apparatus in regard to trade and other social relations is ignored by such writers. In reality, however, the basis of agreements is not simply the rational calculation of abstract individuals with a view to their perceived costs and benefits; it is a combination of both formal legislation and legitimation, and inherited custom and tradition of a less formal kind.

Even in the microcosm of the contractual agreement we find the simultaneous inter-penetration and relative autonomy of civil society and the state. However, such a view can be obtained only by abandoning the liberal demarcation of the state from society. Contrary to the associated idea of 'rational economic man', each individual is enmeshed in a web of customs and traditions which reflect the complex relationship between the two.

Consequently, Williamson's analysis is not only deficient in regard to its view of 'economic man' but also it offers an unconvincing analysis of contractual arrangements in a capitalist society. To develop an alternative view we must first refer to a long tradition of analysis of the exchange relationship by sociological theorists. Regrettably, this tradition has been given negligible attention by economists.

## 7.2   CRITIQUE OF THE UTILITARIAN CALCULUS

Since the rise of capitalism, social theory has been faced with a set of questions which mainstream economists have preferred to ignore. How is it that a complex society with extensive market relations and a high degree of competition can stay together and not disintegrate in the war of each against all? Why does a sufficient measure of social solidarity exist in a society where the bonds of tradition are weakened, where the variety of different occupations and vested interests is increased, and people are encouraged to look first and foremost to their own self-interest? What, in these circumstances, prevents society from ruinous schism or collapse, and promotes a degree of integration in a highly differentiated system?

Many years ago, Hobbes attempted to provide an answer to these questions. However, his idea that the sovereign emerges to maintain social order and cohesion is unconvincing in that it offers no explanation of the stability and continuity of sovereign rule. Hobbes' solution is internally inconsistent in that its own model of individual human behaviour does not extend to the sovereign himself. Why would the supreme ruler act with firmness and benevolence to maintain social cohesion and not, for instance, act in a manner which further promotes the war of all against all? Thus in the case of the sovereign Hobbes implicitly abandons the axiom of crude, individual self-interest which is so important in his theory as a whole.

Classic liberalism conceives of society mainly as a network of contractual relations and as a summation of contracts between individuals. Social integration is said to result from each individual pursuing his or her own interests, perhaps with the addition of some agency outside the contracting parties to enforce agreements. Within certain behavioural limits it is regarded that the devotion to self-interest will generally produce a result that is conducive to the harmony and development of society as a whole. It is clear that the works of the Property Rights School, and those of Williamson as well, fall within this same broad theoretical tradition.

## Durkheim and the impossibility of pure contract

It is in examining and rejecting this liberal-utilitarian argument, that Emile Durkheim provides a very different theory in his classic work *The Division of Labour in Society*. As we shall see below, instead of the *deus ex machina* of the Hobbesian sovereign, Durkheim suggests that the answer to the problem of social integration is found in the microcosm of exchange and contract itself.

As we have noted, a crucial feature of a contract is that it is normally the result of the intentions and agreement of two or more individuals. But is the contract in its entirety simply an expression of the desires and rational calculations of the parties involved? Durkheim's critique of the liberal-utilitarian tradition rests on an assertion of the existence, and indeed necessity, of non-contractual elements in all social relationships even when markets and the division of labour are well developed: 'It is absolutely true that contractual relationships that originally were rare or completely missing are multiplied as labour in society is divided up.' But what the liberal-utilitarian tradition fails to perceive is that 'the non-contractual relationships are developing at the same time' (Durkheim, 1984, pp. 154–5).

Durkheim points out that whilst in general an explicit agreement is necessary to any valid contract, there are elements involved in its creation that cannot be reduced to the expressed intent of any individual.[12] 'For in a contract not everything is contractual' (Durkheim, 1984, p. 158). Whenever a contract exists there are factors, not reducible to the intentions or agreements of individuals, which have regulatory and binding functions for the contract itself. In opposition to the idea that total social cohesion is obtained through the summation of personal agreements, Durkheim poses the existence of an 'organic' social solidarity which is additional to the contractarian bonds.

His key argument is that for all contracts there exists a set of binding rules to which there is no explicit or detailed reference by the parties involved. Some of these rules are legal. In this instance, the parties to the contract accept without discussion the overall regulation of the legal system and the body of law, despite the fact that no contractual agent can be fully aware of all the laws involved, and of the substance of the legal judgement if any issue came to court. The law 'constrains us to respect obligations for which we have not contracted, in the precise meaning of the term, since we have not deliberated upon them or, on occasions, even been aware of them beforehand' (p. 161).

Furthermore, there is the problem of incomplete knowledge that affects any contractual arrangement. It is necessary for the arrangements to be fixed for the entire period of the contractual relationship (the problem addressed by Williamson) and to cover all possible eventualities. It would appear that the formulation of each contract would thus require considerable planning and deliberation. 'Yet we cannot foresee the variety of possible circumstances that may arise during the period our contract will run, nor fix beforehand, by means of simple mental calculation, what will be in every case the rights and duties of each person, save in matters of which we have very special practical experience' (p. 160).

Durkheim writes as a nineteenth-century sociologist, and his text contains some flaws of presentation and argument which will still serve as fuel for the critic and interpreter for years to come. But the message can be easily transformed and made acceptable. Indeed, they can be expressed in the modern language of the Post-Keynesian economist. To put it in this manner: there is an element of uncertainty in all contracts; they are subject to varied possibilities to which we can assign no calculable probability, and thus cannot be envisaged in detailed contractual terms at the outset. Notably, two Post-Keynesian economists argue that 'as rights and duties can be expressed only in terms of the *ex ante* set of states, *no ironclad* (i.e. perfect) *contract can, even in principle, be written*. In a world where one cannot know all possible outcomes, one cannot contract away all (or even most) of the uncertainty of the future' (Williams and Findlay, 1986, p. 37).

Durkheim's succeeding argument can be given a similarly modern ring. To cope with uncertainty, individuals proceed by trial and error, relying in part on experience and habits. If instead 'we had each time to launch ourselves afresh into these conflicts and negotiations necessary to establish clearly all the conditions of the agreement, for the present and the future, our actions would be paralysed' (p. 161). In an uncertain world we are forced to rely on institutional rules and standard patterns of contract, with the assumption, with cannot for practical reasons be confirmed by detailed negotiation, that the other parties will similarly accept the prevailing norms and conventions.

Thus, even in a rapidly changing society, 'the function of contract is less to create new rules than to diversify pre-established rules in particular cases' (p. 162). The formulation of a contract between two parties more often involves an implicit or explicit reference to a set of norms, customs and rules rather than a detailed negotiation *de novo* over every clause and eventuality. Of course, new forms of contract (and new implicit rules) are being developed all the time. But these could not be adopted, due to the complexities involved, in the majority of cases. Adherence to the customary arrangements remains the norm.

Those who are still confined in the classical liberal tradition, like the Property Rights School, put 'principal stress on enforcement of the terms of the agreement themselves, whereas Durkheim's main stress is on the existence of a body of rules which have not been the object of any agreement among the contracting parties themselves but are socially "given"' (Parsons, 1937, p. 312).

Furthermore, as Talcott Parsons suggests, there are important implications in Durkheim's analysis for the conception of the relationship between civil society and the state. Whilst legal stipulations are important elements to any contract, and generally will be enforced, they stand alongside

> a vast body of customary rules, trade conventions and the like which are, in effect, obligatory equally with the law, although not enforceable in the courts. This shading off of law into trade practice indicates that this body of rules is much more closely integrated with the contractual system itself than the individualists would be ready to grant. The latter tended to think of the role of society in these matters, as represented by the state, as one of only occasional intervention to straighten out a difficulty in a machinery which normally functioned quite automatically without 'social' interference. (Parsons, 1937, p. 312–13)

Note that several of these arguments may apply to some contracts more than others, but in principle there is no contract for which uncertainty can be reduced to zero, and all possible future circumstances envisaged at the start. Even at the extreme, involving, for example, the sale of a simple and well-defined product, the complexities and uncertainties are sufficiently great to give Durkheim's argument considerable weight.

Durkheim's analysis is thus both general and forceful in the context of the modern economy. We are not dealing with a minority case of 'extreme' cases which the modellers of 'economic man' can cheerfully ignore. The non-contractual features of exchange agreements are central and functional to any economic system based on trade.

Furthermore, it is not acceptable to argue that any past or future extension of the market system can undermine these non-contractual features to the extent that it would be legitimate to exclude them from the analysis. It would be wrong to argue that the formal, explicit side of the contract can or will gradually erode the customary and informal rules and regulations to the extent that they can be ignored. Indeed, as uncertainty remains undiminished and the dynamism of the capitalist system creates ever greater complexity for the decision-maker, reliance on some informal rules and customs can never decrease to insignificance. The vision of a 'pure' market or capitalist system which has driven out all vestiges of habit and tradition is both theoretically implausible and unrealizable in practice.[13]

## Some special cases of impure contract

Whilst elements of customary practice and 'organic solidarity' are found within every single contractual arrangement, clearly there are many different kinds of contract and these features will vary in their weight and form.

A set of cases discussed by Durkheim are contracts involving the professions. He notes that relationships with professional persons tend to be imbued with strict moral obligations as well as formal contractual arrangements. Even if a doctor works in the private sector, it is expected that he or she will conform to the sprirt of the Hippocratic oath, especially concerning the secrecy of the consultation and the health and welfare of the patients. A teacher is expected to be dedicated to education and the interests of the pupils. A scientist is expected to be driven by a desire to increase the stock of human knowledge, and to maintain an honesty and diligence in research. In all these cases there is a general expectation and assumption that such 'moral' considerations will have some priority.

W. O. Hagstrom in his book *The Scientific Community* (1965) notes that researchers and academics are expected to step outside a contractual or exchange relationship and make 'contributions' to knowledge in general and to academic journals, for which there are normally no monetary rewards. There certainly may be other rewards, such as prestige, improved chances of promotion, and so on, but simply to subsume all this under the individual calculation of gain and loss misses the point. It could even be true that the motives of recognition and personal advancement are prominent in generating research. The point is that if academics were to accept freely that their motive for researching and publishing was personal gain then this would devalue the very content of their work in the eyes of those they were trying to influence.

Following Neil Smelser (1959) and others, Hagstrom argues that academic publication is an example of the more general anthropological phenomenon of 'gift-giving' and that this is typical 'not only of science but of all institutions concerned with the maintenance and transmission of common values, such as the family, religion, and the communities' (Hagstrom, 1965, p. 12). Whilst reward and compensation will often be expected in return for such 'gifts', they are generally not part of any contractual agreement.[14]

Hagstrom argues that the relationships governing professional services are different from the typical contract on the market. In the professions there is an expectation that agents will conform to a set of values or moral codes. The abdication of any moral control would disrupt the system. In particular, such moral values have to be seen to take precedence over any individual or corporate calculation of the costs and benefits of any activity:

> In general, *whenever strong commitments to values are expected, the rational calculation of punishments and rewards is regarded as an improper basis for making decisions.* Citizens who refrain from treason merely because it is against the law are, by that fact, of questionable loyalty; parents who refrain from incest merely because of fear of community reaction are, by that fact, unfit for parenthood; and scientists who select problems merely because they feel that in dealing with them they will receive greater recognition from colleagues are, by that fact, not 'good' scientists. (Hagstrom, 1965, p. 20)

In all of these examples the sanctions against deviance ostensibily do not work. For the deviant the failure is self-evident, and those that do conform do not normally admit that sanctions are having any significant effect in their own case. However, as Hagstrom points out, 'this does not mean that the sanctions are of no importance; it does mean that more than overt conformity to norms is demanded, that inner conformity is regarded as equally, or more, important' (p. 20).

The upshot of this argument is that the calculus of profit and loss may be embedded in such relationships but it is not the whole story, and significantly its existence has to be denied by the participants. The utilitarian model of 'rational economic man' cannot capture the nature and function of the commitment to moral values, nor the complexities of the 'gift' relationship that is typical in this sphere.

Another relevant study is the famous work of Richard Titmuss (1970) on the donation of blood for medical transfusion purposes. His analysis involved a comparison of different systems of blood procurement, processing and distribution in several different countries. In some, such as Britain, the donation of blood involves no pecuniary reward, but in others, such as the US, blood is often exchanged for cash.

Titmuss argues that the unrewarded donation of blood both results from, and helps to reinforce, diffuse sentiments of fellowship and altruism. The relationship is thus one with prominent moral values. By his or her example the unrewarded donor encourages others to give blood, and helps to sustain the values and norms involved. Whilst blood may remain in short supply there is still a viable mechanism for attracting other donors.

The reaction of most economists to the problem of blood shortages would be to establish a more definite system of tangible incentives. In this manner many countries have sought to enlarge the supply of blood by offering money payments. Titmuss shows, however, that this actually has deleterious effects. Once the blood-donor relationship is commercialized, other destructive forces come into play. In general the attendant moral values are eroded, and in particular the important elements of honesty and trust. Titmuss (1970, p. 151) found that paid donors were on average, compared with voluntary donors, 'more reluctant and less likely to reveal a full medical history and to provide information about recent contacts with infectious disease, recent inoculations, and about their diets, drinking and drug habits that would disqualify them as donors'. Consequently, the blood that is procured under a commercialized system is more likely to be infected and unsuitable for donation.

More generally, from his study of the private market for blood in the US, Titmuss concludes that the operation of cash payments 'represses the expression of altruism, erodes the sense of community, lowers scientific standards, limits both personal and professional freedoms, . . . places immense social costs on those least able to bear them – the poor, the sick and the inept – [and] increases the danger of unethical behaviour in various sectors of medical science and practice' (pp. 245–6).

By any reasonable economic criterion, Titmuss shows that the system of exchange of blood for money is actually less efficient than a system where blood is donated as a gift. The operation of tangible incentives actually decreases the efficiency of the system by lowering the average quality of the blood and is arguably less cost effective. It is possible that commercialization may increase the supply of blood, but there are greatly increased risks of infection and a corresponding decline of quality, as well as damaging 'moral' externalities for society as a whole.

## The centrality of impure contract

On the face of it the blood-donor example would appear to be an extreme case, and such considerations would be not nearly so significant in the wider world of industry and trade. Whilst admitting that the blood-donor case does have special features it would be a mistake to suggest that the considerations involved can be elsewhere disregarded. There are both general and specific reasons to support this view.

Consider first the important question of the dissemination of information in a modern, complex economy. The significance of these activities is indicated by Fritz Machlup (1962) who estimates that about 29 per cent of the gross national product in the US is devoted to the production and processing of information and knowledge.

However, it is inappropriate to treat information just like any other commodity because it has very special characteristics. For instance, it is impossible to sell information just like bread or potatoes on the open market. Once the information is sold, any buyer can undercut the seller and ruin trade by reproducing it at little cost. Arguably, any 'market' for information requires special legal or other constraints or protections in order to work. Furthermore, information has the peculiar feature that even if it has been 'sold' it can still remain in the possession of the producer or seller who may know its content after the sale. Information does not fit into the image of a 'normal' commodity which changes hands from seller to buyer in a straightforward manner.

On the demand side there are still more difficulties. As Kenneth Arrow puts it, 'there is a fundamental paradox in the determination of demand for information: its value for the purchaser is not known until he has the information, but then he has in effect acquired it without cost' (Arrow, 1962, p. 616). In sum, information is a strange item, untypical of the world of market trading, which cannot be the object of pure exchange.

Consequently, 'pure' contracts governing the trade of information are generally not feasible. There will always, for instance, be a degree of trust on behalf of the buyer that the information will be worth its price. Its peculiarities give rise to a whole host of restrictions and impurities. The patent system, for example, is a mechanism through which technical information is protected by legal and institutional constraint.

Another common occurrence is the treatment of information as a gift. Even in the most commercialized of capitalist societies there are plentiful sources of free information: bus timetables, sales catalogues, telephone directories, public libraries and the like. Even when we are buying a commodity, normally there is a measure of free information from the vendor as to its characteristics. If such information were denied we would be suspicious about the quality of the goods. Thus, in many cases where a straightforward contract is involved, there are elements of 'gift-giving' on the information side. The seller is normally aware that these 'gifts' will help engender confidence and trust. Thus where the buyers generally lack information about the commodity to be exchanged there will not be a contract in a 'pure' form.

Just as the flows of information are ubiquitous in modern society, so too is the buying and selling of labour power. However, in most, if not all cases, contracts of employment have the feature that they are not, and cannot conceivably be, perfectly or completely specified in advance. This idea can be traced back to Karl Marx's distinction between labour (the activity of work) and labour power (the capacity to work) in *Capital*. The hiring of labour power does not, and cannot, mean that the work performed is automatic or completely specified. The nature of work is so complex and uncertain that complete specification in advance would be impossible.[15]

Neither is it possible to deal with the problem by an *ex post* settling up of accounts between employer and employee. First, the pattern of work is so complicated that such a process would be wasteful and time-consuming. Second, if at the outset there is an imperfectly specified contract then there could be an extensive dispute between employer and employee as to whether the work performed was either useful or required.

It is thus no accident that labour law is rife with custom and precedent. The day-to-day practice of industrial relations is governed largely by mutual submission to extensive, unwritten conventions and rules. These do not form part of the formal contract but they are essential to facilitate practicable working arrangements over long periods of time. They concern the recognition and treatment of authority, the type of relations between management and employee, and the nature and pattern of work itself. Industrial relations are thus governed by a combination of both the force of custom and the open contractual agreement.

Such an observation is not new to labour economics and industrial relations. For example, the work of John Dunlop (1958) stresses the function of formal and informal customs and rules in an industrial relations system. More recently, David Marsden (1986) has argued that such institutional foundations are a necessary condition for the functioning of any 'free' labour market.

In a monumental study of industrial relations, Alan Fox (1974) argues that all job descriptions contain both specific instructions and terms which allow the employee some discretion. Work roles vary enormously in the degree and manner in which these elements are combined, but to some extent the employee is allowed some discretion to deal with complex issues and unforeseen contingencies.

Fox analyses forms of employment relationship in regard to the extent that they are imbued with mutual fellowship and trust. In many cases there is a 'low trust dynamic' where mutual suspicion between employer and employee can lead to conflict or inefficiency, and fails to foster further trust in the future. In contrast, there are cases of a 'high trust dynamic' which promotes cooperation, diligence and efficiency, but may actually undermine managerial control. Thus, to a greater of lesser degree, all employment contracts involve an element of trust which cannot be obtained or expressed simply in contractual terms.

The idea that the labour contract is not purely one of deliberate exchange is well known in the sociological literature but only rarely has it surfaced in the economic. In a recent and exceptional case, George Akerlof (1982) argues that many contracts of employment consist in part of a gift relationship. Noting case studies (e.g. Homans, 1962) of the quite general phenomenon of workers exceeding the work standards of the firm, without cash or promotion incentives, Akerlof argues that this is an example of a partial gift relationship. In line with the anthropological and sociological theory, gifts are given in accord with socially determined traditions and norms. Thus are established such norms as 'a fair day's work' and the appropriate level of pay. The reciprocal nature of the gift (Mauss, 1954) is reflected in these norms and reciprocal ties of allegiance between workers and the management of the firm.[16]

It may be expected that in the case of business people who are more directly and regularly concerned with buying and selling the force of the market will drive out all vestiges of trust and fellowship. Yet a study by Stewart Macaulay (1963) found a reliance on values such as 'common honesty and decency' in making deals. Even when high risks are involved, business people do not necessarily respond by insisting on a formal contract which covers every eventuality. Macaulay carried out a survey which showed that a clear majority of orders did not involve formal contracts, and relied on word of mouth or established relationships between the persons involved.

Indeed, a variety of trust is to be found in relation to one of the most important and characteristic elements of a modern capitalist system. We refer to money. The entire economic system functions on the basis and belief that otherwise near-worthless pieces of paper or metal will retain their acceptability and consequently their value. In holding money we do not put our trust in individuals but implicitly in the system and the state. For example, in accepting credit, people do not simply rely on the legal and other sanctions against default. In addition there has to be an acceptance that money itself will retain its value.

In a monetary system there must be a measure of trust or confidence, both in the state as a guarantor of the value of its currency, and in the fact that other people will accept this value in exchange. This confidence is reinforced by daily observation of monetary transactions; but it, in itself, does not result from contractual agreement between individuals, nor between individuals and the state. It is strange, but in an economy where contracts are expressed in monetary terms, money itself is non-contractual at its core. Money is a means of overcoming uncertainty; in a world of ignorance and complexity it achieves this by promoting confidence and trust in its precarious value.[17]

### General remarks on trust

The existence and function of trust is accepted by many economists. For instance, Kenneth Arrow (1974, p. 23) writes: 'Trust is an important lubricant of the social system. It is extremely efficient; it saves a lot of trouble to have a fair degree of reliance on other people's work. Unfortunately, this is not a commodity which can be bought very easily. If you have to buy it, you already have some doubts about what you've bought.'[18]

To go further, trust and other associated non-contractual values are not simply efficient and convenient; even in a market system the degree of uncertainty and complexity means that they are essential for the system to work at all. As Herbert Frankel (1977, p. 37) puts in his study of the philosophy of money: 'Individuals and societies are dependent on countless symbols, myths, beliefs and institutions which function as indicators of trustworthiness or the opposite.'

Ultimately, however, trust is unprovable and uncalculable. As Niklas Luhmann (1979, p. 26) states: 'In the last resort, no decisive grounds can be offered for trusting: trust always extrapolates from the available evidence; it is . . . a blending of knowledge and ignorance.' If we demand that it shall be measured we find that it slips away from our grasp.

Furthermore, apparent acts of trust are not only a blending of knowledge and ignorance, but also of thought processes at different levels of consciousness, of both conscious deliberation and unconscious habit and routine. We learn from experience in what sort of situation we can normally place our trust, and by becoming familiar with them we begin to act habitually once trust is established. Although trusting in its most meaningful sense is conscious and deliberative, it is also important in that its repeated endorsement by perceived events and symbols gives rise to habit and routine.

These arguments concerning the essential function of trust and other elements in a contractual system undermine the idea that exchange can be described through the utilitarian calculus. Commodity exchange itself always contains elements of a gift and relies to some significant extent on trust. Exchange is always in part a leap into the unknown, it is a *'salto mortale'* (death leap), to quote a phrase of Marx (1971, p. 88; 1976, p. 200).

The argument here is not simply to recognize the world of uncertainty in which such a leap exists. For such a dangerous act to become commonplace it must be enforced to a large degree by routine and guided by a good measure of trust. How else would we make frequent and vulnerable transactions if we were not to assume away many of the volatilities of an uncertain world, or act, on habit, as if they did not exist? The key point is that the rationalistic, utilitarian calculus is limited and constrained within everyday acts of exchange.

## 7.3   THE IMPURITY PRINCIPLE AND THE FATE OF CAPITALISM

To recapitulate: the point established here is that non-contractual elements are essential, whatever their degree of prominence, in any developed system of exchange. A 'pure' market or exchange system, on purely contractarian lines, could not work in practice and is unacceptable in theory.[19]

However, whilst there are always non-contractual elements within any contract, in a developed capitalist system these do not dominate transactions. In some sense the rational calculation of gain and loss is indeed predominant in a modern market economy. The mistakes of neoclassical economics are to conceive of rationality as unbounded in its scope, to assume that rationality is straightforward maximization, to imply that all action results from reason and calculation, to ignore the cognitive framework behind reason, and to assume that all non-contractual elements can be disregarded. In contrast, it is argued here that the analysis of exchange in modern society has to be understood through an examination of the symbiotic realtionship between *both* its contractual and non-contractual features.

### Impurity and cartesian thinking

I have tried to sum up the general features of this kind of argument elsewhere (Hodgson, 1984, chs 6 and 7) and some of these ideas are discussed in more detail in chapter 11 of the present work. Briefly, the 'impurity principle' is the idea that each system (or sub-system) contains 'impurities' which are not typical of the whole, but which are nevertheless necessary for the system to function.

This idea is derived from a consideration of the economic system through the lenses of both economic history and systems theory. In particular there is reference to W. Ross Ashby's (1952, 1956) 'law of requisite variety'. This is basically the notion that an open system has to contain sufficient variety to deal with all the potential variation in its environment. Sufficient complexity and variety within the system is necessary so that the system can survive and deal with variety and unforeseeable shocks from the outside.

What is involved is more than an empirical observation that different types of structure may co-exist within the economic system as a whole. What is involved is an assertion that some of these economic structures are *necessary* for the socio-economic system to function over time.

The impurity principle is combined with a more familiar idea which is titled 'the principle of dominance', i.e. the notion that socio-economic systems generally exhibit a dominant economic structure. Together these two ideas imply a pluralistic view of the economic system and have important consequences for the debate over markets and planning. These will be raised at the appropriate stage below.

Clearly the idea of the impure contract can be placed in this framework. The contractual elements are dominant, but the non-contractual components are necessary features of the contract as a whole; they are necessary impurities. Thus the idea that all contracts contain non-contractual elements can be regarded as an expression of the impurity principle. The principle of dominance is manifest in the supremacy within the contract of the self-seeking calculation of profit and loss.

Notably, however, whilst the general principles of impurity and dominance were substantiated through systems theory, here similar ideas have arisen through an examination of the molecular relations of contract and exchange.

More fundamentally, at the philosophical level, the impurity principle suggests a break from the Cartesian and mechanistic mode of thinking where phenomena are broken down into determinate elements or parts, and through their aggregation we build up a picture of the whole. What is suggested is that the parts themselves are multi-faceted and inter-penetrating. We can identify parts but we are not generally able to given them an unambiguous quality or sign.

Thus, for example, we can identify the features of law and property that flow from custom and tradition. But law and property are not wholly that; they are partly defined and backed by statutory rights and sanctions as well. It is in the complex and evolving relationship between formal legal and customary features that law and property must be adequately defined. Second, we may identify the predominant aspect of contract and exchange as formal agreement by the parties. But the contract is not, and can never be adequately, defined purely in these terms. The contract contains both contractual and non-contractual elements at the same time and its character is determined by the nature and dynamic of their combination.

Most essentially, therefore, we are suggesting a break from black-and-white, hard-and-fast, either/or, once-and-for-all modes of thinking that are characteristic of the Cartesian and mechanistic world view. Things cannot be broken down completely into timeless, atomistic units. The elements of the world are inter-penetrating in time and space: interacting and changing, becoming as well as being. What is suggested here may have a Hegelian or Marxian ring, but it is not outdated for that. Indeed it broadly reflects some recent developments in modern physics (Bohm, 1980; Capek, 1961; Capra, 1982).

Notably, the principles of impurity and dominance suggest an approach to the analysis of exchange relationships which differs strikingly from their compartmentalization into the two exclusive groups of 'social' and 'economic' exchange in much sociological writing. The thrust of Durkheim's analysis seems to undermine the legitimacy of this division, yet it is accepted with little question in both economics and sociology.[20] Yet all so-called 'economic' exchanges exhibit 'social' aspects to some degree. In addition, it has been argued above that many so-called 'social' exchanges do not involve property rights and thus are not best described as 'exchanges' at all.

Furthermore, the compartmentalization of social science itself encourages economists to make the mistake of treating all exchanges as purely 'economic', i.e. to the exclusion of their non-contractual features, whilst the artificial boundaries between the disciplines prevent the 'sociological' critique of Durkheim and others from being heard by economists.

## Contractual impurities: Schumpeter and Marx

Whilst it contains non-contractual elements at its core, the extension of the formalized contract and the development of the cash nexus to some degree has the same effect on society as a whole as private trade in blood in Richard Titmuss's study. The effect is to break down traditional ties of social allegiance and cohesion. However, because of the very unity of contractual and non-contractual elements within the contract itself, this process cannot, in principle, proceed to its limit.

This argument is clearly of importance in assessing the policy statements of classic liberalism and the New Right. The general thrust of many of their arguments is that the more the economy approximates to a pure market system all the better for our freedom and welfare. An elegant and appropriate response is provided by Alan Fox:

> Those devotees of the market and its associated principles and behaviours who see it as the answer to all human problems provided it is applied unblinkingly and unswervingly enough still fail to grasp that even the modern economic system, to which it is assumed to apply *in excelcis*, continues to operate as it does only because the economic exchange of the market has not entirely taken over. (Fox, 1974, p. 374)

Thus it is not inconsistent to argue that, on the one hand, all contracts and exchanges include non-contractual elements such as trust, and, on the other, the extension of market exchange undermines trust, cohesion and solidarity in the system. This can occur because whilst non-contractual elements are always present, generally market exchanges are *dominated* by self-seeking and non-altruistic considerations.

If the capitalist economy proceeds apace and progressively undermines the 'social' or non-contractual elements of exchange, then this would lead to a crisis, involving the destabilization, or even the demise, of the system. Along these lines, Joseph Schumpeter argued that this process would lead to the end of capitalism and to its replacement by socialism. 'Capitalism', he wrote, 'creates, by rationalizing the human mind, a mentality and style of life incompatible with its own fundamental conditions, motives and social institutions' (Schumpeter, 1928, p. 386).

Like Marx, Schumpeter predicts the demise of capitalism, but he differs in his analysis of the processes involved. Whilst with Marx it is the inner logic of capital that leads to the crisis, with Schumpeter it is capitalism's destruction of all trace of its precedents that leads to its difficulties: 'In breaking down the pre-capitalist framework of society, capitalism thus broke not only the barriers that impeded its progress, but also the flying buttresses that prevented its collapse' (Schumpeter, 1976, p. 139). It is therefore the very success of capitalism in dissolving the traditions and institutions of the past that puts its own future in doubt.[21] This is part of Schumpeter's argument that capitalism displays a process of 'creative destruction'.

Clearly, Schumpeter's idea that capitalism is dependent on pre-capitalist elements is compatible with the 'impurity principle' discussed above. But we are not necessarily drawn to his conclusion that the system is destined to collapse because the march of capitalism will destroy such impurities. All that is suggested by the impurity principle itself is that there is an inner tension between different structures in the system, but that some of the non-dominant structures are necessary for the social formation as a whole to survive. In addition there is no cast-iron reason why the collapse or decay of capitalism (if it were to occur) should lead to its replacement by socialism as Schumpeter supposed.[22]

In short, there are many questionable features in Schumpeter's theory. It has been raised here, however, because the initial stages of his argument correspond with the analysis of this chapter. Schumpeter is one of the very few economists who have noted the inner contradictions of the cash nexus. Likewise, in Marx's work there is an analogous tension between the developmental and the destructive features of an economic system based on private property relations and exchange. As Albert Hirschman (1982) has explained so well, it is only through such a 'dialectical' view that the simultaneously civilizing and corrosive features of our modern economic system can be appreciated. When economists desist in their bland and simplistic either pro- or anti-prescriptions on private property and market exchange then all will be better for the subject and humanity as a whole.

# 8

# Markets as Institutions

The market is a place set apart where men may deceive one another.

Anacharsis of Scythia, *c*.600 B.C.

The study of market behaviour is a major theme, if not the major theme, of economic science as we know it. Furthermore, the proposal that markets should be extended, unfettered and made more competitive is a strident policy recommendation of our times. Remarkably, however, definitions of the market in the economic literature are not easy to find, and analytical discussions of the institutional concepts involved are extremely rare. Mathematical models of market phenomena abound, and there is a voluminous literature on the theoretical determinants of market equilibria. Yet if we ask the elementary question – 'What is a market?' – we are given short shrift. An answer is attempted in this chapter, followed by a discussion of the function of markets in an economic system.

Although the question seems elementary, and the answer is fairly straightforward – to define the market itself as a kind of institution – there are implications which diverge profoundly from orthodox theory. Furthermore, they relate to some heterodox literature on price norms and the function of market 'rigidities' which not only undermine the neoclassical 'idea type' of perfect competition but lead to different lines of investigation and types of policy conclusion.

## 8.1 Defining the Market

*The elusive definition*

One of the few economists to attempt to define a market was Alfred

Marshall (1949, Book V, ch.1) who devoted a whole chapter to this task. However, his statement is unsatisfactory because he goes little further than quoting the definitions of Augustin Cournot and William Jevons with approval.

Cournot (1897) describes a market as a 'region in which buyers and sellers are in such frequent intercourse with each other that the prices of the same goods tend to equality easily and quickly'. Jevons (1871) takes a market 'to mean any body of persons who are in intimate business relations and carry on extensive transactions in any commodity'. However, as definitions these are no more than rough and ready first approximations. In Cournot's description the key terms are not further explored and the institutional mechanisms creating the tendency towards price equality are not outlined. Similarly with Jevons: the meaning of 'intimate business relations', and 'extensive transactions' is not made sufficiently clear. There is a vagueness and looseness in both definitions which subsequent writers have not been inclined to remedy.

Even within the Austrian tradition, with its avid pro-market policy recommendations, no satisfactory definition of the market has been found. The closest thing to a definition of the market in Ludwig von Mises' *Human Action* is as follows: 'The market is the social system of the division of labour under private ownership of the means of production . . . The market is not a place, a thing or a collective entity. The market is a process, actuated by the interplay of the actions of the various individuals cooperating under the division of labour' (1949, p. 258). Here too the definition rests on other concepts which are insufficiently clear, and notably any concept of exchange is absent from this passage.

In a popular modern economics textbook Richard Lipsey (1983, p. 69) defines a market as 'an area over which buyers and sellers negotiate the exchange of a well-defined commodity'. This too is vague and insufficient but most of the rival textbooks do not even bother to define the market at all. For too long 'the market' has been taken for granted.

## Markets and institutions

It is not adequate to define a market simply as a place or region where transactions take place and commodities are exchanged. Scott Moss has pointed out that much else is involved:

> Goods and services are exchanged in markets. The process of exchange involves the establishment and publication of prices; it involves informing potential customers that the goods or services produced by the firm are available for sale; it involves informing suppliers that there is a demand

for their products; it involves the transportation of goods and resources required to render services from suppliers to customers. In summary, the process of exchange entails communication and transportation between sellers and buyers of commodities which are to be traded. (Moss, 1981, pp. 1–2)

The strength of this definition[1] is its recognition that markets always involve associated activities including the 'establishment and publication of prices', means of contacting and informing customers, and means of transportation. However, the definition lacks the notion of exchange being dependent upon legal institutions, and involving the exchange of property rights as well as the transfer of goods or services. Furthermore, the institutional aspects of price determination and publication, customer communication, and transport are not mentioned. In short there is a neglect of the customary, legal, political and other social arrangements which are central to all market systems.

Moss' definition needs to be enlarged in line with the stress on social institutions in the present work. The market has to be defined in relation to a wide set of institutions, not concerned solely with legal matters such as the establishment of property rights and adjudication over contracts, but also with transportation and the communication of market-related information. Furthermore, as Todd Lowry (1976) emphasizes, the market creates a forum in which a consensus over prices can be established, which is absent in the isolated purchase or sale. The production of this consensus is facilitated by legal and other rules, customs and practices that are embedded in market institutions.

We shall here define the market as a set of social institutions in which a large number of commodity exchanges of a specific type regularly take place, and to some extent are facilitated and structured by those institutions. Exchange, as defined above, involves contractual agreement and the exchange of property rights, and the market consists in part of mechanisms to structure, organize, and legitimate these activities. Markets, in short, are organized and institutionalized exchange. Stress is placed on those market institutions which help to both regulate and establish a consensus over prices and, more generally, to communicate information regarding products, prices, quantities, potential buyers and potential sellers.

Some institutions within the market are associated with exchange and contracts in an elemental sense (such as the legal system and the customs which govern the contract), as discussed in the preceding chapter. These would be present even if a formal market did not exist. Other institutions are specifically to do with the development of a market, and the coordination of a large number of exchanges in an organized manner.

In many cases the distinction between market transactions and non-market exchange is difficult to draw, especially where the market is not physically defined as a building or an open space. The advertising columns of a newspaper or the handwritten 'for sale' notices in a local shop are in reality an intermediate case between a fully developed market and the set of transactions which are concluded without recourse to advertising or any public forum. However, even with these intermediate examples the exchanges are organized under the aegis of an institution and they could be said to be carried out within a market according to the above definition. Whilst there is a spacious grey area between the market and non-market cases, the 'ideal types' are nevertheless of conceptual significance and of analytical value.

Unfortunately, economists have not only shown a general negligence in defining the market, but also they have been extremely cavalier in their use of the term. Thus, for example, in his analysis of marriage Gary Becker (1976, p. 206) states without any hesitation that 'a *market* in marriages can be presumed to exist' (emphasis in original). Clearly, institutions such as marriage bureaux do exist. However, these are not markets (or at least not markets for marriages *per se*) but agencies with specific (largely informational) services on offer. A marriage itself involves a contractual arrangement between the bride and groom. Even if this takes place alongside family deals involving goods or services it is not the case that marriages themselves are bought or sold, and all these contracts are generally concluded outside any form of market in the strict sense.

In contrast to Becker's work on the family, social convention makes a strong distinction between familial or sexual activities that are, and are not, matters for market or other exchange. Leaving aside the moral or other arguments for and against either marriage, or the family, or prostitution, it should be accepted that the sexual relation between lovers or spouses is different in both form and substance from that between a prostitute and a client. Only in the case of a prostitute can sexual services possibly be procured through a kind of market. Becker and his followers should thus be much more discriminating in their use of the term 'market' in this context.

Another example is the concept of the 'internal labour market' within the firm. In the very act of moving away from neoclassical theory, and in an institutionalist direction, Peter Doeringer and Michael Piore (1971) propose such a concept to help explain such phenomena as wage differentials and job discrimination. However, as David Marsden (1986, p. 162) argues: 'despite the existence of a degree of competition between employees within internal labour markets for certain jobs, internal labour markets offer quite different transaction arrangements, and there is some doubt as to whether they fulfil the role of the markets.'

To put it more strongly, 'internal labour markets' within firms are not markets in the sense defined above, in that no systematic and institutionalized process involving the buying and selling of labour power is normally to be found. As Doeringer and Piore (1971, pp. 1–2) themselves suggest, 'internal labour markets' are not governed primarily by the price mechanism but by 'a set of administrative rules and procedures'. But a consequence of this point is to give strength to the argument that the term 'internal labour market' should be dropped, despite the value of much of the associated analysis, and an alternative such as 'internal labour allocations' should be used instead.[2]

### Types of market institution

An example of a way in which market institutions form a definable substance and boundary for the market is in the case where there is a real-life auctioneer. Auctioning involves the use of a specified method, custom or routine for reaching a price agreement. (A 'Dutch' auction is an example.) Such a routine will structure the bidding and is likely to affect the outcome. In addition, the organization of an auction market will require publicity, clerical work, transportation and storage. Thus an auction market is not simply a region where individual preferences collide. It is a social institution in the fullest sense. Such real auctions are thus very different from the unreal price auction in Walrasian theory.

Arthur Okun (1981, p. 138) contrasts an auction with what he calls a 'customer market': 'The hallmark of auction markets is the absence of price tags; sellers are price takers and not price makers. In fact, most products are sold with price tags set by the seller and through a process of shopping by the buyer.' However, the use of price tags has important implications in terms of market institutions and routine. For example, it enables the continuous selling of large numbers of identical products.

In capitalist societies, most markets involve explicit or implicit legal contracts and the protection of the parties involved through sanction and due process of law. In these cases the legal institutions involved are important adjuncts to the institution of the market itself. Nevertheless, it is possible for there to be illegal or 'black' markets, and it would be wrong to assume that these are not social institutions. The very fact that they are illegal means that there have to be carefully designed or suitably evolved mechanisms for making contacts, vetting participants, and developing the trust that no-one will inform the authorities. An established black market will have all these things, its own customs, and patterns of routine behaviour, making it an institution in its own right.

## Markets and exchange

It is important to emphasize that it is possible for there to be commodity exchange without it being exchange on a market. The market includes a generalized mechanism to establish and publicize prices, and to promote goods and services. In contrast, there are many cases when exchange is established other than through the market, by contact obtained in other spheres of activity. A common example of non-market exchange is the habitually renewed contract to supply a good or service to a regular client. Identical or close substitutes may exist, but the buyer chooses to remain with the same supplier without 'going to the market' to consider an alternative. There is a clear distinction between regularized exchange, or 'relational contracting', of this type, and using the institution of the market as an environment of more immediate competition and choice.

Another case where non-market exchange can arise is where the good or service to be exchanged is unique, such as a custom-built piece of machinery. In some cases, market institutions may serve to put the customer in contact with a potential producer, but the specialized nature of the transaction makes it possible, even likely, that contact will be made through other means, especially through a previously established relationship.

Examples of non-market exchange are a great deal more common in the real world than a literal reading of the literature would suggest. Furthermore, without a clear definition of the market that does not mention or allude to its institutional structure, it is not possible to make an adequate distinction between market and non-market exchange. Despite the increasing recognition of an institutional dimension to economics, the distinction between market and non-market transactions has continued to elude most economists.[3]

## Some immediate theoretical consequences

The institutional definition of the market constructed above has a number of important theoretical consequences, including the following. First, in mainstream economics the market is seen as a kind of natural or normal order, consisting of the aggregation of individual bargains, whereas non-market institutions are regarded as to some extent alien or unnatural. The market is seen as an ether in which individual and subjective preferences relate to each other, leading to the physical exchange of goods or services. Any view that the market is simply an aggregation of bilateral exchanges between individuals, or essentially some kind of reflection of given individual preferences and purposes, is rejected here. All exchange, and particularly market exchange, takes place in, and interacts with, an institutional context. Clearly, if markets too are social institutions which have evolved through time then the naturalistic or ethereal view of the market is flawed.

Second, the argument in this chapter contrasts with the peculiar dichotomy in mainstream economics where markets are 'free', and institutions (by suggestion not including the market) are 'constraints'. The market is seen to evoke mobility, contrasting with the restrictiveness and inertia of institutions. The policy conclusion is often that the constraining influence of institutions should be minimized or removed, or that institutions should remain only to redress the alleged inefficiencies or injustices of the 'free' market. Once, however, the market is regarded as an institution in its own right it becomes reasonable to ask if it imposes constraints of its own, and if it is not, in this sense, completely 'free'. As we should expect with any other social institution, the market too imposes barriers and constraints. Furthermore, as in the case of other social institutions, the market has enabling as well as constraining functions. The misconceived dichotomy between 'free markets' and 'constraining institutions' is rejected.[4]

Third, this ethereal, non-institutional conception of the market enables it to be regarded as the supreme medium for the expression of individual choice. Non-market institutions, by contrast, are seen as being 'collectivist' in nature; they are seen to restrict expression of these preferences and exchange activity based upon them. However, it is argued here that the market has ineradicable social and 'collectivist' aspects as well. Therefore, and in contrast to the popular view, an attachment to a pure and extreme individualism cannot find a direct reflection in the market. Consequently, pure individualism and the advocacy of markets are not entirely consistent with each other. In the present work, of course, there is not attachment to either pure individualism or a 100 per cent market system, so the problem does not arise. It exists, however, for much of orthodox theory, which can in principle have either individualism or markets, but not both to extremes.

Fourth, we are led to the proposition that markets, like other social institutions, play a major role in transmitting information and forming and moulding individual preferences, expectations and actions. This argument has been developed already in general terms in part two. Its particular significance here is that the function of market institutions is not only the transmission of information concerning the prices or quantities of specific products, but also to affect the actions and dispositions of other agents which are gathered under the aegis of the market institution.

The manner in which people are affected by the market as an institution is not merely that it provides information, or merely constraints, but that it structures the process of cognition of the agents involved and can actually affect their preferences and beliefs. Thus in a subtle way, through the operation of market conventions, routines and rules, the individual in the market is to some extent 'coerced' into specific types of behaviour. Consequently, and emphatically in contrast to much of orthodox economics, the market can never be entirely 'free' in the classic liberal sense, and it does not necessarily represent the epitome of freedom for the individual.

The failure of orthodox theory to supply an institutional definition of the market often leads to its treatment as a universal category of human interaction. As discussed in the preceding chapter, in orthodox sociology there is a tendency to subsume all forms of social interaction under the broad heading of 'exchange'. By giving the 'exchange' concept little or nothing against which to oppose itself, this devalues the very concept of exchange in the process. Similarly, some economists have a tendency to find markets everywhere, such as in regard to marriage or inside the firm. The market becomes a universal category; thus this concept too becomes devalued. In contrast, by revealing the ideological underpinnings of the orthodox concept of the market, and by making it a specific and non-universal definition, it is possible to recognize the weight and importance of this central institution in the modern economy.

## 8.2 WHY DO MARKETS EXIST?

As argued above, in orthodox economics the market is regarded as a kind of state of nature, the natural medium through which individual traders interact, existing before and independently of social institutions. From this viewpoint we are not impelled to raise the question as to why markets exist. In contrast, if markets are regarded as either planned or spontaneous social institutions then the question is raised as to why they evolve, survive and spread throughout the modern world. The question has been raised by Ronald Coase (1937) as to why firms exist, but the corresponding analysis of markets has not been given nearly as much attention.

The structure of the argument in the present and preceding chapter points at a more specific version of the question: Why do markets exist as opposed to non-market exchange? In other words, why do markets grow up to coordinate and to structure exchange transactions? Clearly, the word 'market' is used here in the sense defined in this chapter, and not in the sense that prevails in orthodox economic theory, otherwise the questions would not have the same meaning. The questions as to why firms sometimes exist as opposed to markets, and conversely why do markets sometimes exist as opposed to firms, are raised in the next chapter.

*Transaction costs*

An obvious answer to the question why markets exist as opposed to exchange is that non-market exchange imposes costs on the transactors that are reduced in the case of markets. In the phraseology that has followed Coase, markets could be said to economize on transaction costs. However, as is substantiated by further discussion below, the idea of transaction costs has become a kind of catch-all phrase and it is not employed with sufficient precision and clarity. Furthermore, the concept has been developed by Oliver Williamson and others in explicit association with a narrow version of calculating, self-seeking and maximizing 'economic man'. Criticisms of these developments are presented in the next chapter. Consequently, in the meantime, we here deal specifically with the problem as to why markets arise and isolated exchanges do not always remain in an unorganized state.

In fact, Coase points to a number of different kinds of cost that are related to the exchange process. In his famous article he cites, for example, the 'cost of discovering what the relevant prices are' (1937, p. 390) and the 'costs of negotiating and concluding a separate contract which takes place on a market' (pp. 390–1). In short, what are involved here are the costs of obtaining relevant information, the cost of bargaining and making decisions, and finally the costs of policing and enforcing contracts.

However, what Coase and other writers fail to note is that all these costs and difficulties are actually reduced in the market as compared to fragmented, non-market exchange. Thus the 'cost of discovering what the relevant prices are' is reduced dramatically through the creation of a market, which of course is here regarded as an organized form of exchange. Markets help to publicize prices and other relevant infor-mation, or help traders to find out the information more easily by establishing contacts between agents. The creation of regularized access to contacts within the market itself reduces costs, by making it easier 'to discover who it is that one wishes to deal with'.

Bargaining 'costs' are likewise reduced because the market helps establish procedures and conventions for reaching a bargain, and agents more easily establish expectations as to what kind of deal can be struck. Furthermore, the deal is likely to be concluded more rapidly when the pressing option of using alternative buyers and sellers is clear to both parties because they are readily at hand.

In the third case, 'policing and enforcement costs' can sometimes be reduced by the market because of its association with norms of conduct and codes of practice amongst the buyers or sellers. In this case the individual alone does not have to ensure that the contract is carried out, but other agencies may help to protect product quality, maintain prompt delivery, and so on. Alternatively, 'policing and enforcement costs' are reduced in the market because transactions where such costs are likely to be high are normally more suitable to specific exchanges outside the market. If, for example, products are standardized or mass-produced then these costs are reduced or shared between many consumers; and standard products are more amenable to market trade. In contrast, specialist contracts can incur high policing or enforcement costs, simply because of their specialist, one-off, nature; and such deals are not so suited to the market.

Consequently, all the reasons that are cited by Coase to explain why market arrangements are more costly than the firm, serve perfectly well as reasons why the market is less costly than atomized exchange. Whilst the Coasian arguments favour the firm over the market in given situations, the same arguments can be turned in favour of the market as against less-structured exchange.[5]

### On the limits to the growth of the market

In his 1937 article Coase rightly raises the question as to why the cost-reducing mechanism of the firm does not grow to replace all transactions and the market itself. Similarly, the question should be raised as to why the market does not grow to engross all exchanges. In other words, if the market reduces costs why is it that all exchange is not organized within a market structure?

However, the answer to this question is not the same as that Coase gives in regard to the firm. He proposes that with the firm there are decreasing returns to scale, imposing limits to its growth and span of control. But there is no obvious or familiar argument why there should be decreasing returns to scale in the case of the market.

A plausible alternative hypothesis is that non-market exchange survives because of its suitability for specialized contracts and heterogeneous products. It is precisely because large-scale buying and selling does not pertain in these cases that the set-up costs of the market outweigh any possible gains.

In other cases the costs of entering the market may be so high that entrants are deterred. A buyer or seller may thus instead rely on personal contact or word of mouth to promote transactions. It is thus possible in certain circumstances that a number of buyers and sellers can continue to trade without using market institutions. Other things being equal, such behaviour is all the more viable if each unit of the commodity yields a high revenue and the number of units demanded is small. There is in addition the possibility that market forms are concentrated in some spheres and not in others, simply out of routine, or other factors could be involved (see note 7, p. 297).

There are thus some possible reasons why non-market exchange may be preserved, and why markets are not ubiquitous. However, it will be argued in the next chapter that a key reason for the survival of non-market exchange is its promotion and sustenance by the firm, for reasons that will be elaborated. Without the existence of the firm there would be a stronger tendency for the market to grow in organization and subsume more acts of exchange.

## 8.3   MARKETS, PRICES AND NORMS

At the outset, the neoclassical theory of the market faced the problem as to how price adjustments are made, and how the supposed equilibrium of prices and quantities is reached within its theoretical framework. Thus Leon Walras developed the well-known fiction of an auctioneer, calling out sets of prices, and adjusting them in response to differences in supply and demand, until markets cleared and an equilibrium was reached. This *deus ex machina* has been resorted to by neoclassical economists ever since.

Leaving aside the unrealism of this assumption of an omnipotent market coordinator for a moment, it is striking that neoclassical theory had to construct such an *institutional* arrangement for their model of a market to work. Thus, despite the common assumption, the Walrasian framework does not actually present the market as an unstructured ether where free-floating individuals collide and interact. As in the case of other institutions the auction arrangement does not only constrain activity but enables action by processing and broadcasting price information.

However, in the neoclassical model the costs of processing and providing this information are, unrealistically, not taken into account.

Even the minimal institutional presence of the auctioneer is overshadowed by the mechanical maximization of all-knowing, costlessly calculating, economic agents. The auction is simply a framework; there is no evidence of institutions in the rich sense, permeated with habit, culture and routine, and where individuals and institutions carry the marks and preconceptions of a historical past.

In addition, there are serious problems once the imaginary institutional framework of the all-knowing auctioneer is removed. Basing himself on Joan Robinson's (1971, 1974) work, Thanos Skouras (1981, pp. 202–4) has developed a line of argument that raises many questions about the mainstream approach.

Consider a market for a commodity, and assume that it is evident that the quantity supplied exceeds the quantity in demand. A consequent price reduction may result from changes made by individual agents. But, as Skouras argues, there is no necessary reason why people will automatically reduce prices in this way. If, for example, 'historical experience leads buyers and sellers to expect that this is an abnormally low price and that it will most likely be higher in the near future, then the price will not fall' (p. 203). Given such experience and expectations, buyers will be willing to buy more and sellers will be willing to sell less, so that the gap between supply and demand will narrow, and may even be reversed so that demand is in excess. And all this may occur whilst the price remains constant.

What is crucial in Skouras' argument is the idea of an expected normal or equilibrium price which is formed, in part, from historical experience. Furthermore:

> The quantity that buyers would be willing to buy and sellers willing to sell at a particular price will be different depending on whether, (1) this price is seen as the equilibrium price, (2) this price is lower than the expected normal price, or (3) the price is higher than the expected normal price. It is evident that in cases (2) and (3) the drawing of demand and supply schedules presupposes a knowledge of the equilibrium price and cannot serve for its determination. Traditional demand and supply analysis, even when enriched by reaction functions giving rise to fluctuations, is built on case (1): buyers and sellers are assumed to react as if any price that is considered might be the equilibrium price. It is in this way that their memory of the past and their expectations about the future are eliminated and it becomes possible to construct curves the intersection of which determines the equilibrium price. (p. 203)

It is, of course, widely accepted that decisions to buy or sell at a given price depend in part on expected prices in the future. But future prices may themselves fluctuate, so the expectation is in the form of a norm, or range of possible prices, that are assumed to prevail at some future period. The question then is how such an expected norm is established.

### The establishment of norms

The obvious orthodox answer would be to suggest some learning experience, based on observations of moving prices. However, if price adjustments were frequent then there are strong arguments to suggest that agents would have difficulty in establishing some expectation of a norm. Ceaseless, incremental, price fluctuations may appear to the observer as little more than 'noise', and even if a sophisticated statistical analysis were readily at hand then it would not necessarily produce a reliable result. Most of the evidence of judgement under uncertainty (Kahneman, Slovic and Tversky 1982) suggests that people do not make such judgements on the basis of Bayesian probability calculations or statistical regressions. Furthermore, given the amount of information involved and the insufficiency of computational speed and capacity (even in the age of the micro-computer), it is difficult to see how people could carry out such computations every time they were appropriate.

Yet in the absence of such expected norms, decisions to buy and sell would appear hazardous or uncertain. For markets to work, some mechanism to establish norms in the minds and practices of agents is required. In some cases, crudely interpreted past experience can fit the bill. There are a large number of day-to-day commodities for which prices are more-or-less stable, and without deliberating upon it we learn the price level and thus come to expect that future prices will be at about a given level. As George Shackle (1972, p. 227) argues in his chapter on 'prices as conventions', prices which 'have stood at particular levels for some time acquire thereby some sanction and authority'.

As Frederic Scherer (1970, pp. 179–82) has pointed out, prices sometimes tend to gravitate around 'focal points' which are often at or below rounded amounts. Thus we will often encounter prices such as £29.95 or £71.00 but we are not likely to find an item with an advertised price of £9602.56. Price norms are likely to be at focal points rather at any arbitrary level.

In many cases, however, prices will not be stable; and even, in some cases, there will be no established focal points and continuous variation will be the normal practice. But even here a broad or narrow range of prices can serve as a norm or a guide. Prices are then evaluated in relation to their position within or outside this range. We can thus generate expectations on the basis of rough-and-ready experience of price movements through historical time.[6]

Even if the day-to-day price of a commodity shifts decisively above or below its preceding norm, as argued above this does not mean that the expected price norm itself will move automatically in the same direction. Clearly, however, few prices are permanently stable, and at some time or another price changes will force norms to adjust. The question then is through what mechanism is the new norm established?

A partial answer proposed here is that market institutions themselves have an important function in establishing norms. This is frequently overlooked because the prevailing conception of a competitive market is one where agents are continuously higgling and haggling, and moving prices incrementally to their mutual advantage. However, even in markets where price alterations are frequent, trading is often structured and information is published so that the formation of norms is possible, so that most agents may accept them as a guideline or convention.

Take the stock market as an example. This is a case of a potentially volatile market where minute-to-minute, incremental adjustments in prices are common. Nevertheless, the Stock Exchange promotes an official listing of closing stock prices for each day, as a guide for buyers and sellers. Even after the so-called 'Big Bang' of 1986, which incidentally is supposed to make the financial market more 'free' and competitive, the London Stock Market still remains a highly structured institution. For example, instead of all transactions being individually and independently priced and publicized, prices are set and adjusted regularly by no more than three dozen 'market makers' and this information is transmitted to jobber/brokers by computer. In a path-breaking empirical study of the trading networks in a securities network, Wayne Baker (1984, p. 775) argues that: 'Trading among actors exhibited distinct social structural patterns that dramatically affected the direction and magnitude of option price volatility.'[7]

We may conclude that even in a potentially volatile market where dramatic price changes are possible, trading is structured and information is published selectively so as to help the formation of price expectations and norms. Indeed, the very complexity and volatility of the price of stocks impels the market institution to publish or sponsor a great deal of guideline information so that agents can cope. Furthermore, informal trading networks between agents also help to establish trading conventions and norms.

In other cases, where prices are less volatile, price information can more directly contribute towards the formation of a norm. It is because prices are stable, and are perceived by agents to be in equilibrium, that the task facing market institutions is less daunting in this respect. However, market institutions may still have many other functions, such as providing information regarding product quality and the location of potential buyers and sellers, and regulating both the product and the entrants to the market. In fact, a crucial function may be more subtle; by ordering trade under the aegis of some institution, the price and quality of the product may be legitimized at its given level. There is a kind of stamp of institutional approval which may contribute in a powerful manner to the emergence of price norms.

In neoclassical theory the only kind of price norm is the *ex post* equilibrium price. It is presumed to be formed after an extensive process of market adjustment and price signalling in logical rather than historical time. In contrast, although the kind of price norm discussed here may be affected by day-to-day prices, in another respect it exists *ex ante*, embedded in institutions and the expectations of individuals, and thus bears upon current prices in historical time.

It is important to note that price norms acquire a moral dimension in the eyes of the purchaser, which further helps to reinforce them in the market. In a random survey of residents of Toronto, Kahneman et al. (1986) discovered that an overwhelming majority of respondents would regard the behaviour of a hardware store as 'unfair' if it raised the price of snow shovels the day after a heavy fall of snow. The study reveals that a price increase is considered acceptable if it reflects a real cost increase, but not if it is simply a response to scarcity. (See also Frey, 1986.)

It could be supposed that the consuming public accepts the legitimacy of a price norm if it is based on costs with the mark-up of a 'reasonable' margin for profits. Consequently, changes in price are acceptable if and only if they likewise reflect costs in some way. The effect on the producer and retailer would be to give strong incentives to conform to this implied ethic of the cost mark-up, and pay much less attention to price adjustments in response to changes in scarcity or sudden increases in demand.

In addition there is evidence of the existence of moral norms in regard to money wages. The slogan 'a fair day's pay for a fair day's work' has a long history, despite being criticized by Marx and others for invoking standards of fairness which simply reflect rather than challenge the underlying asymmetries in the employment relationship.

### The classical tradition

In rehabilitating a type of *ex ante* price norm, in a sense we are returning to the classical tradition of Adam Smith and David Ricardo, with their 'normal' or 'natural' price, and to subsequent developments such as Karl Marx's 'prices of production', and Piero Sraffa's (1960) system of 'values' based on matrices of input–output coefficients.

However, there are important differences between this tradition and the argument in the present book. In the works of Smith, Ricardo, Marx and Sraffa price norms relate to some kind of notional, long-run stationary state where global profit rates and other adjustments are assumed to be fully worked out. They are sometimes assumed to be the 'centres of gravitation' of day-to-day prices. However, 'institutional' price norms are the outcome of a process in historical time, and a mechanical or gravitational analogy is thus misleading. Price norms depend in part on expectations, and the legitimizing and informational functions of institutions. These features make the processes governing their formation irreversible, unlike the processes of classical mechanics. Information problems and irreversible processes have been given little prominence in the 'classical' tradition from Smith to Sraffa, where the focus is instead on the long-period stationary state.[8]

The concept of a price norm that is produced by a market institution has a relevance for the preceding comparison of market and non-market exchange in terms of transaction costs. Such norms are relevant in any cost comparison of market with non-market institutions. The important point here is that the market creates a benchmark, by establishing and publicizing such norms on a widespread basis. In this respect it differs from other institutions such as the firm, or the isolated agreement to exchange. Such a benchmark is necessary to make such comparisons, but outside the market it is essentially lacking. Some of the implications of this point are raised in the next chapter, concerning specifically the use of the notion of transaction costs in explaining the nature and existence of the firm.

## 8.4 THE IMPOSSIBILITY OF PERFECT COMPETITION

At the extreme, and in stark contrast to the institutional picture, the neoclassical concept of 'perfect competition' removes all structures and conventions from the market. In the neoclassical model the continuous marginal adjustment of prices is possible, and indeed necessary, until a market-clearing equilibrium is reached. Any fixed norm or institutional biasing of prices would in theory act as an impediment to this process. The informational content of the norm itself is thereby ignored in the theory.

Over the years, however, a number of arguments and criticisms have been expressed which begin to undermine the neoclassical model. Most of these relate, in some way, to the informational function of conventions, norms or institutions which was discussed more generally in chapter 6 above. Apparently, however, these arguments have been produced independently, and without knowledge of key precedents, by the economic theorists involved.

Frank Knight's famous distinction between risk and uncertainty is an important starting point. In essence the distinction was reproduced by John Maynard Keynes in his *General Theory* and his 1937 article summarizing its main points. Uncertainty, Keynes writes, applies to a situation where 'there is no scientific basis to form any calculable probability whatever' (Keynes, 1973b, p. 114).

In an uncertain world we are, nevertheless, forced to act. Keynes argues that we act very much on the basis of past experience and established convention: 'Knowing that our own individual judgement is worthless, we endeavour to fall back on the judgement of the rest of the world which is perhaps better informed. That is, we endeavour to conform with the behaviour of the majority or the average' (Keynes, 1973b, p. 114).

Yet Keynes applies his argument mainly to investment decisions and to the Stock Exchange, so as to draw out the implications for the aggregate level of output and employment. Less attention is given by Keynes to the implications for all prices and markets. It is in the hands of later Keynesians, such as Joan Robinson and George Shackle that Keynes's argument is placed in the context of markets and prices in general.

An important contribution by Frank Knight and Thornton Merriam (1948) has been noted already. In a key passage, they implied that continuous, rationally motivated adjustment of prices prevented others from forming clear expectations as to what was to happen and from developing clear guidelines upon which to act. 'Without some procedure for coordination, any real activity on the part of the individual, any departure from past routine, must disappoint the expectations and upset the plans of others who count on him to act in a way predicted from his past behaviour' (p. 60).

### The function of conventions

This argument has clear implications on the question of price adjustments within market institutions. But it has remained underdeveloped in economic theory. Several years passed until similar issues were addressed by G. B. Richardson (1959, 1960). He argues that if neoclassical 'perfect competition' did actually exist it could not function for long. The problem being that no individual agent would be aware of the investment intentions of others. The incentive to invest depends in part on the knowledge of a limited competitive supply from other firms, or the establishment of a belief that others do not possess the information regarding the opportunity that is available to the investor. 'Perfect competition' does not provide this. Precisely because of its 'perfection' it places no limit on the number of firms that can be expected to compete. Richardson writes:

> A profit opportunity which is known by and available to everybody is available to nobody in particular. A situation of general profit potential can be tapped by one entrepreneur only if similar action is not intended by too many others; otherwise excess supply and general losses would result. In other words, a general opportunity of this kind will create a reliable profit expectation for a single entrepreneur only if there is some limitation upon the competitive supply to be expected from other producers. (1959, pp. 233–4)

This turns the conventional, neoclassical view inside out. Richardson argues that '"perfect knowledge" . . . would have been no use to the members of the system even if they could ever be assumed to possess it' (1959, p. 236) and the conditions necessary for adequate information are incompatible with perfect competition. He suggests that producers obtain information about the prospective activities of those to whom they are inter-related in a number of possible ways. First, there is explicit collusion or agreement. Second there is implicit collusion: 'a general understanding that no-one will alter what they are doing'. And Third, there are 'frictions', 'imperfections' and 'restraints', which, although they appear to stand in the way of 'free competition', are actually in some measure necessary to make the market system function at all.

A possible defence of the neoclassical model is that if an efficient futures market were to develop then, by observing this market, agents would be able to calculate the viability of an investment project, and thus the problem of inability to foresee the number of competing investors would be alleviated. The adjustments of supply and demand in such a market would create an equilibrium where future investment projects are neither under- nor over-subscribed.

However, there are a number of reasons why this defence should be rejected. First, a futures market cannot work this efficiently if agents are unable to ascribe a meaningful probability to each future state or event, or even more seriously if the outcome itself is not known to be possible. Furthermore, a futures market cannot exist at all in the case of not-yet-invented commodities which do not exist either in fact or in imagination. Consequently, in a world of uncertainty, where the relevant probabilities are unobtainable, or many possible outcomes are simply unknown, futures markets cannot solve the problem that Richardson identifies.

Finally, if futures markets did exist for every possible state of the world and every conceivable commodity, there is the problem of coping with all the information in the many markets and thereby making a global, rational calculation. The existence of bounded rationality, given the limited computational capacity available, puts such a solution out of reach.[9]

Arguably, therefore, Richardson's argument depends implicitly upon the assumption that uncertainty is present, or that rationality is bounded, or both. In contrast to the fully specified general equilibrium model of Kenneth Arrow and Gerard Debreu, where contracts concerning the future are part of the 'single gigantic once-for-all "higgle-haggle"' (Meade, 1971, p. 166), Richardson's argument takes into account the process of decision-making in real time.

Richardson argues that the model of perfect competition that is found in mainstream economic theory is unconvincing because it does not work. It is readily admitted by neoclassical theorists that perfect competition does not exist. Richardson's argument, however, is that it would not actually be viable if it did.[10]

As a consequence, the mainstream view of rigidities and constraints has to be reversed. Far from always preventing the system from working efficiently, they often play a functional role in a modern economy. This idea is implied in some passages of Keynes' work, but never developed to the full. However, it has been taken up by some modern Post-Keynesians. Thus Jan Kregel (1980) argues that because of uncertainty regarding the future:

> the information required for rational decision making does not exist; the market mechanism cannot provide it. But, just as nature abhors a vacuum, the economic system abhors uncertainty. The system reacts to the absence of the information the market cannot provide by creating uncertainty-reducing institutions: wage contracts, debt contracts, supply agreements, administered prices, trading agreements. Since all are meant to reduce uncertainty over time, it is natural that their value be denominated in the unit whose value is most stable over time – money – or . . . in terms of the durable whose own rate of return declines least rapidly with an increase in demand. (Kregel, 1980, p. 46)

Kregel's presentation of the argument has strong functionalist overtones (e.g. 'the system reacts . . . by creating . . .'), but his point is still well made and it can survive their removal. His discussion of money can find a more obvious connection with the work of Keynes. In chapter 17 of the *General Theory* it is suggested that the rigidity of the money wage is not necessarily disadvantageous. He argues that if money wages fell easily then this might create disruptive expectations of a further fall.

However, these ideas were not fully developed by Keynes, and his microeconomic theory remains largely on marginalist foundations.

The discussion of price norms is again relevant in this context. Without the informational assistance of such norms it would be difficult to establish meaningful expectations of the future. Price norms thus help the market-based economy to operate in a world where agents have limited knowledge.

Consequently, the (partial) rigidity of prices and wages should not be treated as a restrictive assumption to be imposed upon a 'more general' model. Rigidities are not a 'special case'. These so-called 'imperfections' help to impose coherence and order on the market system. Markets function coherently *because of* these 'imperfections', and not *despite* them as mainstream theorists presume. Such 'imperfections' are an integral part of the analysis discussed here.

*The game-theoretic analysis of markets*

The above arguments, gleaned from the work of Knight, Keynes, Richardson and others, are all centred on the concept of uncertainty. It is quite possible, however, to approach some of these conclusions by a different route.

The key development here is the application of game theory to the study of economic institutions and norms, primarily represented by the pioneering work of Andrew Schotter (1981). In a game-theoretic framework agents have the choice of different strategies to obtain the maximum payoff. The model of agent is still that of maximizing 'economic man': the only slight difference being that he or she is no longer programmed by preferences and constraints to achieve a single, determined outcome. Agents maximize, but they may, for example, mix strategies randomly in certain proportions as they seek to optimize.

Schotter does not refer to the preceding works of Richardson and others that are in the same vein. His work follows a development in game theory where agents' strategies are not confined to a single 'game'. Instead the focus is on recurrent supergames, i.e. games that are played repeatedly over and over again.[11] It is argued that as the games 'are repeatedly played, the players develop certain societally agreed to rules of thumb, norms, conventions and institutions which are passed on to succeeding generations of players' (p. 12).

Within this framework, Schotter shows that institutions and routines are, far from being market 'imperfections', actually necessary to supply vital information, particularly about the future strategems of other agents. Whether through evolution or conscious design, institutions provide rich information upon which agents can develop expectations regarding the future behaviour of other actors.

In contrast, if action were unstructured and completely fluid it would be much more difficult, by observing behaviour that was subject to continuous change, to form such expectations. The neoclassical model of price adjustment under perfect competition is a case in point. In this ideal case, information is signalled principally through the price system. This provides information regarding resource supply and demand. In contrast, if there are market restrictions and 'imperfections', much more information is transmitted, and other than through price. The web of institutions within and around the market place serve as 'mechanisms that supply information about the potential actions of other economic agents' (p. 157).

The parallel with the work of Richardson is evident. Both authors give reasons why the model of perfect competition cannot work. Richardson's argument centres on investment, but Schotter's is based on a more general consideraion of the informational function of institutions. Both authors argue that a market where there are 'restrictive' rules and conventions provides more information for agents and is more viable in operation. The attraction of Schotter's argument for many economic theorists will be its extensive formal basis in game theory, and the fact that it does not require that the model of maximizing 'economic man' should be abandoned.

In a later work, Schotter (1985) highlights the important policy conclusions of his theory, in terms of a critique of the 'free-market' economics of the New Right.[12] Clearly, his argument that institutions and rigid conventions are actually functional to the decision-making process, both inside and outside the market, is a counter to the New Right view that as much as possible all such rigidities and conventions should be dissolved.

Consider the New Right crusade to enlarge the sphere of the market at the expense of frictions and rigidities in the system, such as trade unions and fixed exchange rates. The above arguments suggest that these frictions and rigidities are not as dispensable as 'free-market' advocates assume. The vision of a perfectly competitive and 'free' market system is thus an unattainable utopia of the Right.

In Schotter's (1985) work his analysis is described as an 'immanent critique' of neoclassical theory, because it shares some of its basic assumptions but draws untypical conclusions. It is as an internal critique that Schotter's work is best appraised. Arguably, game theory cannot serve as a wider foundation for an economic theory of social institutions, partly because of its continuing adoption of the assumptions of maximizing 'economic man', and partly because it does not fully express the extent of information problems in the real world.

It was noted above that the existence of futures markets could be said to overcome some of the difficulties in forming expectations in the neoclassical theory. However, it was also noted that in a world of uncertainty and bounded rationality such futures markets would not overcome these difficulties, and institutions and conventions would still play an essential role in the formation of expectations of the future. The question then is can Schotter's work be enriched, and protected from the neoclassical counter-argument, by introducing uncertainty and bounded rationality? It would appear that, unlike the work of Richardson, it is difficult to overcome the futures market counter-argument in this manner in Schotter's models, because of their dependence on game theory.

Despite a brief reference to bounded rationality (1981, pp. 148–9), Schotter underlines a standard assumption of game theory that agents make use of '*all* relevant information', and nothing is ignored in the determination of their optimal strategy (p. 160). However, as Herbert Simon argues, such global calculations are impossible because of the limited computational capacity of any computer or human brain. A function of institutions that has been discussed already in chapter 6 is that they facilitate actions when such global calculations are impossible.

Uncertainty does not play a central role in game theory because the actors are aware of both the menu of strategic options and the payoffs in each case. As George Shackle (1972, ch. 36) points out in his critique, game theory excludes the phenomenon of tactical surprise: 'Surprise is the exploitation of the opponent's lack of knowledge, or of his reliance on what he wrongly believes to be knowledge' (p. 423). In reality, Shackle argues, the 'most powerful resource available to a real-life contestant may be to exploit the ignorance of . . . contestants concerning the ultimate conditions of the contest' (p. 426). For this reason the structure of competition and markets is not adequately represented by the game-theoretic tableau.

More generally, Schotter's theory highlights some of the important functions of institutions and conventions, but throws insufficient light on the processes through which an institution grows and dies. It is simply assumed that an institution will arise because it is efficacious in the context of rational behaviour by agents. In excluding surprise, the possibility of institutional breakdown through the disruption of conventions and routines is not explored.[13]

A more adequate theory of institutions will have to place more emphasis on the functions of habit and routine in the growth of transformation of institutions. However, as Richardson's argument suggests, the demonstration of the place of restrictions and constraints in enabling the market system to function is likely to be the centrepiece of such a theory.

In sum, however, we should not underestimate the collective significance of these game-theoretic developments. For the first time they raise a serious and sustained challenge to the treatment of the market in mainstream economics. If they were to be developed and improved then the unrestrained free-market presumptions of much economic theory would be substantially undermined.

# 9

# Firms and Markets

Undoubtedly, labor, land and money markets *are* essential to a market economy. But no society could stand the effects of such a system of crude fictions even for the shortest stretch of time unless its human and natural substance as well as its business organization was protected against the ravages of this satanic mill.

Karl Polanyi (1957, p. 73)

The renewed interest in the economics of institutions has brought fundamental questions about the nature of the firm to the fore. In particular the traditional neoclassical explanation for the existence of the firm has been found to be deficient. It is the purpose of this chapter to address some of these questions and critically review some of the related developments in the literature. Furthermore, we shall raise some aspects of the firm which are neglected both in orthodox theory and some modern developments. A conclusion is that the foundations of the theory of the firm have to be rebuilt radically if we are to take account of these considerations.

First of all, however, it is pointed out that essential to the 'markets-as-institutions' argument in the preceding chapter is a distinction between those institutions which are, and are not, markets. If the distinction has any meaning it is important that these two sets of institutions are examined and compared. An important type of non-market institution is the capitalist firm. As Karl Marx (1976, p. 132) pointed out long ago, within firms there is a division of labour but no internal exchange of commodities between its members. Consequently, the firm is distinguished from the market. Likewise, some recent literature in economics stresses the unique features of the firm, the labour contract, or the labour market, and thus a distinction between market and non-market institutions is in a manner sustained.

A prominent feature of the firm in the work of Marx is that it is characterized by internal authority relations: 'the worker works under the control of the capitalist to whom his labour belongs' (1976, p. 291). This contrasts with the apparent freedom and equality in the market: that 'very eden of the innate rights of man . . . the exclusive realm of Freedom, Equality, Property and Bentham' (p. 280).[1] These ironic phrases suggest that, for Marx at least, the authoritarian relations within the firm are quite different from the freedom and formal equality which in appearance pertain to legal rights in the market. Clearly, in this analysis and others, there is a recognition that two very different types of institution are involved. It is in an important challenge to this essential distinction that discussion in this chapter is commenced.

## 9.1   NEOCLASSICAL PERSPECTIVES ON THE FIRM

*Alchian and Demsetz: the firm as a market*

Challenging this distinction, Armen Alchian and Harold Demsetz (1972) have taken a very different view. They argue that there is no vital distinction between ordinary market exchange and the organization and allocation of resources within the firm.[2] They deny that there is any essential difference between the exchange of everyday commodities in the market and the employment contract within the firm: 'Telling an employee to type this letter rather than to file that document is like my telling a grocer to sell me this brand of tuna rather than that brand of bread' (Alchian and Demsetz, 1972, p. 777). Their article has proved to be highly influential and the characterization of the firm mainly as a set of contracts has been extended in various directions by a number of other theorists.[3]

An important consequence of this argument is a rejection of the idea that there is any specific form of power or authority relation between employer and employee within the firm. Alchian and Demsetz argue repeatedly that the firm

> has no power of fiat, no authority, no disciplinary action any different in the slightest degree from ordinary market contracting between any two people . . . To speak of managing, directing, or assigning workers to various tasks is a deceptive way of noting that the employer continually is involved in renegotiation of contracts on terms that must be acceptable to both parties. (p. 777)

Whilst the management may appear to have authority over the worker, they argue that in reality the relation is symmetrical, it is 'simply a "quid pro quo" contract. Each makes a purchase and a sale' (p. 783). According to Alchian and Demsetz, the employee can be said to 'order' the employer to pay the agreed wage as much as the employer can be said to 'order' the employee to perform certain acts. Just as the employer can terminate the agreement and 'fire' the employee, the conception is that the employee can 'fire' the employer and leave the job.

The only major difference between the firm and the market that is recognized by Alchian and Demsetz is the importance of team production by workers and the consequent difficulty of metering and rewarding their individual contributions to the collective effort. Their argument is that there is a need for a 'monitor' to minimize 'shirking' amongst the workforce. In turn, to ensure that the 'monitor' does his or her job well, the view is expressed that this central party should have the right to enjoy the profits that are made by the firm.

The 'monitor' (i.e. employer) makes profits 'not only by the prices that he agrees to pay the owners of the inputs, but also by observing and directing the actions or uses of those inputs' (p. 782). Thus, one of the important functions of the employer is that of gathering information, including data on the performance of employees. But as a consequence of this very feature 'the firm takes on the characteristic of an efficient market in that information about the productive characteristics of a large set of specific inputs is now more cheaply available' (p. 795). The employer is thereby regarded as an orchestrator of a 'market' within the firm.

As already noted above, Alchian and Demsetz view the employment contract as being subject to 'continuous renegotiation' (p. 794). Indeed, they have to take such a view to deal with the fact that employment contracts are never fully or perfectly specified at the outset, and have to cover complex and unforeseen contingencies. Presumably, therefore, the terms of employment are being 'implicitly' bargained over for every instant of working time.

The problems involved in reckless suggestions of an implicit contract where no explicit negotiation or agreement is involved have been raised in the preceding chapter. Appropriately, Hans Nutzinger (1976, p. 232) draws the parallel between the Alchian and Demsetz treatment of the employment relation and Samuel Seabury's characterization and justification of slavery as an implicit contract between master and slave. It is notable that orthodox economists can claim, on the one hand, such attachment to notions such as choice and individual freedom and then, on the other, over-ride the problem of the lack of explicit individual consent without scruple.

Implicit contracts may be deemed to exist in limited cases. However, it is highly contentious to suggest that they can include instances where a full, explicit contract is impossible. It is in the nature of the employment contract that substantive and detailed negotiation over its every feature is not feasible because of the degree of uncertainty and complexity involved in the labour process.

This is the primary reason why Marx's distinction between labour power (the capacity to work) and labour (the activity of work itself) retains such importance. The arrangement in the employment contract is that labour power is hired, and the worker submits to an authority relation, so that the manager can decide when required the pattern and nature of work. It is the very impossibility of concluding a full, explicit contract in advance that necessitates some such alternative arrangement. The capitalist economy has evolved a solution to the problem in the form of a broad contract of employment which allows the direction of labour by management within the firm, but in a manner that is not completely specified in advance.[4]

By suggesting that the employment contract is one of continuous renegotiation, Alchian and Demsetz fail to note and understand the function of the asymmetrical authority relation inside the firm. Furthermore, their model suggests that the over-riding problem of uncertainty and complexity in the context of the organization of labour can be ignored by its construction of a continuously renegotiated contract. The time and resources wasted in actually renegotiating the contract on the shop floor to the extent suggested would be prohibitive, leaving aside the likely disruption of group consensus and team solidarity amongst the workforce that would result from the near-constant protrusion at work of the higgle-haggle of trade. Again, in cavalier fashion, an article that even has 'information costs' in its title, suggests implicitly that such problems of negotiation and information can be disregarded.

The argument here is that the employment contract is distinctive in that it is not fully or perfectly specified in advance, and in that, and partly for this reason, it invests a measure of authority in the management during working time. It has both explicit and implicit features; but it is not, and cannot be, continuously renegotiated or evaluated by calculating agents in the manner of the Alchian–Demsetz model.

If we were to apply this model elsewhere, not simply to the firm but also to the family, the state and other institutions, it would be discovered that 'markets' were everywhere. If an arrangement as complex and informal as the employment contract can be regarded as a continuously renegotiated implicit contract then we should have no problems with finding 'implicit contracts' elsewhere, such as in relations of marriage, parenthood or government. Essentially, the distinction between exchanges and gifts, and between market and non-market institutions would be lost, and the term 'market', by being universal, would have little substantive meaning.

One reason why the work of Oliver Williamson and his followers is superior to that of Alchian and Demsetz is that a distinction between market and non-market institutions is firmly upheld. Instead of the firm being, in essence, a market, there is a 'creative tension' between markets and hierarchic organizations such as the capitalist firm (Williamson, 1975). The employment relation is said to be different from the grocer–consumer relation because employees have unique personal skills which are not completely known in advance. Such 'job idiosyncracies' rule out, for example, open spot market negotiation of labour contracts on a continuous basis (Williamson, Wachter and Harris 1975). The result is that there is a clear conceptual distinction between the market and other institutions such as the firm. Unfortunately, however, as is elaborated below, there are other serious deficiencies in Williamson's account.

### Why do firms exist?

The earlier work of Ronald Coase (1937) makes an equivalent conceptual distinction between the firm and the market. A question raised by Coase was: Why do firms exist? For him the key feature of the firm is its internal 'supersession of the price mechanism' (p. 389) and the allocation of resources by command rather than price. The question as to why firms exist then becomes the question as to why it is that the price mechanism is not used to allocate resources within the firm itself. For instance, why is it not normally the case that each worker, or group of workers, trades the partly-finished product with colleagues, until it reaches completion? Instead, the firm supplants such a mechanism by organizing relations differently, without such exchanges.

As Coase puts it: 'Outside the firm, price movements direct production, which is co-ordinated through a series of exchange transactions on the market. Within a firm, these market transactions are eliminated and in place of the complicated market structure with exchange transactions is substituted the entrepreneur–co-ordinator, who directs production' (1937, p. 388). Coase's aim was then to explain why this occurred.

His answer is as follows:

> The main reason why it is profitable to establish a firm would seem to be that there is a cost of using the price mechanism. The most obvious cost of 'organising' production through the price mechanism is that of discovering what the relevant prices are . . . The costs of negotiating

and concluding a separate contract for each exchange transaction which takes place on the market must also be taken into account . . . It is true that contracts are not eliminated when there is a firm but they are greatly reduced. A factor of production (or the owner thereof) does not have to make a series of contracts with the factors with whom he is co-operating within the firm, as would be necessary, of course, if this co-operation were as a direct result of the working of the price mechanism. (pp. 390–1)

Following on from this approach, Williamson has developed his central thesis that economic institutions such as the firm 'have the main purpose and effect of economizing on transaction costs' (Williamson, 1985, p. 1). Thus Williamson's explanation of the existence of non-market institutions is that they arise because they are less costly than continuous recourse to the market or exchange. Thus he too endorses a conceptual difference between the market itself and the non-market institution of the firm.

Williamson puts the emphasis onto the crucial concept of 'transaction costs'.[5] But this is not without its problems. As Stanley Fischer (1977, p. 322) writes: 'Transaction costs have a well-deserved bad name as a theoretical device, because solutions to problems involving transaction costs are often sensitive to the assumed form of the costs, and because there is a suspicion that almost anything can be rationalized by invoking suitably specified transaction costs.'

Notably, in a large number of publications in the area of 'transaction costs economics' since the mid-1970s, Williamson has failed to provide an adequate definition of transaction costs themselves. It is not that he has failed to recognize the problem. In one article it is noted that 'the concept wants for definition' (1979, p. 233) but he then proceeds not to define the term but to list a set of 'factors' which relate to the mode of analysis.[6] The nearest that Williamson actually gets to a definition in his latest major work is by quoting Kenneth Arrow's vague characterization of transaction costs as the 'costs of running the economic system' (Arrow, 1969, p. 48). Williamson (1985, p. 19) then follows this with an analogy: 'Transaction costs are the economic equivalent of friction in physical systems.' Whatever the value of this analogy,[7] it is still not a definition. The failure to provide a definition of such a crucial term is symptomatic of the lack of precision in much of Williamson's work.[8]

Carl Dahlman (1979) is much more analytically precise in examining these concepts. He notes that the idea of transaction costs 'has become a catch-all phrase for unspecified interferences with the price mechanism' (p. 144).[9] Furthermore, the typical formal representation of transaction costs among mathematical economists, as a fixed proportion of the value of the goods that are exchanged, is seen to differ 'in no significant way' from a regular transportation cost. This hardly seems to be a sound innovation upon which an economic theory of institutions can be based.

### Transaction costs and lack of information

Usefully, Dahlman turns back to Coase's work to explore the matter further. In an article published in 1960, transaction costs were clarified by Coase in the following terms:

> In order to carry out a market transaction it is necessary to discover who it is that one wishes to deal with, to inform people that one wishes to deal and on what terms, to conduct negotiations leading up to a bargain, to draw up a contract, to undertake the inspection needed to make sure that the terms of the contract are being observed, and so on.

In his commentary on this passage, Dahlman (1979, p. 148) suggests that three types of cost are involved, corresponding to three different, sequential phases of the exchange process, namely: 'search and information costs, bargaining and decision costs, policing and enforcement costs.' However, 'this functional taxonomy of different transaction costs is unnecessarily elaborate: fundamentally, the three classes reduce to a single one – for they all have in common that they represent resource losses due to lack of information'.

Consequently, for example, bargaining and decision costs are seen to represent resources spent in finding information concerning commodities and their supply and demand. 'Policing and enforcement costs are incurred because there is a lack of knowledge as to whether one (or both) of the parties involved in the agreement will violate his part of the bargain.' Thus, in Dahlman's view, all forms of transaction cost reduce to one; essentially a cost incurred due to lack of information. This argument thus reduces the complexity of issues to one dimension alone, providing another example, as noted in a preceding chapter, of 'informational reductionism'.[10]

It can be accepted that for purposes of theoretical clarification, Dahlman's argument is an important step forward; but many problems still remain and it is not entirely clear what a complete reduction of costs to those of information could mean. Indeed it could be fitted neatly into a neoclassical framework. Following the lead of George Stigler's classic (1961) article, search and information costs could be accommodated alongside, and treated similarly to, other costs in a probabalistic framework. In this approach information is treated just like any other commodity, and subject to the marginalist rule that its consumption is optimal when the marginal cost of information search and acquisition is equal to its expected marginal return.

On reflection, however, the very idea of a rational calculus of information costs is open to objection. If we lack a piece of relevant information then how can we have any firm expectation of its marginal return? The very fact that the information is lacking means at most that such expectations are hazy and ill-defined.[11]

Furthermore, with such a treatment of information it is not clear why market contracting is superseded by the organization of the firm. After all, if information is simply a commodity like any other, there is no apparent special rationale for the firm to act as the minimizer of these information-related transaction costs. Seemingly it would be possible to deal with such information problems through the due process of contract and trade.

Consider a model of productive organization of individual contractors all trading semi-finished products with each other, and each making marginal adjustments to deal with information costs along the lines proposed by Stigler. What has to be shown in this case is that some kind of economy of information costs can be obtained by organizing the agents together under an institutional umbrella. But it is still not clear why such an institution should be a firm, and not merely an association of producer-traders who pool relevant information.

More specifically, 'search and information costs' could be reduced substantially by a market research agency under contract from the producer-trader association, 'bargaining and decision costs' could be reduced by a team of consultants, and 'policing and enforcement costs' could be brought down by pooling information regarding the credit, performance and other reliability ratings of the agents involved. It is widely recognized (e.g. Wilson, 1975) that informational economies of scale are substantial, so why is it that such syndicates of independent producers should not arise to minimize the information costs that they would each face on their own, and thus obviate the need for the capitalist firm?

It is not immediately clear that such a syndicate would be more or less efficient than the capitalist firm in reducing such costs, but it is clearly more efficient than a mere aggregation of producer-traders. Thus the 'information costs' version of the transaction costs argument still fails to supply a convincing reason for the existence of the capitalist firm and for the relative rarity of alternative arrangements, such as the syndicate, in real life.

Not only is the above type of argument ineffective in providing a rationale for the firm, but also the treatment of information is itself unsatisfactory. There is no distinction made between sense data and information. There is no regard made to the processes of assessment or computation with given information, which can lead to different conclusions depending on the method of calculation and the cognitive framework. As Robin Matthews (1986, p. 906) points out there are purely cognitive 'costs' of organizing and monitoring transactions, such as the calculation of the bill, which arise even if the honesty of the transacting party is not in doubt. It is well known, for example, that the firm's balance sheet is capable of different interpretations and even different 'bottom line' statements of profit and loss, depending on the interpretations and methodology of the accountant.

These examples raise the problem, as Jim Tomlinson (1986, p. 239) points out, of treating 'information in a "positivist" manner, i.e. as a set of facts, indifferent to any problems of the conceptual frameworks which are necessarily involved'. The conception of transaction costs in the work of Williamson and others ignores the fact that the evidence concerning such costs has to be interpreted by the economic actors, and such interpretations will involve frameworks of cognition that may vary from actor to actor.

Thus, for example, in making a decision as to which production process is superior, 'this is not a case where if enough resources are devoted to acquiring the information the unchallengeable, brute facts can eventually be stated' (Tomlinson, 1986, p. 239). Tomlinson points out that cost figures are inherently the products of particular methods of accounting or calculation, such as on the allocation of overheads and the scale of depreciation. Thus even if we are dealing with past information which is apparently 'given' to the agent, divergences of cognitive interpretation are likely to be involved. Information is not like a fluid which flows from reality to become knowledge stored in a tank in the human brain.

The consequences of this rejection of the positivistic conception of information and knowledge have significance for the conception of transaction costs. It is impossible to reduce them simply to problems of 'information', despite the fact that questions of information and knowledge are indeed central to the existence of the firm.

## 9.2 NOTES TOWARDS AN ALTERNATIVE PERSPECTIVE

### Uncertainty and transaction costs

Richard Langlois (1984) recognizes Dahlman's contribution and tries to overcome the problems in an information-based theory of transaction costs. He takes the view that 'having collapsed all such costs into the lack-of-information category, we now need to make new distinctions within this category if we are to explain internal-organization modes.'

Langlois correctly notes that 'some sorts of lack of information are entirely consistent with a fully price-decentralized market contract mode' (p. 28). For example, a lack of information is implied in a probabalistic or contingent-claims formulation of general equilibrium analysis, and as Brian Loasby (1976) has argued, there is no need in theory for non-market forms of organization in this conception. In other words, the probabilistic version of general equilibrium theory, which implies information problems of a stylized and limited kind, gives no reason why firms, as such, should exist.

Langlois' solution to this problem is to make a distinction between different kinds of information problem which parallels Frank Knight's (1933) famous distinction between risk and uncertainty. Langlois prefers, however, to use the terms 'parametric' and 'structural' uncertainty instead. Parametric uncertainty refers to lack of knowledge regarding the parameters of the problem. This type of uncertainty can exist in the neoclassical model. In this case parametric uncertainty is combined with knowledge of the structure of the problem and all possible states of the world. Structural uncertainty, on the other hand, suggests lack of information about the fundamental nature of the problem and the type of outcomes that are possible. This type of uncertainty is not encompassed by neoclassical theory.

In short, Langlois argues that parametric uncertainty cannot be used to find the source of transaction costs which are relevant to the explanation of the relative efficiency of organizations such as a firm. The Alchian and Demsetz model provides an argument based on parametric uncertainty for internal organization of a limited sort, but it cannot explain the full extent of internal organization within the firm. Langlois proposes that the most solid comparative-efficiency explanations for internal organization ultimately reduce to an explanation based on the existence of incomplete structural knowledge. If the problem were simply lack of parametric knowledge then there would be no need for the firm, as all activities could be covered by contingent contracts and exchanges.

A similar argument is presented by Neil Kay (1984) in a more extensive work. He shows that in a neoclassical world of perfect knowledge the firm is stripped of most, if not all, of its familiar structures and functions. Furthermore, there is no decisive difference if problems of probabilistic risk (or 'parametric uncertainty') are introduced, because there 'is a close affinity between perfect knowledge and risk in terms of homogeneity and replicability of associated events'. He concludes: 'True uncertainty and information costs represent the dominant consideration in areas of firm, market and state organization' (p. 83).[12]

An important feature of this line of argument is that it does not rely on the conception of the human agent as opportunistic. Consider, as an example, the possibility of a person reneging on a half-completed contract. As Langlois (1984) argues, the problem here is not fundamentally one of opportunism *per se*: it is because one party to the contract is uncertain if the other will renege or not. The other person may, or may not, be opportunistic and self-seeking; that is a secondary question.

Indeed, it might even be possible that he or she might break the contract for altruistic rather than selfish reasons, to express solidarity with victims of apartheid or to protest against the fur trade, for example. Strictly, the question of opportunism is not the basic issue. The key point is the existence of the uncertainty as to whether or not the contract will be completed. Consequently, Williamson's emphasis on opportunism as the central element of transaction costs is quite inappropriate.

In the light of the theoretical developments mentioned above, it seems that an answer to Coase's question as to why firms exist is emerging in terms of some radical and non-probabalistic concept of uncertainty. Transaction costs may or may not remain an intermediate category in the argument. But it is clear from the above discussion that transaction costs are not sustainable without some concept of radical uncertainty, and this, either directly or indirectly, seems to be a necessary concept to explain the existence of the firm.

## Uncertainty, institutions and the firm

As suggested elsewhere, the introduction of the concept of real uncertainty makes possible an alternative line of theoretical development along institutionalist lines. The argument, in short, is that in a world of uncertainty, where the probabilistic calculus is ruled out, rules, norms and institutions play a functional role in providing a basis for decision-making, expectation, and belief. Without these 'rigidities', without social routine and habit to reproduce them, and without institutionally conditioned conceptual frameworks, an uncertain world would present a chaos of sense data in which it would be impossible for the agent to make sensible decisions and to act.

In previous chapters it has been noted that such an argument is found, often in elliptic form, in the writings of several Keynesian writers who see uncertainty as a centrepiece of the story. It should be stressed that, contrary to the more frequent interpretation, the argument in this work is not that an emphasis on the concept of uncertainty leads to a subjectivist outlook regarding individual knowledge and the springs of action. In contrast, as Tony Lawson (1985) has argued, there is a view in Keynes' own writings which stresses the function of social conventions in providing a basis upon which to form expectations of the future and to act accordingly. We cope with uncertainty not simply on the basis of our own subjective resources, but with conscious or habitual recourse to the rules and conventions with which we interact.

We may observe the relevance of this for the theory of the firm by asking the question as to the basis upon which any such cost calculations could be carried out. Here the distinction that was made in the preceding chapter between different forms of exchange, including market exchange, is relevant. It was argued that one significant function of market institutions was to create perceptible price norms. In contrast, in the case of non-market exchange, there are no comparable mechanisms for their formation. *A fortiori*, within the firm, where exchange proper is generally absent, price information and price norms are even more elusive. Consequently, rational calculation of costs and benefits becomes less operational as we move away from market institutions, to the extent that it is severely occluded by the absence of information regarding values or costs.

To put it differently: The rational calculus of (transaction) costs is appropriate for the market because it rapidly generates and promulgates (variable) norms and conventions to deal with uncertainty. In contrast, although it is assumed that transaction costs may be reduced, rational calculation on the basis of value and cost is actually much less feasible and meaningful within the firm. There, active agents face all kinds of uncertainties, including those presented under the preceding discussion. But the important point is that the institutional 'solution' to the problems of uncertainty within the firm is not the same as that of the market.

There are at least two major differences. First, market institutions create and legitimate norms through the interaction of relatively autonomous traders typically without long-term commitments to each other. By contrast, the firm is a social institution which generates other conventions and rules (e.g. loyalty) on a more permanent basis. Second, the norms and conventions of the market relate, most crucially, to the matter of price. Within the firm, however, there is no single, clear quantitative expression of a price norm or convention to which actors can relate.

Note that the type of analysis that is presented by Coase and Williamson is essentially neoclassical in that it does not make use of norms and conventions and relies on an ubiquitous calculation of 'costs'. 'In the beginning', writes Williamson (1975, p. 20) 'there were markets'. But there can be no such beginning as the market itself involves socially generated procedures and norms. The market is not a 'state of nature' as Williamson implies, but a social institution. Indeed the procedure that is common to the work of many economists, that one starts from the 'failures' of the competitive market in order to explain the existence of firms and other institutions, ignores the problem that one has first to explain the institutional conditions that are necessary for the establishment of a competitive market itself.

The common view is that the market is a kind of summation of individual actors, without a prior institutional framework. It is also suggested that price information is obtained not through the continuous process of the creation and adjustment of norms, but through the gravitation to equilibrium along neoclassical lines. However, without a theory of rules and norms it is more difficult to explain or interpret the activities within the firm because market adjustments of supply and demand do not occur there. When these activities are explained it is not primarily in terms of prices and costs but in terms of the structures and methods of administration and control. Thus there is a 'measurement problem' in comparing the firm with the market in terms of the relative 'costs' of making transactions.

The consequence is not simply that the actors face uncertainty within the firm, but also that rational calculation of costs and benefits is there, by comparison, much less appropriate. *The function of the firm is, therefore, not simply to minimize transaction costs, but to provide an institutional framework within which, to some extent, the very calculus of costs is superseded.*

In this regard there must be some reservations about any explanation of the nature of the firm in terms of transaction costs. The first is that the concept is based upon the idea of the universal, calculating subject, which, in general terms, has been criticized in part two. The second is that in the particular case of the firm the appropriateness of rational calculation is less than it would be in the case of the market, because calculation must necessarily be based on socially generated cost norms, and these are not readily available as we move away from the market sphere.

These reservations do not dismiss the use of the transaction costs idea altogether, in part because rational calculation has not been dismissed in its entirety. What has been stressed is the functional necessity of additional mechanisms which may be unconscious, habitual or cognitive. And within the firm there is certainly some calculation of the cost and benefits of given activities. The conclusion must be that the idea of transaction costs, whilst illuminating, is not a sufficient basis for a theory of the nature of the firm.

What must be incorporated in the theory is the function of the firm in reproducing and developing the habits and routines which are appropriate as an alternative to the optimizing, rational calculus of profit and loss. The nature of the firm is not simply a minimizer of transaction costs, but a kind of protective enclave from the potentially volatile and sometimes destructive, ravaging speculation of a competitive market. In the market the rational calculus depends upon the fragile price convention, which can often depend on 'whim or sentiment or chance' (Keynes, 1971b, p. 163). Habits and traditions within the firm are necessarily more enduring because they embody skills and information which cannot always or easily be codified or made subject to a rational calculus. What the firm achieves is an institutionalization of these rules and routines within a durable organizational structure. In consequence they are given some degree of permanence, and guarded to some extent from the moody waves of speculation in the market.

As Thorstein Veblen perceived long ago, and Richard Nelson and Sidney Winter (1982) have argued more recently, the firm has an ability to store and reproduce a large number of gene-like habits and routines. Thus the firm contains a great mass of skills and technologies upon which its productive capabilities depend. Whilst the firm too will change and evolve, sometimes even with rapidity, internally it is not subject to the buffeting waves of sometimes inexplicable speculation which are characteristic of volatile markets where agents relate to each other with more tenuous and short-term commitments.

### The comparative efficiency of the firm

Without attempting to create a fully fledged, alternative account of the existence and nature of the firm, some suggestions emerge which in part account for its relative efficiency.

Consider the alternative, hypothetical case of the atomized contracting mode, where the firm does not exist and individual producers each trade their finished or semi-finished products. In this case individual exchanges either take place outside the market and without the use of established norms which are legitimized and in a sense 'checked' by the market, or they take place on the market proper and are subjected to its ebbs and flows of speculation. Both alternatives have disadvantages when compared with the firm.

It is possible to put some of these disadvantages under the heading of 'transaction costs'. But an important difference between the argument here and the type of analysis presented by Coase and Williamson is that theirs involves comparative statics, involving partial equilibrium comparisons along Marshallian lines;[13] whereas the present argument conceives of market and extra-market exchange as an ongoing and variable *process*.

Thus we are not simply dealing with the existence of supposed 'costs' when comparing the 'equilibrium' situations of the market and the firm, it is also being noted that the processes of competition and exchange are potentially corrosive for the habits and routines which transmit skills and keep production going, and the existence of the firm can in part be explained by its ability to protect and sustain these routines within its institutional framework.

The importance of the protective function for the firm is illustrated by the extent to which firms enter into fixed and non-market arrangements with other firms and agencies, and thus place further extended defences between the firm and the open market. G. B. Richardson (1972, p. 883) has drawn attention to this phenomenon, arguing that it refutes the commonplace picture of firms simply as 'islands of planned co-ordination in a sea of market relations'.

In practice, firms build wide and substantial barriers between themselves and such tempestuous seas by entering into all kinds of arrangements or deals with each other. They will often, for instance, make use of traditional ties of loyalty and use personal exchanges of goods or resources, rather than going to the open market and seeking one-off competitive deals. There are also cases, Richardson shows, of firms taking up shareholdings in other firms with which they have a trading relationship. Through these and other means they may be able to influence management policy in the cooperating firm. Often such relationships between firms are unequal, such as the case where small manufacturers are suppliers of components for motor cars that are produced in large, multinational firms. Even in this case, however, the large firm prefers to involve itself in a close relationship with a small firm, rather than to take spot bids in the open market.

These various cases where traditional bonds of loyalty grow up between firms, and to some extent supplant open-market dealings, are known as 'relational contracting'. Furthermore, as Ronald Dore (1983) argues, the case of Japan suggests that the origin of these ties of established trading loyalty is not simply or primarily in vestiges of past tradition, but partly in the growth of new technologies and work relationships where the maintenance of high quality and product flexibility has become of increasing importance. More generally, both Dore and Richardson suggest that the firm does not simply exist in a sea of market relations (nor would it be that efficient if it did) but also in a vital network of established contracting bonds and relations which are partially of its own making.

In a sense, therefore, the question that is posed by Coase and Williamson, as to why firms exist and why production is not organized through market relations, is the wrong way round. The question should be: Why do firms sometimes move outside both their own organization, and even the orbit of relational contracting, and use the volatile market to obtain their supplies? Why, therefore, do open markets exist at all? The point of raising this question is to suggest, contrary to Williamson and Coase, that the onus is as much to explain the existence of the market as it is to explain the existence of the firm.

Also relevant here is the extent to which the firm embodies and sustains a degree of trust between its members. This, of course, should not be exaggerated, because trust and altruism cannot be dominant in an acquisitive and competitive system. But it has been shown already in chapter 7 that a degree of trust is essential for the firm to function at all. Even a hierarchical and non-participatory firm involves a measure of trust between its agents, partly because 'only a small portion of what people actually do on a job can be monitored in detail' (Nelson, 1981b, p. 1038), and the complexity of the production process means that it cannot easily be codified or evaluated by the supervisor.

If trust and cooperation are functional to the efficiency of the firm, then a form of organization or regime in which they were promoted could well be superior in terms of performance. Whilst all firms embody trust and loyalty in some measure, firms which promote these attributes to a greater degree are more likely to be efficient. Thus, for example, the extent to which more participatory forms of organization provide evidence of higher productivity (see Hodgson, 1984, ch. 9; Jones and Svejnar, 1982; Stephen, 1982) suggests that to some extent the performance and efficiency of the firm is positively correlated with the level of cooperation and trust between its members.

More specifically, in a comparative analysis of Japanese firms, Dore (1983) suggests that the relative efficiency and technological dynamism of that country stems in part from 'obligated relational contracting'. This differs from formalized arrangements according to the letter of the written contract, in that it is tempered by duty, trust, and give-and-take, in the context of long-term trading relations. The success of Japanese industry stems largely from established relations of this type, both within and between firms, and not from a mythically ubiquitous market 'flexibility' where each agent forcefully pursues his or own interest solely or mainly in terms of an explicit calculus of individual benefit or loss, and where the literal word of the written contract is taken as the substance of all relations.

In the sphere of the competitive market, and in contrast to the real-world firm, trust and long-term cooperation, whilst present to some degree, are undermined by competition between the many different and transient agents. In the market there is a changing and volatile population, where each individual is pursuing his or her objectives largely in accord with the overt calculus of profit and loss. In distinction, opportunistic and self-seeking behaviour is certainly present and significant within the firm, but, contrary to Williamson, it is diminished and kept under check within its boundaries. The firm, by engendering loyalty and trust to some degree, encourages people to act differently. Without this ability to generate more cohesive and less atomistic behaviour the firm would not be able to function.

A key to understanding the nature of the firm is thus its ability to mould human preferences and actions so that a higher degree of loyalty and trust are engendered. In contrast, following the tradition of individualistic social scientists, Williamson puts forward a model of individual human nature (i.e. 'opportunism') and recklessly assumes that this applies equally to quite different forms of institutional arrangement, and that in particular it applies equally to the market and the firm.[14] No recognition is made of the effect of the institutional environment in moulding actions and beliefs.

Samuel Bowles (1985a) has appropriately described the view of the human agent in this individualistic tradition as one of 'malfeasance', with its obsessions with self-seeking behaviour and with derivative phenomena such as 'shirking' at work. In contrast, as Bowles points out, the work performance function should not be regarded as exogenously given, as partly a consequence of immutable 'human nature'; it is endogenous and partly a function of the institutions and structures involved. We could add here that it is also a function of the general atmosphere of cooperation and trust.

People are often profoundly affected by their circumstances. Even in the same economic system these differ to some degree from the market to the firm. If the selfish version of 'economic man' has some limited relevance for the rational calculations of the marketplace, it has to be substantially modified for the intimate and ongoing social relationship of a social institution within which people work together for much of their lives. Even if they are valid, it is thus a mistake to assume unreservedly that the supposedly self-seeking, rational calculations of the market can be readily transferred from one place to another, and can characterize human relations in a firm to a similar extent. It is not being suggested that capitalist or other firms are institutions of benevolence and philanthropy – far from it. What is being argued is that some extra-contractual elements, including a measure of loyalty and trust, even if small, are essential for the firms to function at all.

Consequently, we are unable to understand the nature of the firm either by excluding non-contractual elements such as loyalty and trust, or by regarding them as dominant and to the exclusion of self-seeking calculation. More accurately, the firm embodies a symbiotic relationship between the bounded rationality of its agents and additional, non-utilitarian dynamics. These are both antagonistic and complementary. As in the more general case of the contract, discussed in chapter 7, the impurity principle may provide a useful conceptual tool to understand this phenomenon.

The role of such extra-contractual arrangements can be observed, often more prominently, in non-market institutions other than the capitalist firm. The family is just one example amongst many. Only very recently has the transaction costs analysis been applied in such a context. In a lengthy article Robert Pollak (1985) shows that such an analysis of families and households is superior to the more traditional view of Gary Becker and others in that the latter ignores their internal organization and structure. What is notable however, is that Williamson's narrow concept of 'opportunism' is lost from view, and Pollack has to emphasize quite different personal attributes such as 'loyalty' and 'altruism' to move the analysis onto this terrain. He fails to notice, however, the implied challenge that this provides to Williamson's own transaction costs analysis of the firm.

*Innovation and transaction costs*

A further problem in regard to the transaction costs analysis is in relation to innovation and technological development. Williamson and other theorists of the firm have recognized that it is difficult to promote and sustain technological innovation in the marketplace. In contrast, the firm provides a kind of protective shelter where in particular long-term research and development can take place.

But can the promotion of research and innovation within the firm and its retreat from the market be explained by the higher transaction costs of using the market mechanism? What do these costs mean in this context? Since we are dealing with developments and innovations which have not yet, and may never, come to fruition, some kind of notional futures market for the innovations and knowledge in the future must be involved, if the market is to be involved at all.

In some cases, however, the innovation will be chanced upon by accident. In others even the nature and application of the project will not be known in advance. The development of future technology is so riddled with radical uncertainty that no comprehensive futures market of this type could exist. We are then entitled to ask what transaction costs are being saved by not using such a non-existent market? In general, this alternative opportunity is absent. There are thus no opportunities foregone, and therefore there is no saving on costs.

Clearly, this underlines once again the argument that it is uncertainty or lack of knowledge which is one of the central factors in accounting for the nature or existence of the firm. The firm as a relatively durable organizational structure is able to deal with the lack of knowledge about the future fruits of research and development and innovation. Its relative internal stability means that it can carry unquantifiable risks which would be eschewed in the volatility of the market. In particular large firms are able to set up and sustain R&D departments with their own funds. It is widely recognized that atomized, small-scale private enterprise is not well able to make such long-term commitments (Freeman, 1974; Kay, 1979, 1984; Nelson, 1981a; Nelson and Winter, 1982).

In addition, another of the preceding points in the discussion above is highlighted by this argument. In investing in R&D and trying to promote internal innovation, the firm is taking a leap into the dark. Management simply does not know if the costs of carrying out such an effort will be rewarded with profits in the future. If calculations of the viability of such efforts are made, then they will be little more than guesses or extrapolations from a past and essentially different performance. In making such commitments the firm has to take future performance on trust. There can be no reliable calculus of risk involved.

It is thus emphasized once again that the significance of the firm as an institution is largely to do with the fact that in its internal routines and arrangements it does not attempt to enforce completely a strict utilitarian calculus. The firm is a social institution which to some extent promotes relationships of loyalty and trust which, by comparison, are not advanced to the same degree on the market. These relationships are essential for technological innovation and growth, particularly in the long term. A firm has no long-term future if it is ever ruled by the short-term vision of its accountants.

### Efficiency, technology and power

Whilst no claim is made here to provide a complete alternative theory of the existence of the firm, the ideas put forward above should be compared with a number of competing types of explanation.

One question is whether the explanation is technological, or in terms of social institutions and relations. By examining the function of habits and routines in transmitting technological skills and information, and in turn the role of the firm in protecting and reproducing these routines, we can see that the 'technological' and the 'social' are inextricably bound together. The argument here thus differs, for example, from the works of Scott Moss (1981) and Axel Leijonhufvud (1986), who put an exclusive emphasis on technology in explaining the existence of the firm. It differs also from the work of Ronald Coase (1937) and Oliver Williamson (1975, 1985) in that here there is a greater emphasis on the technology-preserving functions of routines within the firm. Furthermore, the emphasis here on embedded skills, which are not capable of ready expression in a codified form, and thus do not constitute 'information' in a conventional sense, distances the present work from an interpretation which sees the firm entirely in terms of the lack or availability of appropriate information, as in the work of Neil Kay (1984) and Richard Langlois (1984).

Turning once again to the question of the efficiency of the firm, neoclassical theory takes it for granted that an explanation of its efficiency suffices to explain its actual origins and development. As Edna Ullman–Margalit (1978) shows, however, this is invalid. Strictly, in order to explain the existence of a structure it is neither necessary nor sufficient to show that it is efficient. Inefficient structures do happen to exist; and many possible efficient structures will never actually emerge. Traditionally, neoclassical theory confuses the question of efficiency with existence; the fact of existence is often taken to indicate, usually with the suggestion of some evolutionary mechanism of the 'survival of the fittest', that the structure is optimal in some sense.

Notably, Stephen Marglin (1974) has argued that the nature of the firm is mainly to do with power and not efficiency, and that its existence is explained not by its technology but by its capacity to enlarge the span and degree of control of the capitalist. The firm is thus explained as an institution of power, rather than one that survives due to its cost-cutting efficiency. In contrast, in the Coase–Williamson tradition, the existence of the firm is explained purely in efficiency and cost-minimizing terms.

Recognition of the confusion between explanations of efficiency and explanations of existence is important in untangling the conflict between the type of analysis based on power and the type of analysis based on considerations of efficiency. What Marglin offers, as the seminal author in the former case, is a plausible account of the historical development of the firm. During the industrial revolution, he argues, capitalists established the factory mode of organization to wrest control of textile and other industries from a host of parcellized and unruly semi-autonomous producers. However, in shunning efficiency explanations his account as to why given forms of organization have grown and survived, once they have become established, is less plausible.

In contrast, in the Coase–Williamson tradition and in other varieties of neoclassical theory, the historical question of the initial derivation of a system is ignored, or assumed to have been answered by addressing the question of efficiency. A Darwinian evolutionism is invoked to demonstrate a kind of equivalence between efficiency and existence, in which the existence or non-existence of a particular type of organization is regarded as direct evidence of, respectively, efficiency of inefficiency. However, an explanation of the existence of an organization as a result of its purported theoretical efficiency is difficult to construct. The only argument that comes to mind involves the assumption of random organizational mutations. Over a sufficiently long period of time it could be expected that eventually a theoretically efficient organizational form would be thus generated. It is then assumed that, once given this random chance, it would both prosper above all others and persist.

But there are many problems with the formulation. It amounts to little more than an explanation of the evolution of the firm as a result of the cosmic dice. No explanation comes to mind as to how such random mutations could be generated, nor why a firm should not continue to mutate, perhaps to its disadvantage, once it has become established. If firms can win in the roulette of existence by chancing upon an efficient form of organization in one instant, they can lose out in another by chancing upon failure.

As suggested in chapter 6, the focus on the evolution of the firm in terms of routinized technology and skills, in the manner of the work of Veblen, Nelson and Winter, offers a solution to the problem. The 'routines as genes' idea can explain, unlike the neoclassical-Darwinian theory, the persistence of a given organizational form once it is established. This does not deny questions of efficiency but explains its persistence in a given environment. There would seem to be no reason why some of Marglin's points about the origin of the capitalist firm should not also be incorporated in the account. Notably, however, the questions of efficiency and existence are not conflated as they are in the tradition of Williamson, Coase and other neoclassical theorists.

After all, efficiency is a relative concept, not simply to other entities but to the total environment. It would be mistaken, for example, to describe the dinosaur as inefficient, or to explain its demise through some inefficiency in its design. The dinosaur grew in numbers, diversified and survived for many millions of years. It prospered both in relation to other less enduring species, and to the climatic conditions of the time. When, for whatever reason (possibly the impact of a large meteorite on Earth), the climate changed very rapidly, the species was then wiped out, along with the majority of the other species on this planet. The dinosaur then proved 'unfit' but principally in relation to a marked climatic change, and not relative to the majority of its animal 'competitors'. In this illustrative case it was the dramatic change in the overall environment that mattered.

For this reason it is quite wrong to follow Williamson and others and assume that the survival and growth of the capitalist firm, in terms of both number and average size, explains its superior efficiency over less numerous forms of organization, such as the workers' cooperative or the participatory firm. The most that can be concluded is that there is some evidence of the relative efficiency of the capitalist firm in the context of a given type of social, economic and political environment. The current make-up of financial institutions, government policies, case law, etc., clearly favour the traditional firm. If this environment were to change (and it could) then we may be able to find 'evidence' of the 'superiority' of a quite different form of organization.

In consequence, the real-world 'evidence' of the superiority in numbers of the conventional capitalist firm should not be interpreted as evidence for its universal comparative efficiency. Mere existence, in any quantity, should not be taken to impute universal efficiency without relation to context or environment. Failure to notice this means that economic theory, whatever its degree of formal sophistication, simply remains once again a conservative reflection of the *status quo*.

# 10

# Expectations and the Limits to Keynes

For although Keynes had so much to say about the effects of expectations about the future on present economic behaviour, he seems to be not nearly so informative about the causation of these expectations.

D. G. Champernowne (1963, p. 192)

Knowledge, uncertainty, and the formation of expectations are topics of increasing concern to economists today. After the long decades of mechanistic modelling in which these problems were given insufficient attention or substance, interest has grown rapidly with the rise of the rational expectations hypothesis and renewed attention being given to the Austrian School.

Notably, theoretical work from both these camps has been used in attempts to rebut Keynes and to justify a *laissez-faire* approach to economic policy. Yet for Keynes too the existence of uncertainty in economic life was a central theme of his *General Theory of Employment, Interest and Money*. He was, however, drawn to very different policy conclusions.

It is the aim of this chapter to examine more closely Keynes' view of the relationship between expectations and economic activity with a view to the possible policy implications. We commence with a discussion of the role of expectations in the *General Theory* and related works of Keynes from that period. This is followed by a discussion of the concept of the expecting agent in the firm and elsewhere. It is suggested that Keynes had a psychologistic and rationalist conception of human action which is defective and leads to a mistaken view of government and the state. Furthermore, an alternative, institutionalist approach may be able to account for some of the problems with the application of Keynesian policies to capitalist economies in recent years.

A third section of this chapter is directed at the alternative treatments of expectations by the rational expectations theorists and by the Austrian School. Although it is impossible to discuss them in detail, brief reference to these now fashionable theories is unavoidable. A final section discusses some of the implications of this analysis.

## 10.1  EXPECTATIONS IN THE *GENERAL THEORY*

Expectations, 'upon which business decisions depend', are said in the *General Theory* to 'fall into two groups'. The first, called 'short-term expectation', is the price 'a manufacturer' expects to get from current commenced output. The second, called 'long-term expectation', is concerned with the expected future yield if investment in additional capital equipment takes place (Keynes, 1971b, pp. 46–7).

Keynes devotes considerable attention to the effects of the general state of expectations on the level of economic activity, arguing that past expectations helped to determine the past level of output and investment. Thus they remain 'embodied in to-day's capital equipment with reference to which the entrepreneur has to make to-day's decisions'. For this reason 'it will often be safe to omit express reference to *short-term* expectation, in view of the fact that in practice the process of revision of short-term expectation is a gradual and continuous one, carried on largely in the light of realised results' (1971b, p. 50). This argument enables Keynes to focus attention on 'The State of Long-Term Expectation' (ch. 12). Much significance is attributed to this in the work of many modern Post-Keynesians (e.g. Davidson, 1972; Loasby, 1976; Minsky, 1976; Robinson, 1973a; Shackle, 1972, 1974).

In his 1937 lecture notes, Keynes himself seems to place even greater relative emphasis on the effects of shifting long-term expectations by suggesting that the *General Theory*, if rewritten, should assume at the outset that 'short-period expectations were always fulfilled; and then have a subsequent chapter showing what difference it makes when short-period expectations are disappointed' (1973b p. 181; see also Kregel, 1976).

### Long-term expectations

As Post-Keynesians have emphasized, long-term expectations are formed not merely in the context of risk, to which a definite probability can be attributed, but also of uncertainty regarding future events for which 'there is no scientific basis on which to form any calculable probability whatever' (Keynes, 1973b, p. 114). Long-term expectations are, in Keynes' view, guesses with minimal information regarding future economic and other related events. There is also, Keynes pointed out, the question of the confidence with which we make such forecasts (1971b, p. 148; see also Stohs, 1980). Typically, crucial information is lacking to make sound estimates of future investment yields. The confidence of any estimate will depend on the quantity and quality of the information that is available. Given that these estimates are usually little more than guesses, they are tentative and precarious by nature. Lacking firm evidence and sound calculation they can be revised with startling rapidity with any shift in the economic or political wind.

Keynes' theory of long-term investment is not ahistorical. Noting the 'separation between ownership and management which prevails to-day' and the 'development of organised investment markets', Keynes (1971b, p. 150) argues that decisions to invest in financial terms are no longer irrevocable, and are being constantly revalued on the stock market. This adds to the instability of the system. Keynes indicated that he regarded his theory as having greatest relevance to a capitalist system with large-scale enterprises and a developed and relatively autonomous financial sector.

Despite the precariousness of investment decisions in an uncertain world, 'the necessity for action and decision' compels the investor to act *as if* he or she had 'a good Benthamite calculation of a series of prospective advantages and disadvantages, each multiplied by its appropriate probability, waiting to be summed'. What guidelines are to be used for action in the face of such uncertainty?

> We assume that the present is a much more serviceable guide to the future than a candid examination of past experience would show it to have been hitherto . . . (and) that the *existing* state of opinion as expressed in prices and the character of existing output is based on a *correct* summing up of future prospects . . . Knowing that our own individual judgement is worthless, we endeavour to fall back on the judgement of the rest of the world which is perhaps better informed. That is, we endeavour to conform with the behaviour of the majority or the average. (1973b, p. 114)

In both the *General Theory* and the 1937 *Quarterly Journal of Economics* summary of its main points (from which the above is quoted) Keynes refers to the 'psychology' of a large group of individuals, each trying to copy or anticipate the others. Decisions are then taken, he argues, on the basis of past convention. This, however, is not always stable:

> A conventional valuation which is established as the outcome of the mass psychology of a large number of ignorant individuals is liable to change

violently as the result of a sudden fluctuation of opinion . . . the market will be subject to waves of optimistic and pessimistic sentiment, which are unreasoning and yet in a sense legitimate where no solid basis exists for a reasonable calculation. (1971b, p. 154)

According to Keynes, human beings are rational but they live and act in a world where widespread uncertainty places severe limits on the capacities of individuals to make detailed, rational calculations about the future. Actions flow from judgements about the future which often lack an objective empirical foundation other than by observation of 'the convention' that is formed by the actions of others.

### Keynes' policy conclusions

Keynes' above remarks form the basis for his famous critical judgement on stock-market speculation: 'When the capital development of a country becomes a by-product of the activities of a casino, the job is likely to be ill-done' (1971b, p. 159). The policy conclusions are well known: government intervention to regulate the overall level of effective demand and the propensity to consume, and the 'socialisation of investment'. Government steps in, as it were, to change 'the convention' that currently dominates entrepreneurial activity, and to fix it at a level which would create and maintain full employment. In Keynes' view the market mechanism cannot achieve this on its own. The limits to rational calculation within the market system have to be overcome by the reason and action of wise government.

Keynes is careful to note that the formation of economic conventions is not entirely chaotic and unstable. If it were, successful state intervention to maintain full employment would be unlikely for prolonged periods. He ends chapter 12 of the *General Theory* with assurances of the possibility of stability:

> We should not conclude . . . that everything depends on waves of irrational psychology. On the contrary, the state of long-term expectation is often steady, and, even when it is not, the other factors exert their compensating effects. We are merely reminding ourselves that human decisions affecting the future, whether personal or political or economic, cannot depend on strict mathematical expectation, since the basis for making such calculations does not exist. (1971b, p. 162–3)

Once the government has backed and regulated the level of effective demand so as to reach full employment, then, Keynes suggests, the market will come into its own: 'I see no reason to suppose that the existing system seriously misemploys the factors of production which are in use . . . It is in determining the volume, not the direction, of actual employment that the existing system has broken down' (1971b, p. 379).

Implicit in Keynes' theory is the idea that a sustained 'convention' corresponding to full employment cannot depend on government action alone. In addition 'average opinion' would have to 'correctly' identify economic indicators as being consistent with the preservation of full employment and bouyant effective demand, and the actions of economic agents would have to be 'rational' and consistent with this perception. Without this, government action would be unable to achieve any kind of full employment equilibrium; its objectives would be thwarted by 'irrational' behaviour on behalf of investors and managers. To support its policy conclusions, therefore, Keynes' theory has to bring a qualified notion of economic stability and a conception of rational actions once again to the fore of the stage.

## 10.2 SOME LIMITATIONS OF THE THEORY

Keynes' theory of the relationship between expectations and the level of production and employment is, of course, a major landmark in the history of economic thought. It is a clear break from the self-regulating equilibrium models of the still-prominent neoclassical school, and it is in advance of the mechanistic approach that is found in some Marxist economic theory.[1] Both these traditions neglect the role of uncertainty and limited knowledge in the modern economy, mechanically relating the actions of economic agents to past and present stimulii alone, without giving due consideration to their (essentially indeterminate) expectations. Pre-Keynesian economics finds its analogue in the classical mechanics of Newton; in contrast, Keynes' work has been compared to the physics of Einstein where information is no longer obtainable without cost (Leijonhufvud, 1968, p. 397).

With his theory of investment and employment, Keynes is able to argue, even more clearly than Marx did before, that the capitalist system is potentially unstable, containing no automatic machinery of self-regulation which can move it always towards full employment and optimal output. This message remains poignant and relevant today, even if it is not universally accepted. However, without detracting from the enduring value of Keynes' analysis, on close inspection there are some gaps. It is the aim of this section to bring some of these into view. The object is not to destroy the whole Keynesian argument but to suggest a plan for restoration and extension.

The forthcoming discussion starts with the topic of the expecting agent ('the entrepreneur' in Keynes' work) and this is then related to firms and financial institutions. Next, a consideration of Keynes' methodological standpoint is followed by a critique of his view of government. Although these topics are wide-ranging, it shall be argued that they connect together as a whole, forming a qualified critique of Keynes which has important policy implications.

### The expecting agent

It is notable how frequently Keynes' discussion of expectations is phrased in terms of the first person plural. 'We' calculate, 'we' reason and 'we' form our expectations. This understandable literary device raises a more serious question: Who is the expecting agent to which Keynes refers? Does he mean everyone involved in the economy, or a single group or class?

The actor that appears most frequently in his argument is 'the entrepreneur' and it appears that his discusssion of expectations is related primarily to this person. Keynes adopts a distinction between 'entrepreneurs' and 'rentiers', redolent of his Marshallian background. However, these terms are not used with sufficient precision in the *General Theory*. In one passage 'the entrepreneur' is the owner-manager of the firm. In another he is an investor on the stock market. In another still the separation of ownership and control is observed, and the process of expectations-formation is split between the financier and the directors of the firm.

What is apparent from chapters 11 and 12 of the *General Theory* is that the agent which Keynes has in mind has money capital to invest, and is making comparisons between its expected yield if it is converted into means of production, and the expected future rates of interest if this money is lent to financial institutions. However, this economic agent is not the Marshallian entrepreneur, nor one who is necessarily making the actual decisions concerning the scale of output, investment and employment in the firm. Joan Robinson (1971, pp. 31–2) has pointed out that 'Keynes rather lost his grip on the distinction between the rentier and the entrepreneur. His discussion of "the state of long-term expectations" is devoted to Stock Exchange rather than to the accumulation of means of production.'

A clear definition of 'the entrepreneur' and other crucial actors may have eluded Keynes because of an assumption that his account of expectations-formation applies more or less equally to all economic agents, or at least to those with ready money to invest or exchange. This would help to explain his frequent reference to 'psychology' in his discussion of the formation of expectation. Keynes' account was, it appears, based on a view of human nature, rather than institutional structures or social relations, despite its concrete references to the nature of modern capitalism.

The problem is not simply one of defining the expecting agent. In Keynes' work there is also a failure to consider the processes through which expectations are formed and the social culture and structures which give them colour and substance. This omission is not atypical of the overwhelming majority of economic theorists, but it is all the more acute for Keynes who made uncertainty and expectations central to his analysis. Instead, Keynes made use of favourite analogies to explain the 'mass psychology' of expectations-formation. Chapter 12 mentions the game of snap, of old maid, musical chairs and a beauty contest, illustrating the process of 'anticipating what average opinion expects average opinion to be' (1971b, p. 156). Important possible distortions or limitations in the perception and cognition of 'average opinion', and the institutions through which such opinions are processed and refracted, are not considered.

Sir John Hicks (1969, p. 313) has made his misgivings in this area clear:

> When I reviewed the *General Theory*, the explicit introduction of expectations was one of the things which I praised; but I have since come to feel that what Keynes gave with one hand, he took away with the other. Expectations do appear in the *General Theory*, but (in the main) they appear as *data*; as autonomous influences that come in from outside, not as elements that are moulded in the course of the process that is being analyzed.

### Firms and financiers

Taken literally, Keynes' theory would apply at first sight to such institutions as the organized investment market where 'average opinion' is communicated more readily to all agents involved. But once matters are complicated by adding other institutions and more complex mechanisms, then the general applicability of Keynes' account of expectations-formation is put into doubt. What if, for example, finance is provided through the banks, as well as or instead of through the sale of stock? Unless it is assumed that there is near-perfect, financial-market competition between the banks and the stock market then 'average opinion' and 'conventions' in one will not be the same as in the other.

Some of the implications of this possible divergence are discussed further below. But the example should indicate that the nature and structure of economic institutions is at least as relevant as 'psychology' in the determination of real-world expectations. This is illustrated most graphically with the firm itself. Keynes only partly came to terms with the fact that the Marshallian entrepreneur is a rare if not extinct species of capitalist. Thus the agency forming expectations within the firm is rarely a single, commanding individual. In any case, the firm should not be treated as a purely psychological entity. Decisions to invest and to expand the firm's output and employment are taken by a number of individuals in structured social interaction, which psychology alone cannot explain.

Of course, 'the end of *laissez-faire*' and the growth of the large enterprise was recognized by Keynes himself. So too has the postwar literature on the theory of the firm. But the descriptive idea of the firm as an entrepreneur is still prominent. This is because economists have continued to believe that the firm has a set of consistent objectives which are the matter of rational calculation, or assumed that the firm performed 'as if' this were the case. In this way the relevant expectations and objectives of a large and complex enterprise are reduced to those of a single individual. In this guise the ghost of the entrepreneur still haunts the firm of economic theory.

Nevertheless, in modern heterodoxy there is an increasing awareness of the importance of the organization and internal structure of the firm. In some accounts it is no longer treated as a unitary being ('the entrepreneur') but as a complex system. This innovation is apparent, for example, in the work of management-systems-theorists such as Stafford Beer (1972) where the firm is not regarded as having a single objective function. Its agents are motivated in a number of different and often conflicting ways. The enterprise contains a number of functional organizations (production, research, marketing, financing, etc.) which are part of an overall complex structure, but they may not be in harmony with each other. Richard Nelson (1981b, p. 1036) argues forcefully that the firm should be regarded as a 'social system' rather than a 'machine'. Likewise, Grahame Thompson (1982, p. 235) has suggested that: 'Instead of conceiving of the enterprise or firm as a relatively homogeneous, organic, functioning *unity* typified by a universal calculating subject ("management")' it should be regarded as 'a heterogeneous non-unitary, dispersed and fractured *entity* or social agency'.

Furthermore, there are a number of possible types of structured relationship between the management and the workforce of the firm, and these are likely to influence productivity and performance in different ways (Kilpatrick and Lawson, 1980; Nelson, 1981b; Hodgson, 1982a) and thereby have a feedback effect on the motivations, objectives and expectations of management. Class conflict within the enterprise is likely to have a crucial effect on expectations and performance.

Consequently, the idea that the performance of the firm relates to a single set of individual expectations can no longer be readily accepted.

This does not mean, however, that expectations and objectives within the firm can be disregarded. But these too are dispersed and non-unitary within the firm; their formation reflecting the structure and routine of the institution itself. We have left the unitary entrepreneur, pondering and acting in an uncertain world of atomistic individuals, a long way behind.

Similar considerations apply to the financier and financial institutions, although structures and motivations will be different. An earlier work by Thompson is relevant here. He notes that the gearing ratio of fixed-interest capital to risk capital is over five times greater in Japan than in the UK. Thus the acceptance of risky investment projects by Japanese financial institutions is much greater. Is it 'psychologistic attitudes to "risk" which are supposed to underlie the determination of the most appropriate level of gearing for any company in given circumstances'? Keynes' predeliction for psychological formulations has been noted. In contrast, Thompson (1977, p. 286) answers in the following manner: 'In fact it is precisely the structural relationships between the financial and industrial sector which "enables" a much higher level of gearing to be acceptable, not some psychologistic aversion or otherwise to risk.'

Psychological issues should not be excluded from any complete explanation. But it is important, in contrast to a tendency in Keynes' work, to put adequate stress on the institutional frameworks which both influence and constrain economic action in the real world. As institutions and habitual practices are diverse, both between and within countries, then so too will divergences of expectations and objectives between economic agents be likely.

It is important to emphasize that the existence of non-unitary structures and institutions does not simply mean that expectations have to be related to a multiplicity of economic agents. It also means that the formation of expectations is affected by institutions and structures themselves. The very perceptions of economic agents are moulded by institutions, culture and routine.

It has been noted already that it is not the intention here to propose a kind of structural determinism in which the ideas and actions of economic agents are completely determined by the appropriate structures and institutions. Due recognition should be made for insight, will, flair, accident and the like. But whilst a deterministic position is unacceptable, so too is an outlook which assumes that the firm or the financial institution can be equated with a single subject, especially one that functions largely on the basis of rational calculation.

The point being stressed here is that culture, habits and institutions colour perception and judgement, and play a very important part in the formation of expectations. In turn they help to explain the persistence of apparently 'irrational' expectations which do not appear to be based on a sound assessment of existing information, or of divergent expectations between agents who may be placed in a different institutional setting. Whilst recognizing supplementary (largely indeterminate) influences in the process of expectations-formation, expectations are not here treated as exogenous as they are in the work of Keynes.

### Keynes' rationalist conception of action

It has been argued above that Keynes' theory involves the assumption that actions of economic agents are, as far as possible, governed by reason and calculation. His important qualification of this principle was the addition of the element of uncertainty about the future, which in many circumstances made rational calculation meaningless or impossible. Despite this qualification, a rationalist conception of action remains. Keynes' picture is of a world that is governed by entrepreneurial speculation, and to a much lesser extent by tradition and routine. In his work, reason and calculation are highlighted; rational agency is over-stressed with a neglect of habits and institutions.

Keynes too was never led to challenge directly the rationalist conception. Strictly, he was not a philosophical rationalist, but like many other economists he held to a rationalist conception of action.[2] And the type of so-called 'Keynesian' theory which prevailed after the Second World War relegated the issue even further by shifting the concept of uncertainty from the centre of the stage. However, Keynes' own account of uncertainty leads, as we have seen, to some emphasis on the formation of 'the convention' and its role in decision and action. Consequently, there is a thread in Keynes' work which leads in a more fruitful and challenging direction.

It is important to note that the orthodox economists' belief that human action is based on rational calculation is allied to empiricist assumptions about the perception and cognition of the real-world data upon which such calculations are based. There is a notion of 'evidence' out there, which can be appraised independently of concepts and theories, and which is the substance of individual processes of rational decision-making.

To a significant extent, a similar methodological combination of empiricism with a rationalist conception of action is found in the work of Keynes. Arguably, he had strong empiricist leanings, albeit of a sort more sophisticated than those found in the writings of many other economists. Empiricist interpretations can be made of several passages from his earlier *Treatise on Probability*, such as those where he suggests that through perception we may have 'direct acquaintance' with some facts and that sense data carries meaning for the subject, without any mention of the language, the symbolic order, or the conceptual framework through which they are perceived (e.g. 1973a, p. 12).

In the same work Keynes criticizes the 'Empiricist School', but only for their alleged assumption that 'the data of experience' are sufficient to derive 'judgements of probability without the aid either of intuition or of some further *a priori* principle' (1972a, p. 94). Such an assumption would be invalid. but it is made only by the most extreme and vulgar of empiricists, and not by other empiricist philosophers. Furthermore, contrary to Keynes' implication, 'the data of experience', even with the addition of appropriate intuition and *a priori* principles, are *not* sufficient. A conceptual or symbolic framework is required as well, otherwise cognition of the sense data is not possible.

Indeed, the very argument within Keynes' *Treatise on Probability* proposes some sort of logical relation between evidence and conclusion. The thesis is that the probability of a proposition can be inferred, in certain circumstances, directly from evidence. However, it is often the case that evidence can be interpreted in different ways, each suggesting a different conclusion to the observer.[3]

There is a third and related element in Keynes' methodology which should be mentioned here. His combination of a rationalist view of human action with an empiricist epistemology is closely related to an over-estimation of the powers of reason and persuasion in affecting and changing economic policy. Donald Moggridge (1976, pp. 38–9), an editor of Keynes' collected writings, has pointed out: 'Keynes always believed that "a little clear thinking" or "more lucidity" could solve almost any problem . . . reform was achieved by the discussion of intelligent people . . . using the method of persuasion.' Similar criticisms of Keynes have been made by others with quite different views.[4]

Keynes' faith in reason and persuasion was fractured on two important occasions. The first was the Versailles negotiations after the First World War (Keynes, 1971a). The second was the response of the national government to the deep slump of the early 1930s (Keynes, 1972a). These failures to 'face facts' and to bring reason to bear, are frequently described by Keynes as 'lunacy' or 'madness'. When clear thinking and persuasion failed to bring about the desired result, it seems that Keynes lost patience and was driven to suggest that his adversaries should be certified as incapable of rational appraisal and action. Keynes' equilibrium position was the optimism of a rationalist. Yet on occasions this was disturbed by frustration and doubt, especially, and to some extent understandably, in times of crisis.

It was late in his life that Keynes began to put his earlier conception of human action under more critical scrutiny. Writing in 1938 he accused himself and his colleagues of misunderstanding

> human nature, including our own. The rationality which we attributed to it led to a superficiality, not only of judgement, but also of feeling. It was not only that intellectually we were pre-Freudian, but we had lost something which our predecessors had without replacing it. I still suffer incurably from attributing an unreal rationality to other people's feelings and behaviour (and doubtless my own too). (1972b, p. 448)

This commendable self-critisism can be directed at some of the ideas in the *General Theory*, as well as Keynes' own personality. Also it is appropriate to ask why Keynes' affliction remained 'incurable' even when he was aware of it himself. Perhaps one reason was his tendency to view the issue as primarily psychological and philosophical, rather than it being in addition a general under-estimation of the force of vested interests and institutions in social life.

## Government action

Another related area where Keynes' work has been open to criticism is his treatment of government and the state. His neglect of vested interests and the influence of institutions led him to assume that goverment could always be persuaded to act in the common interest, even if more self-centred motives such as the pursuit of profit and monetary reward prevailed throughout the rest of society. This rather elitist and somewhat unrealistic view has been criticized from both the New Right and the Marxist Left.[5] One does not necessarily have to accept either the New Right view of the egoistic social actor, nor to assume, along with some Marxists, that the state exclusively represents the interests of the capitalist class, to see the serious limitations of Keynes' view of government. Like the classic liberals of old, he assumed a hermetic division between the state and civil society. Self-interest prevailed in the latter, but 'philosopher kings' guided by reason ruled the state. Such a view is clearly inconsistent, and has to be rejected.

In an early, perceptive and since neglected assessment of the *General Theory*, A. L. Rowse criticized Keynes' trust in the potency of ideas and reason. Rowse went on to argue that in the political sphere 'it is the control of power . . . that matters; it is not what a party says or thinks that indicates what it will do: that depends almost entirely upon what it *is*, what is its social basis, what are the implications of its make up' (Rowse, 1936, p. 58). From this point he goes on to criticize Keynes' now-famous dictum that 'the power of vested interests is vastly exaggerated compared with the gradual encroachment of ideas' (1971b, p. 383). Instead, Rowse (pp. 60–1) argues that

> ideas of action and policy do not operate *in vacuo*; they have to work in a field which is made up of pre-existing interests, group-interests and self-interests, economic, political, social and so on . . . But what makes these ideas effective in and for society, is, apart from their own internal tests, (coherence, clarity, consistency, etc.), the body of interest they express or elicit, themselves acting as the medium in which those interests communicate and struggle against each other.

Rowse's background, as a historian, leads him to recognize and emphasize social relations, power and vested interests in economic behaviour. The 'rationalist fallacy' in Keynes' work led him not only to give an individualistic and inadequate picture of the process of expectations formation in finance and industry. It also sustained a naive optimism concerning the influence of reason and persuasion on government policy. Both stem from the assumptions that where uncertainty is not present the given facts are unambiguous and readily available, and that the overwhelming majority of political and economic agents will reach common, rationally based conclusions in regard to the available information. Problems of divergent interpretations of given facts, of 'cognitive dissonance', of highly parcellized information, and the blind inertia of institutions, including the firm and the government department, are pushed to one side. Persuasion and reason were potentially supreme, Keynes thought, not only within the world, but in regard to theories about the world, including his own. The powers of vested interests and government could be tamed and controlled by reason.

It is suggested in this chapter that Keynes' empiricist epistemology, his rationalist conception of action and his faith in persuasion are connected in the following manner:

1 From *A Treatise on Probability* to the *General Theory* there is an empiricist assumption of a more or less direct relationship between sense data and the perception of 'facts' about the outside world.
2 This directly appraised factual knowledge is the substance of calculation and reason by economic agents, giving a common, economy-wide foundation for the formation of the 'convention' and 'average opinion'.
3 Keynes' distinctive innovation is to recognize that rational calculation, whilst remaining central to individual action, is severely limited by the existence of uncertainty about the future. But he implies that if uncertainty were to be removed (which of course is impossible outside mainstream economic theory), the formation of

expectations would be an objective and rational process, based on empirically given facts about the world.

4   His faith in persuasion arises in areas where uncertainty is not apparent. Keynes tends to assume that in these circumstances reason, and objective assessment of the evidence, would then lead intelligent people to reach shared conclusions about economic theory and policy, outside the sway of mere intuition or personal whim.

5   The power of reason applies to the entrepreneurs in the sense that they will tend to form and conform to an 'average opinion' of the state of the economy on the basis of commonly appraised facts.

6   The power of reason and persuasion applies to the state for similar reasons and due to the assumption that narrow, and possibly conflicting, self or vested interests do not prevail in this arena.

## 10.3   AUSTRIAN AND RATIONAL EXPECTATIONS ALTERNATIVES

It is neither necessary nor possible to give a full survey of the main approaches to expectations theory. However, two important alternatives to the work of Keynes are sketched in outline here, for they help to clarify the issues involved. First, however, the question of the exogeneity or endogeneity of expectations is raised, as this has been a matter of inspiration for the rational expectations theorists.

### The Endogeneity of Expectations

A crucial weakness of the *General Theory* in comparison with the rational expectations hypothesis is Keynes' treatment of long-term expectations as exogenous to the model. In fact, his theory divides the economic world into two parts: determinate relationship between investment, output, employment, income, saving, etc., on the one hand, and indeterminate long-term expectations, governed by uncertainty, on the other. Keynes constructs a model which is partitioned between the determinate and the indeterminate. As Shackle (1972, p. 233) puts it:

> The *General Theory of Employment, Interest and Money* proceeds in terms of functions, and regards variables as in some sense 'dependent' on each other. But this dependence of many variables upon each other, in a web of mutual determination, is vain for the defence of the traditional standpoint. For *one* variable is left unchained. Investment . . . is at the mercy, not of the other variables, firmly clasping its shoulder in a

function-grip, but of the ever-dissolving and re-appearing will-o-the-wisp of expectation . . . Investment is the maverick variable not fully harnessed into the team.

For at least two decades after the Second World War, the very treatment of expectations and investment as the undetermined variables in the Keynesian system created the theoretical possibility of constructive government intervention, and prevented the resurgence of the 'self-adjusting' ideas of *laissez-faire*. However, eventually Keynes' failure to consider the processes through which expectations were actually formed and investment determined, became a weakness rather than a strength. Rational expectations theorists, alarmed by the apparent schizophrenia in the Keynesian system, broke down the division by ignoring real uncertainty and hauling expectations into the determinate camp, possibly with the addition of an element of probabilistic variation or risk. With this closed and complete model, the rational expectations theorists stormed through the gap in the Keynesian system, claiming to have an adequate theory to explain expectations where Keynes did not.

It has become typical of rational expectations theorists to associate Keynes with the adaptive expectations hypothesis, which was prominent in postwar macroeconomic modelling before the rational expectations 'revolution'. However, as Tony Lawson (1981) has shown, the adaptive expectations hypothesis is not consistent with the work of Keynes himself, who argued that 'it is in the nature of long-term expectations that they cannot be checked at short intervals in the light of realised results' (1971b, p. 51). This shows that Keynes' long-term expectations are *not* adaptive, but it fails to explain how such expectations *are* formed. The gap is not filled in Keynes' work, and it is this void which has now made the Keynesian system vulnerable; when in the past the same gap served to vindicate the Keynesian policy position.

## The rational expectations hypothesis

The rational expectations hypothesis is frequently described by its proponents as being the assumption that economic agents make the best use of all the information they have, or that they 'do not make systematic mistakes in forecasting the future' (Begg, 1982, p. xi). These 'weak' versions of the hypothesis, as Gustavo Gomes (1982) and others have pointed out, do not tell us very much. A wide variety of 'best' uses of information is conceivable for different agents. As we know from experience, much perplexing or ambiguous information may be best ignored. And the nature of a 'mistake', systematic or otherwise, is a matter of great potential controversy. In practice, advocates of 'rational expectations' follow Robert Lucas (1972) and assume that the expectations of economic agents are formed on the basis of the complete economic model that is being proposed. It is this 'strong' version of the hypothesis that concerns us here.

Behind the 'strong' rational expectations hypothesis there are a number of assumptions. Consider the following:

1 James Tobin (1980), David Begg (1982) and James Wible (1982–3) have drawn attention to the almost universal assumption of market clearing in rational expectations models. Thus it is assumed what many of the theorists set out to prove markets 'work' and that government intervention is not required.
2 The idea of 'rational', optimizing behaviour is usually explicit. Along with most neoclassical theorists, it is assumed that agents are optimizing exclusively for their own gain (or that of their household), without even a tinge of autonomous altruism.
3 As Willem Buiter (1980), Jagdish Handa (1982) and others have made clear, it is assumed that economic agents are virtually omniscient, in that they are assumed to know the basic elements of the 'objective underlying model' of the economy (which is usually presumed to be a neoclassical and monetarist one). Even in less cavalier versions of the hypothesis it is assumed that all economic agents are aware of, and implicitly agreed upon, the essential, 'reduced-form' mechanisms of the model.

Each one of these assumptions is open to doubt. It has been widely argued by Marxists and Keynesians of all varieties that markets will not necessarily clear in a monetary economy. In an uncertain world people may wish to hold on to money, creating an excess demand for that commodity, and corresponding to a glut of unsold non-money commodities. As Keynes emphasized in the *General Theory*, this excess demand for will not in general lead to greater output and employment to satisfy that demand. On these grounds Say's Law will break down. (See also Marx, 1969, pp. 501–5; Leijonhufvud, 1968; Sowell, 1972.)

However, there is some common ground between Keynes' views and assumptions 2 and 3. As we have seen, the idea of the rational agent is central to his work. But the key difference is that Keynes regarded rational, calculating action as severely limited by considerable uncertainty about the future. Thus Keynes does not regard economic agents as 'optimizers' in the strict neoclassical sense. Consequently, after some common concessions to rationalist models of action there is a significant divergence between Keynes and the rational expectations theorists.

to the 'true
limited exte
expectation
empirical r
accepted m

In taking
convention
information
rational ex
readily avai
an identica
frameworks
information
similar but

It is now
creates seve
and further
others that
Metcalfe (
differently
three such g
their assum
are, to som
least one o
'rational' b
they demon
behaviour a

Andrea
divergent e
difficulties
may be ca
imbued wit
spending by
Whereas th
pessimistic
a world in
sectors of t
reflation no
restore gro
divergent e
sianism and

Unwittin
Keynes in t

Recent work has underlined the significance of introducing time and uncertainty in rational choice models. Herbert Simon (1976) echoes Keynes by arguing that 'rule of thumb' or 'heuristics' are appropriate with uncertainty and limited information. Behavioural experiments indicate that people do not make full use of all the information that is available, and they react to new information often by making only small changes in their routines. As Alan Garner (1982) points out, this evidence contradicts the rational expectations hypothesis and is more in tune with the work of Keynes and some of his followers, such as George Shackle. Paul Davidson (1982–3) argues that agents who wish to avoid making persistent errors through real time will *not* use all the information that is available to them. Randall Bausor (1983) rejects rational expectations thinking after consideration of the epistemics of time. True uncertainty about the future in the sense of Keynes, rather than mere risk to which a calculable probability can be attributed, is not compatible with the rational expectations hypothesis.

Turning to assumption 3, the problem of uncertainty and limited information is still relevant. R. J. Shiller (1978) and others have argued that, contrary to the rational expectations theorists, most individuals do not have sufficient knowledge to form coherent economic models of the real world. Keynes' work contradicts 3 in the sense that he clearly believed that the economic system can work in ways which are counter to intuition and popular assumption. In particular, some recognition is given to the 'fallacy of composition'; the whole does not always correspond to the sum of the parts.

Most importantly, Keynes sees counter-intuitive relationships in macroeconomics which can be the reverse of those to which they correspond at the microeconomic level. Examples include the well-known 'paradox of saving' (1971b, pp. 358–71) where saving by individuals may increase personal wealth, but not necessarily the wealth of the community as a whole. This is a clear example of the fallacy of composition: what is true for individuals or households within the nation is not necessarily true by summation for the nation as a whole. For Keynes, aggregate saving meant a reduction in effective demand and could lead to a reduction in business expectations and a general contraction of economic activity.

Another example relates to the employment of labour. The neoclassical 'law of demand' states that the demand of a commodity is inversely related to its price. It is still popular to apply this principle, with little or no qualification, to the aggregate labour market. Thus it is suggested that the demand for labour can be increased by a reduction in wages, and indirectly by a removal of impediments to atomistic competition in the labour market, for example minimum-wage legislation and trade

to the 'true' relationship between the economic variables. Thus, to a limited extent, Keynes shares the confidence and optimism of the rational expectations theorists who believe that with sufficient reason and empirical research we can construct a 'true' and almost universally accepted model of the economic system.

In taking the view that investors will tend to reach and share a common convention and consensus, based on rational appraisal of shared information, Keynes makes a slight but significant concession to the rational expectation theorists who assume that crucial information is readily available to everyone, and is used to make 'rational' decisions on an identical basis. However, for reasons due to differing cognitive frameworks or information-processing capabilities, agents will appraise information in different ways and form expectations which are not always similar but can diverge.

It is now recognized that the existence of divergent expectations creates severe theoretical difficulties for the rational expectations model and furthermore completely undermines the conclusion of Lucas and others that government intervention is impotent. David Peel and Stanley Metcalfe (1979) develop a model where expectations are formed differently for different groups of agents. In particular, they identify three such groups: workers, managers and financiers, showing that under their assumptions the conditions for self-righting stability of the economy are, to some extent, undermined. Furthermore, if it is assumed that at least one of these groups form their expectations on an adaptive, non-'rational' basis, and in other cases expectations are formed rationally, they demonstrate that the economy can generate the same qualitative behaviour as one in which all expectations are formed adaptively.

Andrea Boltho (1983) has argued that the Peel–Metcalfe model of divergent expectations may be able to explain some of the current difficulties with Keynesian policies. He suggests that Western Europe may be caught in an 'expectations trap' where the financial sector, imbued with monetarist orthodoxy, responds to the expansion of public spending by speculating against the domestic currency in fear of inflation. Whereas the industrial sector will respond to deflation by generating pessimistic expectations of the future. There is thus 'the possibility that in a world in which divergent expectations are formulated in different sectors of the economy neither traditional nor Keynesian measures of reflation nor orthodox monetarist policies of deflation may be able to restore growth and employment' (p. 1). The general possibility of divergent expectations creates difficulties for both orthodox Keynesianism and the standard rational expectations model.

Unwittingly, the possibility of divergent expectations is suggested by Keynes in the *General Theory*, for he assumes that entrepreneurs form their long-term expectations in the way described in chapter 12, but consumers, on the other hand, think and act differently, as suggested in chapters 8–10. In the former case they are dominated by an uncertain future, in the latter they are prevailed upon by habit.

If divergent expectations were present not only between investors and consumers, but also between different investing institutions, then the possibility of an 'expectations trap' can be entertained. There may be a partial or general 'stickiness' in the formation of optimistic expectations, and in different degrees throughout the economy, in response to the demand-inducing policies of government. If so, no longer will production, employment and output respond almost mechanically to a shift in effective demand.[6] Keynesian policies, whilst not necessarily without effect, will perhaps have a limited and patchy response. They may require complementary action of a more radical kind to stimulate production and raise employment. This policy issue is rejoined in the next chapter.

In another relevant contribution, John Haltiwanger and Michael Waldman (1985) consider the possibility of variations in the information-processing abilities of agents. Thus their model embodies the realistic idea that agents are heterogeneous in regard to cognition and calculation. They show that, depending on certain assumptions, it is possible for the 'sophisticated' or the 'naive' information-processors to have a disproportionate effect on the system as a whole. Not only does this undermine the standard conclusions of the Lucas model, but also rehabilitates the idea of adaptive or other apparently less 'rational' processes of expectations formation. Despite the prominence of the latter in the old-style Keynesian literature, it should be noted that the Haltiwanger–Waldman model achieves this result by making assumptions about the heterogeneity of rational processes, in contrast to the assumptions made by Keynes.

A further irony is that the rational expectations model, which is most often associated with an ultra-individualist political philosophy, assumes that every individual is alike in his or her capacity to appraise and interpret the facts. Consequently, this 'individualistic' outlook assumes a grey uniformity between individuals. By introducing divergent expectations and heterogeneous agents not only is the argument of the rational expectations theorists for *laissez-faire* undermined, but also the richness and diversity of human individuality is emphasized.

## The Austrian theory of expectations

Where Keynes splits the theoretical system into two parts – one determined, the other indeterminate, rational expectations theorists attempt to construct a completely determined system. The approach of the 'Austrian School' differs profoundly from both. The economy is disaggregated into its individual parts, bonded by the regular communication of subjectively based information through the market mechanism. For Post-Keynesians the Austrian approach is not without its insights, particularly its critique of the concept of economic equilibrium and of general equilibrium analysis, and its stress on the importance of information and knowledge in the economic system. And, despite widespread misconception, it should be stressed that Austrian theory is very different from the rational expectations framework, within which the notion of long-run equilibrium is supreme.

However, some serious deficiencies in the Austrian position undermine their case. Particularly in regard to its view of the human agent, Austrian economics shares some common ground with neoclassical theory and it has been thus criticized in part two of this work. In addition, it has also been pointed out that whilst the Austrian argument that it is impossible to centralise all information is valid, it is wrong to assume that all knowledge is individual in character. Some information (often information about the location of other information) is necessarily centralized and institutionalized (e.g. in a telephone directory). It is thus doubtful that the 'decentralized' market can provide an effective signalling device for all information and all activities in a complex economic system.[7]

Another deficiency concerns the Austrian treatment of the firm and the sphere of production. A stylized picture of 'the entrepreneur' pervades the analysis. As in the work of Keynes, this enables the Austrian School to put great emphasis on entrepreneurial expectations. Similarly, little attention is given to the nature and functions of the large and complex firm. The expectations of non-entrepreneurial agents within production are not considered in great detail, for it is deemed that the active agent is not the worker but the entrepreneur. As with Keynes, the analysis bypasses the shopfloor and there is silence about the real processes of production. This error is compounded by Austrian theorists who choose to relegate the concept of the division of labour in favour of the 'division of knowledge'.

As Fernando Carvalho (1983–4, p. 270) points out, for the Austrian School there is an unsolved problem of explaining the existence of regularity and order in economic life. The Austrians

> take the 'freedom' of the agent to its ultimate consequences. The individual mind is the ultimate source of all action and this makes the future completely unpredictable . . . If, however, there is no order beyond the individual, decision is empty and powerless. The future then

cannot be 'created' except as a result of accidental interactions of otherwise unrelated individuals.

It is significant that Friedrich Hayek's more recent work represents a sustained endeavour to grapple with this problem. His concept of 'spontaneous order' is an attempt at a solution, but it is notable that it represents a move away from classical liberalism to stress the function of tradition and routine in imparting cohesion to social and economic life. Other Austrians remain closer in spirit to an atomistic individualism but have failed to tackle the problem of the persistence of regularity and order in society.

In Keynes' theory the sphere of indeterminacy in economic life corresponds to those involved in the process of investment: beyond them there are more regular relations between cause and effect. In the Austrian scheme indeterminacy governs all market relations. In the intersection of the two lies the common ground. Shackle (1972, 1974) is the most important explorer of this intellectual territory, attempting a synthesis of the work of Keynes with that of the Austrian School. But to this synthesis some of the above objections still remain.

There have been recent, illuminating developments following this synthesis of Keynes' work with some aspects of the Austrian School, involving in some cases the behaviouralists as well (Loasby, 1976; Earl, 1983). These choice-theoretic approaches are still largely future-oriented, emphasizing the effects of uncertainty about the future on current imagination and choice. The past is a bygone. Its marks on human behaviour, transmitted through institutions and embodied in habits and the conceptual frameworks of cognition, are unexplained. Instead, social behaviour is explained ahistorically, and soley on the basis of individual imagination or choice. The past then appears principally in the form of institutional barriers or constraints.

As it has been argued in part two of this work, such individualistic and psychologistic conceptions pay insufficient attention to the work of sociologists and others, who have argued at great length that through social routine and the medium of institutions the past has a tremendous effect, not only on the constraints of choice and action, but on perception and reason itself.

Without the insertion of adequate defences against subjectivism, Keynes' theory of expectations is liable to further decomposition into Austrian, atomistic terms. This is especially true because Keynes sets out his theory of expectations in ahistorical terms and without reference to institutions. To be fair, this latter defect is typical of mainstream economics as a whole, and it is not confined to Keynes. However, this does not prevent an effective takeover of Keynesian expectations theory by the more consistent individualism of the Austrian School, especially because the latter provides an alternative to the mechanical determinism of much of neoclassical economics.

In addition there are insufficient defences against an Austrian critique of the role of persuasion in proselytizing a consensus view of the world. If it is accepted that a great amount of information must remain decentralized, and for that reason, at least, conceptions of the world are likely to vary from person to person, then persuasion will no longer be paramount. Furthermore, expectations of economic agents, even with similar information, can be on divergent, habit-ridden grooves, making government manipulation of 'the convention' or 'average opinion' more difficult than Keynes did suggest.

## 10.4 Lessons for Post-Keynesian Economics

On the grounds of analytic improvement, as well as self-defence, a number of modifications are necessary to the Keynesian theory of expectations and investment. These are related, in the main, to giving greater weight to the role of institutions in the economic system. An alternative to Austrian subjectivism, and to the much greater uniformity of expectations-formation with the rational expectations hypothesis, is to use the building block of specific social institutions rather than the anonymous and abstract individual.

In some ways the rival alternative approaches of the rational expectations theorists and the Austrian School are more consistent. The former erects a kind of systemic determinism; the latter the indeterminacy of a mass of colliding individuals. In comparison, Keynes' uneasy juxtaposition of the determinism of his Post-Marshallian model of the economy with the indeterminacy of expectations is unlikely to endure. For its apparent inconsistency of these crucial issues it is likely to be steadily eroded by Austrians and rational expectations theorists from both sides.

The argument in this chapter is that the ability of Keynesian theory to survive may well depend on its ability to abandon its individualistic and exclusively psychologistic precepts, and incorporate a theory of expectations based on a functional and historical study of political and economic institutions. Such an alternative framework for Keynesianism is not yet worked out in detail, although important elements are already present in the work of several Keynesians. It is far beyond the scope of this work to attempt to complete such a massive task. But an example which illustrates the importance of the institutionalist dimension to Keynesian theory follows.

## The imperfectionist interpretation

Consider the discussion in chapter 8 of the present work regarding the 'stickiness' of wages or prices. Keynes discusses the rigidity of money wages in chapter 17 of the *General Theory* (1971b, pp. 232–7), noting that if this were not so their fall might disrupt expectations regarding future costs and other related variables. Keynes' main point here has been widely misinterpreted as an assertion that, given the real world as it is, wages happen to be sticky. Thus 'Keynesian economics' is interpreted as being a theory that is applicable to a market economy with unfortunate 'imperfections'. Keynes' *General Theory* thus is rendered a 'special case' of a more general, and therefore more attractive, (neoclassical) theory which allows an unbounded range of variable flexibility in the wage and price mechanisms.

In this case the validity of Keynes' approach becomes simply a matter of empirical tests of the real-world inflexibility of wages and prices. Furthermore, even if wage and price rigidity is observed, the policy conclusion could equally be to attempt to remove all these 'imperfections' and move towards a 'free' and completely flexible real-world market, rather than the adoption of Keynesian policies. The 'imperfectionist' version of Keynesianism can easily lead to economic policies far removed from those of Keynes himself.

A much stronger version of Keynesian theory involves the adoption of an institutional approach. Keynes' point in chapter 17 could be interpreted in institutionalist terms. Not only are institutions necessary to provide information, but also rigidity and routine are to some extent required to reduce uncertainty and to make meaningful decision-making possible. As Tony Lawson (1985) argues in a discussion of Keynes' concept of uncertainty, people obtain knowledge about future outcomes and current choices by involvement in social practices and observation of the habits and routines that are the texture of social and economic life. Furthermore, as argued in chapter 8 of the present work, non-market institutions and rigid 'imperfections' play a necessary role in enabling the market system to operate.

Keynes did not explicitly reach all these conclusions, and his general emphasis is on individual psychology rather than institutions. For example, trade unions are mentioned only once in the chapter on 'Changes in Money-Wages' and three times in the *General Theory* as a whole. However, the treatment of expectations and uncertainty in Keynes' work points to a possible institutionalist interpretation, and one, furthermore, which strengthens the Keynesian case.

## Conclusion

The argument here suggests that there exists a foundation for an extension of Post-Keynesian theory along institutionalist lines. We do not have to start from scratch, but a start has to be made. For without major renovation and extension, and particularly with the inclusion of an endogenous theory of expectations formation, the Keynesian theoretical system is likely to continue to decline in terms of popularity and academic support.

It has always been a weakness of Keynesian theory that it lacked a basic microeconomic framework, and Keynes was usually forced to rely on Marshallian concepts and ideas. But likewise in Keynes there is a concern to treat the economic system as a whole, to generate a practical and realistic analysis, and to avoid a narrow compartmentalization of study. The challenge for modern Post-Keynesians is to rebuild Keynes' theory on more adequate, and non-individualistic, theoretical foundations.

# 11

## Directions and Policy Implications

It is nevertheless true that lessons, perhaps the only substantial ones, on
how to transcend the static framework have come from Marx, Veblen and
Schumpeter.

Nicholas Georgescu-Roegen (1971, p. 321)

A major theme of this work has been its challenge to the core
assumption of orthodox economic theory that both the tastes and
preferences of individuals, and the characteristics of production, are
given and exogenous to the theoretical system. Clearly, for orthodoxy,
these core assumptions imply a specific type of policy approach. Take,
for example, the economics of welfare. The policy focus of neoclassical
economics is in regard to the allocation, rather than the production, of
resources. Measurements of welfare are based on the given preference
functions, with the economy in a supposed position of equilibrium.
Despite the limitations of this narrow static framework, orthodox theory
seems to have no hesitation in extending its analysis to contentious
policy issues, to prescribe for example an extension of both markets and
private-property relations.

In some respects the theoretical framework of Austrian theory is an
improvement, in the sense that its approach is more dynamic and
process-oriented, rejecting the paradigm of general equilibrium and
focusing on the conditions for entrepreneurship and the creative use of
individual knowledge. But the conditions for the generation of
entrepreneurial ability itself, and the cultural influences on the cognition
of relevant information, are expressedly ignored. Once again the
circumstances moulding individual tastes, expectations and actions are
left outside the analysis.

A more fundamental rejection of the equilibrium approach would not
take tastes and technology as given, because these too are in a process of
continuous transformation, and not at rest. The replacements to the

static approach must go further than the arena and processes of economic exchange. If economics is to become fully dynamic it must engross the institutions of production and the formation of goals and tastes as well.

It is characteristic of an institutional approach, therefore, that the area of study in economics is not rigidly divided off into separate compartments. Although equilibrium analysis may be of some limited use, it is necessary to examine the processes of interaction between tastes, technology and the remainder of the socio-economic system. In consequence the institutional approach is process-oriented and evolutionary, rather than static and equilibriating.

Likewise, there is no attempt here to erect a Chinese Wall between the positive and normative aspects of economic study. Neoclassical theory attempts to make such a division, but, as we have seen, it fails in that its theoretical presuppositions remain deeply influenced by classic liberal ideology. The utilitarian attempt to separate off means from ends, and by this gambit to push value judgements to one side, is unacceptable too in that it fails again to consider the interaction of means and ends in the economic process. It focuses simply on the necessary means for a fixed equilibrium of ends. It is a more realistic and open approach to accept the interaction of judgements of fact and value in any social science.

With such normative questions in view, this chapter proceeds to draw out some implications of the type of analysis that is presented in this present work. At this stage it is possible to do little more than suggest the appropriate directions that future theoretical and policy development may take. Fortunately, however, there is now a substantial body of heterodox theory that may be useful in this regard.

We start with a consideration of some basic questions of human need and economic welfare. Some recent work in this area has some relevance for the recurrent policy questions which concern economists, such as the appropriate mix of markets and planning, and the limits to private enterprise and the state. The second section of this chapter suggests a general theoretical framework that is derived from systems theory for approaching these questions, before moving on, in the third section, to draft some guidelines concerning economic organization by using elements of the analysis from earlier chapters of this book.

## 11.1 NEEDS AND WELFARE

### A road to serfdom?

One prominent feature of this work is to look 'behind' the individual and to take his or her institutional circumstances into account. Institutions are regarded not merely as ridigities or constraints, but as structures and routinized activities which affect the dispersal and cognition of data and mould individual preferences and actions in many other ways.

The reader versed in orthodox economic theory, and influenced by its connections with classical liberal ideology, may be worried by the apparent policy implications of this line of argument. Does an awesome totalitarianism lurk in its wings? If humans are malleable and the supremacy of their expressed preferences is disconfirmed, is this not the cue for the entrance of a dictator to interpret needs according to whim or ideology and to disregard all contrary expressions of need or want? Is the denial of this finality of the individual the signpost for a road to serfdom in which the population as a whole is suppressed?

Arguably, such fears lie behind the continuing assumption by orthodox economics of the exogeneity of tastes and preferences and the assertion that the individual is the best judge of his or her welfare. In all likelihood these fears lurk in the background, despite the fact that they are not often made explicit.

Undeniably, there is some substance in the concerns expressed by the New Right. There are various traditions of paternalism, centralism and authoritarianism in social philosophy which deny or over-ride the right or ability of the individual to develop an understanding of his or her needs. Nevertheless, these dangers are not effectively countered by assuming that preferences are exogenous and that the expressed views of the individual are always sacrosanct.

Furthermore, the contrary view itself offers no ground for an authoritarian state, for several reasons. First, the assertion of some degree of individual malleability gives no *moral* justification for any form of dictatorship, or even a general or particular disregard for individual preferences and purposes. Furthermore, the assertion of the exogeneity of preferences and the subjectivity of purpose is itself no discouragement to a dictator who may (subjectively) believe that he or she has knowledge of what people really want, and (purposefully) acts accordingly.

Surely an important counter-argument to an authoritarian or paternalist view is that if it is sometimes difficult to know and express our own needs then it is many more times difficult to do so for the whole of society. If the individual is not always the best judge of his or her preferences then that is good reason to be sceptical of a paternalist of a dictator who expresses a belief about what society as a whole might need.

The latter argument can, however, be strengthened by underlining the problems relating to how a dictator, or anyone else for that matter, in principle 'knows' what is wanted by a number of individuals. Wants and needs are complex, and any serious attempt to express them involves large amounts of information. It is simply impossible to express all this information completely and adequately in either single or multiple cases. Whilst some very elemental and basic needs may be known (e.g. vitamins, oxygen), once we begin to describe the broader range of wants and needs they become varied and highly complex. Needs at a slightly higher level (e.g. clothing, shelter) can be known in broad terms, but not for everyone in complete detail. Consequently, whilst some specific or broadly defined needs can be appraised by a central authority, it is inconceivable that information relating to all needs could be gathered and processed on a centralized basis for society as a whole.

Notably, the latter kind of argument has been put forward by Friedrich Hayek (1935, 1937, 1945) and other Austrian thinkers, partly as a component of their forcible case against complete central planning by the 'socialist' state. This, of course, was the subject of debate in the 1920s and 1930s between Ludwig von Mises and Friedrich Hayek, on the one hand, and Oskar Lange and Frederick Taylor, on the other. As I have argued elsewhere (Hodgson, 1984), one important aspect of the Austrian position is incontrovertible: complete central planning is impossible because of the insuperable problems of gathering and processing the large amount of necessary information, even with the assistance of the largest foreseeable computers.[1]

Notice, however, that the Austrian writers go much further, by denying the value or viability of *all* economic planning by governments and even of the desirability or long-term feasibility of the so-called 'mixed economy'. In addition the very idea of general welfare or social needs in the traditional sense is denied. Some of their insights regarding problems of information and uncertainty should be accepted, but there is no need to follow them in their extreme and untenable views.

Inadvertently, however, by stressing problems of information and the complexities of human interaction, the Austrian thinkers have provided a strong argument against those who may see a 'road to serfdom' in a theory which dares to consider the forces that mould the purposes and preferences of individuals. This is because the amount of information involved rules out any theoretical justification for a single, paternal authority. We are thus not impelled to put the analysis of those forces beyond the boundaries of economic analysis.

## Needs and economic analysis

Furthermore, even the most avowedly subjectivist of economic theorists end up asserting a number of objective or universal needs pertaining to society as a whole.[2] Indeed, the whole thrust of the economic policies of the New Right is for the 'need' for individual 'freedom' to be maximized by minimizing constraints on all human actors. Other 'needs' are derived, such as for individual autonomy, private property rights and an extensive market mechanism. The point here is not the validity or otherwise of these 'needs' but the fact that any economic analysis that makes policy proposals must have a set of implicit or explicit 'needs' or values at its core.

Herein lies an internal contradiction in much New Right analysis. If it were as absolutely individualistic or subjectivist as claimed then it would have to abandon any rational argument to persuade others of the policy proposals to which it is attached. This inner contradiction caused by combining extreme subjectivism with rational argument was identified by Michael Oakeshott (1962, p. 21) when he wittily described Hayek's work as 'a plan to resist all planning'.

A pure and extreme subjectivism, if such a thing were possible, would put any analysis of needs or policies beyond the bounds of discourse, given that discourse is always between two or more individuals. Rational argument about policy would be a matter for the individual alone. Consequently, and against the traditions of both neoclassical and Austrian economics, an extreme subjectivism would not indulge in any extended rational dialogue. As a result of this conflict, either extreme subjectivism, or rational discourse, or both, have to be abandoned.

Instead, the route taken here is to accept that it is possible and desirable, if due care is taken, to establish objective or universal human needs. Perhaps one of the most important contributors in this regard is the psychologist Abraham Maslow (1970). We shall also draw upon the recent work on needs by social theorists Len Doyal and Ian Gough (1984, 1986). Doyal and Gough are keen to attack purely relativist or subjectivist concepts in this area and assert the universality of some bedrock concepts of both need and human nature.

Despite the popular perception that they are poles apart, here there is an uncanny similarity between orthodox economists and the New Right, on the one hand, and some Marxist writers, on the other. Both eschew psychology and any idea of human nature as a foundation for their analysis.[3] Both dismiss the possibility of any general or objective theory of need, asserting that needs are essentially relative, transient of subjective.[4] As Doyal and Gough (1984 pp. 6–9) show, it is relatively easy to find examples of such an unacceptable verdict from the Right, Left and Centre of the political spectrum.

Orthodox economists, true to their subjectivist intellectual pedigree, usually make no distinction between needs and wants and refer exclusively to the latter. Yet in ordinary language we often make such a distinction. A want, for instance, often suggests mere whim or fancy. In contrast, the word 'need' refers to a general requirement pertaining to the human condition, which would apply to anyone else in the same position. Needs are thus objective and universalizable, whereas wants are not. Consequently, to discover and evaluate needs we have to study the nature of the human conditon and its context.

It is interesting to note that there have been mild flirtations by economists with some idea of an objective ranking of needs. Remarkably, in 1871 Carl Menger proposed in his *Principles of Economics* such a ranked list, consisting of water, food, clothing, shelter, coach (transportation) and tobacco. Apart from the insult to the non-smoker, this particular ranking of objective needs is an embarrassment to the modern Austrian economists with their ultra-subjectivist view of needs or wants. It is common for the Austrian theorists to emphasize that their lineage starts with Menger, but often they pay little attention to such discontinuities in their own tradition.

Likewise, the neoclassical theorists, eager to stress the continuity of their outlook with classical writers such as David Ricardo and Adam Smith, see the classical concept of 'use-value' as being effectively identical to the neoclassical 'utility'. What is ignored, as I have argued elsewhere (Hodgson, 1982c, pp. 41–4), is that by 'use-value' the classical economists meant something different from subjective utility, relating to the objective use of or need for the commodity in a social context.[5]

As Lutz and Lux (1979, ch. 2) show, there is an undercurrent in the history of economics which asserts some idea of need in distinction from the variable whims or wants that an individual may express. For example, John Stuart Mill objects to Jeremy Bentham's failure to admit the possibility of 'higher needs' in the utilitarian framework, and stresses the need for education and personal development. A similar undercurrent is present in the writings of Alfred Marshall (1949, p. 72) who sees mere wants as 'the rulers of life among the lower animals' whilst human beings are progressively seeking some greater notion of advancement. Expressions of objective need are not always clear or adequate, but they are there, even in the works of a neoclassical economist such as Marshall and an Austrian such as Menger.

## Theories of needs

It should be clear from this work that its argument depends to a significant degree upon developments in psychology and anthropology. The above discussion of rationality, of habits, and the hierarchical nature of consciousness in part two drew in part from such material. A consequence is to reject the utilitarian foundations of orthodox welfare economics, plus the subjectivist arguments of the Austrians against social welfare *per se*, and to attempt instead to establish some objective conception of human need. A valuable starting point in this regard is Maslow's 'hierarchy of needs' (1970).

Maslow argues that at the first and lowest level of the hierarchy each individual has a number of basic physiological needs, particularly air, water, food, shelter and sleep. These needs must be satisfied in order to survive, and if there is an acute deficiency then the individual will react by directing most of his or her conscious energies towards obtaining the food, shelter, etc., that is required. However, once a basic need is satisfied, then concentration on a higher need becomes possible as the next step in a developmental process.

Consequently, ample gratification of such physiological needs means that the struggle for their satisfaction is submerged from conscious priority. The next set of needs in the hierarchy dominate human action. These higher material needs are regarded by Maslow as being safety and security.

Once all material needs are relatively satiated then the human organism will put priority on needs which have a pronounced social dimension. The first of these is the need for belongingness, consisting of needs for love, affection and acceptance. A higher social need is the need to establish self-esteem, partly on the basis of the recognition and esteem of others for the individual concerned.

Maslow regarded the satisfaction of all the above needs as fundamental to the physical and mental health of all humans. Further to these basic material and social needs there are others, at the apex of the hierarchy, called 'self-actualization' needs. Once all serious deficiencies are met in terms of material and social needs then the person may move on to the creative and most rewarding phase of personal development.

At the higher, 'self-actualization' level there is the need for truth, service, perfection and meaning in human life. Such creative needs are paramount in a mature and healthy adult. However, they are unlikely to be prioritized if the person is constantly seeking after other, lower-level needs. Maslow regards such a block in the developments process as resulting either from material poverty, or from social isolation or insecurity, or from an aberrant fixation on lower-level needs when in other respects a person is ready to progress to a higher level. Thus there is no simple, mechanical relationship between income levels and personal development up the hierarchy of needs. A rich person can still be fixated with the search for personal wealth, or with the accumulation of individual power.

The notion that there are basic human needs which must be satisified before humans can function effectively creates a problem for the utilitarian analysis of orthodox economics. This analysis assumes that the opportunity to choose, act, imagine, conjecture and be entrepreneurial is available to all; there are simply individual differences in ability, situation and knowledge. Yet in reality those that are faced with hunger have little alternative or inclination but to seek satisfaction of this need, literally on a hand-to-mouth basis; those that are sick or disabled are often preoccupied with the problems associated with their condition; and those more fortunate but mentally and physically exhausted by menial, repetitive work naturally have no entrepreneurial inclination when they retire exhausted from the day's toil. Before 'economic man' can choose and act he must be fed, clothed, rested and be healthy. The choosing, acting agent of the textbooks has basic needs that must be satisfied before he can calculate, bargain and choose in the manner in which he or she is supposed. Thus there are material preconditions for the existence of the economic agent that are subsumed or neglected in the orthodox approach.[6] These correspond to Maslow's 'material needs'.

Maslow's work has been used by Branko Horvat (1980, 1982) and Mark Lutz and Kenneth Lux (1979) as a strong argument for the greater involvement of individuals in the decisions that affect them, so as satisfy the higher-order needs of self-esteem, self-respect and self-actualization. As a great deal of life is involved with work, the importance of economic democracy or self-management in the workplace is stressed by these writers. Thus in policy terms a great distance is covered with the use of Maslow's powerful psychological analysis.

A problem, however, is that being based upon psychology alone such an analysis excludes the historical and institutional dimension in the analysis of needs. Whilst there is no justification for a Chinese Wall between economics and psychology, this does not mean that psychology alone is sufficient. There should also be no impassable barrier between economics and the other social sciences.

Consequently, despite Maslow's contribution, the rebuilding of economics exclusively upon psychology is a mistake, and this is one reservation regarding Lux and Lutz's stimulating and valuable book. We need to look further.

On the basis of Doyal and Gough's work (1984, 1986, in press) it is possible to be fairly optimistic about the further progressive development of the theory of human need. They point out that needs are crucially linked with goals, and they define 'basic individual needs' as 'those goals which must be achieved if any individual is to achieve any other goal – however idiosyncratic or culturally specific those other goals are' (1984, p. 10). These 'basic human needs' include survival and autonomy: 'in order to act successfully, people need physically to survive and need enough sense of their own identity and autonomy to inititate actions on the basis of their deliberations' (1986, p. 69). Under these categories come an array of further needs relating to physical and mental health and personal development.

Individual needs such as these generate a further category called 'basic societal needs'. Doyal and Gough are not asserting that society has needs but that 'societal needs' are 'those social preconditions for the achievement of the individual needs' (1984, p. 18; 1986, p. 71) that they describe. Consequently there is a 'basic human need' for food and a 'societal need' for an economic system which can produce and distribute food to the entire population. In addition, an economy is required that will produce adequate clothing, shelter and other items to meet basic needs. Further to this, as autonomous self-development is another basic human need, there is also a 'societal need' for a child-rearing and education system which enables people to learn and develop their own capacities.

Unlike Maslow's work, Doyal and Gough do not rank needs in a simple one-dimensional hierarchy. They erect a demarcation between 'basic human' and 'societal' needs and impose upon this a more complex, inter-active system of needs. Thus the theoretical system of their work is an inter-related web, rather than simple hierarchy. Whilst some needs are self-evident, the character of others, not least the best arrangement for satisfying 'societal needs', is to some extent open-ended and subject to continuing debate. On the one hand, Doyal and Gough reject a purely psychologistic conception of human need which abstracts people from their social and historical location and works from a static idea of the 'human essence'. But also, on the other hand, they reject accounts which result in an entirely relativist conception of need, or which make it an entirely subjective issue.

Clearly, a theory of needs cannot be separated from a wider analysis of the workings of the politico-economic system. Just as it is unwarranted to develop such an analysis in the belief that it is unlikely to point to a set of prescriptive and non-subjective needs, it is also unwarranted to develop a theory of needs in isolation from a general politico-economic analysis.

Because the argument is not rooted simply in the psychological characteristics of human beings, Doyal and Gough are able to go further than Maslow in the prescription of the best kind of society to meet individual needs. For example, such a society will require a well-developed system of communication so that they are able to learn the theories and practices that are needed for material production and human care. They go further to argue for some sort of political authority, ultimately backed up by sanctions, that will ensure that the rules necessary for the functioning of the society are followed.

Whilst the Doyal and Gough line of argument is not fully explored and there are many problems to be resolved, it clearly offers a dynamic and sophisticated approach to the theory of human needs. A feature of their analysis is that it is open-ended, in that they do not claim to provide a formula to mark out the totality of human needs, but to build an analytical engine which has scope to adapt and change in the light of evolving debate. While there is flexibility in this approach there is still an over-riding goal: 'of healthy, educated individuals struggling equally together to look after themselves and each other in ways which fairly maximize their creative potential' (Doyal and Gough, 1984, p. 29).

The break that is made in this present work from the individualist and subjectivist approach to economics clearly has implications for the economics of welfare. The non-subjectivist theory of need outlined above demonstrates that the consequence of this break is not to embrace a paternalistic or arbitrary dictatorship which simply imposes its conception of need over others. In fact, Maslow, Doyal and Gough all stress the development of both individual autonomy and choice as aspects of human need.

However, contrary to orthodox theory, choice is not absolute. When it comes to practical economic and political decisions any government, however liberal or individualistic, is bound to impose its overall conception of need in some areas, and not leave it all to individual choice and the market. Notably, none of the New Right governments that have emerged in the 1980s has suggested that hard drugs, pornography or prostitution are simply matters for individual choice. Every New Right government has asserted the 'need' for law and order and strong national defence. Clearly, there is a major conflict here between government practice and the implications of the subjectivist analysis of their economic advisers.

In sum it is necessary to avoid the false polarity between the proposition, on the one hand, that all needs are subjective, and on the other, that need can be determined by an all-knowing benevolent political party or despot. A dynamic and open-ended conception of need suggests that the institutions determining, evaluating and assessing needs must be flexible and responsive to both individual claims and public debate.

This approach is fundamentally different, therefore, from both statist paternalism and classic liberalism. The former presumes that all or most needs can be known and evaluated by a central authority. Classic liberalism, on the other hand, assumes that there is little possibility of any general knowledge of needs, and on all or most matters the individual remains the best judge of his or her welfare. The former outlook is normally associated with the policy prescription of comprehensive central planning, the latter with the policy of *laissez-faire*.

In contrast, the type of analysis adopted here recognizes that the nature and evaluation of needs will vary depending on the type of need involved. For most needs, however, the approach is both analytic and educative, in that it is accepted that in outline some general analysis of needs is possible, but also their evaluation is to some extent dynamic and open-ended, depending in part on the education and self-awareness of the individual.

Thus there is a societal need for a fully participatory politico-economic system. Participatory democracy, as it has been argued elsewhere (Pateman, 1970; Hodgson, 1984); is not merely a means, it is also an end. It is required as a type of institutional framework within which people can become educated and self-aware as to their needs.

Thus to pose the problem of designing the economic framework within which needs can best be satisfied as being one of simply finding the right mix of market arrangements and public provision misses the point. First, the fact that the determination of needs is itself a dynamic process should augur caution as to the design of static 'optimal' frameworks, whatever the mix between private and collective provision. Second, it should not be ignored that a crucial problem is to establish flexible and open institutions through which human needs can be articulated, clarified, evaluated and prioritized. Thus it is not simply a question of markets and the state; it is also a matter of enhancing democracy within society so that this educative process can flourish.

## 11.2   SYSTEMS, IMPURITY AND DOMINANCE

We now move on to consider in outline the type of society that would best satisfy social needs as discussed above. Whilst it would be impossible to complete this task in anything but the barest outlines, we are able to reach some conclusions by combining some of the arguments in preceding chapters with a more general theoretical framework derived from systems theory. It is to the derivation of this framework that we now turn.

It has been acknowledged already that the problems of information that were highlighted in the Great Planning Debate of the 1920s and 1930s rule out any attempt at 100 per cent intervention or planning by the central state. At the other extreme, concerning the market, in chapters 7 and 8 it was shown that a pure market system is not feasible because the market itself contains 'impurities' and it itself consists of structures and institutions. Consequently, neither, on the one hand, a pure *laissez-faire* market economy, nor on the other hand, an economy that is planned entirely from the centre (either by dictators or by democratically elected representatives), is feasible in practice.

However, this is not a call for a theory or policy formed by mixing together, in desired proportions like ingredients in a stew, the ideas and policies of these two extremes. In this work an attempt has been made to develop a theoretical framework which transcends the type of analysis that is involved in both these extreme cases.

Thus, for example, the question of the appropriate degree of state intervention is not best approached by searching for a 'mix' between intervention and non-intervention. The arguments against a pure market system in earlier chapters of this work do not simply undermine the philosophy of *laissez-faire*; they also show that the market itself is a social institution. Furthermore, the pursuit of a 'free-market' philosophy necessarily involves state intervention to set up the institutions which are necessary to make the market work, and to sanction and sometimes regulate the social relations of the market itself.

In particular, one of the arguments in chapter 7 is that exchange and property relations, whilst being based to a large extent on custom and tradition, have an essential statutory component in a modern society. Thus a market system is necessarily penetrated through the regulation and intervention of the state. As Oakeshott (1962, p. 55) remarks: 'if effective competition is to exist it can do so only by virtue of a legal system which promotes it . . . unregulated competition is a chimera.'

Almost paradoxically, therefore, the idea of a strict non-interventionist economic policy is misconceived. The market functions through a web of institutions which are inevitably entwined with the state and government. As in the Britain of the nineteenth century (see Polanyi, 1944), and under contemporary Western governments of the '*laissez-faire*' New Right, the attempt to create a 'free' market system involves continuous juridical, political and institutional meddling by the central authorities. Note, for example, the cases of wage and working-day legislation in the nineteenth century, and the frequent amendments to trade-union law and corporate competion policy in Britain under the government of Margaret Thatcher in the 1980s.

Consequently, the main argument is not really between intervention and non-intervention, but which type of intervention is to be carried out, and for which ends. Intervention is necessarily institutional in character. To some extent this contrasts with the kind of Keynesian perspective which prevailed for three decades after the Second World War, and which focused impractically and almost entirely on overall, aggregate measures (e.g. taxes, public expenditure, economic growth) to the neglect of structural and institutional considerations.

Nevertheless, some foremost questions of structure for a modern economy are, of course, the appropriate structured combination of market institutions and planning, and between common and private ownership. It is to these questions we now turn. They are approached, however, by first giving an account of a meta-theoretical framework which has first been outlined elsewhere (Hodgson, 1984, chs 6 and 7). After a restatement of these ideas they are developed further in the context of the present work.

### Economic systems as diversified pluralities

If we examine the major economic systems of the past it is clear that none are pure and simple in the sense that they are composed of a single type of economic structure. Classical antiquity included extensive markets, organized manufacture, and a state-planned infrastructure as well as the ubiquitous master–slave relationship on the large agricultural estates. Likewise, the typical serf–lord relationship on the feudal domain existed alongside a developing market, the urban guilds, and the parallel hierarchy of the church. Third, every modern capitalist system contains elements of state intervention, resilient domestic production in the household, as well as markets and private corporations. Finally, in the Eastern Bloc, markets and a degree of private ownership exist alongside the central plan. All economic systems, it appears, are diversified pluralities.

The question is, does the concurrence of these different forms of economic organization within a given social formation represent a kind of accidental or incidental accretion of elements? Clearly, as the social formation changes and evolves, all economic systems are bound to contain residues from the past. Or do we take an additional and stronger view, in that some such elements may be *necessary* for the system as a whole to function? Is it simply a historical likelihood that different structures will co-exist; or can we say more? Do some of these structures play an essential, functional role?

It has been argued elsewhere (Hodgson, 1984, pp. 67–104) that some of these co-existing structures are in fact necessary for the system to operate and reproduce itself through time. Thus in the ancient world some market trade was necessary. Whilst the typical location of slave labour in Ancient Greece and Rome was not in state organizations but in large, privately owned estates, the state still played an indispensible and central part in the economic system, by conquering territory, capturing more slaves, and developing the politico-economic infrastructure.

Similarly, whilst the market was not central at least in the early stages of feudal society, and many products were either consumed directly or appropriated as rents and tithes, the market played an essential function. It was first necessary as part of a trading system to bring scarce commodities from other regions. Later it became even more important with the growth of money rents, as the serfs or peasants had then to sell part of their product on the market in order to obtain cash.

Turning from the past to the present, the type of economic system that is found in the Eastern Bloc provides plentiful evidence of the essential contribution of different economic structures. This is even in an economy where there is apparent acceptance of an ideology which aims to bring most production under a single, central, rational plan. It is well known but worth repeating, however, that problems regarding the quantity and type of information make it impossible to plan completely a complex, modern economy on a central basis. I have calculated elsewhere (Hodgson, 1984, p. 170) that it would take at least 18 years to carry out one of the most basic computational operations for formulating a complete central plan, even with the fastest computers available.

Consequently, central planning can proceed only on the basis of aggregate indicators and targets. This, in turn, can create problems, as there will be insufficient discrimination over quality and insufficient attention to the different types of product involved. Attempts to fulfill aggregate plan targets can lead to shortages of specific types of product and to the creation of items of inferior quality.

The upshot is that either by design or default, legally or illegally, markets or exchanges play an essential part in any system that is centrally planned. Thus, in the Soviet Union, there is a thriving black market and a whole group of people, known as *tolkachi* who make a living by supplying plant managers and others with the materials and spare parts that they need. The planning system is too cumbersome and slow to deal with these individual requests, and there is thus a widespread reliance on these illegal deals.

In the case of Hungary and China, however, and more recently in the Soviet Union itself, there have been attempts to acknowledge this problem and to accept that markets are essential even in an economy which is regulated by an overall, central plan. Thus there have been a tentative endorsement and legalization of types of market and exchange transactions, by public firms, private firms, cooperatives or individuals.

Consequently, just as there are practical limitations to the extent of the market, there are similar limitations to central planning as well. And just as the market requires 'imperfections' to operate, central planning may be able to function only through the conjunction of market and other forms.

## The principles of impurity and dominance

In general, what is involved is more than an empirical observation that different structures and systems have co-existed through history. What is involved is an assertion that some of these economic structures were *necessary* for the socio-economic system to function over time.

The idea that an impurity may be necessary for the socio-economic system to function does not always mean that no other impurity could do the job as well. In some cases, such as the market in a planned economy, there may be no essential substitute for this impurity. In other cases, such as the role of the church under feudalism, there may be in theory an alternative. Thus the word 'necessary' in the preceding paragraph can have either an exclusive or non-exclusive connotation, depending on the concrete circumstances.

The various economic structures that intrude in different types of economic system, such as the market or the state in Classical Antiquity, the market or the church under feudalism, and the market in a centrally planned economy, are called impurities. The idea that they are essential for the system as a whole to function is called the impurity principle.

The impurity principle is combined with a more familiar idea which is conveniently titled 'the principle of dominance', i.e. the notion that socio-economic systems generally exhibit a dominant economic structure. It is expressed by Marx when he writes:

> In all forms of society there is one specific kind of production which predominates over the rest, whose relations thus assign rank and influence to the others. It is a general illumination which bathes all the other colours and modifies their particularity. It is a particular ether which determines the specific gravity of every being which has materialized within it. (Marx, 1973, pp. 106–7)

Whilst the principle of dominance is found in Marxist writings the impurity principle is essentially incompatible with Marxism. It was not a slip of the pen when Marx and Engels wrote in *The Manifesto of the Communist Party* that eventually production would be 'concentrated in the hands of a vast association of the whole nation'. They envisage a society which can be completely structured and ordered according to the dictates of reason, once the vested interests of the minority class are removed. However, whether or not it is desirable, the idea of ordering society as a single and undiversified 'vast association' is not feasible.

*Cybernetics and the impurity principle*

Part of the justification for the impurity principle can thus be derived from an analysis of past socio-economic formations in history. But additional and related arguments can be derived from systems theory or cybernetics. Here there is a set of ideas concerning variety and complexity in relation to the system and its environment. One of the most important is W. Ross Ashby's (1952, 1956) derivation of the 'law of requisite variety'.

The shortest and most frequently quoted version of this law is 'only variety can destroy variety': that is, if a stable target outcome is to be attained, then the variety of the controlling system must be at least equal to that of the activity which it is directing. For example, an air-conditioning system which is meant to keep both the temperature and the humidity of the air within a desired range must have two or more controlling instruments, namely a thermostat and a hygrometer. One instrument will, in general, be insufficient to keep two elements in target range. This general result can be demonstrated mathematically using a matrix structure with rows and columns representing the different possible environmental states, and the different possible responses by the system (Ashby, 1956, ch. 11; Emery, 1981, vol. 1, pp. 100–20).

It is not generally recognized, but in form Ashby's law is nearly identical to the economic policy rule first derived in the work of Jan Tinbergen (1952). In a book published in the same year as Ashby's original work, Tinbergen showed that the number of policy instruments (e.g. government expenditure, taxation levels, etc.) must be equal to or greater than the number of policy targets (e.g. full employment, balance of payments equilibrium, etc.). In their application, of course, Ashby's law and Tinbergen's rule are not identical, as the former is a more general statement than the latter. Their uncanny formal similarity, however, should nevertheless suggest a fruitful application of cybernetics and systems theory to economics.

Some management-systems theorists, notably Stafford Beer (1964), John McEwan (1971), and Raul Espejo and Nigel Howard (1982), have developed and amended Ashby's law and applied it to human organizations. Espejo and Howard point out that what is involved here is not a mathematical truism with *a priori* validity, but a different proposition which could possibly be false.[7] This is the proposition that every viable system is exposed to environmental contingencies with which it cannot cope. In other words, for each system there is a possible disturbance for which there is no response that will lead to a target outcome. To distinguish this from Ashby's law, Espejo and Howard call this the 'law of insufficient variety'.

Consequently, to minimize the chances of disruption an open system has to contain sufficient variety to deal with all the potential variation in its environment. Complexity and variety within the system is necessary so that the system can survive and deal with complexity, variety and unforeseeable shocks in the real world.

The impurity principle is a special case of this corollary. It is a broader idea than Tinbergen's rule, and one narrower than Ashby's general law, which applies to all open systems. The impurity prinicple does not relate simply to economic policy, but also to the composition and complexity of the socio-economic formation as a whole. The idea is that there must always be a plurality of economic structures, so that the socio-economic formation as a whole has requisite variety to promote and cope with change. Thus if one type of structure is to prevail (e.g. central planning), other structures (e.g. markets, private firms) are necessary to enable the system to function.

There is a further difference with Ashby's law and its immediate extensions. In Ashby's exposition 'requisite variety' is derived from the variety of the environment which is *external* to the system. In social terms this translates into the proposition that a social system has to contain sufficient variety to deal with potential shocks from its natural and international environment. But in the case of social systems there is a further source of threatening variety: from *within* the system itself. In part two of this work it has been argued that there is a degree of indeterminacy in human action. Consequently there is 'internal' potential variety emanating from these partially indeterminate human acts. Clearly the existence of 'internal' as well as external potential variety is an important distinguishing feature in comparing social with other systems[8]

The impurity principle is thus substantiated in a double sense, both by the complexity of the external environment and, within limits, the inner indeterminacy of much human behaviour. Human organizations thus present an extra dimension of diversity which is not present in a mechanistic system. To distinguish between these two sources of variety and potential shock to the system we refer below to environmental and agent variety, respectively. The application of this distinction is taken up below.

### Illustrations of the impurity principle

Clearly, the impurity principle provides an initial theoretical framework to support a policy of economic pluralism. However, it does not lead to the same type of policies as presented by the major postwar theoreticians of the 'mixed economy'. For instance, in the work by Anthony

Crosland (1956) in this genre, no notion is present of the *necessary* combination of planning with markets, of markets with plans. The 'mixed economy' is presented as an ethical ideal, not as a functional necessity. The combination of the principle of dominance with the impurity principle again distances the theoretical standpoint here from that of Crosland. The notion of a heterogeneous structured whole, in which one type of economic structured is dominant, is not present in his work.

We have suggested already that the policy outlook that is implied by the impurity principle differs from a not uncommon Marxist intention to suppress completely all vestiges of markets and private enterprise from a socialist system. Such statist and non-pluralistic versions of socialism are typically inspired by a utopian rationalism which assumes that society can be ordered in its entirety according to the dictates of reason.

Clearly, in such a conception the problems of gathering and processing information, and of cognitive divergences between agents, are downplayed or ignored. Otherwise, when such problems arise they are attributed to differences of class outlook and interest which at some ideal future stage will be removed. However, whilst such issues as class are very likely to exacerbate divergences of information and cognition, it is simply utopian to suggest that the latter can be reduced to insignificance, even with the abolition of class differences in society.

Although the impurity principle itself points us towards such an anti-statist conclusion, there are additional features of the present work which tie in with the latter argument. The emphases on problems of information, and of cognitive divergences between agents even when similar phenomena are observed, all undermine the rationalistic outlook which is associated with proposals for a complete and all-embracing central plan. These problems are compounded in a complex industrial society, especially when the territory and population are large. Furthermore, the fact that the actions of individual agents are largely routinized and habitual often makes central-planning adjustments difficult. The existence of 'tacit knowledge' associated with acquired and habitual skills means that much information of this sort can never be known or appreciated by the centre.

Clearly, some of the arguments in the preceding pararaph have an Austrian ring, and others are reminiscent of statements against planning from Michael Polanyi (1957, 1967), Michael Oakeshott (1962) and others. However, whilst these arguments work against the proposition for complete planning by the central state, they do not imply an attachment to policies of an opposite extreme. No support can be derived here for the complete abolition of central planning and a complete reliance instead on the market mechanism. Such conclusions are further examples of promising and rounded arguments being forced into square, pre-existing, ideological holes.

At the general level, the impurity principle and the derivative arguments for economic pluralism can obviously be directed against the New Right and advocates of a 'pure' market system. An extreme case of the latter is Ludwig von Mises (1949, p. 259) who writes: 'The market economy or capitalism, as it is usually called, and the socialist economy preclude one another. There is no mixture of the two systems possible or thinkable; there is no such thing as a mixed economy, a system that would be in part capitalist and in part socialist'.

Both Friedrich Hayek and Milton Friedman have proposed that the market and capitalist elements in the Western 'mixed economy' should be dramatically increased. While a pure market economy ostensibly involves a decentralization and parcellization of economic power, it is non-pluralistic in the important sense that it involves a largely uniform set of social and property relations: a plurality of agency but not of structure.

As a further illustration of the critical relevance of this broad approach consider Don Lavoie's forceful presentation (1985a) of a New Right case against national planning and for a market-based economic system.[9] An impressive feature of this work is its emphasis, following Michael Polanyi, on the function of habit and tradition in preserving and transmitting complex 'practical knowledge' within the economy. In this respect there are strong common features with parts of the present study. As we shall show, however, there are wide divergences as well.

Early in his book Lavoie identifies just three types of economic coordination process: tradition, market and planning. In some passages he seems to recognize that any social system is necessarily a combination of some of these three elements. Thus he writes that 'no human society is conceivable that is dissociated from traditions altogether' (p. 29).

However, this hint of pluralism is not replicated in regard to planning. Unlike the other two categories, 'Planning' is defined in a pure and all-embracing form; it 'aims at the complete replacement of Market and Tradition by a fundamentally different method of organization' (p. 29).

Clearly, Lavoie has erected a straw man to knock down with ease. He does not seem to notice that if either 'Market' or 'Tradition' were defined in such an all-embracing and exclusive manner then we would likewise have no difficulty in rejecting them too as organizing principles. Lavoie starts by recognizing the inter-penetration of markets and tradition, but rejects at the outset any complex combination or symbiotic relationship between planning and markets, or planning and tradition.

A few pages later he asserts, however, that as organizing principles tradition and markets are 'incompatible' (p. 39). This may seem to contradict his preceding statement. On the other hand it could mean that, in the language of the present work, either tradition or market may be dominant, but not both. Lavoie seems to lack a conceptual framework to express this clearly. He wants to retain tradition in its fundamental role but to make the market the supreme organizing principle. In other words he seems to wish to recognize tradition as a necessary impurity in a market system.

Consideration or development of an impurity-dominance type of framework is made much more difficult because of Lavoie's treatment of planning at the outset. If this were given a fair crack of the whip within Lavoie's argument then he would have to consider the possibility of planning playing a necessary function alongside tradition. The contentious issue would then be whether or not the system is to be dominated by the market.

However, Lavoie's reliance on the Austrian School prevents him from adopting anything approaching an impurity principle. Not only would the recognition of planning as a necessary impurity go against von Mises' statement against the mixed economy quoted above, but for Lavoie there would be a much more difficult theoretical task on hand. He is quite right to emphasize the triumph of the Austrians in their demonstration that complete central planning, whether desirable or not, is simply impossible in practice. However, that is all they did demonstrate. They did not show convincingly that a mixture of planning and market was not feasible, despite dogmatic statements to the contrary.

## Extending the impurity principle

Consequently the impurity principle leads to a direct rejection of Marxist statism, New Right free markets, and the Crosland-type mixed economy. However, as developed so far, the impurity principle is not sufficient on its own to provide detailed demarcation criteria for policy purposes, so as to design the appropriate combination of market, planning and other economic mechanisms.

In preceding works the impurity principle has been applied simply to socio-economic systems as a whole, with the above conclusions regarding economic pluralism. It should be stressed, however, that with complex and open systems the demarcation of 'parts' and 'wholes' is, to some extent, a matter for the level of theoretical abstraction. Thus, for example, a given national economy is part of a world economic system, which in turn is part of a world eco-system, and so on. Ashby's law would suggest that the impurity principle could be applied to these other levels as well.

Working, as it were, in the other direction, each system is composed of sub-systems which themselves display the properties of complete, open systems. We shall apply this argument to the firm, and then to the market. This consideration of sub-systems will enable us to draw some further conclusions.

## 11.3　Guidelines for Economic Organization

### The firm as a system

The firm is a system. Although systems theory has been applied more frequently to the firm by management theorists such as Stafford Beer (1972), there are examples of economists following this approach, such as the work of Neil Kay (1979). Directly from Ashby's law, Beer draws the conclusion that the firm must be structured internally with sufficient variety to cope with the complexity and variety of its environment.

As Beer argues, in part this shows a need for some degree of hierarchy within the firm; any given level of hierarchy has insufficient variety to deal with environmental complexity and variation. Different levels of the hierarchy imply different practices and routines and different methods for dealing with problems. For example, the mechanic on the shopfloor may simply repair a piece of supplied machinery that is defective. In contrast the manager will address the problem as to whether or not the same supplier is to be used again. The hierarchical organization of the firm thus creates the possibility and likelihood of different types of response to the same eventuality, thus giving the firm some resilience to mishaps or external changes.

Notably, this is despite the fact that reactions are often routinized or habitual. A response through global calculation is normally impossible because the lack of information and the complexity of the problem. Despite this the firm can to some extent cope with variety and change: not only breakdowns and mishaps but also virulent competition and technological transformation.

Management hierarchy, furthermore, permits and endorses a distinction between long-term stategists and relatively short-term tacticians; the former concerned with general decisions concerning strategy and the latter with their implementation. As Alfred Chandler (1962, 1977) points out, firms have found it useful to adopt an organizational structure which separates strategic decision-makers from those concerned with more immediate tactics and the implementation of the strategy.

There is also a distinction between formal and informal structures within the firm. Consequently, as John McEwan (1971) and Richard Nelson (1981b) and others have argued, whilst hierarchy may be necessary, management at any level cannot have complete control over any tier of the system. In part, the existence of informal structures prevents this, but it has the additional positive feature that it creates diversity. More generally, Michael Dietrich (1986, p. 322) has pointed out that 'the development of future economic activities within complex organizations involves a strategic planning system and an informal system, whether the latter is recognized or not'. A progressive management will not try to repress or extinguish informal structures, nor ignore them whilst wishing they would go away, but try to make them as responsive and flexible as possible.

In addition, of course, there are many other sources of complexity and diversity within the firm. A common and widely appreciated response to a complex and uncertain environment is for the firm to diversify, so that as the market for each product fluctuates the firm as a whole is more resilient. Diversification is thus a response to potential variety which consists in increasing the variety of activities within the firm.

In contrast, vertical integration is a response in terms of reducing the potential variety in the environment by widening the boundaries of the system itself. However, whilst this can alleviate one set of problems it can create another. The firm may itself ossify, and its own sub-systems may themselves begin to function in an independent, unresponsive and sometimes conflicting manner. As Kay (1984, p. 170) puts it: 'risk avoidance and over-emphasis on vested interests and the status quo are well recognized problems of an insulated bureaucracy.' The distinctive problem for an ossified firm of this type is not to do with lack of information and uncertainty: it is that internal routine has begun to run on inflexible grooves, and there is no stimulus for managers or workers to develop broader aspirations, to innovate, and to improve.

The application of the extended impurity principle to this particular system thus suggests that there are broadly two types of response by the firm to change, complexity, variety and uncertainty regarding its external environment.

1  The firm may respond by creating internal structural variety to match the variety from outside. This can occur by product diversification, of by organizational subdivision of a horizontal or vertical type.
2  The firm can attempt to reduce the external variety by increasing the span of control. This can occur through the firm's own growth and

increasing dominance of the market, or closer cooperation and longstanding arrangements with associated companies, or through takeovers or mergers with other firms.

However, whilst the above are partial solutions they create further problems of their own. Internal structural diversification breaks the firm down into parts which in turn can become ossified and lead to overall inflexibility. On the other hand, any increase in the span of control may itself lead to problems as there may be reduced stimulii from the market and the firm's environment, reducing the impetus for innovation and growth. Thus the very success in dealing with variety for a period of time may itself lead to problems of rigidity and inertia, making the firm actually more vulnerable to different environmental shocks in the future. As Kay (1984, p. 171) puts it:

> The problem becomes one of throwing system boundaries around potential transactors as far as possible to prevent the appearance of independent sub-systems with their attendant potential for sub-system allegiance, loyalty, identification and opportunistic treatment of other sub-systems – and yet system boundaries must not be thrown far enough to eliminate market incentives to compete, as in the case of monopoly and command systems.

Given these considerations, a stress on the more flexible methods of increasing the span of influence of the firm seems apposite, such as through extended relational contracting and attempts to create longstanding and quality-responsive relations with customers and other firms. These have the benefit that they both encourage some degree of loyalty and stability and at the same time sufficient flexibility and responsiveness to enhance product development and quality control.

The problem of agent variety – due to the indeterminate element in human behaviour – is even more complex. Because the individuals are part of the system, their potential variety is not an external threat to be matched or controlled. The problem is one of variety in a relationship not between the firm and the environment but between the individual and the firm.

A convenient theoretical procedure for dealing with this problem is first to invert the terms in the relationship, and view the issue not from the point of view of the firm but from that of the individual. The 'problem' then is not one of the firm coping with the agent variety of indeterminate behaviour, but of the individual dealing with the potential variety of the 'environment' that now consists of the firm itself.

There are two types of response by the individual to the variety provided by the firm, parallel to those discussed for the firm-environment relation above. First, the individual can respond by creating potential variety. This suggests a combination of education and training procedures to create a flexible repertoire of transferable skills. These skills would range from the analytic, conceptual and problem-solving to the detailed, routinized skills concerning proficiency with language, machinery and communication.

Second, the individuals can respond by increasing their control over their 'environment', i.e. the firm. This suggests an increase in the democratic control of the firm by its members – the extension of industrial democracy and worker participation. The democratic influence of the group over the firm thus reduces potential difficulties of individuals coping with the structured environment of the firm itself. In addition to extending group control, participation of this kind is likely to aid, and be enhanced by, the personal education and development discussed in the preceding paragraph. There is plentiful evidence that worker participation can lead to substantial increases in productivity, motivation and efficiency (e.g. Blumberg, 1968; Espinosa and Zimbalist, 1981; Hodgson, 1984; Jones and Svejnar, 1982; Stephen, 1982; Vroom and Deci, 1970).

Note that this specific type of solution effectively undermines the assumption by orthodox economists that both tastes and technology are exogenous. Tastes and preferences become highly inter-dependent and interactive; and technology – which involves the mode of organization of work – changes through participation in decision-making. This further undercuts some of the neoclassical arguments against some kind of collective, participatory involvement. For instance, as Felix FitzRoy and Kornelius Kraft (1986, pp. 115–16) point out, arguments against collective schemes based on the so-called 'free-rider' problem of an agent shirking and thus benefitting from the efforts of others in the collective, have a fundamental flaw in that interaction in the group is neglected. A cooperative atmosphere is likely to 'mobilize peer-group pressure *against* shirking and encourage "consummate cooperation" with group incentives'.

Industrial participation and democracy cannot be fully successful unless they also involve changes in the labour contract itself. Inevitably this means putting work relations many steps beyond the threat of unemployment and the haggling of the labour market. Threats of redundancy are not conducive to the development of a sense of community and belongingness at work. Job-tenure rights, which in Britain may in some cases result mainly from the behest of strong trade unions, should not be regarded as an unfortunate rigidity, but as an opportunity for developing participation and identification with the organization, as exemplified to some extent in Japan, and to varying degrees in the professional or academic communities in most advanced industrial countries.

We recollect that the original formulation of the problem was of the firm dealing with the agent. It is clear, however, that by inverting the question and finding an answer the original problem has been tackled as well. If the individual can cope with the variety of the firm then this implies that there is a relatively stable realtionship between the two. Consequently, to summarize, we have two further ways for the firm to attempt to deal with potential variety, in this case the variety of the agent:

3   The firm may respond by promoting the education, training and self-development of the workforce, so as to increase flexibility and the acquisition of transferable skills.
4   The firm may respond by increasing internal democracy and worker participation, to develop a unitary style of organization where there is group influence or control over the structure as a whole.

However, these two responses may themselves have their problems. The educative process, combined with the dynamics of the participating group, may create further agent variety of a threatening type. Education and self-development, combined with industrial democracy, may lead to challenges to private ownership of the firm and the concentrations of residual power. As Juan Espinosa and Andrew Zimbalist (1981, p. 21) have argued, participatory and work humanization schemes will promote

> labour's identification with capital . . . only as long as the initiative and direction of the program remain with the capitalists . . . There is ample evidence that, once given a taste of control over their work, workers go after more. If this occurs, the capitalists' control over the program is lost and their control over the entire production process becomes threatened.

Consequently, 'solutions' to the problem of variety within the existing framework of power and property themselves pose a threat to those arrangements themselves. The application of such solutions may be perceived by management as a threat to their position and security, and be aborted. The result is often a retreat to the old authoritarian methods with all their attendant problems (Hodgson, 1982–3; 1984, p. 136). Thus the 'law of insufficient variety' applied to the firm has this particular sting in its tail: attempts to minimize the problem result either in fundamental threats to the existing system, or a conservative retreat to patterns of power and authority which not only are less productive but also have chronic difficulties in adjusting to change.

An outstanding task for economists is to try to develop a method of analysis which can explain and evaluate such fundamental transformations in the relations and distribution of power. The marginalism of orthodoxy is ill suited to this task. In merely attempting to consider marginal adjustments to the *status quo*, orthodoxy has neglected the fundamentals. Answers to such vital questions are normally dealt with by invoking the attendant ideology, rather than by referring to a well-developed theoretical analysis.[10]

## The conditions for innovation

Considering further the question of the form of ownership of the firm, the most important arguments in favour of markets and private ownership come from the Austrian School. Their approach is not to compare static equilibria but to consider the dynamic conditions and processes of change. This approach is illustrated with the following argument from the Austrian-inspired work of Stephen Littlechild:

> Compared to private ownership, regulation and nationalization impose a different kind of filter on the imaginative vision, as well as on the choice of project. Different objectives will be paramount in designing projects; different weights will be attached to predictions of the future; different time-horizons will be relevant. In particular, there will be pressure to put forward and choose those projects that are demonstrably acceptable, those for which there is a 'proven need'. Projects that rely on imaginative vision or hunch will find it more difficult to gain acceptance, despite the importance (from the RS [radical subjectivist] perspective) of this element in long-term decision making. (Littlechild, 1986, p. 37)

Despite some germs of truth in the argument, it is essentially one-sided and does not consider all the conditions relating to the question. Consistent with the Austrian approach, the conditions behind the agent, moulding his or her decision-making, are not put into the picture. The individual is taken as given; we are simply asked to address the matter of the receptiveness of the system to the immanent 'imaginative vision' of the agent. The conditions that engender and mould the entrepreneur's purpose and imagination are themselves ignored. Of course, imagination and entrepreneurship are not completely determined by the environment, and they certainly depend on elements of flair and intuition which are unpredictable and essentially indeterminate. But they also have material and social preconditions, and they are likely to be partly moulded by culture and institutions.

It is thus no accident that in history bursts of innovative or intellectual activity are associated with the development of specific cultures. How else can we explain, for example, the Renaissance, the Scottish Enlightenment, the commercial and academic prowess of the Jewish people, and the technological ferment during and after the British Industrial Revolution?

Consequently, any comparison between different forms of enterprise must also consider whether or not the institutional ground is fertile for the promotion of imagination and innovation of this type. There is no obvious relationship between the pattern of private or public ownership, on the one hand, and the fertility of these conditions, on the other. Thus the Austrian focus on the form of ownership here misses the point. What is more important is the type and level of social culture, the level of technical and general education, and the material and institutional supports for entrepreneurial activity.

As well as the preconditions for innovation the conditions for its establishment and acceptance must also be considered. Indeed, the two may interact. If an innovation is deemed to have little chance of acceptance it will be stillborn. Alternatively, for example, small-firm entrepreneurship can be promoted by the existence of a large-scale potential purchaser, such as a public corporation, or the state itself. (This has typically been the case with state defence procurements.) In this respect the greater stability and funding of public enterprise can often have advantages, even if it may be at the cost of some dynamic efficiency within the purchasing enterprise.

Furthermore, the existence of some degree of economic planning may also provide entrepreneurs with a sense that although their own product may or may not be accepted, there is likely to be a general demand for products of their type. Likewise, we can here find support for the Keynesian argument that it is not only the imagination of the entrepreneurs that matters, but also the existence of a perceived general level of effective demand for the products that they may create.

In addition, the relationship between the financial and industrial sectors has to be brought into consideration. Any business is affected by the financial environment, including the availability of finance and the level of interest rates. Arguably, a stable financial environment, committed to the long-term growth of the economy as a whole, would help create favourable conditions for entrepreneurial activity and technological development. Indeed, the increasing instability of the world financial system has been cited as a reason for slower rates of growth of output and productivity throughout the Western world (Grahl, 1986; Kindleberger, 1978; Minsky, 1982).

It is in a sense paradoxical that dynamism and entrepreneurship may require some background of stability and routine to prosper. It is true nevertheless, and a conclusion that can be drawn from G. B. Richardson's (1959, 1960) argument, as discussed in preceding chapters. A world where the actions of each firm are unstable and unpredictable to others is an anarchic world where investment and innovation are discouraged. Some inflexibility and predictability is required in the system, for there to be adequate incentives for firms to take risks. Whilst to go to the extreme of a completely routinized, tradition-based economic system would mean the end of innovation and technical advance; the alternative extreme of anarchy would be no better in practice.

An important point to appreciate is that the required degree of stability that may be provided, for example, by some institutional rigidities or by a given level of effective demand, is more often at a general rather than a specific level. General informational guidelines of this type can be appreciated widely, but specific, context-related information cannot be dispersed on such a broad basis.

Thus it is possible to conceive of a combination of both stability and temporal variety in a complex system. Stability will relate more closely to the general levels, whilst continuous change and variety will be apparent in more narrow and specific contexts. Thus the managers of a firm may know the general conditions in an economy or region, and make decisions of location and overall scale on that basis. But the choice of product type and the approach to marketing it will require much more specific information that requires particular, detailed reserch, and this information will not be widely known.

Consequently, the promotion of innovation is not achieved either by global, central planning nor by total *laissez-faire*. A dynamic and innovative system will require a structured combination of variety and rigidity, of stasis and change, of centralized guidance and decentralized autonomy. Neither the liberal ideology of the free market, nor the statism of much of the traditional Left, lend themselves to this type of policy approach.

## Institutional intervention

This multi-levelled character of the informational signals in a complex economy contrasts with some of the ultra-subjectivist defences of the market system. In these arguments, information is treated as essentially subjective in character, and divided amongst individuals. Thus, according to these views, there is no alternative to the completely decentralized market system which alone reflects this parcellization of knowledge. However, not all information is of the same rank or generality. Whilst individuals are privy to detailed information which cannot all be aggregated and processed by a central authority, some sorts of information can be collected and handled centrally in a meaningful way.

In particular there are important informational economies of scale. This is apparent when we consider the function of a telephone directory, which contains specific pieces of information of a general form and type. Another example is a library. Despite the fact that no individual can appreciate more than a small fraction of the information it contains, the location of the library will be widely known, and one is able to find specific pieces of information in books and journals by consulting its catalogue and reference systems.

Knowledge in society is implanted in a network of structured institutions. Furthermore, information itself is of different degrees of generality. The structured nature of information leads to an apparent paradox. A decentralized market system reflects the dispersed nature of much information in society, but for a market system to work effectively, centralized information-gathering and purveying institutions are required as well.

It is important to note that the general type of economic order that emerges from society itself will have extremely important cultural and information-purveying functions. Relevant illustrations of this are found in an article by Michael Best (1982). As a pertinent case, Best shows that in the US the motor car, tyre and oil companies systematically bought up and dismantled rail and tram lines so as to create a market for the private car. Thus a general social culture was created that was oriented towards that mode of transport. Both the cultural texture and the informational signals within society changed. It became both 'desirable' and 'rational' for the individual to own and use the car, and the whole socio-economic system became locked into that style and pattern of industry and life.

Information is not ranked simply in terms of to the generality or specificity of its content. Economic systems contain information concerning different time horizons as well. This is most obviously the case with financial markets, where the short-term orientation of much speculative activity has dangers for an economic system which sees the stock market as its supreme regulator. Despite the existence of futures markets the financial system is unable to provide sufficient overall stability for long-term decision-making, because of a lack of the necessary general guidelines and constraints.

With such considerations of the time horizon in mind, Richard Nelson (1981a) argues that research and development and long-term investment projects are not best promoted by a completely decentralized, private-enterprise system. In fact, in most advanced capitalist countries including the US, a great number of important technological innovations emanate from institutions which rely a great deal on state funding, such as the universities. This is most obvious in the case of the space programme and defence, but it is also true for a large number of additional research and development projects.

Whilst considerable decentralization is required to ensure that the economy remains flexible and responsive, long-term, research-oriented and knowledge-intensive industries require the stability and support provided by an overall framework. At a minimum the central institutions that could be relevant here are some form of indicative planning (Estrin and Holmes, 1983; Hare, 1985) combined with an interventionist industrial policy to prioritize and coordinate economic activities (Best, 1986; Carter, 1981; Cowling, 1987; Gruchy, 1984; Hughes, 1986; Rapping, 1984). All long-term economic problems are essentially structural and institutional: institutions affect not only the framework of economic growth but also the ideology and culture which prevail in society, plus the purposes and goals to which people aspire.

What criteria are relevant in determining the appropriate mix between markets and planning and public and private institutions? Janos Kornai (1971) suggests that with high industrial concentration, decisions involving major structural modifications, essential indivisibilities, increasing returns and longer time horizons give favourable grounds for overall planning, whereas their absence may favour the fuller operation of the market system. Alec Nove (1983) makes similar points, stressing the criterion of 'plannability' which relates to such factors as the measurability and homogeneity of the product.

However, the choice is not simply a technical matter. In choosing the appropriate combination of planning and markets consideration has also to be given to the question of the devolution and distribution of economic power, for an over-centralized economy does not simply threaten economic efficiency in the narrow sense, but also political pluralism, local democracy and autonomy. Furthermore, a number of decisions have to be taken concerning societal and individual needs, and the respective ranking of priorities. The economic objective is not simply 'progress' or 'growth'. These objectives are not as simple or uni-dimensional as they appear. Even if such bland terms could be defined satisfactorily, they would not be acceptable as the sole targets of economic policy.

Furthermore, if Ronald Dore's arguments (1983) about the importance of trust relations and relational contracting in the development of a modern economy are to be accepted, then the projection of radical economic policy objectives has to have features of a moral crusade. To use Fred Hirsch's phrase (1977), the revival of an 'ethos of social obligation' has to become both an economic means and an end. The removal of the market from the prestige position of supreme arbiter in matters of allocation and worth, does not mean its replacement by the moral numbness of centralized bureaucracy. Instead, the market must be tempered by legislation and social practices that enhance considerations of fairness and cooperation rather than the anonymous forces of supply and demand.

In particular, as Dore and others have argued, this means clutching the nettle of an incomes policy. The market-oriented approach of 'free collective bargaining' is not acceptable in these terms. But neither is a restrictive and punitive incomes policy which keeps down the wages of the lower-income earners but not those of the rich, which has most often been the case with incomes policies in Britain in the past. The determination of wages has to be done outside the 'free' market, in part to establish norms of fairness; but the consequent incomes policy has itself to have a strong egalitarian ethos for it to be regarded as fair and to be accepted on a more permanent basis. Any permanent incomes policy has to be flexible rather than punitive and rigidly authoritarian, and project a high moral profile. Otherwise it is likely to fail, on both ethical and practical grounds.

More generally, it should be emphasized that institutional intervention has to be both broad and deep, to lead to some basic changes in social relationships and personal goals, if it is to have a chance of success in dealing with the kind of crisis which is affecting some of the stagnating economies of the Western world. There is now an impressive set of theoretical and empirical studies on the conditions for growth or decline in modern economies. Despite wide differences in ideological viewpoint, remarkably similar conclusions have been reached. They all suggest that change has to be wide and substantial if it is to be effective.

For instance, in a short but widely quoted study, Sir Henry Phelps Brown (1977) argues that one of the main problems with the British economy is that it missed the 'fresh start' of sweeping institutional change that would be promoted by invasion or revolution. Past success in the old methods, whilst being cossetted by the old imperial trading system, made managers and administrators reluctant to learn the new. Twentieth-century minds became bounded by the methods, processes and products of the nineteenth century.

A similar but more detailed argument is developed by Bernard Elbaum and William Lazonick (1986a, p. 2) who attribute the relative decline of the British economy on the twentieth century to

> rigidities in the economic and social institutions that developed during the nineteenth century, a period when Britain was the world's leading economic power and British industry was highly atomistic and competitive in organization . . . Britain's distinctiveness derived less from the conservatism of its cultural values *per se* than from a matrix of rigid institutional structures that reinforced these values and obstructed individualistic as well as collective efforts at economic renovation.

Of course, relative to Britain, the US has enjoyed a superior economic performance. But it still faces the problem of the slowdown in productivity growth and the erosion of its share of world trade. In this case institutional arguments again seem to be more convincing. In a Marxist-inspired study focusing on the institutional and political nature of the accord between labour and capital, Samuel Bowles, David Gordon and Thomas Weisskopf (1985) argue that the related inflexibility in structures and practices has been a major cause of the slowdown in growth.[11]

Other studies, some of a more general nature, such as by Simon Kuznets (1959, 1979) and Nathan Rosenberg (1982b) have also emphasized the dual role of innovation and institutional flexibility in promoting growth. Furthermore, in an extensive comparative study on *The Rise and Decline of Nations*, Mancur Olson (1982) argues that sweeping radical change, particularly resulting from internal revolution or defeat in war, has in the past helped to promote economic growth by overcoming the inertia of ossified, growth-retarding institutions.

These analyses, by far the most convincing of all the many attempts to explain national economic growth or relative decline, all suggest that radical solutions are required to the deep-seated problems that beset many of the leading industrial nations. The unitary remedies of the past will not work. The extension of markets and competition itself is unlikely to succeed. The Keynesian solution of demand management is necessary, but far from sufficient. The imposition of central planning and state control on its own, without sweeping change elsewhere, will fail to bring substantial results. It is only a radical and structured combination of different methods, at different levels of the economy, that has any chance of success. The complexity and variety within the economic process requires a multiplicity of regulatory mechanisms.

As well as substantial political and economic decentralization, with widespread use of the market mechanism where appropraite, structural and institutional intervention on this scale is likely to take place in the context of national and supra-national planning which is partly indicative, partly regulatory and partly directive in character. The task for economists is to apply the wide literature on, and experience of, planning, industrial organization, financial structures and the management of production in a way that is appropriate for economic and social objectives.

The concrete application of institutionalist theory to practical problems requires detailed and painstaking study of institutions and their development. At the theoretical level, such an approach implies interdisciplinary scholarship which is neither fashionable nor encouraged at present by the structure or goals of academia. It requires the lateral thinking and sweep of mind that is often frowned upon by the burrowing, half-blind, mole-like specialists.

These may be formidable and arduous tasks, and sometimes lacking formal elegance and glamour. But for those concerned about the undiminished problems of mass unemployment, poverty and famine, and the wasting of the environment and of human creative potential, an institutional economics may well prove to be the only feasible alternative.

# Notes

PREFACE

1 Notably, a recent study of the stagnation of the American economy by
Samuel Bowles, David Gordon and Thomas Weisskopf (1985) is influenced
by both the Marxian literature on the labour process and broader
institutional considerations. They produce a plausible account of the
productivity slowdown with some impressive econometric corroboration.
2 *Wall Street Journal*, 26 December 1985. I am grateful to Francis Green for
supplying this quotation.
3 Tony Aspromourgos (1986) questions the use of the term 'neoclassical' to
describe mainstream theory. However, the term is now so widely used that it
is difficult, if not impossible, to expunge it from the literature, and it remains
in use here. Furthermore, it is used in a fairly broad sense to cover the class
of economic theory here described, thus removing some of the difficulties in
applying the term more narrowly. Nevertheless, the definition is not
sufficiently broad to put the Austrian School in the neoclassical stable, for
their rejection of equilibrium theorizing and their distinctive emphasis on
knowledge and the economic process should place them apart.
4 For an excellent summary of this debate see Geoff Harcourt (1972).
5 For a sophisticated example of such 'Marxian' theory see John Roemer
(1981). Likewise, some developments of Sraffian linear analysis, rather than
being presented (like Sraffa's own work) as a 'prelude to a critique of
economic theory' are claimed to be a more-or-less adequate foundation for
an alternative paradigm. Notably, however, in Sraffian analysis, questions of
rationality, knowledge and uncertainty, and processes through time are
ignored. As Geoff Harcourt (1985) shows, Joan Robinson became acutely
aware of the limitations of these approaches in her last years. Whilst some of
her followers have regarded these remarks as an aberration of later life, on
the contrary they seem to be evidence of her continuing capacity for deep
self-criticism and her still lively, constructive intelligence in the months
before her death in 1983.

uld not be overlooked that the Austrian School is superior to the
... assical in many respects, particularly in their stress on problems of
information and in their rejection of the orthodox conception of equilibrium.
See in particular Friedrich Hayek (1937, 1945).

2 These three themes are inspired by and developed from Richard Langlois'
introduction (1986b, pp. 5–6) to a highly relevant collection of essays.

3 This move away from a 'pure-market' philosophy, and with a greater
emphasis on the informational and other functions of rules and conventions
in economic life, is evident even in works of an avid pro-marketeer such as
Friedrich Hayek (1982) in his later writings.

4 In taking this view the author acknowledges the influence of the feminist
movement, and its insistence that reason and calculation do not comprise the
entirety of discourse and communication in social life.

5 For example, Piero Mini (1974, p. 42) has pointed out that: 'Predictable and
precise reactions can hardly be expected of individuals and groups that are
truly free . . . In economic theory freedom is spoken of, but in reality the
economic agents act as slaves.' Mini refers to Jeremy Bentham's famous
statement, of man being governed by 'two sovereign masters, *pain* and
*pleasure*' (Bentham, 1823, p. 1). From different viewpoints, James Buchanan
(1969), Spiro Latsis (1972) and George Shackle (1969) have all noted the
lack of real choice in, and the deterministic nature of, neoclassical theory.

6 For a survey of this literature see Jack Hirshleifer and John Riley (1979).

7 Note, for instance, the application of W. Ross Ashby's (1952, 1956) 'law of
requisite variety' to the study of socio-economic systems in chapters 7 and 11
of the present work and elsewhere (Hodgson, 1984, chs 6 and 7).

8 For other adoptions of a systems view by economists see, for example, Kurt
Dopfer (1976), Neil Kay (1979, 1982), Janos Kornai (1971), Alec Nove
(1979, pp. 148–52), H. Thoben (1982), Roger Troub (1983) and Walter
Weisskopf (1979). Earlier discussions relating economics to a systems
perspective are found in Adolph Lowe (1951) and G. Sebba (1953).

9 Namely Samuel Bowles (1985a), Herbert Gintis (1972, 1974), Sergio
Parrinello (1984) and Ian Steedman (1980). See also Mary McNally (1980).

10 See for instance, Kenneth Boulding (1985), Donella Meadows et al. (1974),
Paul Ekins (1986), Bertram Schefold (1985).

## 2 ON METHODOLOGY AND ASSUMPTIONS

1 See, in particular, Ernest Nagel (1963), Alan Coddington (1979), Bruce
Caldwell (1980b; 1982, pp. 175–86), Alan Musgrave (1981), Donald
McCloskey (1983). Other critics are noted by Eugene Rotwein (1973),
Lawrence Boland (1979a) and Bruce Caldwell (1982, 1984b).

2 Instead of the term 'instrumentalism', Alan Coddington uses 'pragmatism' to
describe this aspect of Milton Friedman's methodology. Pragmatism is

defined as the view that 'the only way of assessing the adequacy of an assumption is by using and applying the theory in which the assumption appears, and seeing how well the theory performs' (Coddington, 1979, p. 2). This seems pretty close to instrumentalism to me. Coddington's little-discussed article antedates Lawrence Boland's now-famous 'defence' of Friedman by one month.

3 Although explicit statements are not that numerous, examples of this 'ideological instrumentalism' are not foreign to the contemporary academic community of social scientists and emanate from authors from the Left, Centre and Right of the political spectrum. An example would be the rejection of Hans Eysenck's researches into intelligence or E. O. Wilson's theories of sociobiology for ideological reasons by many on the left, and the obverse ideological acceptance of such theories by many on the far Right. (For a refreshing counter to both these stances see Hirst and Woolley, 1982, and for a carefully argued critique of Eysenck's and Wilson's work see Rose et al, 1984).

   Of course, in totalitarian countries explicit examples of the use of ideological criteria in the acceptance and rejection of theories are more numerous. (For examples from the Soviet Union see Popovsky, 1980.) Under more liberal regimes the question should be raised as to whether 'ideological instrumentalism' is more frequently a *hidden* criterion in the selection or rejection of theories than would appear at first sight. In some later passages of the present work evidence is cited to suggest that it is.

4 Like many positivists and empiricists, Milton Friedman is evidently aware that there can be no atheoretical perception of the data, for he writes: 'A theory is the way we perceive "facts", and we cannot perceive "facts" without a theory' (Friedman, 1953, p. 34). However, he is neither the first nor the last empiricist to fail to see the anti-empiricist consequences of this point. Note in particular the discussion of Karl Popper below.

5 For a selection of modern critiques of empiricism and positivism see Louis Althusser and Ethienne Balibar (1970), James Feibelman (1972), Richard Grandy (1973), Norwood Hanson (1958), Barry Hindess (1977c), Martin Hollis and Edward Nell (1975), and David Willer and Judith Willer (1973).

6 Notably by Paul Feyerabend (1975), Thomas Kuhn (1962), Imre Lakatos (1970), Karl Popper (1959, 1965), Michael Polanyi (1957, 1967) and Stephen Toulmin (1973).

7 For two examples of such a position see Roy Bhaskar (1975) and Alan F. Chalmers (1982). Chalmers describes his position as 'unrepresentative realism'.

8 Some of the present author's earlier works contain an attempt to sustain a realist methodology which is flawed by the implicit or explicit suggestion that some theories are demonstrably closer to the real world than others. John King (1982, pp. 175–6) has criticized such passages in my work, making the point that there is no self-evident criterion as to which theory is 'closer' to reality than another. Whilst I do not accept all the arguments in his article, I accept this criticism without reservation.

9 Whether or not Friedman's methodology is essentially Popperian, amongst economists there has been a near universal failure to apply Popperian criteria

to theory testing. E. R. Canterbery and R. J. Burkhardt (1983) have carried out a survey of no less than 542 empirical articles in the 1973–8 period from four top-ranking articles, namely the *American Economic Review*, the *Journal of Political Economy*, the *Quarterly Journal of Economics* and the *Economic Journal*. Their results show that only three of these articles attempted to falsify the hypotheses being tested.

However, we should not draw the conclusion, along with some Post-Keynesians and others, that all would be well if Popper's methodology was put into practice. It is argued here that Popper's methodology is internally inconsistent and practically inoperable.

10 This account of events does not, however, stand up to close examination. According to the standard view, in 1905 Albert Einstein proposed the theory of relativity in order to explain the otherwise unaccountable results of the 1887 Michelson–Morley experiment. However, Michael Polanyi (1957, pp. 9–15) and Gerald Holton (1969, pp. 133–97) have shown that the experiment does not in fact bear out the thesis it was supposed to illustrate. Neither this nor any other controlled experiment played any significant role in the development of Einstein's theory, nor any creditable scientific part in its initial acceptance. Indeed the original experiment (and the many replications of it by D. C. Miller from 1902 to 1926) actually did not give the results required by the theory of relativity. But this evidence was simply ignored by the scientific community that had already become converted to the relativity idea. Subsequently, the idea that the Michelson–Morley work was a 'crucial experiment' in favour of the theory became a myth of modern science.

Consequently, whilst there are cases of evidence playing an important role in the development of science, the procedure is rarely, if ever, along Popperian lines, and there are many cases (in physics as well as economics) of awkward evidence being simply ignored.

11 Whilst it is possible to construct a Popperian defence of neoclassical theory, it should be noted that Popperian methodology does not necessarily lead in that direction (see Boland, 1982). Indeed, the non-falsifiable character of many neoclassical propositions, such as the maximization hypothesis (Boland, 1981), makes them vulnerable to a strict Popperian attack. Furthermore, influential non-neoclassical economists such as Joan Robinson (1964, p. 8) and Friedrich Hayek (1967) have broadly accepted the methodology of Popper.

12 Karl Popper's progress from a 'naive' to a 'sophisticated' falsificationist is discussed in the famous article by Imre Lakatos (1970).

13 See the excellent discussion of the Duhem–Quine thesis by Rod Cross (1982b), and his attempt (1982a) to apply the methods of appraisal developed by Imre Lakatos to different theoretical justifications for economic policies in the UK.

Lakatos' starting point was to break from the idea of isolated hypotheses and single, crucial experiments. Hypotheses are always tested as structured wholes and a part of a 'scientific research programme' which is evolving through time. At the centre of this theoretical system is a subgroup of hypotheses known as the 'hard core'. These are protected from empirical challenge by a 'negative heuristic', i.e. a set of rules which ensures that the 'hard-core' assumptions are not undermined.

In effect, regarding single hypotheses, Lakatos virtually reverses Popper's emphasis on falsification. Empirical evidence is brought to bear on the hypotheses of the protective belt, where as often as not they are endorsed by verification, rather than through non-falsification in Popperian terms.

Instead, the appraisal of a research programme derives from observation of its evolution through time and the series of particular theories which it is able to generate. A 'progressive' research programme is one which steadily increases the range of predictions which are subject to empirical corroboration and is successful in that these predictions are confirmed by the facts. In contrast, a research programme is 'degenerating theoretically' if amendments to protective-belt hypotheses reduce the empirical content in terms of predictions given, and 'degenerating empirically' if predictions do not meet with empirical confirmation. Instead of a single observation falsifying a theory, a theory in the series is 'falsified when it is superceded by a theory with higher corroborated content' (Lakatos, 1970, p. 118).

There are a number of problems with Lakatos' methodology, but in many respects it is an advance on the work of Popper. In particular, it would appear that a Lakatosian methodological regime would be more pluralistic in spirit and more tolerant of rival research programmes than the strict application of Popperian criteria of falsification. Under the latter, and in a peculiar manner contrary to Popper's intent, non-falsifiable statements can be given too much credence (see e.g. Lawrence Boland, 1981, and the discussion in chapter 4 of the present work), and promising research programmes which generate a number of ostensibly false predictions can be recklessly discarded.

14 For a related set of criticisms of Popper see Karel Williams (1975).

15 McCloskey (1983, p. 484n.) notes that a version of Kelvin's dictum is inscribed on the front of the Social Science Research Building at the University of Chicago. Frank Knight is said to have remarked on it one day: 'Yes, and when you *can* express it in numbers your knowledge is of a meagre and unsatisfactory kind'.

16 After this witty and powerful critique of the Official Methodology of economics, it is somewhat surprising that McCloskey draws rather conservative conclusions. His recommendation seems to be that whilst the Official Methodology is fatally wounded, there is no alternative methodological basis for the appraisal of theories. Consequently, he suggests, neoclassical theorists can simply carry on doing what they do.

As Bruce Caldwell and A. W. Coats (1984) demonstrate, this is a highly unsatisfactory argument. In particular it ignores recent, non-positivist and non-prescriptive developments in the philosophy of science. If science cannot develop in the manner that the prescriptive methodologists would desire, there are nevertheless very good reasons why it does frequently change and evolve. The lack of a single, guiding methodological authority is not an excuse for a retreat into conservatism; it is often the signal of and opportunity for theoretical change.

Furthermore, it is rather naive to suggest that after decades when neoclassical theory has been defended with the use of the Official Methodology the demise of the latter will leave neoclassical theory unscathed. As Larry Laudan (1977) argues, methodological considerations are often central to the conceptual appraisal of a theory by its practitioners as well as its opponents. 'It is precisely for that reason that perceived methodological weaknesses have constituted serious, and often acute conceptual problems for any theory exhibiting them' (p. 59).

17 Some of the few discussions of the relationship between quantum physics and the Heisenberg uncertainty principle, on the one hand, and economics on the other include Kenneth Boulding (1970), H. Thoben (1982) and Walter Weisskopf (1979). For a general discussion of the philosophical impact of contemporary physics see Milic Capek (1961). Highly readable presentations of modern physics with popular discussions of further possible implications are found in Fritjof Capra (1975, 1982).

18 Alternatively, we may be tempted to take on board the ideas of Paul Feyerabend. In his *Against Method* he comes to the conclusion that: 'The only principle that does not inhibit progress is: *anything goes*' (1975, p. 23).

The trouble is that any methodology opposed to method itself is self-contradictory. Furthermore, if 'anything goes' in the pursuit of progress we are inclined to ask what is progress itself? On this, Feyerabend is evasive. He writes that 'my frequent use of such words as "progress", "advance", "improvement", etc., does not mean that I claim to possess special knowledge about what is good and what is bad in the sciences and that I want to impose this knowledge upon my readers. *Everyone can read the terms in his own way* and in accordance with the tradition to which he belongs' (p. 27).

This amounts to an admission that what is one person's progress is another's regress, and vice versa. Feyerabend's *Against Method* contains the assumption that 'progress' in some form is desirable. But if the principle were to be applied, by what criteria would we know that progress had taken place?

Notably, Feyerabend's main illustration that a more 'anarchistic' methodological approach would assist 'progress' in science is the work of Galileo. His arguments are important, for they show that Galileo's work was sometimes 'irrational', that it often relied on base rhetoric rather than sound argument, and it certainly did not conform to any mediaeval or modern methodology of science. In particular, Galileo did not falsify Ptolemy and instate Copernicus as many Popperians presume. This example is effective against Popper, and perhaps even Lakatos as well. But does it work in favour of Feyerabend? It can only be cited in support of the 'anything goes' precept if it is deemed, by some criterion, that Galileo's work marked clear and unambiguous 'progress' for science. Thus to make his 'anything goes' methodology work, Feyerabend has to assert a single and perhaps dogmatic set of criteria for 'progress' in science.

It is quite possible to argue, however, that Galileo's work combined features which allowed science to develop in some ways, but actually to regress in others. In particular, as Arthur Koestler (1959) argues in his excellent study, the influence of Galileo can be considered negative in at least two respects. One was the highest priority he gave to formalistic and mathematical methods of presentation, which indeed has been seminal but not entirely positive for all subsequent science. The other was the imposition in thought of hermetic divisions between science and mysticism, reason and intuition, and science and morality, all of which emanate from the scientific culture of the seventeenth century. Whilst it would be rash to deny that Galileo's work in dynamics did mark a kind of progress for humanity, there are at least two influential aspects of his thought for which it is possible to make a partially negative case.

Note in particular the asymmetry in the burden of argument that Feyerabend takes upon himself. His one-sided aim is to show that the only principle that does not inhibit progress is 'anything goes'. He thus focuses solely on the 'positive', and not the 'negative' side of this precept: there is no debit side to the balance sheet. Indeed, it is possible to read Feyerabend's very own account of alleged 'progress' in science and be drawn to the conclusion that 'anything goes' has often inhibited 'progress' in some of its forms.

The central difficulty of the 'anything goes' position is illustrated perfectly by Feyerabend's admission that 'progress' may in some cases be assisted by political dictat. He argues in some cases for 'political interference' so as to ensure 'a balanced development' (p. 216) or a healthy 'proliferation' of competing theories (p. 51). But can political 'interference' be anything else but prescriptive? By administrative directive, denial of funds, or whatever, it must involve shifting some scientists from doing this to doing that.

Such a problematic contradiction within libertarianism is familiar to political philosophers. Does anarchism or libertarianism, in proclaiming complete freedom of action to be the ultimate, allow some people to act if the effect is to diminish the freedom of others? Furthermore, a paradox in the market-oriented variety of libertarianism, which proclaims its central aim of 'rolling back' the state, is that it can only succeed in its goal by investing the state with still more powers. Without these it cannot abolish or break up market restrictions, traditional arrangements, trade unions and other impediments to so-called 'free competition'. Feyerabend's 'methodological anarchism' has the same kind of philosophical problems as anarchism and market libertarianism in the political sphere.

The similarities between this argument against methodological *laissez-faire* and the later argument in this book against the theoretical and practical possibility of a 'pure' market system should be noted. See in particular chapter 8.

## 3  BEHIND METHODOLOGICAL INDIVIDUALISM

1 Fritz Machlup (1978, pp. 454, 472), Mark Blaug (1980, p. 49).
2 See May Brodbeck (1968, ch. 4), I. C. Jarvie (1972, pp. 173–8), Leonard Krimerman (1969) and J. O'Neill (1973) for summaries.

3 For statements to support the view that Marx was not a methodological individualist, despite his conception of the purposeful individual, see Marx (1973, esp. pp. 84–5, 156–7, 161–5, 196–7, 264–5). However, Jon Elster (1982) and John Roemer (1982) claim to use 'methodological individualism' as a basis for a game-theoretic analysis of Marxian class struggle. This is a long way from the intentions of the Austrian School, and it is not clear whether or not the term is being employed in the same manner. Arguably, it is not; for instance see the critique of game theory in largely 'Austrian' terms by George Shackle (1972, ch. 36).

A more extended attempt to show that Marx was a 'methodological individualist' is found in an odd book by D. F. B. Tucker (1980, p. 14), where he views methodological individualism as comprising:

1 The idea 'that human nature and reason are much the same throughout history and, consequently, that we can understand different historical periods in terms of how we would expect individuals to behave'; thus the aim is to produce 'a science of society which is universal'.
2 The idea that the 'study of human behaviour can be conducted in a scientific way' despite 'the fact that human agents have conscious awareness of what they do'.
3 A scepticism 'of all explanations which attribute to social entities purpose apart from the concerns of the persons who function within them'.

In response to Tucker's argument two points must be made. First, this is not a definition of methodological individualism which is either sufficiently precise or in accord with the prevailing view in the literature. His account differs from the definition adopted here and at least for this reason Tucker's assertions can be pushed to one side. In addition we may note that there is no dispute here with the second and third of Tucker's propositions. Indeed, it would be difficult to find many social scientists who disagreed with proposition 2.

Second, it is highly dubious that Marx would have agreed with either the first or the third of Tucker's propositions cited above. For example, concerning the first proposition, Marx attacked classical economics for the universalism of its precepts, and, concerning the third, he frequently ascribed purposefulness to social entities such as the bourgeoisie or the proletariat. Notably, Tucker's maverick interpretation of Marx is supported by very few citations from the work of Marx himself.

Elsewhere there is a similar lack of sufficient care and clarity in over-enthusiastic attempts to discover vestiges of 'methodological individualism' in the works of Thorstein Veblen (Seckler, 1975; Rutherford, 1984b).

4 For a discussion of the topic of contract law by an eminent legal theorist see Grant Gilmore (1974).

It should be added that, as the modern business system has developed, the law has come to treat whole companies, composed of many individuals, as unitary actors with rights and responsibilities, just as nation states are so regarded in modern international law. However, in these contexts it is still legal practice to ascribe intent to individuals. Corruption in a large company is traced to individuals, not to the company or shareholders as a whole. Speaking literally and not in any figurative sense, it was the mass murderers, not the whole German nation, who were put on trial in Nuremberg after the Second World War.

5 The unacceptable idea of the purposeful collective is often associated with a functionalist perspective, as found in many writers including Hegel and Marx, and modern sociologists such as Talcott Parsons. Functionalism itself has been widely criticized elsewhere (e.g. Elster, 1979, 1982; Giddens, 1982a, 1984; Gough, 1975, 1979). But it would be wrong to suggest that the rejection of functionalism necessarily leads to methodological individualism, or that advocates of the latter are incapable of making errors of a functionalist kind. These are reasons why the question of functionalism can be left on one side.

6 Illustrations are numerous but see, for example, Andras Angyal (1941), Solomon Asch (1952), Richard Eiser (1980) and Stanley Milgram (1974).

7 For different recent elaborations of this point by economists see Lawrence Boland (1979b) and Ian Steedman (1980).

8 Notably, this question of determinacy is a matter for debate within the Austrian camp. For example, by accepting a measure of mathematical modelling into their theory some neo-Austrians qualify the scope for indeterminacy.

9 In relation to methodological individualism we may briefly consider the neoclassical general equilibrium model of Kenneth Arrow and Gerard Debreu, in which according to James Meade (1971, p. 166) all trading is reduced to a 'single gigantic once-for-all "higgle-haggle" in which all contingent goods and services . . . are bought and sold once and for all now for money payments now'.

Such 'big bang' models of economic behaviour that condense all determinants of future action into one first instant of time offer no solace to a strict methodological individualist. Given that everything within the model, including individual choice, is predetermined at the outset, and everything depends on everything else, it is arbitrary to assume that individual agency has any primacy. The equations could be transposed so as to make it look as if other factors were the driving force behind the model, and that individuals were simply passive reactors. Both alternatives would be arbitrary within the theory.

10 It is interesting to note how the 'chicken-and-egg' problem arises in relation to the controversy over the labour theory of value. It is not uncommon for Marxist economists to argue that 'all commodities are produced by labour', claiming that this can be shown by tracing back both the past and present labour employed in their production. However, just as labour enters into the production of goods, some goods (e.g. food, housing, etc.) enter into the production of labour. The problem of arbitrariness arises once again. Unless good reason can be found to single out labour (and many Marxists would claim to have such a reason) then it is no less legitimate to single out, for example, water, steel or land as the basis of value. For a more extensive discussion of this issue see Hodgson (1982c).

11 For two recent examples of this broad approach see the work of Anthony Giddens (1984) in sociology and Tony Lawson (1985) in economics on the theory of 'structuration' or 'societal interactionism'. These works both adopt a balanced and sophisticated position in regard to the relation between agency and structure in human action.

12 Similar points are stressed in several Post-Keynesian writings. For a particularly clear example see Sheila Dow (1985).

13 The hypothesis that the wider acceptance of methodological individualism amongst economists in the 1970s is somehow related to the rise of the political individualism of the New Right should not, of course, be ruled out. The preferences of economists themselves are not immune to the pressure of political and cultural developments such as this.

4 THE MAXIMIZATION HYPOTHESIS

1 See, for example, Benn and Mortimore (1976), Harrison (1979), Hindess (1984), Hollis (1977), Hollis and Lukes (1982) and Wilson (1970).

2 We shall leave on one side the long discussion about whether 'rational economic man' can be altruistic or not, for as neoclassical economists Alfred Marshall (1949), Lionel Robbins (1937) and Philip Wicksteed (1910) all argue, there is no reason, in principle, why economics should assume that people are entirely selfish. The accusation is not that 'rational economic man' *cannot* be altruistic within a neoclassical framework, but that most often it is assumed that he is not. (See Collard, 1978; Margolis, 1982; Sen, 1976–7.) The pursuit of this allegation, whilst itself important, would lead us off the trail. Our task is to understand the core assumption of rationality that is common to all neoclassical theory.

3 See, for example, the empirical studies and discussions found in Arrow (1982), Koo (1963), Koo and Hasenkamp (1972), May (1954), Sensat and Constantine (1975), Slovic and Lichtenstein (1983) and Tversky and Kahneman (1981).

4 See Bharadwaj (1968), Majumdar (1958), von Mises (1949, p. 103) Robinson (1964, p. 51) and Wong (1978). Amartya Sen (1973) argues persuasively that this problem demonstrates that more than behaviour is required to explain behaviour. Faith in the axioms of revealed preference is not vindicated by observation of behaviour through time, but has to be supported by a further belief that (consistent) behaviour results from the actual preference of the consumer. The latter, of course, is not given any empirical test.

5 See Green (1971, p. 24), Shone (1975, p. 25) and Walsh (1970, pp. 84–6).

6 Ajit Singh (1975) finds the empirical support for the view that a 'natural selection' process operates through takeovers to be 'very weak'.

7 The arguments of both Shackle and Simon in this vein are synthesized by Earl (1983). Making use of a similarly important book by Brian Loasby (1976), and of non-maximizing models such as the lexicographic theory of choice (Georgescu-Roegen, 1954; Fishburn, 1974; Tversky, 1969), Earl

attempts to erect an alternative theoretical structure with an explicit rejection of the maximization hypothesis.

8  See Chase and Simon (1973), de Groot (1978), Newell and Simon (1972) and Simon (1976).

9  See, for example, the studies of cognitive processes in politics in Axelrod (1976), and the case study of the Pearl Harbour attack in Wohlstetter (1962).

10  See, for example, Dudycha and Naylor (1966), Edwards (1968), Feldman (1963), Gettys, Kelly and Peterson (1973), de Groot (1978), Hogarth (1975), Howell and Burnett (1978), Kahneman and Tversky (1973, 1979, 1984), Lichtenstein and Slovic (1971, 1973), Newell and Simon (1972), Nisbett and Ross (1980), Slovic, Fischhoff and Lichtenstein (1977), Slovic and Lichtenstein (1971), Schoemaker (1980, 1982) and Tversky and Kahneman (1973, 1974, 1981). For a recent and longer bibliography see Slovic and Lichtenstein (1983).

11  The tenor of his remarks does not suggest that Arrow believes that neoclassical theory is invulnerable on the grounds that it has never *claimed* to be realistic. His explicit rebuttal of the evolutionary argument in the context of the example suggests that Arrow believes that there is a problem with neoclassical theory.

12  In response to Caldwell's appeal for a less narrow definition of 'criticism', Boland (1983, p. 829) claims to have discovered a logical contradiction. To the 'reasonable' proposition that 'theories cannot be proven absolutely true or false' Boland retorts: 'The statement that theories are not true or false is itself a statement – one which is claimed to be true!' But to say that (most) theories cannot be *proven* absolutely true or false is not inconsistent with the proposition that theories *are* actually true or false.

13  The philosophical basis of the demarcation between ends and means is, of course, utilitarianism. By assigning all direct value judgements solely to purposes and ends, the means can ostensibly be assessed with the canons of positive, or value-free, social science. Values are attached to the means only indirectly, via the values relating to the ends which the means can serve. (Myrdal, 1958, ch. 10)

14  Neglected passages from Alfred Marshall's *Principles of Economics* indicate that not all neoclassical economists were willing to take ends as given. Marshall freely admitted that there are social and cultural factors influencing both the character of the individual and his or her goals. For example, he suggested (Marshall, 1949, p. 1) that 'character is being formed' during the hours of paid employment by relations with associates at work. In the same book he argues that 'although it is man's wants in the early stages of his development that give rise to his activities, yet afterwards each new step upwards is to be regarded as the development of new activities giving rise to new wants, rather than of new wants giving rise to new activites' (p. 76). This amounts to an assertion that means and ends cannot be considered in separation, as the activities required to reach ends will alter the latter in the process. (Note the discussion of Marshall's thought on this point thought by Parsons, 1937, ch. 4; and Chasse, 1984.) Marshall's argument has some resonance with the recent anthropological study of modern consumer society

by Mary Douglas and Baron Isherwood (1980) where consumption is seen not as the end-point in the economic process but as the sphere where a segment of social culture and individual wants are generated.

15 Note that whilst it is legitimate to make use of some of Jon Elster's arguments in this section, in broader terms there are important differences between Elster's work and the perspective adopted here. First, Elster proclaims an unsubstantiated adherence to 'methological individualism', in part because he wrongly suggests that it flows from a forceful rejection of functionalism and a crude holism. Second, although Elster successfully identifies a number of problems with the utilitarian conception of human action, his approach is still largely grounded in a 'rational choice' paradigm which uses the choices and preferences of individuals as the starting point. This is a more valid reason for adopting the 'methodological individualism' label but it is not one which is consistent with his residual attachment to Marxism or the themes of the present work. In fact it has much more in common with the rational actor of neoclassical theory.

5　The Rationalist Conception of Action

1 Note also the development within political theory of positions opposed to the rationalist conception of action, e.g. Graham Allison (1969, 1971), Robert Axelrod (1976) and Michael Oakeshott (1962). For historical case studies of political and military agencies acting apparently against their 'self-interest' see Barbara Tuchman (1984).

2 If players did act in such a fashion then there would be not much of a contest between them. The player advantaged by the first turn would proceed to pot all the balls and win all the points. Only rarely do games happen like that because in reality there is the possibility of error and surprise.

3 Since the early 1970s, Friedrich Hayek, in what has been described as his 'third phase' (Bosanquet, 1983, pp. 36–41), has moved some distance away from his earlier position. Hayek's later writings (e.g. 1978a, 1982) involve critiques of Cartesian rationalism and a reduced stress on individual purposefulness in favour of an evolutionary explanation based on the survival and adaptation of traditions and rules. Von Mises, in Hayek's recent judgement, 'was of course a rationalist utilitarian in which direction . . . I cannot follow him' (1982, vol. 3, p. 205). In Hayek's view his later work represents 'a new beginning' (Hayek, 1982, vol. 3, p. 176). It appears that Hayek has moved slightly away from the classic liberalism of the New Right and towards a traditional conservatism based on the preservation of traditions and rules (e.g. Hayek, 1978a, p. 19). Most of his illusions in the market, however, remain.

Another interesting view is presented by Donald Lavoie (1985a) in which he attempts a synthesis between Austrian economic theory and Michael Polanyi's notion of 'tacit knowledge'. However, in recognizing the importance of habit and the functional nature of tradition, Lavoie does not seem to realize that he has travelled a long way from classical liberalism and

Austrians such as Ludwig von Mises and Carl Menger. The pro-market arguments of Hayek, Lavoie and others are discussed further in chapters 8 and 11.

4 See Nicholas Georgescu-Roegen (1954), Amos Tversky (1969), Peter Fishburn (1974) and Peter Earl (1983).

5 While the behaviouralist approach has a great deal to offer, its literature is not entirely consistent or adequate. For example, in one essay Herbert Simon makes the important point that we cannot 'rule out the possibility that the unconscious is a better decision-maker than the conscious' (1955, p. 104), but in another work he regards 'the simplest movement – taking a step, focusing the eyes on the object – as purposive in nature' (1957b, p. 85). It is strange to admit the possibility of 'unconscious' habits in human behaviour, but then to regard cognitive and other lower-level acts as 'purposive'. The general question of habits is discussed in more detail in the next chapter.

6 A notable and extremely rare recent exception is Ronald Heiner (1986, pp. 95–7) who makes a brief acknowledgment of both habits and unconscious mental processes. Generally, such statements are more common in sociology, psychology and political science.

7 A sample of further references to recent and related developments in cognitive psychology could include J. R. Anderson (1980), Noam Chomsky (1980), R. G. Crowder (1976), N. Geschwind (1980), James Gibson (1979) and S. Glucksberg and M. McCloskey (1981).

8 On the question of multiple degress or levels of consciousness see the exchange between Arthur Koestler and Friedrich Hayek in Koestler and Smythies (1969, p. 326). Hayek's reticence on the point is unfortunate, but it is explicable in terms of his acceptance of a developed version of Cartesian dualism.

9 See, for example, Andras Angyal (1941, 1965), W. Ross Ashby (1952) and G. Sommerhoff (1974). On the general theory of living systems see A. Koestler and J. R. Smythies (1969), James Miller (1978) and Herbert Simon (1968).

10 Thus in a highly stimulating behaviouralist work on the firm, Neil Kay (1984) reduces almost every problem to one of information. As an example he writes that the 'main distinguishing feature between types and grades of labour is *informational* . . . Remove informational barriers and the main distinguishing feature or type of labour disappears' (pp. 36–7). In reality, however, skill differences are partly cognitive and conceptual, and partly a matter of embedded habit, and cannot be reduced to the transmission of raw data or information alone.

## 6 ACTION AND INSTITUTIONS

1 Noam Chomsky (1959) has proposed that learning through stimulus and response cannot fully account for the acquisition of language, arguing that the environment of a child is too complex and unstructured to convey the rules of grammar, and the capacity to do this must to some extent be

genetically endowed. This controversial position cannot be assessed here. What is more important for our purposes is the overall consensus among cognitive theorists regarding the general process of acquisition of concepts and the conceptual nature of knowledge itself.

2 See, for example, Peter Berger and Thomas Luckmann (1967), Mary Douglas (1973), J. M. McLeod and Steven Chaffee (1972) and J. P. Spradley (1972). For an interesting essay on the active role of linguistic structure in the presentation and development of economic theory see Richard Fritz and Judy Fritz (1985).

3 Of course it is possible to 'explain' acceptance of authority or adherence to the law within a neoclassical framework. In addition, perhaps, it could be argued that it is reasonable to accept the norms and rules of established authority, because by virtue of its social position and manifest ability to survive and prosper, it offers information as to the 'best' course of action for the agent. However, it is argued in this work that such explanations are unsatisfactory. It is unreasonable to propose that people feel obliged to keep mostly within the law, and to accept the apparent wisdom of authority, because they have carried out, or are acting 'as if' they have carried out, rational calculation as to the costs and benefits of each case.

Partial recognition of the pressure to conform and other social influences on individual action is found in a work by Stephen Jones (1984). However, whilst Jones does not adopt a straightforward cost-minimizing interpretation in which conformism and emulation are strategems to gain information from the experience of others, the topic is still approached largely within a neoclassical theoretical framework. The social pressure to conform simply becomes an argument in the utility function to be maximized. Thus, as if one eye to developments within psychology and sociology were open, but the other closed, 'conformism' is modelled in terms of rational calculation and utility-maximizing choice. If the subject matter of cognitive social psychology and sociology were to be taken seriously the very use of such functions would be put into question.

4 Notions related to that of practical knowledge are important for some developments in the non-neoclassical theory of the firm. For instance, the concept of 'unteachable knowledge' is central to the work of Edith Penrose (1959, esp. pp. 44–9). She argues that every manager will have practical skills and knowledge of techniques, markets and so on which are not easily codified and require immersion in experience to acquire. More recently, Richard Nelson and Sidney Winter (see below pp. 140–4) have developed a theory of the firm which lays great stress on the acquisition and transmission of routinized practical skills.

5 From extensive studies of business behaviour Katona concludes that rigid pricing rules often prevail, and: 'Habitual pricing rules may extend to such measures as rebates, markdowns, promotions and clearance sales' (Katona, 1975, p. 321). He argues that rigid pricing mechanisms may be operative even if prices are fluctuating or flexible, or if there is rapid inflation.

Whilst, to repeat, no amount of evidence can prove its existence, there is a great weight of data in favour of the theory of full cost pricing. See, for example, Hall and Hitch (1939), Andrews (1949), Sylos-Labini (1969), Eichner (1976) and Lee, (1984a, b). The repeated operation of full cost pricing methods could plausibily be explained through the existence of routinized pricing procedures within the organization.

6 See Thorstein Veblen (1964). A recent discussion by Lamar Jones (1986) of the espousal of Charles Darwin by Thorstein Veblen and the other early institutionalists fails to discuss in depth the possible rationale for their evolutionary views. However, Jones is inadvertently correct in suggesting that the appropriate biological mentor for an evolutionary economics is not Darwin himself. This point is taken up below, pp. 140–4.

In a more positive discussion of this topic Alan Dyer (1984) finds a gap in Veblen's theory, where it fails to explain how specific habits conflict. This Dyer fills with Charles Peirce's theory of signs (Peirce, 1955; Greenlee, 1973). Peirce argues that the signs or patterns through which raw sense data is interpreted are generally imprecise and ambiguous, and he discusses the manner in which social interactions (and habits) develop through such an ambiguous assembly of signs. Dyer could equally have drawn upon the work of modern cognitive theorists to reach similar conclusions.

7 Surprisingly, despite some considerable similarity between Nelson and Winter's approach and the theories of Veblen and the early American institutionalists, Nelson and Winter, make no reference to any of Veblen's works.

8 Note in this context Ronald Heiner's work (1983, 1985, 1985–6) on the origin of rules, norms and predictable behaviour. Like the work of Herbert Simon, one of its valuable features is its stress on the difference between computational competence and the complexity of everyday choices and problems in economic life. However, for Heiner, 'observed regularities of behaviour . . arise because of uncertainty . . . [and] . . . predictable behaviour will evolve only to the extent that uncertainty prevents agents from successfully maximizing' (1983, p. 561). Thus rules and norms arise because of 'uncertainty' and if 'uncertainty' were absent they would not exist.

Heiner's argument depends upon the presupposition that a hypothetical, 'omniscient agent with literally no uncertainty in identifying the most preferred action under any conceivable condition . . . would benefit from maximum flexibility to use all potential information or to adjust to all environmental conditions' (p. 563).

However, the fact that behaviour *could* be more flexible does not imply that it will *necessarily* be so. Consequently, rule-bound and predictable behaviour is possible in the absence of uncertainty. Taking his example of the Rubic Cube, an omniscient agent with a high degree of mathematical competence could unscramble the cube in the shortest possible number of moves. In this case such behaviour would have predictable qualities. The complete lack of uncertainty (in the sense Heiner uses the word) can still give rise to predictable behaviour.

In addition, the next step in Heiner's argument is also flawed. He claims that less flexibility to choose (which in his view flows from uncertainty) must give rise to less complex behaviour. Take, for example, the case of a person that after many months shopping in Town A finds that there is a very good shopping centre in nearby Town B with much lower prices. Such increased knowledge of options clearly can lead to a simple switch in the shopping venue, and behaviour does not necessarily become more complex as a result.

Thus Heiner's argument is misleading in its claim to identify 'the origin of predictable behaviour' in uncertainty. What Heiner does show is that given the realities of the human mind (or today's computers), optimizing behaviour is ruled out by the competence–difficulty gap. The fact that rule-bound and less flexible behaviour may have a value for dealing with this uncertainty does not itself explain the origins of predictable behaviour in all cases, including those in which uncertainty may not exist.

9  We note here some other recognitions of the informational functions of institutions and routine. Geoffrey Newman writes extensively of 'the extent to which institutional structures themselves supply information for decision-making'. He notes correctly that this question 'has received little attention yet it is absolutely fundamental to the analysis of information supplied in markets' (Newman, 1976, p. 474).

Newman's collaborator, Lawrence Boland, notes that: 'One of the roles that institutions play is to create knowledge and information for the individual decision maker. In particular, institutions provide social knowledge which may be needed for *interaction* with other individual decision makers' (Boland, 1979b, p. 963).

Working from a sophisticated and inventive game-theoretic perspective, Andrew Schotter writes that: 'Social and economic institutions are informational devices . . . (and they) convey information about the expected actions of other agents . . . In addition, we see that institutions tend to "codify memory" for the agents in the economy and thereby transform the game they are playing from a game of imperfect recall into one that has what we will call *institution-assisted perfect recall*' (Schotter, 1981, p. 109).

Related ideas are found in the work of Herbert Simon: 'our institutional environment like our natural environment surrounds us with a reliable and perceivable pattern of events . . . The stabilities and predictabilities of our environment, social and natural, allow us to cope with it within the limits set by our knowledge and our computational capacities' (Simon, 1983, p. 78).

More recently, Richard Langlois has commented that 'institutions have an informational-support function. They are, in effect, interpersonal stores of coordinative knowledge; as such, they serve to restrict at once the dimensions of the agent's problem-situation and the extent of the cognitive demands placed upon the agent' (Langlois, 1986a, p. 237).

A number of related further references, from the particular perspective of the analysis of the operation of markets, are noted in chapter 8.

10  Of course, the (slightly) hidden agenda behind the theory of 'spontaneous order' is to provide further classic liberal arguments for the minimal state. Whilst in some important cases, such as the emergence of language, the

theoretical argument carries considerable force, in others, such as the evolution of money, the legitimizing and statutory functions of the state are downplayed. There is a further discussion of the tendency of classic liberal economists to underestimate the role of the state in the next chapter.

11 On this point see for example Karl Marx and Frederick Engels (1976, p. 174) and Paul Sweezy (1968, p. 21).

12 For further discussions of this issue see Edith Penrose (1952), Milton Friedman (1953), Tjalling Koopmans (1957, esp. pp. 1239–42).

13 The writings of the Austrian School are notable for their emphasis on both the intended and unintended consequences of purposive acts. However, because such writers regard all action as purposive, the stress is almost wholly on the process through which unintended consequences result from the interaction with other agents in possession of subjective insight and knowledge. There is much less consideration of the 'unintended' moulding of action by habit and routine.

In contrast, the behaviouralist economists fail to deliberate on the unintended consequences that result from the actions of agents blocking one another. As Richard Langlois (1986a, p. 236) points out, the work of Herbert Simon and his followers puts supreme emphasis on the explanation of the behaviour of the single agent, and neglects problems that arise when agents interact with one another in society. But, as Langlois asserts, the prime goal of social science is not to explain individual behaviour but the unintended as well as intended results of actions of many agents. Diverse economists, including Marxists, Keynesians and Austrians, all accept that the interaction of individual actions may have consequences which were not willed by any one individual.

7 CONTRACTS AND PROPERTY RIGHTS

1 For a collection of broadly neoclassical essays on *Economics and Social Institutions* see Karl Brunner (1979), which is introduced explicitly as an alternative to the 'allure of an encompassing vision' (p. vii) found in Marxian thought.

In his neoclassical critique of the $X$-efficiency theory of Harvey Leibenstein, Louis De Alessi (1983) regards the works of Armen Alchian, Ronald Coase, Harold Demsetz, Oliver Williamson and others as 'revisions', 'extensions' or 'generalizations' of neoclassical theory, rather than a turn in a different direction. As De Alessi points out, such contributions still focus 'on the individual as the basic unit of analysis' (p. 76); he thus underlines the survival of this core neoclassical conception in the Alchian–Coase–Demsetz–Williamson work, and illustrates the unacceptability to orthodoxy of the mildly heretical challenge to this core that is presented by Leibenstein's $X$-efficiency idea.

2 See for example J. Hirshleifer (1979, p. 12), and the criticisms in D. M. Nuti (1972).

3 Another example of undue universalization is the mainstream conception of 'the economic problem' as involving scarce resources and unlimited wants. In his study of a 'stone age' economy, Marshall Sahlins (1972) shows that tribal economies differ from capitalism in that they do not generate ever-increasing wants. In addition, and in contrast to capitaism, tribal, hunter-gatherer societies in tropical regions are faced with such an abundance of food and other necessities that resources are, for practical purposes, unlimited. Thus, and against the mainstream view, it is possible for there to be vast resources and scarce wants. Once again a concept or argument that is typified in a capitalist society is extended without warrant by orthodoxy to all forms of socio-economic system.

4 For the theory of 'implicit contracts' of this type see Baily (1974), Azariadis (1975) and Azariadis and Stiglitz (1983). These authors recklessly ignore the question of the verification of the contractual nature of the supposed arrangement.

At least two highly contentious issues are involved. First, is this in fact an implicit contract between employer and employee, or does it lie in the tradition of Samuel Seabury and others who argued that slavery was justified as it was an implicit contract between slave-owner and slave? Second, is the theory successful in explaining the phenomena, such as wage levels and employment, which it purports to explain? The first question has largely been ignored, and as yet the answers to the second are unsatisfactory. See, for instance, Robert Flanagan (1984).

Interestingly, David Laband (1986) notes that the Azariadis (1975) article has been one of the most frequently cited from the years 1974–6.

5 Alan Randall (1978) argues that Ronald Coase's (1960) paper was essentially an attack on the last justification for state intervention in Pigovian welfare economics.

6 See the account of the development of the concept of property in C. B. Macpherson's (1973, pp. 120–40) stimulating essay 'A Political Theory of Property'. The theme is taken up in Kamenka and Neale (1975).

7 As we have seen, liberal political theory wrongly regards the state as being separable from civil society. But there is also a obverse error. For example, some Marxists, such as Louis Althusser (1971) and others, suggest that in modern capitalism there is negligible real autonomy of the individual or civil society from the state.

This argument is subjected to a devastating critique by Anthony Polan who notes that by notionally absorbing civil society into the state, Althusser's theory serves as an awesome apologia for Soviet dictatorship. By suggesting that this fusion exists under capitalism, the theory 'subverts criticism that in the Soviet Union the state is identical with society, i.e. no institution exists which is not part of the state, no activity occurs which is not directed by the state and made to serve its purpose' (Polan, 1984, p. 35). Thus an obverse of the liberal position that civil society and the state are clearly divided, also leads to error.

For a collection of recent and sophisticated articles on the theory of the state see Peter Evans, Dietrich Rueschemeyer and Theda Skocpol (1985).

8 Note that there is a connection here between the social institutional character of the concept of property and the social character of the concept of value in the work of Marx. Leaving aside the quantitative aspect of the determination of value, it is seen as a relationship between persons as well as between things.

In addition, the social aspect of the property concept is emphasized in the institutionalist tradition. Richard Ely, for instance, argued that even in the case of 'private property' there are two sides, the individual and the social. The social side must be regarded as essential: 'The two necessarily go together, so that if one perishes the other must perish. The social side limits the individual side, and as it is always present there is no such thing as absolute private property' (Ely, 1914, pp. 136–7). For a discussion see Larry Reynolds (1985).

9 It is hard to avoid the observation that just as in his (1983, 1984) analysis of exchange, Oliver Williamson pushes the state to one side, his lengthy (1975) analysis of *Markets and Hierarchies* simply ignores the possibility that a 'transaction costs' analysis can lead to a theoretical justification for the state as well as the firm. Curiously, he is blind to the argument, put neatly by William Dugger, that 'the transaction cost analysis he uses to explain why the firm replaced the market in many economic activities can also be used to explain why the developmental process of minimizing transaction costs could be continued by *replacing the firm with the state* in many areas where the firm earlier replaced the market' (Dugger, 1983, p. 107).

10 However, some of the legal theorists that are quoted by Williamson in support of his extreme view do not actually bear it out. For example, Williamson (1985, pp. 4–5) discusses Karl Llewellyn's distinction between 'iron rules' and 'yielding rules' in a contract and quotes him as follows:

> . . . the major importance of legal contract is to provide a framework for well-nigh every type of group organization and for well-nigh every type of passing or permanent relation between individuals and groups . . . – a framework highly adjustable, a framework which will almost never accurately indicate real working relations, but which affords a rough indication around which such relations vary, an occasional guide in cases of doubt, and a norm of ultimate appeal when the relations cease in fact to work. (Llewellyn, 1931, pp. 736–7)

Plainly, this quotation does not support the suggestion by Williamson that it is a 'precursor' to the idea of 'private ordering' where contractual 'governance' is a matter simply for calculating individuals without the formal legal apparatus of the central state. In fact, Llewellyn's point matches more closely the perspective adopted in the present work that the formal stipulations of the law penetrate civil society but they do not completely dominate it and subsume it. They provide rules and guides, but they do not direct nor rigidly constrain every act.

11 However, there is a slight sign that Williamson may be beginning to move away from his version of neoclassical 'economic man'. He has introduced the concept of individual 'dignity', arguing that it has 'important social

consequences'. Furthermore: 'Parties who devise governance structures in view only of their private utilitarian calculus will thus undervalue dignity in relation to its social importance' (Williamson, 1986a, p. 178). Not only is this a departure from pure, individualistic utilitarianism but also, if taken to its logical conclusion, it would fracture the concept of the self-seeking 'economic man' at the core of his earlier analysis.

Williamson himself recognizes on the same page that his revised view could lead to the conclusion that some extension of worker participation could now be regarded as acceptable. This contrasts with the prominent argument in his earlier work that in general the subversion or democratization of capitalist hierarchy will undermine efficiency.

12 The validity of Durkheim's point should not be obscured by some of the defects in its formulation, and some of the more general problems with his theoretical contribution as a whole. For instance, Durkheim often writes of 'society' as if it were a purposeful agent in itself, and much of his thought has a distinct functionalist tone. Such errors can be rectified without damage to his central thesis of the non-feasibility of a society based on pure contract alone.

13 Note that this point is different from the issue as to whether such a state of affairs is desirable. Notably, the New Right wish to move as close as possible to a 'pure' market system, and the traditional Left view is that the extension of markets is the antithesis of socialism. However, both ideologies share the belief that such an extension of markets is theoretically feasible. Just as Ludwig von Mises (1949, p. 259) suggested that a 'mixed economy' was impossible, in *Capital*, Karl Marx entertained the view that the extension of market relations in capitalist society could proceed to the extent that traditional institutions, such as the family, were dissolved. On this general point and the contrasting 'impurity principle' see Hodgson (1984, chs 6 and 7) and chapter 11 of the present work.

14 Whilst the concept of the gift or grant is alien to most economists a general theory of grants has been developed by Kenneth Boulding (1973). However, the grant is a wider concept than the pure gift in that grants are sometimes based on contractual obligation, such as a pension or a student grant. Boulding notes that grants such as payments to charity, inherited wealth, retirement pensions and unemployment benefits play a highly significant role in the modern economy. In fact it has been estimated that between one-fifth and one-half of the US economy is run on a system of grants rather than exchanges.

Boulding argues that there are two types of grant. There is the 'gift', arising out of 'love'; and the 'tribute' arising out of 'fear'. An example of the tribute is the payment of taxes. An example of the gift is the resources devoted to child-rearing within the family. In both these cases, although through different processes, the effect is to provide integration and cohesion within society.

Boulding is right to point out the existence of grants as well as exchanges in a modern economy. His work is an antidote to, in Marx's famous phrase (1976, p. 163), 'the fetishism of commodities' where all services and objects are seen as actual or potential items of exchange. That, however, is not the whole point. The proposition here is not simply that there is a distinction between grants and exchanged commodities, nor even that gifts and grants are essential for social cohesion, but that commodity exchange itself normally contains elements of a gift and always relies to some extent upon trust.

15 Herbert Simon (1951) has developed a model of the employment contract where contracts are not definitely specified in advance. Approaches to this topic from a Marxian or Post-Marxian perspective include Bowles (1985a, b), Gintis (1976), and Hodgson (1982c, chs. 16 and 17).

However, Marx did not emphasize the relation between, on the one hand, the important distinction between labour and labour-power and, on the other, the existence of complexity and uncertainty in a capitalist economy. Furthermore, his tendency was to ignore all the non-contractual elements in the system. The very logic and structure of *Capital* suggest that capitalism is moving relentlessly towards a more purified form, and thus destroying all vestiges of the past. In contrast, some modern Marxist writers have gone some way to rectify these deficiencies, by emphasizing the functional autonomy of institutions such as the family and the state.

16 Almost inevitably, Akerlof introduces his argument in a formal utility-maximizing framework. Nevertheless, his results are impressive. For instance, unlike Doeringer and Piore (1971) he does not simply take the segmentation of labour markets as given but explains them one stage further. There is, in his view, a fundamental distinction between those segments of the labour market where the gift component of both labour input and wages is sizeable, and those where they are not.

Clearly labour markets where the gift components are significant will not be market-clearing. Hence Akerlof's analysis has implications as well for the study of involuntary unemployment. Perhaps its main significance, however, is the introduction of sociological and anthropological concepts which are alien to neoclassical theory into a prestigious economic journal. This is indeed the thin end of a long and very useful wedge.

17 Worries that the value of money is not maintained through the normal contractual mechanisms, and the belief that, if any, the last institution that can be trusted is the state, lead to a variety of responses by individualistic writers. Arguably, concern about inflation by individualistic theorists such as Milton Friedman is more to do with the *exposé* of state 'incompetence' or 'malpractice' or 'unaccountability' than the problem of rising prices *per se*.

From a similar ideological outlook, Friedrich Hayek has proposed that the state monopoly in the production of money should be abolished. Instead, private banks or individuals would be free to produce their own token money, with its own denominations and units of account. Hayek (1978b, p. 44) asserts: 'The kind of trust on which private money would rest would not be very different from the trust on which today all private banking rests'.

However, in general, trust in the continuing existence or viability of an individual or a bank is not likely to be the same as trust in the state, with its legitimacy, symbolic significance, and attendant power. Whilst the state is far from being infallible in matters of monetary policy, and its powers are often abused, it does have clear advantages in its capacity to encourage confidence in a currency system. Hayek's proposal that similar or adequate levels of confidence can be generated by private individuals or groups at best seems rather naive.

Furthermore, Hayek seems to neglect the symbolic significance and social convenience of having a single unit of account in a complex economy, and underestimates the computational and cognitive problems involved in a chaotic world of multiple currencies and units of account for the millions of commodities at the level of day-to-day trade.

As both Karl Marx (1973) and Georg Simmel (1978) have argued at length, money has a social character that is not reducible to individuals. Marx, 1973, p. 160) saw money as 'an *objectified relation* between persons' and Simmel (1978, p. 129) regarded it as 'an individual thing whose essential significance is to reach beyond individuals'. If multiple currencies exist these 'objective' bonding functions of a single currency are undermined. For a further commentary on Simmel, and an extended discussion of the place of trust in monetary relations see Herbert Frankel (1977).

18 Indeed, the fact that trust and love are devalued if they are subjected to bribe or purchase is, of course, a major dramatic theme of Shakespeare's *King Lear*.

19 Most economists have acted as if they were unaware of the existence of non-contractual elements in any contract. To their credit, in their major work on general equilibrium theory Kenneth Arrow and Frank Hahn (1971, p. 23) raise them explicitly. But they then wrongly assume that they can be safely ignored.

20 In particular, the distinction is used uncritically by Alan Fox (1974).

21 Note John Elliot's useful (1980) article where he stresses the similarities, rather than the differences, between Schumpeter and Marx.

22 This point is developed by Warren Samuels (1985) in his persuasive critique of Schumpeter's *Capitalism, Socialism and Democracy*.


## 8 MARKETS AS INSTITUTIONS

1 Scott Moss (1984, p. xi) claims to have formulated the 'first' economic definition' of markets 'in modern times'. Whilst the above citations from other works show that his claim is inaccurate, the positive features of Moss' definition should not be overlooked.

2 Such a term is certainly less glamorous, but in a work of science the choice between glamour and theoretical precision should be lexical and in favour of the latter, rather than a trade-off between the two:

'How with this rage shall beauty hold a plea,
Whose action is no stronger than a flower?'

(Shakespeare, *Sonnets*, 65)

3 Note the similar points made by Todd Lowry (1976).

4 David Marsden (1986, p. 231) has emphasized: 'Labour markets, and especially those for skilled labour, are institutional phenomena in that they

depend upon an institutional underpinning.' However, this observation is not extended to markets in general.

5 Robert Clower (1967, 1969a) argues that the reduction of 'bargaining costs' is the main fact in determining the relative efficiency of a monetary over a barter economy. The parallel with transaction costs is obvious. It suggests that there are arrangements outside the conventional, money-based market for which transacting involves *higher* costs.

6 The fact that severe price inflation can disrupt this everyday establishment of expected price norms is one reason why inflation *is* a problem in a capitalist society. The irony, however, is that orthodox theory – as Frank Hahn (1982) demonstrates – gives no reason why inflation should be a problem at all. In contrast, a non-neoclassical theory that highlights the function and importance of price norms clearly suggests why unpredicted inflation creates difficulties, in part because it subverts the process through which such conventions are established. Serious price inflation thus distorts perceptions in the marketplace, and is thereby a problem, even if its solution may not have priority over, for example, unemployment. For an argument along related lines see Axel Leijonhufvud (1977).

7 Contrary to orthodox microeconomic theory, Baker (1984, pp. 803–4) concludes from his analysis that there is no necessary positive correlation between market competitiveness and size. He finds that larger markets exhibit more structural differentiation, and because of this and their size tend to impede the flow of information among all market actors. His conclusion is that smaller and more stable market size is more conducive to heightened competitiveness. Given this conclusion perhaps it is no accident that his article was not published in an economics journal but in the *American Journal of Sociology*. But there is no good reason why this work should be described as 'sociology' rather than 'economics'. For some related studies see Adler and Adler (1984).

8 Writing from this Smith–Ricardo–Marx–Sraffa tradition, John Eatwell (1979, pp. 39–41) argues that questions of uncertainty are not central to Keynes' work, and thereby relegates them from his own sphere of concern. However, Paul Davidson (1972), Hyman Minsky (1975), Alexander Dow and Sheila Dow (1985) and others have argued convincingly that the concept of uncertainty holds both an implicit and explicit central position in Keynes' thought. Consequently, in important respects Keynes' work must be regarded as a break from the classical tradition and at least some of its modern derivatives.

In an extremely interesting paper, Geoff Harcourt (1985) shows that towards the end of her life Joan Robinson was disenchanted with some of the uses of Sraffian long-period analysis and in particular with the idea of Sraffian prices as centres of gravitation for price fluctuations.

9 There is an additional problem with an Arrow–Debreu model of complete futures markets. As Mario Nuti (1972) points out, in a developed capitalist system where, by definition, slavery is prohibited, there cannot be a futures market for labour power. If there were, the workers would be in substance enslaved. See also Hodgson (1982c, chs 16 and 17).

10 Peter Earl (1983, p. 7) interprets Richardson's argument as being about the functional role of 'imperfections of knowledge' in helping the market system work. This, however, is misleading, because Richardson is pointing at explicit and implicit collusion, and suggesting that such institutional arrangements help agents obtain *more* information about the likely behaviour of others. As in the work of Neil Kay (1984) there is a tendency towards what might be called 'informational reductionism', i.e. the reduction of all major problems and issues to ones of information, in some laudable attempts to bring neglected questions of information or knowledge to the fore.

11 Other recent work on the theory of repeated games has some additional relevance here. Robert Axelrod (1980a, b, 1981, 1984) organized a tournament to find the best competing strategy for a series of repeated Prisoners' Dilemma games. One interesting conclusion was that the most successful strategy was one of the simplest – the so-called 'tit-for-tat' strategy in which each player repeats what his or her opponent did in the preceding period. Thus cooperation is met with cooperation, and non-cooperation is met by punishment that is swift and sure. Significantly, such a successful strategy is very simple and it amounts to a clear behavioural norm for other players to watch and imitate. For a further discussion see D. Kreps et al. (1982).

12 In this later work, Schotter describes his game-theoretic argument as an 'immanent critique' of orthodoxy, because it starts from neoclassical assumptions and proceeds to show that conventional neoclassical conclusions are unwarranted. This is a slight change of tack, because his earlier work is described as a 'first word' in the development of the economic theory of social institutions (1981, p. 19).

13 Although an optimal strategy in a game-theoretic model may consist of a random choice from a set of mixed strategies, the probability of each choice is still determined by the characteristics of the model and the preferences of the agents. Thus, in a game-theoretic model, action – or more loosely its probability distribution – is still determined, even if not in the manner of the agent in the marginalist and non-linear manner of neoclassical theory. Consequently, there is limited scope for any spontaneity and indeterminacy in human behaviour. The institutionalist emphasis in the present work, as it was argued in part two, does not mean that such indeterminate elements in human behaviour should be excluded.

## 9   FIRMS AND MARKETS

1 For an important and influential discussion of this topic see Bob Rowthorn (1974).

2 The ensuing discussion (especially pp. 196–9) is influenced by the work of Hans Nutzinger (1976, 1982) and Jim Tomlinson (1986).

3 See, in particular, Michael Jensen and William Meckling (1976) and Eugene Fama (1980) – all members of the Property Rights School.

4 A limited but useful model of the employment relationship along these lines has been developed by Herbert Simon (1951). For relevant discussions and elaborations see Samuel Bowles (1985a), Herbert Gintis (1976) and Hodgson (1982c).

5 Note that the phrase 'transaction costs' does not itself appear in Coase's original article. Furthermore, Coase's (1937) argument that there is a 'cost' of 'discovering what the relevant prices are' can be interpreted in different ways. It could mean the 'cost' of obtaining and analysing the relevant price information rather than the complete 'cost' of carrying out the transactions themselves.

6 Williamson's immediate response to this admitted need for a definition of transaction costs is as follows:

> Among the factors on which there appears to be developing a general consensus are: (1) opportunism is a central concept in the study of transaction costs; (2) opportunism is especially important for economic activity that involves transaction-specific investments in human and physical capital; (3) the efficient processing of information is an important and related concept; and (4) the assessment of transaction costs is a comparative institutional undertaking. Beyond these general propositions, a consensus on transaction costs is lacking. (Williamson, 1979, p. 234)

However, nothing amounting to a definition of transaction costs is supplied in Williamson's work. On this score the above paragraph is both too vague and too narrow. It is too vague in that it fails to define the term but simply explicates its context, and it is too narrow in that it is related to the specific behavioural concept of 'opportunism', i.e. 'self-interest seeking with guile'. For these and other reasons, to be raised later, the account and treatment of transaction costs in Williamson's work is defective. For instance, it is shown later that the essence of the transaction cost idea does not depend upon the assumption of self-seeking behaviour.

7 It would be an error to suggest that by concentrating on the market rather than the firm earlier versions of neoclassical theory could legitimately exclude this 'friction' because, according to Williamson, the state where transaction costs are minimized is the firm, not the market. By adopting an analytical sequence where 'in the beginning there were markets' Williamson (1975, p. 20) moves from a sphere where transaction costs are relatively high to one where they are reduced. This is the reverse of the procedure in classical mechanics where the frictionless state is the datum, to be amended by the addition of frictional forces. The analogy of transaction costs with friction is thus misleading in some respects.

8 Whilst Williamson's contribution to postwar economic theory is of significant net value, it is marred by a terminological and analytical imprecision and the use of confusing and sometimes obscurantist jargon.

For example, in a recent book (1985, p. 49) Williamson proposes that 'obedience is tantamount to non-self-interest-seeking'. However, obedience under threat may well be regarded as self-interest. Williamson's attempt to contrast 'self-interest' with 'obedience' thus fails under the simplest analytic scrutiny, and puts some doubt upon what he means by his central concepts of 'self-interest' and 'opportunism' in the first place.

As a second and equally important example he frequently misuses the term 'bounded rationality' with statements of the form: 'Economizing on transaction costs essentially reduces to economizing on bounded rationality' (Williamson, 1979, pp. 245–6; see also e.g. Williamson, 1985, p. 32). Whilst it is possible to work out what Williamson is likely to mean by such phrases, they are nonetheless unsatisfactory. After all, 'bounded rationality' is not a scarce resource, not something that can be 'economized', but a term which itself refers to the limited capacity for computation and rationalizing of the human brain.

If we are to take Williamson's idea of 'economizing on bounded rationality' to mean 'economizing on the time and effort spent on reason and computation (which happens to be bounded or scarce)' then that in turn raises a question which is eluded by the previous formulation: the economizing on 'rationality' itself involves reason and calculation, so how can we economize on economizing itself? This raises further questions about Williamson's continuing allegiance to the paradigm of 'rational economic man' and the idea that all such actions flow from rational, economizing deliberation.

The use of obscurantist jargon is unlikely to be a deliberate attempt to prevent such questions being raised, but it certainly has the function of preventing their full exposure.

9 The indiscriminate use of the term 'transaction costs', and as yet without an adequate definition of the term, is redolent of the following dialogue from Lewis Carroll, *Through the Looking Glass*:

> 'When *I* use a word,' Humpty Dumpty said, in rather a scornful tone, 'it means just what I choose it to mean – neither more nor less.'
>
> 'The question is,' said Alice, 'whether you *can* make words mean so many different things.'
>
> 'The question is,' said Humpty Dumpty, 'which is to be master – that's all.'

10 This tendency to reduce all or most economic problems to the lack or scarcity of information is not uncommon amongst those economists who, quite rightly, and in reaction against former neoclassical assumptions of 'perfect information', wish to bring problems of information and knowledge to the fore. An informational reductionist aspect of Neil Kay's otherwise stimulating (1984) work was raised in note 10 to chapter 5.

11 The argument that has been already put forward in the present work, as in the work of Keynes (1971b, 1973b), is that in such circumstances we fall back on 'the convention', or 'average opinion'. But this itself implies limits to the rational calculus, as demonstrated in part two.

12 Note also Brian Loasby's (1976) demonstration that in a neoclassical general equilibrium model with contingent contracts there is no explanation of any need or basis for any non-market form of organization.

It is remarkable that, by emphasizing uncertainty (as opposed to risk), but with different features and qualifications, Loasby, Kay and Langlois are returning to Frank Knight's *Risk, Uncertainty and Profit* and a core idea in its discussion of the firm that its 'existence in the world is the direct result of the fact of uncertainty' (1933, p. 270). As I have briefly noted in an earlier work (Hodgson, 1982c, pp. 190–2), Coase (1937) gives slight acknowledgment of this point but seems reluctant to take it fully on board. In addition, whilst making copious references to Knight he nowhere distinguishes between uncertainty and risk in this article.

13 Hans Nutzinger (1982) has argued convincingly that:

> The cost of coordinating activities by different devices are not independent of the given distribution of market and non-market coordination mechanisms; if at all, they can only be determined *ceteris paribus* for a given institutional arrangement . . . This leads to the fundamental problem that all conjectures and comparisons in terms of efficiency, based on transactions costs, can only be carried out by starting from a real or imaginary *status quo*, and they hold only in the environment of the initial situation; hence all comparisons of transactions costs, are *local*. (p. 180)

Consequently, analysis of the Williamson type 'has to be confined to models of partial equilibrium in the tradition of Marshall' (p. 181).

14 This point is clearly of importance in rejecting Williamson's (1975, 1980, 1985) argument which purports to show why the participatory firm should be expected to be inefficient.


10   EXPECTATIONS AND THE LIMITS TO KEYNES

1 Examples of mechanistic economic modelling in the Marxian tradition are, unfortunately, not difficult to find. From this standpoint some Marxists (e.g. Bob Sutcliffe, 1977, p. 173) completely exclude expectations as partial determinants of the level of economic activity, because of their allegedly 'subjective' nature. Not only is this view misconceived in its exclusion of expectations, it is argued below that it is wrong to regard them as purely subjective in character. Sutcliffe sees the Keynesian explanation of booms and slumps, based as it is on expectations, as being 'methodologically' equivalent to the sunspots theory of William Stanley Jevons and worthy of similar disdain.

2 Note the distinction between these two: the rationalist conception of action is not an epistemological standpoint but an aspect of some models of human behaviour, i.e. the view that all action is dominated by rational calculation; whereas philosophical rationalism is the idea that reason is the ultimate epistemological authority. Of course, there may be connections between these two sets of ideas, but nevertheless they are still different in substance.

3 Anna Carabelli (1985, pp. 155–6) demonstrates that Keynes' view was that experience does not provide 'a criterion by which to judge whether on given

evidence the probabilities of two propositions are or are not equal' (Keynes, 1973a, p. 94); that Keynes rejected the view of some English empiricists that probability is 'a quality belonging to the entities of phenomenal experience'; and that Keynes was concerned with 'logical relevance' rather than whether logical connection was reflected in 'really material causal laws' (1973a, p. 183).

On these grounds, and on these grounds alone, Carabelli mistakenly concludes that Keynes was 'anti-empiricist'. In reality, however, all that she has shown is that Keynes did not believe that the probability of propositions can be read directly from 'given evidence'; that Keynes distanced himself from some English empiricists who apparently believed that probability belonged to phenomenal experience; and that he refrained from advancing any view on the relation between logic and cause.

From the references that Carabelli musters it is possible to conclude that Keynes was not a vulgar empiricist, but it is not legitimate to conclude that he was against all forms of empiricism. Indeed, Keynes' very idea of 'given evidence' which has widespread use in his treatise on probability, and which is included in one of Carabelli's quotations (see above), demonstrates an empiricist outlook. For an anti-empiricist there is no such thing as 'given evidence' that is independent of the theoretical and conceptual framework of the observer, and of propositions which are previously established.

These points should not detract from the validity of much of Carabelli's remaining argument and her important conclusion that Keynes' 'contributions on economic method, theory and policy are characterized by a sense of what is possible rather than what which is necessary' (Carabelli, 1985, p. 151).

4 Friedrich Hayek reported that Keynes 'was really supremely confident of his powers of persuasion and believed that he could play on public opinion as a virtuoso plays on his instrument'. When Hayek saw Keynes for the last time, in 1946, Keynes explained that if his theories 'should ever become harmful, [Hayek] could be assured that [Keynes] would quickly bring about a change in public opinion' (Hayek, 1972, pp. 103–4). Clearly, Keynes did not here consider any alternative proposal which could survive his death, which was to occur in the same year.

5 See, for example, Buchanan et al. (1978), and Paul Sweezy's (1946, p. 303) portrayal of 'Keynes' habit of treating the state as a *deus ex machina* to be invoked whenever his human actors, behaving according to the rules of the capitalist game, get themselves in a dilemma from which there is apparently no escape'.

6 For a discussion of this point and the so-called 'Keynesian dichotomy' see Alan Coddington (1983).

7 For arguments that are relevant to this point see Janos Kornai (1971) and Andrew Schotter (1981).

11   Directions and Policy Implications

1 On this point there is agreement here with the dominant view in the modern re-assessment of the planning debate (Vaughn, 1980; Murrell, 1983; Lavoie,

1985b) as well as with the arguments of many socialist scholars familiar with the Eastern Bloc economies (Brus, 1975; Horvat, 1982; Kornai, 1971, 1972; Nove, 1983).

2 Note this tension within Friedrich Hayek's recent writings. Whilst always claiming to be an ultra-subjectivist, in a recent work Hayek (1982) develops his liberal argument in terms of the need for some universal and enduring social conventions and norms. Thus, as noted above, Hayek moves some distance from classic liberalism in the direction of a traditional conservatism. At the same time he acknowledges some of the strain on his rationalist values that is caused by his continuing assertion of extreme subjectivism. Thus the acknowledgement of conventions has eroded his former extreme liberalism, whilst in turn the rational arguments for both are undermined by the implications of his unqualified subjectivism. Even an eloquent theorist of Hayek's stature cannot have it three ways at the same time.

3 However, as Norman Geras (1983) demonstrates with rigour, Marx did have an enduring view of human nature and by implication a partially non-relativist conception of human need, contrary to many statements by his followers.

4 Similarly, as noted in the preceding chapter, some Marxist writers take a similar view to the Austrian theorists in wrongly regarding expectations as purely subjective.

5 How else would we have the so-called water–diamonds paradox? Smith and Ricardo could not have said that the use-value of water was high and that of diamonds was low if by use-value they had in mind a subjective concept along the lines of neoclassical utility or satisfaction. In the neoclassical system the utility of water or diamonds can be either high or low, depending on the utility function of the individual. The 'paradox' is not solved by equating exchange-value with marginal utility and use-value with total utility. What then has to be explained is why the classical economists assumed that the total utility of diamonds was low and not high. Arguably, instead of subjective utility, they had some objective concept of general social 'need' in mind.

6 This can be taken as a strong argument in favour of the unorthodox but persuasive idea of a 'basic income allowance' which would be paid by the state to everyone in society irrespective of wealth, apart from the fact that it would grossly simplify the administration of the social security, unemployment, tax allowance, student grant and pension schemes (see Ekins, 1986, ch. 10; Roberts, 1983).

7 In an earlier work (Hodgson, 1984, p. 108), I attribute the statement to Espejo and Howard that this law is 'potentially falsifiable'. This is wrong on two counts. First, Espejo and Howard do not use the phrase themselves; instead they simply say that it is an 'empirical' law. Second, my statement is wrong because whilst the law is possibly false it is not potentially falsifiable, even if we accept the feasibility of a Popperian test. There is no possible event in the real world which would show the law to be false.

To demonstrate the latter point consider the law in question. The law simply states that every viable system is exposed to environmental contingencies with which it cannot cope. Now, a system is either coping or not coping. If a system is coping with variation in its environment that does not mean that it will always cope in the future. Thus in this case the law is not falsified. In the other case, if a system is not coping, then clearly the law is not falsified but supported.

Contrary to Popperian criteria, however, this does not mean that the law is unscientific. It is argued here that it has value as a meta-theoretical framework for organizing further statements and theories about real-world systems. Furthermore, whilst the law is not falsifiable it is not a truism or tautology. It could be false, in that a viable system could exist for which there were no environmental contingencies with which it could not cope. It is in this sense that Espejo and Howard regard it as an 'empirical' law.

Note also that the most abstract version of the neoclassical maximization hypothesis has a similar epistemological status. As Lawrence Boland (1981) has pointed out, this too is non-falsifiable but not a tautology. (See chapter 4 of the present work.) Most, if not all, theoretical systems have similar 'meta-theoretical' statements at their core. Their epistemological status alone thus offers no grounds for their acceptance or rejection.

Whilst the law of insufficient variety, and its special case the impurity principle, have a similar epistemological status, there are still factors that distinguish between them. The grounds for rejecting the maximization hypothesis are partly that it does not easily explain some experimental evidence, such as that concerning choice under risk; and partly that it is directed towards equilibrium explanations and is not a suitable theoretical assumption for explaining economic transformation and growth. On these points the impurity principle is superior.

8 I have noted elsewhere (Hodgson, 1984, p. 161) that this notion of the particular indeterminacy of individual behaviour, and some of the problems it brings for a system-wide response, were brilliantly illuminated by George Eliot in her novel *Felix Holt*. Despite the work being well over a century old (it was first published in 1866), she wrote using the strikingly modern analytic metaphor of the game:

> Fancy what a game of chess would be if all the chessmen had passions and intellects, more or less small and cunning: if you were not only uncertain about your adversary's men, but a little uncertain also about your own; if your knight could shuffle himself on to a new square by the sly; if your bishop, in disgust at your castling, could wheedle your pawns out of their places; and if your pawns, hating you because they are pawns, could make away from their appointed posts that you might get checkmate on a sudden. You might be the longest-headed of deductive reasoners, and yet you might be beaten by your own pawns. (Eliot, 1972, p. 383)

It has recently been brought to my attention that a strikingly similar metaphor was used by Adam Smith a century before that, and by this Eliot may have been inspired in writing the above passage. In his *Theory of Moral Sentiments* (published in 1759) Smith writes: 'The man of system . . . seems to imagine that he can arrange the different members of a great society with as much ease as the hand arranges the different pieces upon a chessboard.' However 'every single piece has a principle of motion of its own, altogether different from that which the legislature might choose to impress upon it' (Smith, 1976, pp. 233–4).

Of course, to make such individual 'passions and intellects' and 'principles of motion' meaningful we have to assume that there is some degree of indeterminacy in human decision-making and action, and that the individual is not a programmed machine.

9 Don Lavoie's work is not picked for its weakness as a representation of a New-Right position but for its strength. Furthermore, its challenging argument should make it required reading for social scientists across the political spectrum. Notably, it is an antidote to the ill-informed view, more prominent for historical reasons in Britain than in the US, which associates all forms of New-Right thinking with authoritarianism and militarism. Lavoie makes it absolutely clear that he opposes both, including the reckless military spending and much of the foreign policy of the US, explicitly including the Reagan administration. Such a work should help to convince the British Left that the New Right as a whole cannot be countered simply with the old anti-conservative slogans and assertions of the past. Hence the taunting ambiguity of his (1985a) subtitle: 'What is Left?'

10 Thus, for example, as Louis Putterman (1984) demonstrates, orthodox economics still has not managed to develop an adequate and convincing explanation of why labour is hired by the representatives of capital, and not the other way round.

11 Of course, a distinction must be made between attempts to explain long-term slowdown or relative decline, covering several decades, and explanations of short-period economic downturn or recession. The strength of the institutionalist arguments is, at present, most apparent in regard to the former.

# Bibliography

Ackoff, R. L. and Emery, F. E. (1972) *On Purposeful Systems* (London: Tavistock).

Adler, P. and Adler, P. (eds) (1984) *The Social Dynamics of Financial Markets* (Greenwich, CT: JAI Press).

Agassi, J. (1960) 'Methodological Individualism', *British Journal of Sociology*, 11, pp. 244–70.

Agassi, J. (1975) 'Institutional Individualism', *British Journal of Sociology*, 26, pp. 144–55.

Aglietta, M. (1979) *A Theory of Capitalist Regulation* (London: NLB).

Akerlof, G. A. (1970) 'The Market for "Lemons": Quality Uncertainty and the Market Mechanism', *Quarterly Journal of Economics*, 84, pp. 488–500. Reprinted in Akerlof (1984).

Akerlof, G. A. (1980) 'A Theory of Social Custom, of which Unemployment may be One Consequence', *Quarterly Journal of Economics*, 94, pp. 749–75. Reprinted in Akerlof (1984).

Akerlof, G. A. (1982) 'Labor Contracts as Partial Gift Exchange', *Quarterly Journal of Economics*, 97(4), pp. 543–69. Reprinted in Akerlof (1984).

Akerlof, G. A. (1983) 'Loyalty Filters', *American Economic Review*, 73(1), pp. 54–63.

Akerlof, G. A. (1984) *An Economic Theorist's Book of Tales* (Cambridge: Cambridge University Press).

Akerlof, G. A. and Dickens, W. T. (1982) 'The Economic Consequences of Cognitive Dissonance', *American Economic Review*, 73(3), pp. 307–19. Reprinted in Akerlof (1984).

Akerlof, G. A. and Yellen, J. L. (1985) 'A Near-Rational Model of the Business Cycle with Wage and Price Inertia', *Quarterly Journal of Economics*, *100* (supplement), pp. 823–38.

Alchian, A. A. (1950) 'Uncertainty, Evolution and Economic Theory', *Journal of Political Economy*, 58, pp. 211–22.

Alchian, A. A. and Demsetz, H. (1972) 'Production, Information Costs, and Economic Organization', *American Economic Review*, 62, pp. 777–95. Reprinted in Putterman (1986).

Aldrich, J. (1977) 'Participation and the Nature of the Firm', in D. Heathfield (1977, pp. 122–34).

Allison, G. T. (1969) 'Conceptual Models and the Cuban Missile Crisis', *American Political Science Review*, 63, pp. 689–718.

Allison, G. T. (1971) *Essence of Decision* (Boston: Little, Brown and Co.).

Althusser, L. (1971) *Lenin and Philosophy and Other Essays* (London: NLB).

Althusser, L. and Balibar, E. (1970) *Reading Capital* (London: NLB).

Amsden, A. H. (ed.) (1980) *The Economics of Women and Work* (Harmondsworth: Penguin).

Anderson, J. R. (1980) *Cognitive Psychology and Its Implications* (San Francisco: Freeman).

Andrews, P. W. S. (1949) *Manufacturing Business* (London: Macmillan).

Angyal, A. (1941) *Foundations for a Science of Personality* (New York: Commonwealth Fund).

Angyal, A. (1965) *Neurosis and Treatment* (New York: Wiley).

Anshoff, H. I. (1968) *Corporate Strategy* (Harmondsworth: Penguin).

Aoki, M. (1984) *The Cooperative Game Theory of the Firm* (Oxford: Oxford University Press).

Aoki, M. (1986) 'Horizontal *vs.* Vertical Structure of the Firm', *American Economic Review*, 76(5), pp. 971–83.

Arrow, K. J. (1962) 'Economic Welfare and the Allocation of Resources for Invention', in *The Rate and Direction of Inventive Activity: Economic and Social Factors,* National Bureau of Economic Research, pp. 609–25 (Princeton NJ: Princeton University Press). Reprinted in Lamberton (1971).

Arrow, K. J. (1968) 'Mathematical Models in the Social Sciences', in Brodbeck (1968, pp. 635–67).

Arrow, K. J. (1969) 'The Organization of Economic Activity: Issues Pertinent to the Choice of Market Versus Nonmarket Allocation', in *The Analysis and Evaluation of Public Expenditure: the PPB System*, vol. 1, US Joint Economic Committee, pp. 59–73 (Washington DC: US Government Printing Office).

Arrow, K. J. (1974) *The Limits of Organization* (New York: Norton).

Arrow, K. J. (1975) 'Gifts and Exchanges', in Phelps (1975, pp. 13–28).

Arrow, K. J. (1978) 'The Future and the Present in Economic Life', *Economic Inquiry*, 16(2), pp. 157–69.

Arrow, K. J. (1982) 'Risk Perception in Psychology and Economics', *Economic Inquiry*. 20(1), pp. 1–9.

Arrow, K. J. and Hahn, F. H. (1971) *General Competitive Analysis* (Edinburgh: Oliver and Boyd).

Artis, M. J. and Miller, M. H. (1981) *Essays in Fiscal and Monetary Policy* (Oxford: Oxford University Press).

Asch, S. E. (1952) *Social Psychology* (New York: Prentice-Hall).

Ashby, W. R. (1952) *Design for a Brain* (New York: Wiley).

Ashby, W. R. (1956) *Introduction to Cybernetics* (New York: Wiley).

Aspromourgos, A. (1986) 'On the Origins of the Term "Neoclassical"', *Cambridge Journal of Economics*, 10(3), pp. 265–70.

Auerbach, P. (1985) *Market Structure and Firm Behaviour: An Empty Box?* (London: Thames Papers in Political Economy).

Axelrod, R. (ed.) (1976) *Structure of Decision* (Princeton, NJ: Princeton University Press).

Axelrod, R. (1980a), 'Effective Choice in the Prisoner's Dilemma', *Journal of Conflict Resolution*, 24, pp. 3–25.

Axelrod, R. (1980b) 'More Effective Choice in the Prisoner's Dilemma', *Journal of Conflict Resolution*, 24, pp. 379–403.

Axelrod, R. (1981) 'The Emergence of Cooperation Among Egoists', *American Political Science Review*, 75, pp. 306–18.

Axelrod, R. (1984) *The Evolution of Cooperation* (New York: Basic Books).

Ayres, C. E. (1978) *The Theory of Economic Progress*, new edn, (Kalamazoo, Mich.: New Issues Press).

Azariadis, C. (1975) 'Implicit Contracts and Underemployment Equilibria', *Journal of Political Economy*, 83, pp. 1183–202.

Azariadis, C. and Stiglitz, J. E. (1983) 'Impicit Contracts and Fixed Price Equilibria', *Quarterly Journal of Economics*, 98(supplement), pp. 1–22.

Baily, M. N. (1974) 'Wages and Unemployment Under Uncertain Demand', *Review of Economic Studies*, 41, pp. 37–50.

Baker, W. (1984) 'The Social Structure of a National Securities Market', *American Journal of Sociology*, 89(4), pp. 775–811.

Barber, B. (1983) *The Logic and Limits of Trust* (New Brunswick, NJ: Rutgers University Press).

Barnes, B. (ed.) (1972) *Sociology of Science: Selected Readings* (Harmondsworth: Penguin).

Barry, B. M. (1970) *Sociologists, Economists and Democracy* (London: Collier-Macmillan).

Baumol, W. J. (1959) *Business Behavior, Value and Growth* (New York: Macmillan).

Baumol, W. J., Panzar, J. C. and Willig, R. D. (1982) *Contestable Markets and the Theory of Industry Structure* (New York: Harcourt Brace Jovanovich).

Bausor, R. (1983) 'The Rational-Expectations Hypothesis and the Epistemics of Time', *Cambridge Journal of Economics*, 7(1), pp. 1–10.

Beam, R. D. (1983) 'Towards a System-Based Unified Social Science', in Machlup and Mansfield (1983, pp. 607–18).

Bear, D. V. T. and Orr, D. (1967) 'Logic and Expediency in Economic Theorising', *Journal of Political Economy*, 75, pp. 188–96.

Becker, G. S. (1976) *The Economic Approach to Human Behavior* (Chicago: University of Chicago Press).

Beer, S. (1964) *Cybernetics and Management* (London: Science Editions).

Beer, S. (1972) *Brain of the Firm* (London: Allen Lane).

Begg, D. K. H. (1982) *The Rational Expectations Revolution in Macroeconomics: Theories and Evidence* (Oxford: Phillip Allen).

Bell, D. and Kristol, I. (eds) (1981) *The Crisis in Economic Theory* (New York: Basic Books).

Belshaw, C. S. (1965) *Traditional Exchange and Modern Markets* (Englewood Cliffs, NJ: Prentice-Hall).

Benello, C. G. and Roussopoulos, D. (eds) (1971) *The Case for Participatory Democracy* (New York: Viking Compass).

Benn, S. I. (1976) 'Rationality and Political Behaviour', in Benn and Mortimore (1976, pp. 246–67).

Benn, S. I. and Mortimore, G. W. (eds) (1976) *Rationality in the Social Sciences* (London: Routledge and Kegan Paul).

Bentham, J. (1823) *An Introduction to the Principles of Morality and Legislation* (London: Frourde).

Berger, P. L. and Luckmann, T. (1967) *The Social Construction of Reality* (Harmondsworth: Penguin).

Bertalanffy, L. von (1950) 'The Theory of Open Systems in Physics and Biology', *Science*, 111, pp. 23–9. Reprinted in Emery (1981).

Bertalanffy, L. von (1971) *General System Theory: Foundation Development Applications* (London: Allen Lane).

Best, M. H. (1982) 'The Political Economy of Socially Irrational Products', *Cambridge Journal of Economics*, 6(1), pp. 53–64.

Best, M. H. (1986) 'Strategic Planning, the New Competition and Industrial Policy', in Nolan and Paine (1986, pp. 182–97).

Bharadwaj, K. (1968) 'The Collected Scientific Papers of Paul A. Samuelson', *Indian Economic Journal*, pp. 501–26.

Bhaskar, R. (1975) *A Realist Theory of Science* (Leeds: Leeds Books).

Bhaskar, R. (1979a) 'On the Possibility of Social Scientific Knowledge and the Limits of Naturalism', in Mepham and Ruben (1979, pp. 107–39).

Bhaskar, R. (1979b) *The Possibility of Naturalism* (Brighton: Harvester).

Blau, P. M. (1964) *Exchange and Power in Social Life* (New York: Wiley).

Blauberg, I. (1979) 'Systems and Wholeness Concepts', *Social Sciences*, 10, pp. 65–79.

Blaug, M. (1978) *Economic Theory in Retrospect*, 3rd edn (Cambridge: Cambridge University Press).

Blaug, M. (1980) *The Methodology of Economics: Or How Economists Explain* (Cambridge: Cambridge University Press).

Block, F. L. (1977) *The Origins of International Economic Disorder* (Berkeley: University of California Press).

Blumberg, P. (1968) *Industrial Democracy: The Sociology of Participation* (London: Constable).

Boehm, S. (1982) 'The Ambiguous Notion of Subjectivism: Comment on Lachmann', in Kirzner (1982, pp. 41–52).

Bohm, D. (1980) *Wholeness and the Implicate Order* (London: Routledge and Kegan Paul).

Boland, L. A. (1979a) 'A Critique of Friedman's Critics', *Journal of Economic Literature*, 17, pp. 503–22. Reprinted in Caldwell (1984b).

Boland, L. A. (1979b) 'Knowledge and the Role of Institutions in Economic Theory', *Journal of Economic Issues*, 13(4), pp. 957–72.

Boland, L. A. (1981) 'On the Futility of Criticizing the Neoclassical Maximization Hypothesis', *American Economic Review*, 71, pp. 1031–36. Reprinted in Caldwell (1984b).

Boland, L. A. (1982) *The Foundations of Economic Method* (London: George Allen and Unwin).

Boland, L. A. (1983) 'The Neoclassical Maximization Hypothesis: Reply',

*American Economic Review*, 73(4), pp. 828–30. Reprinted in Caldwell (1984b).

Boland, L. A. (1986) *Methodology for a New Microeconomics: The Critical Foundations* (London: Allen and Unwin).

Boland, L. A. and Newman, G. (1979) 'On the Role of Knowledge in Economic Theory', *Australian Economic Papers*, 18, pp. 71–80.

Boltho, A. (1983) 'Is Western Europe Caught in an Expectations Trap?', *Lloyds Bank Review*, April, pp. 1–13.

Bosanquet, N. (1983) *After the New Right* (London: Heinemann).

Boulding, K. E. (1956) *The Image: Knowledge in Life and Society* (Ann Arbor: University of Michigan Press).

Boulding, K. E. (1970) *Economics as a Science* (New York: McGraw-Hill).

Boulding, K. E. (1973) *The Economy of Love and Fear* (Belmont, CA: Wadsworth).

Boulding, K. E. (1981) *Evolutionary Economics* (Beverly Hills, CA: Sage Publications).

Boulding, K. E. (1985) *The World as a Total System* (Beverly Hills, CA: Sage Publications).

Bowles, S. (1985a) 'The Production Process in a Competitive Economy: Walrasian, Neo-Hobbesian, and Marxian Models', *American Economic Review*, 75(1), pp. 16–36. Reprinted in Putterman (1986).

Bowles, S. (1985b) 'State Structures and Political Practices: A Reconsideration of the Liberal Democratic Conception of Politics and Accountability', in Coe and Wilber (1985, pp. 147–90).

Bowles, S., Gordon, D. M. and Weisskopf, T. E. (1985) *Beyond the Waste Land: A Democratic Alternative to Economic Decline* (London: Verso).

Bradley, I. and Howard, M. (eds) (1982) *Classical and Marxian Political Economy* (London: Macmillan).

Brainard, W. and Perry, G. (1981) 'Editors' Summary', *Brookings Papers in Economic Activity*, no. 1, pp. i–xv.

Brodbeck, M. (ed.) (1968) *Readings in the Philosophy of the Social Sciences* (New York: Macmillan).

Bromley, D. W. (1985) 'Resources and Economic Development: An Institutionalist Perspective', *Journal of Economic Issues*, 19(3), pp. 779–96.

Brothwell, J. F. (1986) '*The General Theory* after Fifty Years: Why are We Not All Keynesians Now?', *Journal of Post Keynesian Economics*, 8(4), pp. 531–47.

Brown-Collier, E. K. (1985) 'Keynes' View of an Organic Universe: The Implications', *Review of Social Economy*, 43(1), pp. 14–23.

Bruner, J. S. (1973) *Beyond the Information Given* (London: George Allen and Unwin).

Brunner, K. (ed.) (1979) *Economics and Social Institutions* (Boston: Martinus Nijhoff).

Brus, W. (1975) *Socialist Ownership and Political Systems* (London: Routledge and Kegan Paul).

Buchanan, J. M. (1968) 'Frank H. Knight', *International Encyclopedia of the Social Sciences*, vol. 8, pp. 424–8 (New York: Macmillan).

Buchanan, J. M. (1969) 'Is Economics the Science of Choice?', in Streissler (1969, pp. 47–64).

Buchanan, J. M. (1982) 'The Domain of Subjective Economics: Between Predictive Science and Moral Philosophy', in Kirzner (1982, pp. 7–20).

Buchanan, J. M. and Tullock, G. (1962) *The Calculus of Consent* (Ann Arbor: University of Michigan Press).

Buchanan, J. M., Wagner, R. E. and Burton, J. (1978) *The Consequences of Mr Keynes* (London: Institute of Economic Affairs).

Buckley, W. (1983) 'Signals, Meaning, and Control in Social Systems', in Machlup and Mansfield (1983, pp. 601–6).

Buiter, W. H. (1980) 'The Macroeconomics of Dr Pangloss: A Critical Survey of the New Classical Macroeconomics', *Economic Journal*, 90, pp. 34–50.

Burman, P. (1979) 'Variations on a Dialectical Theme', *Philosophy of the Social Sciences*, 9, pp. 357–75.

Butler, R. J. (1983) 'Control through Markets, Hierarchies and Communes: A Transactional Approach to Organisational Analysis', in Francis et al. (1983).

Caldwell, B. J. (1980a) 'Positivist Philosophy of Science and the Methodology of Economics', *Journal of Economic Issues*, 14(1), pp. 53–76.

Caldwell, B. J. (1980b) 'A Critique of Friedman's Methodological Instrumentalism', *Southern Economic Journal*, 47, pp. 366–74. Reprinted in Caldwell (1984b).

Caldwell, B. J. (1982) *Beyond Positivism: Economic Methodology in the Twentieth Century* (London: Allen and Unwin).

Caldwell, B. J. (1983) 'The Neoclassical Maximisation Hypothesis: Comment', *American Economic Review*, 73(4), pp. 824–7. Reprinted in Caldwell (1984b).

Caldwell, B. J. (1984a) 'Praxeology and its Critics: An Appraisal', *History of Political Economy*, 16(3), pp. 363–79.

Caldwell, B. J. (ed.) (1984b) *Appraisal and Criticism in Economics* (London: Allen and Unwin).

Caldwell, B. J. and Coats, A. W. (1984) 'The Rhetoric of Economics: A Comment on McCloskey', *Journal of Economic Literature*, 22, pp. 575–78.

Canterbery, E. R. and Burkhardt, R. J. (1983) 'What Do We Mean By Asking Whether Economics is a Science?', in Eichner (1983b, pp. 15–40).

Capek, M. (1961) *The Philosophical Consequences of Contemporary Physics* (New York: Van Nostrand).

Capra, F. (1975) *The Tao of Physics: An Exploration of the Parallels Between Modern Physics and Eastern Mysticism* (London: Wildwood House).

Capra, F. (1982) *The Turning Point: Science, Society and the Rising Culture* (London: Wildwood House).

Carabelli, A. (1985) 'Keynes on Cause, Chance and Probability', in Lawson and Pesaran (1985, pp. 151–80).

Carling, A. (1986) 'Rational Choice Marxism', *New Left Review*, no. 160, pp. 24–62.

Carter, C. (ed) (1981) *Industrial Policy and Innovation* (London: Heinemann).

Carvalho, F. (1983–4) 'On the Concept of Time in Shacklean and Sraffian Economics', *Journal of Post Keynesian Economics*, 6(2), pp. 265–80.

Casson, M. C. (1982) *The Entrepreneur: An Economic Theory* (Oxford: Basil Blackwell).

Chalmers, A. F. (1982) *What is This Thing Called Science?* (Milton Keynes: Open University Press).

Champernowne, D. G. (1963) 'Expectations and the Links Between the Economic Future and the Present', in Lekachman (1964, pp. 174–202)

Chandler Jr, A. D. (1962) *Strategy and Structure: Chapters in the History of the American Industrial Enterprise* (Cambridge MA: MIT Press).

Chandler Jr, A. D. (1977) *The Visible Hand: The Managerial Revolution in American Business* (Cambridge MA: Harvard University Press).

Chandler Jr, A. D. and Daems, H. (eds) (1980) *Managerial Hierarchies: Comparative Perspectives on the Rise of the Modern Industrial Enterprise*, (Cambridge, MA: Harvard University Press).

Chase, W. G. (ed.) (1973a) *Visual Information Processing* (New York: Academic Press).

Chase, W. G. and Simon, H. A. (1973b) 'The Mind's Eye in Chess' in Chase (1973a, pp. 215–81)

Chasse, J. D. (1984) 'Marshall, the Human Agent and Economic Growth: Wants and Activities Revisited', *History of Political Economy*, 16(3), pp. 381–404.

Cheung, S. N. S. (1983) 'The Contractual Nature of the Firm', *Journal of Law and Economics*, 26(1), pp. 1–22.

Chipman, J. S. (1971) 'Consumption Theory Without Transitive Indifference' in Chipman et al. (1971, pp. 224–53).

Chipman, J. S., Hurwicz, L., Richter, M. K. and Sonnenschein, H. F. (eds) (1971) *Preferences, Utility and Demand* (New York: Harcourt Brace Jovanovich).

Chomsky, N. (1959) 'Review of B. F. Skinner's *Verbal Behavior*', *Language*, 35, pp. 26–58.

Chomsky, N. (1980) 'Rules and Representations', *Behavioral and Brain Sciences*, 3, pp. 1–61.

Churchman, C. W. (1979) *The Systems Approach and Its Enemies* (New York: Basic Books).

Clark, L. H. (ed.) (1954) *Consumer Behavior, Vol. I, The Dynamics of Consumer Reaction* (New York: New York University Press).

Clark, L. H. (ed.) (1955) *Consumer Behavior, Vol. II, The Life Cycle of Consumer Behavior* (New York: New York University Press).

Clower, R. W. (1967) 'A Reconsideration of the Microfoundations of Monetary Theory', *Western Economic Journal*, 6, pp. 1–9. Reprinted in Clower (1969b).

Clower, R. W. (1969a) 'Introduction' in Clower (1969b, pp. 7–21).

Clower, R. W. (ed.) (1969b) *Monetary Theory* (Harmondsworth: Penguin).

Coase, R. H. (1937) 'The Nature of the Firm', *Economica*, 4, pp. 386–405. Reprinted in Putterman (1986).

Coase, R. H. (1960) 'The Problem of Social Cost', *Journal of Law and Economics*, 3, pp. 1–44.

Coase, R. H. (1972) 'Industrial Organization: A Proposal for Research', in Fuchs (1972, pp. 59–73).

Coates, D. and Hillard, J. (eds) (1986) *The Economic Decline of Modern Britain: The Debate Between Left and Right* (Brighton: Harvester).

Coats, A. W. (1954) 'The Influence of Veblen's Methodology', *Journal of Political Economy*, 62, pp. 529–37.

Coats, A. W. (1976) 'Economics and Psychology: Death and Resurrection of a Research Programme', in Latsis (1976b, pp. 43–64).

Coddington, A. (1979) 'Friedman's Contribution to Methodological Controversy', *British Review of Economic Issues*, 2(4), pp. 1–13.

Coddington, A. (1983) *Keynesian Economics: The Search for First Principles* (London: George Allen and Unwin).

Coe, R. D. and Wilber, C. K. (eds) (1985) *Capitalism and Democracy: Schumpeter Revisited* (Notre Dame, Indiana: University of Notre Dame Press).

Cohen, G. A. (1978) *Karl Marx's Theory of History: A Defence* (Oxford: Oxford University Press).

Cohen, M. D. and Axelrod, R. (1984) 'Coping with Complexity: The Adaptive Value of Changing Utility', *American Economic Review*, 74, pp. 30–42.

Cohn, M. D., March, J. G. and Olsen, J. P. (1972) 'A Garbage Can Model of Organizational Choice' *Administrative Science Quarterly*, 17, pp. 1–25.

Collard, D. (1978) *Altruism and Economy: A Study in Non-Selfish Economics* (Oxford: Martin Robertson).

Collins, H. (1986) *The Law of Contract* (London: Weidenfeld and Nicolson).

Commons, J. R. (1924) *Legal Foundations of Capitalism* (New York: Macmillan).

Commons, J. R. (1934) *Institutional Economics: Its Place in Political Economy* (Madison: University of Wisconsin Press).

Commons, J. R. (1950) *The Economics of Collective Action* (New York: Macmillan).

Conlisk, J. (1980) 'Costly Optimizers Versus Cheap Imitators', *Journal of Economic Behavior and Organization*, 1, pp. 275–93.

Copi, I. M. (1972) *Introduction to Logic*, 4th edn (New York: Macmillan).

Cournot, A. (1897) *Research into the Mathematical Principles of the Theory of Wealth*, translated by Nathaneil Bacon from the French edition of 1838 (New York: Macmillan).

Cowling, K. (1987) 'An Industrial Strategy for Britain: The Nature and Role of Planning', *International Review of Applied Economics*, 1(1), pp. 1–22.

Crosland, C. A. R. (1956) *The Future of Socialism* (London: Jonathan Cape).

Cross, R. (1982a) *Economic Theory and Policy in the UK: An Outline and Assessment of the Controversies* (Oxford: Martin Robertson).

Cross, R. (1982b) 'The Duhem-Quine Thesis, Lakatos and the Appraisal of Theories in Macroeconomics', *Economic Journal*, 92, pp. 320–40. Reprinted in Caldwell (1984b).

Crowder, R. G. (1976) *Principles of Learning and Memory* (Hillsdale, NJ: Erlbaum).

Cyert, R. M. and De Groot, M. H. (1975) 'Adaptive Utility' in Day and Groves (1975, pp. 223–36).

Cyert, R. M. and March, J. G. (1963) *A Behavioral Theory of the Firm* (Englewood Cliffs NJ: Prentice-Hall).

Dahlman, C. J. (1979) 'The Problem of Externality', *Journal of Law and Economics*, 22(1), pp. 141–62.

Davidson, D. (1980) *Essays on Action and Events* (Oxford: Oxford University Press).

Davidson, D. (1985) *Inquiries into Truth and Interpretation* (Oxford: Oxford University Press).

Davidson, P. (1972) *Money and the Real World* (London: Macmillan).

Davidson, P. (1982–3) 'Rational Expectations: A Fallacious Foundation for Studying Crucial Decision-Making Processes', *Journal of Post Keynesian Economics*, 5(2), pp. 182–98.

Day, R. H. and Groves, T. (eds) (1975) *Adaptive Economic Models* (New York: Academic Press).

De Alessi, L. (1983) 'Property Rights, Transactions Costs, and X-Efficiency: An Essay in Economic Theory', *American Economic Review*, 73(1), pp. 64–81.

Debreu, G. (1959) *Theory of Value* (New York: Wiley).

Demsetz, H. (1967) 'Towards a Theory of Property Rights', *American Economic Review (Proceedings)*, 57, pp. 347–59.

Demsetz, H. (1969) 'Information and Efficiency: Another Viewpoint', *Journal of Law and Economics*, 12(1), pp. 1–22. Reprinted in Lamberton (1971).

Desai, M. (1981) *Testing Monetarism* (London: Pinter).

Dietrich, M. D. (1986) 'Organisational Requirements of a Socialist Economy: Theoretical and Practical Suggestions', *Cambridge Journal of Economics*, 10(4), pp. 319–33.

Dillard, D. (1980) 'A Monetary Theory of Production: Keynes and the Institutionalists', *Journal of Economic Issues*, 14(2), pp. 255–73.

Dillard, D. (1982) 'Rewriting the Principles of Economics', *Journal of Economic Issues*, 16(2), pp. 577–85.

Dixon, R. (1986) 'Uncertainty, Unobstructedness and Power', *Journal of Post Keynesian Economics*, 8(4), pp. 585–90.

Doeringer, P. B. and Piore, M. J. (1971) *Internal Labour Markets and Manpower Analysis* (Lexington, MA: Heath).

Dolan, E. G. (ed.) (1976) *The Foundations of Modern Austrian Economics* (Kansas City: Sheed and Ward).

Dopfer, K. (ed.) (1976) *Economics in the Future* (London: Macmillan).

Dore, R, (1973) *British Factory–Japanese Factory: The Origins of National Diversity in Industrial Relations* (Berkeley and Los Angeles: University of California Press).

Dore, R. (1983) 'Goodwill and the Spirit of Market Capitalism', *British Journal of Sociology*, 34(4), pp. 459–82.

Douglas, M. (ed.) (1973) *Rules and Meanings* (Harmondsworth: Penguin).

Douglas, M. and Isherwood, B. (1980) *The World of Goods: Towards an Anthropology of Consumption* (Harmondsworth: Penguin).

Dow, A. and Dow, S. C. (1985) 'Animal Spirits and Rationality', in Lawson and Pesaran (1985, pp. 46–65).

Dow, S. C. (1985) *Macroeconomic Thought: A Methodological Approach* (Oxford: Basil Blackwell).

Downs, A. (1957) *An Economic Theory of Democracy* (New York: Harper).

Doyal, L. and Gough, I. (1984) 'A Theory of Human Needs', *Critical Social Policy*, 10, pp. 6–38.

Doyal, L. and Gough, I. (1986) 'Human Needs and Strategies for Social Change' in Ekins (1986, pp. 69–80).

Doyal, L. and Gough, I. (in press) *On Human Needs* (London: Macmillan).

Dudycha, L. W. and Naylor, J. C. (1966) 'Characteristics of the Human Inference Process in Complex Choice Behaviour Situations', *Organizational Behavior and Human Performance*, 1, pp. 110–28.

Duesenberry, J. S. (1949) *Income, Saving and the Theory of Consumer Behavior* (Cambridge MA: Harvard University Press).

Dugger, W. M. (1979) 'Methodological Differences Between Institutional and Neoclassical Economics', *Journal of Economic Issues*, 13(4), pp. 899–909.

Dugger, W. M. (1982) 'The Alleged Value Neutrality of Economics: An Alternative View', *Journal of Economic Issues*, 16(1), pp. 75–106.

Dugger, W. M. (1983) 'The Transaction Costs Analysis of Oliver E. Williamson: A New Synthesis?', *Journal of Economic Issues*, 17(1), pp. 95–114.

Dunlop, J. T. (1958) *Industrial Relations Systems* (New York: Holt).

Durkheim, E. (1984) *The Division of Labour in Society*, translated from the French edition of 1893 by W. D. Halls with an introduction by L. Coser (London: Macmillan).

Dworkin, G., Bermant, G. and Brown, P. G. (eds) (1977) *Markets and Morals* (Washington, DC: Hemisphere).

Dyer, A. W. (1984) 'The Habit of Work: A Theoretical Exploration', *Journal of Economic Issues*, 18(2), pp. 557–64.

Earl, P. E. (1983) *The Economic Imagination: Towards a Behavioural Analysis of Choice* (Brighton: Wheatsheaf).

Earl, P. E. (1984) *The Corporate Imagination: How Big Companies Make Mistakes* (Brighton: Wheatsheaf).

Earl, P. E. and Kay, N. M. (1985) 'How Economists Can Accept Shackles's Critique of Economic Doctrines Without Arguing Themselves Out of Jobs', *Journal of Economic Studies*, 12 (1/2), pp. 34–48.

Eatwell, J. (1979) *Theories of Value and Employment* (London: Thames Papers in Political Economy).

Edwards, W. (1968) 'Conservatism in Human Information Processing' in B. Kleinmuntz (1968, pp. 17–52). Reprinted in Kahneman et al. (1982).

Eichner, A. S. (1976) *The Megacorp and Oligopoly* (Cambridge: Cambridge University Press).

Eichner, A. S. (1983a), 'Why Economics Is Not Yet a Science', *Journal of Economic Issues*, 17(2), pp. 507–20.

Eichner, A. S. (ed.) (1983b) *Why Economics Is Not Yet a Science* (London: Macmillan).

Eichner, A. S. (1985) *Toward A New Economics* (London: Macmillan).

Eiser, J. R. (1980) *Cognitive Social Psychology: A Guidebook to Theory and Research* (London: McGraw-Hill).

Ekins, P. (1986) *The Living Economy: A New Economics in the Making* (London: Routledge and Kegan Paul).

Elbaum, B. and Lazonick, W. (1986a) 'An Institutional Perspective on British Decline', in Elbaum and Lazonick (1986b, pp. 1–17).

Elbaum, B. and Lazonick, W. (eds) (1986b) *The Decline of the British Economy* (Oxford: Oxford University Press).

Eliot, G. (1972) *Felix Holt, The Radical* (Harmondsworth: Penguin).

Elliot, J. E. (1980) 'Marx and Schumpeter on Capitalism's Creative Destruction: A Comparative Restatement', *Quarterly Journal of Economics*, 94, pp. 45–68.

Elster, J. (1979) *Ulysses and the Sirens* (Cambridge: Cambridge University Press).

Elster, J. (1982) 'Marxism, Functionalism and Game Theory: The Case for Methodological Individualism', *Theory and Society*, 11, pp. 453–82.

Elster, J. (1983a) *Sour Grapes: Studies in the Subversion of Rationality* (Cambridge: Cambridge University Press).

Elster, J. (1983b) *Explaining Technical Change* (Cambridge: Cambridge University Press).

Elster, J. (1985) *Making Sense of Marx* (Cambridge: Cambridge University Press).

Elster, J. (ed.) (1986) *Rational Choice* (Oxford: Basil Blackwell).

Ely, R. T. (1914) *Property and Contract in Their Relation to the Distribution of Wealth* (New York: Macmillan).

Emery, F. E. (ed.) (1981) *Systems Thinking*, vols 1 and 2 (Harmondsworth: Penguin).

Emmet, D. and MacIntyre, A. (eds) (1970) *Sociological Theory and Philosophical Analysis* (London: Macmillan).

Espejo, R. and Howard, N. (1982) 'What is Requisite Variety? A Re-Examination of the Foundation of Beer's Method', *University of Aston Management Centre Working Paper no. 242*, September.

Espinosa, J. G. and Zimbalist, A. S. (1981) *Economic Democracy: Workers' Participation in Chilean Industry, 1970–1973*, updated student edn (New York: Academic Press).

Estrin, S. and Holmes, P. (1983) *French Planning in Theory and Practice* (Londen: Allen and Unwin).

Evans, P. B., Rueschemeyer, D. and Skocpol, T. (eds) (1985) *Bringing the State Back In* (Cambridge: Cambridge University Press).

Fabian, R. G. (1967) 'An Empirical Principle for Deductive Theory in Economics', *Southern Economic Journal*, 34(1), pp. 53–66.

Fama, E. F. (1980) 'Agency Problems and the Theory of the Firm' *Journal of Political Economy*, 88, pp. 288–307. Reprinted in Putterman (1986).

Farmer, M. K. (1982) 'Rational Action in Economics and Social Theory: Some Misunderstandings', *Archives européennes de sociologie*, 23, pp. 178–96.

Fazzari, S. M. (1985) 'Keynes, Harrod, and the Rational Expectations Revolution', *Journal of Post Keynesian Economics* 8(1), pp. 66–80.

Feibelman, J. K. (1972) *Scientific Method* (The Hague: Martinus Nijhoff).

Feigenbaum, E. A. and Feldman, J. (eds) (1963) *Computers and Thought* (New York: McGraw-Hill).

Feiwel, G. R. (1975) *The Intellectual Capital of Michal Kalecki* (Knoxville: University of Tennessee Press).

Feldman, J. (1963) 'Simulation of Behavior in the Binary Choice Experiment', in Feigenbaum and Feldman (1963, pp. 329–46).

Ferber, R. (1955) 'Factors Influencing Durable Goods Purchases', in Clark (1955, pp. 75–112).

Festinger, L. (1957) *A Theory of Cognitive Dissonance* (Stanford, CA: Stanford University Press).

Feyerabend, P. K. (1975) *Against Method: Outline of an Anarchistic Theory of Knowledge* (London: NLB).

Fischer, S. (1977) 'Long-Term Contracting, Sticky Prices, and Monetary Policy: A Comment', *Journal of Monetary Economics*, 3, pp. 317–23.

Fishburn, P. S. (1974) 'Lexicographic Orders, Utilities and Decision Rules: A Survey', *Management Science*, 20, pp. 1442–71.

FitzRoy, F. R. and Kraft, K. (1986) 'Profitability and Profit Sharing', *Journal of Industrial Economics*, 35(2), pp. 113–30.

Flanagan, R. J. (1984) 'Implicit Contracts, Explicit Contracts, and Wages', *American Economic Review (Papers and Proceedings)*, 74(2), pp. 345–9.

Flemming, J. S. (1981) 'The Role of Expectations in Fiscal and Monetary Policy', in Artis and Miller (1981, pp. 88–94).

Forbes, I. (ed.) (1986) *Market Socialism: Whose Choice?*, Fabian Tract 516 (London: Fabian Society).

Foucault, M. (1977) *Discipline and Punish* (London: Allen Lane).

Fox, A. (1974) *Beyond Contract: Work, Power and Trust Relations* (London: Faber and Faber).

Francis, A., Turk, J. and Willman, P. (eds) (1983) *Power, Efficiency and Institutions; A Critical Appraisal of the 'Markets and Hierarchies' Paradigm* (London: Heinemann).

Frankel, S. H. (1977) *Money: Two Philosophies; The Conflict of Trust and Authority* (Oxford: Basil Blackwell).

Frantz, R. S. (1980) 'On the Existence of X-efficiency', *Journal of Post Keynesian Economics*, 2(4), pp. 509–27.

Freeman, C. (1974) *The Economics of Industrial Innovation* (Harmondsworth: Penguin).

Freeman, R. B. and Medoff, J. L. (1979) 'The Two Faces of Unionism', *The Public Interest*, 57, pp. 69–93.

Freud, S. (1922) *Introductory Lectures on Psycho-Analysis*, translated by J. Riviere with a Preface by E. Jones (London: George Allen and Unwin).

Frey, B. S. (1986) 'Economists Favour the Price System – Who Else Does?', *Kyklos*, 39, pp. 537–63.

Friedman, B. (1979) 'Optimal Expectations and the Extreme Information Assumptions of "Rational Expectations" Macromodels', *Journal of Monetary Economics*, 5, pp. 23–41.

Friedman, M. (1953) 'The Methodology of Positive Economics', in *Essays in Positive Economics* (Chicago: University of Chicago Press), pp. 3–43.

Friedman, M. (1962) *Capitalism and Freedom* (Chicago: University of Chicago Press).

Friedman, M. (1967) 'The Role of Monetary Policy', *American Economic Review*, 58(1), pp. 1–17.

Friedman, M. (1977) 'Nobel Lecture: Inflation and Unemployment', *Journal of Political Economy*, 85(2), pp. 451–72.

Fritz, R. G. and Fritz, J. M. (1985) 'Linguistic Structure and Economic Method', *Journal of Economic Issues*, 19(1), pp. 75–101.

Fuchs, V. R. (ed.) (1972) *Policy Issues and Research Opportunities in Industrial Organization* (New York: National Bureau for Economic Research).

Furnham, A. and Lewis, A. (1986) *The Economic Mind: The Social Psychology of Economic Behaviour* (Brighton: Wheatsheaf).

Furubotn, E. G. and Pejovich, S. (eds) (1974) *The Economics of Property Rights* (Cambridge, MA: Ballinger).

Fusfeld, D. R. (1980) 'The Conceptual Framework of Modern Economics', *Journal of Economic Issues*, 14(1), pp. 1–52.

Galanter, M. (1981) 'Justice in Many Rooms: Courts, Private Ordering, and Indigenous Law', *Journal of Legal Pluralism*, 19, pp. 1–47.

Galbraith, J. K. (1958) *The Affluent Society* (London: Hamish Hamilton).

Galbraith, J. K. (1969) *The New Industrial State* (Harmondsworth: Penguin).

Garfinkel, H. (1967) *Studies in Ethnomethodology* (Englewood Cliffs, NJ: Prentice-Hall).

Garner, C. A. (1982) 'Uncertainty, Human Judgement, and Economic Decisions', *Journal of Post Keynesian Economics*, 4(3), pp. 413–24.

Garner, C. A. (1983) '"Uncertainty" in Keynes' *General Theory:* A Comment', *History of Political Economy*, 125(1), pp. 83–6.

Georgescu-Roegen, N. (1954) 'Choice, Expectations and Measurability', *Quarterly Journal of Economics*, 68(4), pp. 503–34.

Georgescu-Roegen, N. (1971) *The Entropy Law and the Economic Process* (Cambridge, MA: Harvard University Press).

Georgescu-Roegen, N. (1978) 'Mechanistic Dogma in Economics', *British Review of Economic Issues*, no 2, pp. 1–10.

Georgescu-Roegen, N. (1979) 'Methods in Economic Science', *Journal of Economic Issues*, 13(2), pp. 317–28.

Geras, N. (1983) *Marx and Human Nature* (London: Verso).

Geschwind, N. (1980) 'Neurological Knowledge and Complex Behaviors', *Cognitive Science*, 4, pp. 185–94.

Gettys, C. F., Kelly, C. and Peterson, C. R. (1973) 'The Best Guess Hypothesis in Multistage Inference', *Organizational Behavior and Human Performance*, 10, pp. 364–73. Reprinted in Kahneman et al. (1982).

Gibson, J. (1979) *The Ecological Approach to Visual Perception* (Boston, MA: Houghton Mifflin).

Giddens, A. (1976) *New Rules of Sociological Method* (London: Hutchinson).

Giddens, A. (1982a) *A Contemporary Critique of Historical Materialism* (London: Macmillan).

Giddens, A. (1982b) *Profiles and Critiques in Social Theory* (London: Macmillan).

Giddens, A. (1984) *The Constitution of Society: Outline of the Theory of Structuration* (Cambridge: Polity Press).

Gilmore, G. (1974) *The Death of Contract* (Columbus, OH: Ohio State University Press).

Gintis, H. (1972) 'A Radical Analysis of Welfare Economics and Individual Development', *Quarterly Journal of Economics*, 86, pp. 572–99.

Gintis, H. (1974) 'Welfare Criteria With Endogenous Preferences: The Economics of Education' *International Economic Review*, 15(2), pp. 415–30.

Gintis, H. (1976) 'The Nature of Labor Exchange and the Theory of Capitalist Production', *Review of Radical Political Economics*, 8, pp. 36–54.

Glucksberg, S. and McCloskey, M. (1981) 'Decisions About Ignorance: Knowing That You Don't Know', *Journal of Experimental Psychology: Human Learning and Memory*, 7, pp. 311–25.

Goldberg, V. P. (1976) 'Toward an Expanded Theory of Contract', *Journal of Economic Issues*, 10(1), pp. 45–61.

Goldberg, V. P. (1980) 'Relational Exchange: Economics and Complex Contracts', *American Behavioral Scientist*, 23(3), pp. 337–52. Reprinted in Putterman (1986).

Goldberg, V. P. (1984) 'A Relational Exchange Perspective on the Employment Relationship', in Stephen (1984, pp. 127–44).

Gomes, G. M. (1982) 'Irrationality of "Rational Expectations"', *Journal of Post Keynesian Economics*, 5(1), pp. 51–65.

Gordon, W. C. (1980) *Institutional Economics: The Changing System* (Austin: University of Texas Press).

Gorman, W. M. (1967) 'Tastes, Habits and Choices', *International Economic Review*, 8, pp. 218–22.

Gough, I. (1975) 'State Expenditure in Advanced Capitalism', *New Left Review*, no. 92, pp. 53–92.

Gough, I. (1979) *The Political Economy of the Welfare State* (London: Macmillan).

Gowdy, J. M. (1985–6) 'Rational Expectations and Predictability', *Journal of Post Keynesian Economics*, 8(2), pp. 192–200.

Graaff, J. de V. (1957) *Theoretical Welfare Economics* (Cambridge: Cambridge University Press).

Grahl, J. (1986) *Productivity Slowdown and Financial Tensions* (London: Thames Papers in Political Economy).

Grandy, R. (ed.) (1973) *Theories and Observation in Science* (Englewood Cliffs, NJ: Prentice-Hall).

Granovetter, M. (1985) 'Economic Action and Social Structure: The Problem of Embeddedness', *American Journal of Sociology*, 91(3), pp. 481–510.

Green, F. (1977) *Empiricist Methodology and the Development of Economic Thought* (London: Thames Papers in Political Economy).

Green, F. (1979) 'The Consumption Function: A Study of a Failure in Positive Economics' in Green and Nore (1979, pp. 33–60).

Green, F. (1984) 'A Critique of the Neo-Fisherian Consumption Function', *Review of Radical Political Economics*, 16(2/3), pp. 95–114.

Green, F. and Nore, P. (eds) (1977) *Economics: An Anti-Text* (London: Macmillan).

Green, F. and Nore, P. (eds) (1979) *Issues in Political Economy: A Critical Approach* (London: Macmillan).

Green, H. A. J. (1971) *Consumer Theory* (Harmondsworth: Penguin).

Greenlee, D. (1973) *Peirce's Concept of Sign* (The Hague: Mouton).

Grether, D. M. and Plott, C. R. (1979) 'Economic Theory of Choice and the

Preference Reversal Effect', *American Economic Review*, 69 p. 623–38.

Groot, A. D. de (1978) *Thought and Choice in Chess* (The Hague: Mouton).

Grossman, S. J. (1977) 'The Existence of Futures Markets, Noisy Rational Expectations and Informational Externalities', *Review of Economic Studies*, 64, pp. 431–49.

Grossman, S. J. and Stiglitz, J. E. (1976) 'Information and Competitive Price Systems', *American Economic Review*, 66(2), pp. 246–53.

Grossman, S. J. and Stiglitz, J. E. (1980) 'The Impossibility of Informationally Efficient Markets', *American Economic Review*, 70(2), pp. 393–408.

Gruchy, A. G. (1972) *Contemporary Economic Thought: The Contributions of Neo-Institutionalist Economics* (Clifton, NJ: Augustus Kelley).

Gruchy, A. G. (1984) 'Uncertainty, Indicative Planning, and Industrial Policy', *Journal of Economic Issues*, 18(1), pp. 159–80

Habermas, J. (1976) *Legitimation Crisis* (London: Heinemann).

Hagstrom, W. O. (1965) *The Scientific Community* (New York: Basic Books).

Hahn, F. H. (1981) 'General Equilibrium Theory', in Bell and Kristol (1981, pp. 123–38).

Hahn, F. H. (1982) *Money and Inflation* (Oxford: Basil Blackwell).

Hahn, F. H. and Hollis, M. (eds) (1979) *Philosophy and Economic Theory* (Oxford: Oxford University Press).

Hall, R. L. and Hitch, C. J. (1939) 'Price Theory and Business Behaviour', *Oxford Economic Papers*, 2, pp. 12–45. Reprinted in Wilson and Andrews (1951).

Haltiwanger, J. and Waldman, M. (1985) 'Rational Expectations and the Limits of Rationality: An Analysis of Heterogeneity', *American Economic Review*, 75(3), pp. 326–40.

Hammond, P. J. (1976a) 'Changing Tastes and Coherent Dynamic Choices', *Review of Economic Studies*, 43, pp. 159–73.

Hammond, P. J. (1976b) 'Endogenous Tastes and Stable Long-Run Choice', *Journal of Economic Theory*, 17, pp. 159–73.

Handa, J. (1982) 'Rational Expectations: What Do They Mean? – Another View', *Journal of Post Keynesian Economics*, 4(4), pp. 558–64.

Hanson, N. R. (1958) *Patterns of Discovery* (Cambridge: Cambridge University Press).

Harcourt, G. C. (1972) *Some Cambridge Controversies in the Theory of Capital* (Cambridge: Cambridge University Press).

Harcourt, G. C. (ed.) (1977) *The Microeconomic Foundations of Macroeconomics* (Boulder, Co: Westview Press).

Harcourt, G. C. (1985) 'On the Influence of Piero Sraffa on the Contributions of Joan Robinson to Economic Theory', *Economic Journal (Conference Papers)*, 96, pp. 96–108.

Hare, P. (1985) *Planning the British Economy* (Basingstoke: Macmillan).

Hargreaves Heap, S. P. (1986–7) 'Risk and Culture: A Missing Link in the Post Keynesian Tradition', *Journal of Post Keynesian Economics*, 9(2), pp. 267–78.

Harris, M. (1979) *Cultural Materialism: The Struggle for a Science of Culture* (New York: Random House).

Harrison, R. (ed.) (1979) *Rational Action* (Cambridge: Cambridge University Press).

Harsanyi, J. C. (1968) 'Individualistic and Functionalistic Explanations in the Light of Game Theory: The Example of Social Status', in Lakatos and Musgrave (1968, pp. 305–22).

Havighurst, H. C. (1961) *The Nature of Private Contract* (Evanston, IL. Northwestern University Press).

Hayek, F. A. (ed.) (1935) *Collectivist Economic Planning* (London: Routledge and Kegan Paul).

Hayek, F. A. (1937) 'Economics and Knowledge', *Economica*, 4, pp. 33–54. Reprinted in Hayek (1948).

Hayek, F. A. (1945) 'The Use of Knowledge in Society', *American Economic Review*, 35(4), pp. 519–30. Reprinted in Hayek (1948) and Putterman (1986).

Hayek, F. A. (1948) *Individualism and Economic Order* (Chicago: University of Chicago Press).

Hayek, F. A. (1952a) *The Counter-Revolution of Science* (Glencoe IL: Free Press).

Hayek, F. A. (1952b) *The Sensory Order: An Inquiry into the Foundations of Theoretical Psychology* (London: Routledge and Kegan Paul).

Hayek, F. A. (1967) *Studies in Philosophy, Politics and Economics* (London: Routledge and Kegan Paul).

Hayek, F. A. (1972) *A Tiger by the Tail: The Keynesian Legacy of Inflation* (London: Institute of Economic Affairs).

Hayek, F. A. (1978a) *New Studies in Philosophy, Politics, Economics and the History of Ideas* (London: Routledge and Kegan Paul).

Hayek, F. A. (1978b) *Denationalisation of Money – The Argument Refined*, 2nd edn (1st edn 1976) (London: Institute of Economic Affairs).

Hayek, F. A. (1982) *Law, Legislation and Liberty*, 3-volume combined edn (London: Routledge and Kegan Paul).

Heathfield, D. (1977) *The Economics of Co-Determination* (London: Macmillan).

Hegel, G. W. F. (1969) *Hegel's Science of Logic*, translated by A. V. Miller from the German edition of 1831 (London: George Allen and Unwin).

Heiner, R. A. (1983) 'The Origin of Predictable Behavior', *American Economic Review*, 73(4), pp. 560–95.

Heiner, R. A. (1985) 'Origin of Predictable Behavior: Further Modelling and Applications', *American Economic Review*, 75, pp. 391–6.

Heiner, R. A. (1985–6) 'Rational Expectations When Agents Imperfectly Use Information', *Journal of Post Keynesian Economics*, 8(2), pp. 201–7.

Heiner, R. A. (1986) 'Uncertainty, Signal-Detection Experiments, and Modeling Behavior', in Langlois (1986b, pp. 59–115).

Hey, J. D. (1979) *Uncertainty in Microeconomics* (Oxford: Martin Robertson).

Hicks, J. R. (1969) 'Automatists, Hawtreyans and Keynesians', *Journal of Money, Credit and Banking*, 1, pp. 307–17.

Hicks, J. R. (1979) *Causality in Economics* (Oxford: Basil Blackwell).

Hicks, J. R. and Weber, W. (eds) (1973) *Carl Menger and the Austrian School of Economics* (Oxford: Oxford University Press).

Hill, C. W. L. (1985) 'Oliver Williamson and the M-Form Firm: A Critical Review', *Journal of Economic Issues*, 19(3), pp. 731–51.

Hindess, B. (1977a) 'Humanism and Teleology in Sociological Theory', in Hindess (1977b, pp. 157–89).

Hindess, B. (ed.) (1977b) *Sociological Theories of the Economy* (London: Macmillan).

Hindess, B. (1977c) *Philosophy and Methodology in the Social Sciences* (Brighton: Harvester).

Hindess, B. (1984) 'Rational Choice Theory and the Analysis of Political Action', *Economy and Society*, 13(3), pp. 255–77.

Hirsch, F. (1977) *The Social Limits to Growth* (London: Routledge and Kegan Paul).

Hirsch, F. And Goldthorpe, J. H. (eds) (1978) *The Political Economy of Inflation* (Oxford: Martin Robertson).

Hirschman, A. O. (1970) *Exit, Voice and Loyalty: Responses to Decline in Firms, Organisations and States* (Cambridge MA: Harvard University Press).

Hirschman, A. O. (1977) *The Passions and the Interests* (Princeton, NJ: Princeton University Press).

Hirschman, A. O. (1982) 'Rival Interpretations of Market Society: Civilizing, Destructive or Feeble?', *Journal of Economic Literature*, 20, pp. 1463–84.

Hirshleifer, J. (1970) *Investment, Interest and Capital* (Englewood Cliffs, NJ: Prentice-Hall).

Hirshleifer, J. and Riley, J. G. (1979) 'The Analytics of Uncertainty and Information – An Expository Survey', *Journal of Economic Literature*, 17, pp. 1375–421.

Hirst, P. Q. and Woolley, P. (1982) *Social Relations and Human Attributes* (London: Tavistock).

Hobbes, T. (1929) *Leviathan* (Oxford: Oxford University Press).

Hodgson, G. M. (1982a) 'Marx Without the Labor Theory of Value', *Review of Radical Political Economics*, 14(2), pp. 59–65.

Hodgson, G. M. (1982b) 'Theoretical and Policy Implications of Variable Productivity', *Cambridge Journal of Economics*, 6(3), pp. 213–26.

Hodgson, G. M. (1982c) *Capitalism, Value and Exploitation* (Oxford: Martin Robertson).

Hodgson, G. M. (1982–3) 'Worker Participation and Macroeconomic Efficiency', *Journal of Post Keynesian Economics*, 5(2), pp. 266–75.

Hodgson, G. M. (1984) *The Democratic Economy* (Harmondsworth, Pelican).

Hodgson, G. M. (1985a) 'Persuasion, Expectations and the Limits to Keynes', in Lawson and Pesaran (1985), pp. 10–45).

Hodgson, G. M. (1985b) 'The Rationalist Conception of Action', *Journal of Economic Issues*, 19(4), pp. 825–51.

Hodgson, G. M. (1986) 'Behind Methodological Individualism', *Cambridge Journal of Economics*, 10(3), pp. 211–24.

Hogarth, R. M. (1975) 'Cognitive Processes and the Assessment of Subjective Probability Distributions', *Journal of the American Statistical Association*, 70, pp. 271–89.

Hollis, M. (1977) *Models of Man* (Cambridge: Cambridge University Press).

Hollis, M. (1981) 'Economic Man and Original Sin', *Political Studies*, 29(2), pp. 167–80.

Hollis, M. and Lukes, S. (eds) (1982) *Rationality and Relativism* (Oxford: Basil Blackwell).

Hollis, M. and Nell, E. (1975) *Rational Economic Man: A Philosophical Critique of Neo-Classical Economics* (London: Cambridge University Press).

Holton, G. (1969) 'Einstein, Michelson and the "Crucial Experiment"', *Iris*, 60, pp. 133–97.

Homans, G. C. (1961) *Social Behaviour: Its Elementary Form* (London: Routledge and Kegan Paul).

Homans, G. C. (1962) *Sentiments and Activities* (New York: Free Press).

Horvat, B. (1980) 'Searching for a Strategy of Transition', *Economic Analysis and Workers' Management*, 14(3), pp. 311–23.

Horvat, B. (1982) *The Political Economy of Socialism: A Marxist Social Theory* (Oxford: Martin Robertson).

Houthakker, H. S. and Taylor, L. D. (1966) *Consumer Demand in the United States, 1929–1970: Analysis and Projections* (Cambridge MA: Harvard University Press).

Howell, W. C. and Burnett, S. A. (1978) 'Uncertainty Measurement: A Cognitive Taxonomy', *Organizational Behavior and Human Performance*, 22, pp. 45–68.

Hughes, A. (1986) 'Investment Finance, Industrial Strategy and Economic Recovery', in Nolan and Paine (1986, pp. 198–233).

Humphries, J. (1977) 'Class Struggle and the Persistence of the Working Class Family', *Cambridge Journal of Economics*, 1(3), pp. 241–58. Reprinted in Amsden (1980).

Hunt, E. K. and Schwartz, J. G. (eds) (1972) *A Critique of Economic Theory* (Harmondsworth: Penguin).

Hutchison, T. W. (1939) *The Significance and Basic Postulates of Economic Theory* (London: Macmillan).

Hutchison, T. W. (1981) *The Politics and Philosophy of Economics: Marxists, Keynesians and Austrians* (Oxford: Basil Blackwell).

Jaffé, W. (1976) 'Menger, Jevons and Walras De-homogenized', *Economic Inquiry*, 14, pp. 11–24.

Jarvie, I. C. (1972) *Concepts and Society* (London: Routledge and Kegan Paul).

Jensen, M. C. and Meckling, W. H. (1976) 'Theory of the Firm: Managerial Behaviour, Agency Costs and Ownership Structure', *Journal of Financial Economics*, 3, pp. 305–60. Reprinted in Putterman (1986).

Jensen, M. C. and Meckling, W. H. (1979) 'Rights and Production Functions: An Application to Labor-Managed Firms and Codetermination', *Journal of Business*, 52(4), pp. 469–506.

Jevons, W. S. (1871) *The Theory of Political Economy* (London: Macmillan).

Jones, D. C. and Svejnar, J. (eds) (1982) *Participatory and Self-Managed Firms* (Lexington, MA: Heath).

Jones, L. B. (1986) 'The Institutionalists and "On the Origin of Species": A Case of Mistaken Identity', *Southern Economic Journal*, 52(4), pp. 1043–55.

Jones, S. R. G. (1984) *The Economics of Conformism* (Oxford: Basil Blackwell).

Jussawalla, M and Ebenfield, H. (eds) (1984) *Communication and Information Economics: New Perspectives* (Amsterdam: North-Holland).

Kaen, F. R. and Rosenman, R. E. (1986) 'Predictable Behavior in Financial Markets: Some Evidence in Support of Heiner's Hypothesis', *American Economic Review*, 76(1), pp. 212–20.

Kagel, J. H., Battalio, R. C., Rachlin, H. and Green, L. (1981) 'Demand Curves for Animal Consumers', *Quarterly Journal of Economics*, 96, pp. 1–16.

Kahneman, D., Knetsch, J. and Thaler, R. (1986) 'Fairness as a Constraint on Profit Seeking: Entitlements in the Market', *American Economic Review*, 76(4), pp. 728–41.

Kahneman, D., Slovic, P. and Tversky, A. (eds) (1982) *Judgement Under Uncertainty: Heuristics and Biases* (Cambridge: Cambridge University Press).

Kahneman, D. and Tversky, A. (1973) 'On the Psychology of Prediction', *Psychological Review*, 80, pp. 237–51. Reprinted in Kahneman et al. (1982).

Kahneman, D. And Tversky, A. (1979) 'Prospect Theory: An Analysis of Decision Under Risk', *Econometrica*, 47, pp. 263–91.

Kahneman, D. and Tversky, A. (1984) 'Choices, Values and Frames', *American Psychologist*, 39, pp. 341–50.

Kalecki, M. (1943) *Studies in Economic Dynamics* (London: George Allen and Unwin).

Kamenka, E. and Neale, R. S. (eds) (1975) *Feudalism, Capitalism and Beyond* (London: Edward Arnold).

Kanel, D. (1985) 'Institutional Economics: Perspectives On Economy and Society', *Journal of Economic Issues*, 19(3), pp. 815–28.

Kant, I. (1929) *Critique of Pure Reason*, translated from the second German edition of 1787 by N. K. Smith (London: Macmillan).

Kapteyn, A., Wansbeck, T. and Buyze, J. (1979) 'Maximizing or Satisficing?'. *Review of Economics and Statistics*, 61, pp. 79–91.

Katona, G. (1951) *Psychological Analysis of Economic Behaviour* (New York: McGraw-Hill).

Katona, G. (1964) *The Mass Consumption Society* (New York: McGraw-Hill).

Katona, G. (1975; *Psychological Economics* (New York: Elsevier).

Katona, G. and Mueller, E. (1954) 'A Study of Purchase Decisions' in Clark (1954).

Katouzian, H. (1980) *Ideology and Method in Economics* (London: Macmillan).

Kay, N. M. (1979) *The Innovating Firm: A Behavioural Theory of Corporate R&D* (London: Macmillan).

Kay, N. M. (1982) *The Evolving Firm: Strategy and Structure in Industrial Organisation* (London: Macmillan).

Kay, N. M. (1984) *The Emergent Firm: Knowledge, Ignorance and Surprise in Economic Organisation* (London: Macmillan).

Keegan, J. (1976) *The Face of Battle: A Study of Agincourt, Waterloo and the Somme* (London: Jonathan Cape).

Keynes, J. M. (1971a) *The Collected Writings of John Maynard Keynes*, vol. II, 'The Economic Consequences of the Peace', first published 1919 (London: Macmillan).

Keynes, J. M. (1971b) *The Collected Writings of John Maynard Keynes*, vol. VII, 'The General Theory of Employment, Interest and Money', first published 1936 (London: Macmillan).

Keynes, J. M. (1972a) *The Collected Writings of John Maynard Keynes*, vol. IX, 'Essays in Persuasion', first published 1931 (London: Macmillan).

Keynes, J. M. (1972b) *The Collected Writings of John Maynard Keynes*, vol. X, 'Essays in Biography', first published 1933 (London: Macmillan).

Keynes, J. M. (1973a) *The Collected Writings of John Maynard Keynes*, vol. VIII, 'A Treatise on Probability', first published 1921 (London: Macmillan).

Keynes, J. M. (1973b) *The Collected Writings of John Maynard Keynes*, vol. XIV, 'The General Theory and After: Defence and Development' (London: Macmillan).

Keynes, J. N. (1891) *The Scope and Method of Political Economy* (London: Macmillan).

Kilpatrick, A. and Lawson, A. (1980) 'On the Nature of the Industrial Decline in the UK', *Cambridge Journal of Economics*, 4(1), pp. 85–102.

Kindleberger, C. P. (1978) *Manias, Panics and Crashes: A History of Financial Crises* (New York: Basic Books).

Kindleberger, C. P. and Laffargue, J. P. (eds) (1982) *Financial Crises: Theory, History, Policy* (Cambridge: Cambridge University Press).

King, J. E. (1982) 'Value and Exploitation: Some Recent Debates', in Bradley and Howard (1982, pp. 157–87).

Kirzner, I. M. (1976a) *The Economic Point of View*, 2nd edn (Kansas City: Sheed and Ward).

Kirzner, I. M. (1976b) 'On the Method of Austrian Economics', in Dolan (1976, pp. 40–51).

Kirzner, I. M. (1981) 'The "Austrian" Perspective on the Crisis', in Bell and Kristol (1981, pp. 111–22).

Kirzner, I. M. (ed.) (1982) *Method, Process and Austrian Economics* (Lexington, MA: Heath).

Kirzner, I. M. (ed.) (1986) *Subjectivism, Intelligibility and Economic Understanding* (New York: New York University Press).

Klamer, A. (ed.) (1983) *The New Classical Macroeconomics: Conversations with New Classical Economists and Their Opponents* (Brighton: Wheatsheaf).

Klant, J. J. (1984) *The Rules of the Game: The Logical Structure of Economic Theories* (Cambridge: Cambridge University Press).

Klein, B. H. (1977) *Dynamic Economics* (Cambridge, MA: Harvard University Press).

Kleinmuntz, B. (ed.) (1968) *Formal Representation of Human Judgement* (New York: Wiley).

Knetsch, J. and Sinden, J. A. (1984) 'Willingness to Pay and Compensation Demanded: Experimental Evidence of an Unexpected Disparity in Measures of Value', *Quarterly Journal of Economics*, 99(3), pp. 507–21

Knight, F. H. (1924) 'The Limitations of Scientific Method in Economics', in Tugwell (1924, pp. 229–67).

Knight, F. H. (1933) *Risk, Uncertainty and Profit*, 2nd edn (London: London School of Economics).

Knight, F. H. (1935) *The Ethics of Competition and Other Essays* (London: Allen and Unwin).

Knight, F. H. (1947) *Freedom and Reform: Essays in Economic and Social Philosophy* (New York: Harper). Reprinted 1982 with a Foreword by J. M. Buchanan (Liberty Press: Indianapolis).

Knight, F. H. and Merriam, T. W. (1948) *The Economic Order and Religion* (London: Kegan Paul, Trench Trubner).

Koestler, A. (1959) *The Sleepwalkers: A History of Man's Changing Vision of the Universe* (London: Hutchinson).

Koestler, A. (1967) *The Ghost in the Machine* (London: Hutchinson).

Koestler, A. and Smythies, J. R. (eds) (1969) *Beyond Reductionism: New Perspectives in the Life Sciences* (London: Hutchinson).

Koo, A. Y. C. (1963) 'An Empirical Test of Revealed Preference Theory', *Econometrica*, 31(4), pp. 646–64.

Koo, A. Y. C. and Hasenkamp, G. (1972) 'Structure of Revealed Preference: Some Preliminary Evidence', *Journal of Political Economy*, 80(4), pp. 724–44.

Koopmans, T. C. (1957) *Three Essays on the State of Economic Science* (New York: McGraw-Hill).

Kornai, J. (1971) *Anti-Equilibrium: On Economic Systems Theory and the Tasks of Research* (Amsterdam: North-Holland).

Kornai, J. (1972) 'Mathematical Programming as a Tool of Socialist Economic Planning' in Nove and Nuti (1972, pp. 475–88).

Kornai, J. (1982) *Growth, Shortage and Efficiency* (Oxford: Basil Blackwell).

Kregel, J. A. (1976) 'Economic Methodology in the Face of Uncertainty', *Economic Journal*, 86, pp. 209–25.

Kregel, J. A. (1980) 'Markets and Institutions as Features of a Capitalistic Production System', *Journal of Post Keynesian Economics*, 3(1), pp. 32–48.

Krelle, W. (1973) 'Dynamics of the Utility Function' in Hicks and Weber (1973, pp. 92–128).

Kreps, D. M., Milgrom, P., Roberts, J. and Wilson, R. (1982) 'Rational Cooperation in the Finitely Repeated Prisoner's Dilemma', *Journal of Economic Theory*, 27, pp. 245–52.

Krimerman, L. I. (ed.) (1969) *The Nature and Scope of Social Science: A Critical Anthology* (New York: Meredith).

Kuhn, T. (1962) *The Structure of Scientific Revolutions* (Chicago: Chicago University Press).

Kunreuther, H. et al. (1978) *Disaster Insurance Protection: Public Policy Lessons* (New York: Wiley).

Kuznets, S. (1959) *Six Lectures on Economic Growth* (Glencoe, IL: Free Press).

Kuznets, S. (1979) *Growth, Population and Income Distribution* (New York: Norton).

Laband, D. N. (1986) 'Article Popularity', *Economy Inquiry*, 24, pp. 173–80.

Lachmann, L. M. (1969) 'Methodological Individualism and the Market Economy', in Streissler (1969, pp. 89–103). Reprinted in Lachmann (1977).

Lachmann, L. M. (1977) *Capital, Expectations, and the Market Process*, edited with an introduction by W. E. Grinder (Kansas City: Sheed Andrews and McMeel).

Lakatos, I. (1970) 'Falsification and the Methodology of Scientific Research Programmes', in Lakatos and Musgrave (1970, pp. 91–195).

Lakatos, I. and Musgrave, A. (eds) (1968) *Problems in the Philosophy of Science* (Amsterdam: North Holland).

Lakatos, I. and Musgrave, A. (eds) (1970) *Criticism and the Growth of Knowledge* (Cambridge, Cambridge University Press).

Lamberton, D. M. (ed.) (1971) *Economics of Information and Knowledge* (Harmondsworth: Penguin).

Lange, O. (1945) 'The Scope and Method of Economics', *Review of Economic Studies*, 13, pp. 19–32.

Lange, O. (1965) *Wholes and Parts: A General Theory of Systems Behaviour* (London: Pergamon Press).

Lange, O. and Taylor, F. M. (1938) *On the Economic Theory of Socialism* (New York: McGraw-Hill).

Langlois, R. N. (1983a) 'Systems Theory, Knowledge, and the Social Sciences', in Machlup and Mansfield (1983, pp. 581–600).

Langlois, R. N. (1983b) 'On the Reception of Noise: A Rejoinder' in Machlup and Mansfield (1983, pp. 631–7).

Langlois, R. N. (1984) 'Internal Organization in a Dynamic Context: Some Theoretical Considerations', in Jussawalla and Ebenfield (1984, pp. 23–49).

Langlois, R. N. (1985) 'Knowledge and Rationality in the Austrian School: An Analytical Survey', *Eastern Economic Journal*, 9(4), pp. 309–30.

Langlois, R. N. (1986a) 'Rationality, Institutions and Explanation', in Langlois (1986b, pp. 225–55).

Langlois, R. N. (ed.) (1986b) *Economics as a Process: Essays in the New Institutional Economics* (Cambridge: Cambridge University Press).

Langlois, R. N. (1986c) 'Coherence and Flexibility: Social Institutions in a World of Radical Uncertainty', in Kirzner (1986, pp. 171–91).

Latsis, S. J. (1972) 'Situational Determinism in Economics', *British Journal for the Philosophy of Science*, 23, pp. 207–45.

Latsis, S. J. (1976a) 'A Research Programme in Economics', in Latsis (1976b, pp. 1–41).

Latsis, S. J. (ed.) (1976b) *Method and Appraisal in Economics* (Cambridge: Cambridge University Press).

Laudan, L. (1977) *Progress and its Problems: Towards a Theory of Scientific Growth* (London: Routledge and Kegan Paul).

Lavoie, D. (1985a) *National Economic Planning: What is Left?* (Washington, DC: Cato).

Lavoie, D. (1985b) *Rivalry and Central Planning: The Socialist Calculation Debate Reconsidered* (Cambridge: Cambridge University Press).

Lawson, A. (1981) 'Keynesian Model Building and the Rational Expectations Critique', *Cambridge Journal of Economics*, 5(4), pp. 311–26.

Lawson, A. (1985) 'Uncertainty and Economic Analysis', *Economic Journal*, 95, pp. 909–27.

Lawson, A. and Pesaran, M. H. (eds) (1985) *Keynes' Economics: Methodological Issues* (London: Croom Helm).

Lazonick, W. (1981) 'Factor Costs and the Diffusion of Ring Spinning in Britain

Prior to World War I', *Quarterly Journal of Economics*, 95, pp. 89–109.

Lee, F. S. (1984a) 'Full Cost Pricing: A New Wine in a New Bottle', *Australian Economic Papers*, 24, pp. 151–66.

Lee, F. S. (1984b) 'The Marginalist Controversy and the Demise of Full Cost Pricing', *Journal of Economic Issues*, 18(4), pp. 1107–32.

Leibenstein, H. (1976) *Beyond Economic Man: A New Foundation for Microeconomics* (Cambridge, MA: Harvard University Press).

Leibenstein, H. (1979) 'A Branch of Economics is Missing: Micro-Micro Theory', *Journal of Economic Literature*, 17, pp. 477–502. Reprinted in Caldwell (1984b).

Leibenstein, H. (1982) 'The Prisoners' Dilemma and the Invisible Hand: An Analysis of Intrafirm Productivity', *American Economic Review (Papers and Proceedings)*, 72, pp. 92–7. Reprinted in Putterman (1986).

Leibenstein, H. (1983) 'Property Rights and X-Efficiency: Comment' *American Economic Review*, 73(4), pp. 831–42.

Leijonhufvud, A. (1968) *On Keynesian Economics and the Economics of Keynes: A Study in Monetary Theory* (London: Oxford University Press).

Leijonhufvud, A. (1977) 'Costs and Consequences of Inflation', in Harcourt (1977, pp. 265–312).

Leijonhufvud, A. (1986) 'Capitalism and the Factory System', in Langlois (1986, pp. 202–23).

Lekachman, R. (1964) *Keynes' General Theory: Reports of Three Decades* (London: Macmillan).

Lerner, M. (ed.) (1948) *The Portable Veblen* (New York: Viking Press).

Lewis, D. (1969) *Convention: A Philosophical Study* (Cambridge: Harvard University Press).

Lichtenstein, S. and Slovic, P. (1971) 'Reversals of Preference Between Bids and Choices in Gambling Decisions', *Journal of Experimental Psychology*, 89, pp. 46–55.

Lichtenstein, S. and Slovic, P. (1973) 'Response-Induced Reversals of Preference in Gambling: An Extended Replication in Las Vegas', *Journal of Experimental Psychology*, 101, pp. 16–20.

Lilienfeld, R. (1978) *The Rise of Systems Theory: An Ideological Analysis* (New York: Wiley).

Lipsey, R. G. (1983) *Positive Economics*, 6th edn (London: Weidenfield and Nicolson).

Little, I. M. D. (1949) 'A Reformulation of the Theory of Consumer's Behaviour', *Oxford Economic Papers*, 1, pp. 90–9.

Littlechild, S. C. (1978) *The Fallacy of the Mixed Economy* (London: Institute of Economic Affairs).

Littlechild, S. C. (1986) 'Three Types of Market Process', in Langlois (1986b, pp. 27–39).

Llewellyn, K. N. (1931) 'What Price Contract? An Essay in Perspective', *Yale Law Journal*, 40, pp. 704–51.

Lloyd, B. B. (1972) *Perception and Cognition* (Harmondsworth: Penguin).

Lloyd, D. (1964) *The Idea of Law* (Harmondsworth: Penguin).

Loasby, B. J. (1971) 'Hypothesis and Paradigm in the Theory of the Firm',

*Economic Journal*, 81, pp. 863–85. Reprinted in Caldwell (1984b).

Loasby, B. J. (1976) *Choice, Complexity and Ignorance: An Enquiry into Economic Theory and Practice of Decision Making*, (Cambridge: Cambridge University Press).

Loasby, B. J. (1986) 'Competion and Imperfect Knowledge: The Contribution of G. B. Richardson', *Scottish Journal of Political Economy*, 33(2), pp. 145–58.

Lofthouse, S. and Vint, J. (1978) 'Some Conceptions and Misconceptions Concerning Economic Man', *Rivista Internationale di Scienze Economiche e Commerciale*, 25, pp. 586–615.

Lovell, M. C. (1986) 'Tests of the Rational Expectations Hypothesis', *American Economic Review*, 76(1), pp. 110–24.

Lowe, A. (1951) 'On the Mechanistic Approach in Economics', *Social Research*, 18, pp. 403–34.

Lowe, A. (1965) *On Economic Knowledge: Toward a Science of Political Economics* (New York: Harper and Row).

Lowry, S. T. (1976) 'Bargain and Contract Theory in Law and Economics', *Journal of Economic Issues*, 10(1), pp. 1–22. Reprinted in Samuels (1979).

Lucas Jr, R. E. (1972) 'Expectations and the Neutrality of Money', *Journal of Economic Theory*, 4(2), pp. 102–24.

Luhmann, N. (1979) *Trust and Power* (Chichester: Wiley).

Lukes, S. (1968) 'Methodological Individualism Reconsidered', *British Journal of Sociology*, 19, pp. 119–29. Reprinted in Emmet and MacIntyre (1970).

Lukes, S. (1971) 'The Meanings of "Individualism"', *Journal of the History of Ideas*, 32, pp. 45–66.

Lukes, S. (1973) *Individualism* (Oxford: Basil Blackwell).

Lukes, S. (1974) *Power: A Radical View* (London: Macmillan).

Lutz, M. A. and Lux, K. (1979) *The Challenge of Humanistic Economics* (Menlo Park, CA: Benjamin/Cummings).

Macaulay, S. (1963) 'Non-Contractual Relations in Business: A Preliminary Survey', *American Sociological Review*, 28(1), pp. 55–67.

Machlup, F. (1946) 'Marginal Analysis and Empirical Research', *American Economic Review*, 36(3), pp. 519–54.

Machlup, F. (1955) 'The Problem of Verification in Economics' *Southern Economic Journal*, 22(1), pp. 1–21. Reprinted in Caldwell (1984b) and Machlup (1978).

Machlup. F. (1962) *The Production of Information and Knowledge* (Princeton, NJ: Princeton University Press).

Machlup, F. (1972) 'The Universal Bogey: Economic Man', in Peston and Corry (1972, pp. 99–117). Reprinted in Machlup (1978).

Machlup, F. (1978) *Methodology of Economics and Other Social Sciences* (London: Academic Press).

Machlup, F. and Mansfield, U. (eds) (1983) *The Study of Information: Interdisciplinary Messages* (New York: Wiley).

MacKay, D. M. (1969) *Information, Mechanism and Meaning* (Cambridge, MA: MIT Press).

Macneil, I. R. (1974) 'The Many Futures of Contract', *University of Southern California Law Review*, 67, pp. 691–816.

Macneil, I. R. (1978) 'Contracts: Adjustments of Long-Term Economic Relations under Classical, Neoclassical and Relational Contract Law, *Northwestern University Law Review*, 72, pp. 854–906.

Macpherson, C. B. (1962) *The Political Theory of Possessive Individualism: Hobbes to Locke* (Oxford: Oxford University Press).

Macpherson, C. B. (1973) *Democratic Theory: Essays in Retrieval* (Oxford: Oxford University Press).

Maital, S. (1982) *Minds, Markets and Money* (New York: Basic Books).

Majumdar, T. (1958) *The Measurement of Utility* (London: Macmillan).

Malcomson, J. M. (1984) 'Efficient Labour Organization: Incentives, Power and the Transactions Cost Approach', in Stephen (1984, pp. 119–25)

Mandeville, B. (1970) *The Fable of the Bees*, edited with an introduction by P. Harth from the first complete edition of 1724 (Harmondsworth: Penguin).

Marglin, S. A. (1974) 'What Do Bosses Do? The Origins and Functions of Hierarchy in Capitalist Production', Part I, *Review of Radical Political Economics*, 6(2), pp. 60–112. Reprinted in Putterman (1986).

Marglin, S. A. (1984) 'Knowledge and Power', in Stephen (1984, pp. 146–64).

Margolis, H. (1982) *Selfishness, Altruism and Rationality* (Cambridge: Cambridge University Press).

Marr, W. L. and Raj, B. (eds) (1983) *How Economists Explain: A Reader in Methodology* (Lanham, MD: University Press of America).

Marris, R. (1964) *The Economic Theory of 'Managerial' Capitalism* (London: Macmillan).

Marschak, J. and Radner, R. (1972) *Economic Theory of Teams* (New Haven: Yale University Press).

Marsden, D. (1984) 'Homo Economicus and the Labour Market', in Wiles and Routh (1983, pp., 121–53).

Marsden, D. (1986) *The End of Economic Man? Custom and Competition in Labour Markets* (Brighton: Wheatsheaf).

Marshall, A. (1949) *Principles of Economics*, Reset 8th edn (London and Basingstoke: Macmillan).

Marx, K. (1969) *Theories of Surplus Value*, Part II (London: Lawrence and Wishart).

Marx, K. (1971) *A Contribution to the Critique of Political Economy*, translated by S. W. Ryazanskaya from the German edition of 1859 (London: Lawrence and Wishart).

Marx, K. (1973) *Grundrisse: Foundations of the Critique of Political Economy*, translated by M. Nicolaus (Harmondsworth: Pelican).

Marx, K. (1976) *Capital*, vol. 1, translated by B. Fowkes from the fourth German edition of 1890 (Harmondsworth: Pelican).

Marx, K. and Engels, F. (1975) *Karl Marx and Frederick Engels, Collected Works*, vol. 3 (London: Lawrence and Wishart).

Marx, K. and Engels, F. (1976) *Karl Marx and Frederick Engels, Collected Works*, vol. 6 (London: Lawrence and Wishart).

Marx, K. and Engels, F. (1977) *Karl Marx and Frederick Engels, Collected Works*, vol. 9 (London: Lawrence and Wishart).

Marx, K. and Engels, F. (1979) *Karl Marx and Frederick Engels, Collected*

*Works*, vol. 11 (London: Lawrence and Wishart).

Maslow, A. (1970) *Motivation and Personality* (New York: Harper and Row).

Matthews, R. C. O. (1986) 'The Economics of Institutions and the Sources of Growth', *Economic Journal*, 96(4), pp. 903–18.

Mauss, M. (1954) *The Gift: Forms and Functions of Exchange in Ancient Societies*, translated by I. Cunnison (London: Cohen and West).

May, K. O. (1954) 'Transitivity, Utility, and Aggregation in Preference Patterns', *Econometrica*, 22, pp. 1–13.

Mayhew, A. (1985) 'Dangers in Using the Idea of Property Rights: Modern Property Rights Theory and the Neo-Classical Trap', *Journal of Economic Issues*, 19(4), pp. 959–66.

McCloskey, D. N. (1983) 'The Rhetoric of Economics', *Journal of Economic Literature*, 21, pp. 481–517. Reprinted in Caldwell (1984b).

McCloskey, D. N. (1985) *The Rhetoric of Economics* (Madison: University of Wisconsin Press).

McEwan, J. D. (1971) 'The Cybernetics of Self-Organising Systems, in Benello and Roussopoulos (1971, pp. 179–94).

McFarland, F. B. (1985) 'Thorstein Veblen Versus the Institutionalists', *Review of Radical Political Economics*, 17(4), pp. 94–105.

McGuinness, A. (1983) 'Efficiency and Industrial Organization' in Shepherd et al. (1983, pp. 8–29).

McLeod, J. M. and Chaffee, S. H. (1972) 'The Construction of Social Reality', in Tedeschi (1972, pp. 50–99).

McNally, M. (1980) 'Consumption, Utility, and Social Process', *Journal of Post Keynesian Economics*, 2(3), pp. 381–91.

Meade, J. E. (1970) *The Theory of Indicative Planning* (Manchester: Manchester University Press).

Meade, J. E. (1971) *The Controlled Economy* (London: Allen and Unwin).

Meadows, D. H., Meadows, D. L. Randers, J. and Behrens, W. W., III (1974) *The Limits to Growth* (London: Pan).

Menger, C. (1963) *Problems of Economics and Sociology*, translated by F. J. Nock from the German edition of 1883 (Urbana, IL: University of Illinois Press).

Menger, C. (1981) *Principles of Economics*, translated by R. Dingwall and B. F. Hozelitz from the German edition of 1871 (New York: New York University Press).

Mepham, J. and Ruben, D.-H. (eds) (1979) *Issues in Marxist Philosophy. Vol. III: Epistemology, Sciences, Ideology* (Brighton: Harvester).

Merton, R. K. (1957) *Social Theory and Social Structure* (Glencoe, IL: Free Press).

Metcalfe, J. S. and Peel, D. A. (1980) 'Growth Expectations and Inflation Expectations in a Simple Macro Dynamic Model', *Metroeconomica*, 32(2–3), pp. 93–114.

Middleton, E. (1986) 'A Behavioral Model of "Animal Spirits"', *Metroeconomica*, 38(1), pp. 39–51.

Milgram, S. (1974) *Obedience to Authority* (London: Tavistock).

Mill, J. S. (1844) *Essays on Some Unsettled Questions of Political Economy* (London: Longman, Green, Reader and Dyer). Reprinted 1948 by the London School of Economics.

Mill, J. S. (1871) *Principles of Political Economy with Some of Their Applications to Social Philosophy*, 7th edn (London: Longman). Reprinted 1965 by the University of Toronto Press and Routledge and Kegan Paul.

Mill, J. S. (1875) *A System of Logic*, 9th edn, 2 vols (London: Longman).

Miller, D. and Estrin, S. (1986) 'Market Socialism: A Policy for Socialists', in Forbes (1986, pp. 3–12).

Miller, J. G. (1978) *Living Systems* (New York: McGraw-Hill).

Mini, P. V. (1974) *Philosophy and Economics* (Gainesville, Florida: University of Florida Press).

Minsky, H. P. (1976) *John Maynard Keynes* (London: Macmillan).

Minsky, H. P. (1982) 'The Financial Instability Hypothesis: Capitalist Processes and the Behaviour of the Economy', in Kindleberger and Laffargue (1982, pp. 13–39).

Mises, L. von (1935) 'Economic Calculation in the Socialist Commonwealth; in Hayek (1935, pp. 89–130).

Mises, L. von (1949) *Human Action: A Treatise on Economics* (London: William Hodge).

Mises, L. von (1957) *Theory and History: An Interpretation of Social and Economic Evolution* (New Haven: Yale University Press).

Mises, L. von (1960) *Epistemological Problems of Economics*, translated by G. Reisman (Van Nostrand: New York).

Mitchell, W. C. (1918) 'Bentham's Felicific Calculus', *Political Science Quarterly*, 33, pp. 161–83. Reprinted in Mitchell (1937).

Mitchell, W. C. (1924) 'The Prospects of Economics', in Tugwell (1924, pp. 8–34).

Mitchell, W. C. (1937) *The Backward Art of Spending Money and Other Essays* (ed. J. Dorfman) (New York: McGraw-Hill).`

Moe, T. (1984) 'The New Economics of Organization', *American Journal of Political Science*, 28(4), pp. 739–77.

Moggridge, D. E. (1976) *Keynes* (London: Fontana).

Moore Jr, B. (1978) *Injustice: The Social Bases of Obedience and Revolt* (London: Macmillan).

Morgenbesser, S. (1967a) 'Psychologism and Methodological Individualism', in Morgenbesser (1967b, pp. 160–74).

Morgenbesser, S. (1967b) *Philosophy of Science Today* (New York: Basic Books).

Moss, S. J. (1981) *An Economic Theory of Business Strategy: An Essay in Dynamics Without Equilibrium* (Oxford: Martin Robertson).

Moss, S. J. (1984) *Markets and Macroeconomics: Macroeconomic Implications of Rational Individual Behaviour* (Oxford: Basil Blackwell).

Murrell, P. (1983) 'Did the Theory of Market Socialism Answer the Challenge of Ludwig von Mises? A Reinterpretation of the Socialist Controversy', *History of Political Economy*, 15(1), pp. 92–105.

Musgrave, A. (1981) '"Unreal Assumptions" in Economic Theory: The F-Twist Untwisted', *Kyklos*, 34, pp. 377–87. Reprinted in Caldwell (1984b).

Myrdal, G. (1953) *The Political Element in the Development of Economic Theory* (London: Routledge and Kegan Paul).

Myrdal, G. (1957) *Economic Theory and the Underdeveloped Regions* (London: Duckworth).

Myrdal, G. (1958) *Value in Social Theory* New York: Harper).

Myrdal, G. (1972) *Against the Stream: Critical Essays on Economics* (New York: Pantheon).

Myrdal, G. (1976) 'The Meaning and Validity of Institutional Economics', in Dopfer (1976, pp. 82–9).

Myrdal, G. (1978) 'Institutional Economics', *Journal of Economic Issues*, 12(4), pp. 771–84.

Nagel, E. (1963) 'Assumptions in Economic Theory', *American Economic Review Papers and Proceedings*, 53, pp. 211–19.

Nagel, E. and Newman, J. R. (1959) *Gödel's Proof* (London: Routledge and Kegan Paul).

Neale, W. C. (1984) 'Technology as Social Process: A Commentary on Knowledge and Human Capital', *Journal of Economic Issues*, 18(2), pp. 573–80.

Neisser, U. (1967) *Cognitive Psychology* (New York: Appleton-Century-Crofts).

Neisser, U. (1976) *Cognition and Reality* (San Francisco: Freeman).

Nell, E. J. (1972) Quoted in *Annals of the American Academy of Science*, p. 447.

Nell, E. J. (ed.) (1984) *Free Market Conservatism: A Critique of Theory and Practice* (London: George Allen and Unwin).

Nelson, R. R. (1981a) 'Assessing Private Enterprise: An Exegesis of Tangled Doctrine', *Bell Journal of Economics*, 12(1), pp. 93–111.

Nelson, R. R. (1981b) 'Research on Productivity Growth and Productivity Differences: Dead Ends and New Departures', *Journal of Economic Literature*, 29, pp. 1029–64.

Nelson, R. R. and Winter, S. G. (1974) 'Neoclassical *vs* Evolutionary Theories of Economic Growth: Critique and Prospectus', *Economic Journal*, 84(4), pp. 886–905.

Nelson, R. R. and Winter, S. G. (1977) 'In Search of a Useful Theory of Innovation', *Research Policy*, 6, pp. 36–76.

Nelson, R. R. and Winter, S. G. (1982) *An Evolutionary Theory of Economic Change* (Cambridge, MA: Harvard University Press).

Newell, A. and Simon, H. A. (1972) *Human Problem Solving* (Englewood Cliffs: Prentice Hall).

Newman, G. (1976) 'An Institutional Perspective on Information' *International Social Science Journal*, 28, pp. 466–92.

Newman, J. W. and Staelin, R. (1972) 'Prepurchase Information Seeking for New Cars and Major Household Appliances', *Journal of Marketing Research*, 9, pp. 249–57.

Nisbett, R. and Ross, L. (1980) *Human Inference: Strategies and Shortcomings of Social Judgement* (Englewood Cliffs, NJ: Prentice-Hall).

Nolan, P. and Paine, S. (eds) (1986) *Rethinking Socialist Economics* (Cambridge: Polity Press).

North, D. C. (1977) 'Markets and Other Allocation Systems in History: The Challenges of Karl Polanyi', *Journal of European Economic History*, 6, pp. 703–16.

North, D. C. (1978) 'Structure and Performance: The Task of Economic History', *Journal of Economic Literature*, 16, pp. 963–78.

Nove, A. (1979) *Political Economy and Soviet Socialism* (London: George Allen and Unwin).

Nove, A. (1983) *The Economics of Feasible Socialism* (London: George Allen and Unwin).

Nove, A. and Nuti, D. M. (eds) (1972) *Socialist Economics* (Harmondsworth: Penguin).

Nozick, R. (1974) *Anarchy, State, and Utopia* (Oxford: Basil Blackwell).

Nozick, R. (1977) 'On Austrian Methodology', *Synthese*, 36, pp. 353–92.

Nuti, D. M. (1970) '"Vulgar Economy" in the Theory of Income Distribution', *De Economist*, 118, pp. 363–9. Reprinted in Hunt and Schwartz (1972).

Nuti, D. M. (1972) 'Postscript' to Nuti (1970) in Hunt and Schwartz (1972, pp. 229–32).

Nutzinger, H. G. (1976) 'The Firm as a Social Institution: The Failure of the Contractarian Viewpoint', *Economic Analysis and Workers' Management*, 10, pp. 217–37.

Nutzinger, H. G. (1982) 'The Economics of Property Rights – A New Paradigm in Social Science?', in Stegmuller et al. (1982, pp. 169–90)

O'Driscoll, G. P. and Rizzo, M. J. (1985) *The Economics of Time and Ignorance* (Oxford: Basil Blackwell).

O'Neill, J. (1973) *Modes of Individualism and Collectivism* (London: Heinemann).

Oakeshott, M. (1962) *Rationalism in Politics and Other Essays* (London: Methuen).

Okun, A. M. (1981) *Prices and Quantities* (Oxford: Basil Blackwell).

Olshansky, R. W. and Granbois, D. H. (1979) 'Consumer Decision Making? Fact or Fiction?', *Journal of Consumer Research*, 6, pp. 93–100.

Olson Jr, M. (1965) *The Logic of Collective Action* (Cambridge, MA: Harvard University Press).

Olson Jr, M. (1982) *The Rise and Decline of Nations* (New Haven: Yale University Press).

Ouchi, W. G. (1980) 'Markets, Bureaucracies and Clans', *Administrative Science Quarterly*, 25, pp. 129–41.

Pareto, V. (1935) *The Mind and Society*, 4 vols, translated from the Italian edition of 1923 by .A. Bongiorno and A. Livingston, and edited by A. Livingston (London: Jonathan Cape).

Pareto, V. (1971) *Manual of Political Economy*, translated from the French edition of 1927 by A. S. Schwier, and edited by A. S. Schwier and A. N. Page (New York: Augustus Kelley).

Parker, D. (1985) 'Is the Private Sector More Efficient? A Study in the Public *v* Private Debate', *Public Administration Bulletin*, August, pp. 2–23.

Parrinello, S. (1984) 'Adaptive Preferences and the Theory of Demand', *Journal of Post Keynesian Economics*, 6(4), pp. 551–60.

Parsons, K. H. (1985) 'John R. Commons: His Relevance to Contemporary Economics', *Journal of Economic Issues*, 19(3), pp. 755–78.

Parsons, T. (1937) *The Structure of Social Action*, 2 vols, (New York: McGraw-Hill).

Parsons, T. (1940) 'The Motivation of Economic Activities', *Canadian Journal of Economics and Political Science*, 6, pp. 187–203. Reprinted in Smelser (1965).

Parsons, T. (1960) 'Durkheim's Contribution to the Theory of Integration of Social Systems', in Wolff (1960, pp. 118–53).

Parsons, T. (1971) *The System of Modern Societies* (Englewood Cliffs, NJ: Prentice-Hall).

Pashukanis, E. B. (1978) *Law and Marxism: A General Theory* (London: Ink Links).

Pasinetti, L. (1981) *Structural Change and Economic Growth* (Cambridge: Cambridge University Press).

Pateman, C. (1970) *Participation and Democratic Theory* (Cambridge: Cambridge University Press).

Pearce, I. F. (1977) 'Participation and Income Distribution', in Heathfield (1977, pp. 26–35).

Peel, D. A. and Metcalfe, J. S. (1979) 'Divergent Expectations and the Dynamic Stability of Some Simple Macro Economic Models', *Economic Journal*, 89, pp. 789–98.

Peirce, C. S. (1955) *Philosophical Writings of Peirce*, ed. J. Buchler (New York: Dover Publications).

Pejovich, S. (1982) 'Karl Marx, Property Rights School and the Process of Social Change', *Kyklos*, 35, pp. 83–97.

Penrose, E. T. (1952) 'Biological Analogies in the Theory of the Firm', *American Economic Review*, 42, pp. 804–19.

Penrose, E. T. (1959) *The Theory of the Growth of the Firm* (Oxford: Basil Blackwell;.

Perrow, C. (1986a) *Complex Organizations: A Critical Essay*, 3rd end (New York: Random House).

Perrow, C. (1986b) 'Economic Theories of Organization', *Theory and Society*, 15, pp. 11–45.

Pesaran, M. H. (1987) *The Limits to Rational Expectations* (Oxford: Basil Blackwell).

Peston, M. (1967) 'Changing Utility Functions' in Shubik (1967).

Peston, M. and Corry, B. (eds) (1972) *Essays in Honour of Lord Robbins* (London: Weidenfeld and Nicolson).

Peterson, W. C. (1977) 'Institutionalism, Keynes and the Real World', *Journal of Economic Issues*, 11(2), pp. 201–21.

Petr, J. L. (1984a) 'Fundamentals of an Institutionalist Perspective on Economic Policy', *Journal of Economic Issues*, 18(1), pp. 1–17.

Petr, J. L. (1984b) 'An Assault on the Citadel: Is a Constructive Synthesis Feasible?', *Journal of Economic Issues*, 18(2), pp. 589–97.

Phelps, E. (ed.) (1975) *Altruism, Morality and Economic Theory* (New York: Sage Publications).

Phelps Brown, H. (1977) 'What is the British Predicament?', *Three Banks Review*, 116, pp. 3–29. Extracted in Coates and Hillard (1986).

Phillips, A. W. (1958) 'The Relationship Between Unemployment and the Rate of Change of Money Wage Rates in the United Kingdom, 1861–1957', *Economica*, 25, pp. 283–99.

Phillips, R. J. (1985–6) 'Marx, the Classical Firm, and Economic Planning', *Journal of Post Keynesian Economics*, 8(2), pp. 266–76.

Piaget, J. (1969) *The Mechanisms of Perception* (New York: Basic Books).

Piaget, J. (1972) *Psychology and Epistemology: Towards a Theory of Knowledge* (Harmondsworth: Penguin).

Piaget, J. and Inhelder, B. (1969) 'The Gaps in Empiricism' in Koestler and Smythies (1969, pp. 118–48).

Piore, M. J. (1973) 'Fragments of a "Sociological" Theory of Wages', *American Economic Review*, 63(2), pp. 377–84. Reprinted in Piore (1979).

Piore, M. J. (ed.) (1979) *Unemployment and Inflation: Institutionalist and Structuralist Views* (Armonk, NY: M. E. Sharpe).

Polan, A. J. (1984) *Lenin and the End of Politics* (London: Methuen).

Polanyi, K. (1944) *The Great Transformation* (New York: Rinehart).

Polanyi, M. (1957) *Personal Knowledge: Towards a Post-Critical Philosophy* (London: Routledge and Kegan Paul).

Polanyi, M. (1967) *The Tacit Dimension* (London: Routledge and Kegan Paul).

Pollak, R. A. (1970) 'Habit Formation and Dynamic Demand Functions' *Journal of Political Economy*, 78, pp. 745–63.

Pollak, R. A. (1985) 'A Transaction Cost Approach to Families and Households', *Journal of Economic Literature*, 23, pp. 581–608.

Popovsky, M. (1980) *Science in Chains: The Crisis of Science and Scientists in the Soviet Union Today* (London: Collins and Harvill).

Popper, K. R. (1945) *The Open Society and its Enemies*, 2 vols (London: Routledge).

Popper, K. R. (1959) *The Logic of Scientific Discovery* (London: Hutchinson).

Popper, K. R. (1965) *Conjectures and Refutations: The Growth of Scientific Knowledge*, 2nd edn (London: Routledge and Kegan Paul).

Pratt, J. W., Wise, D. A. and Zeckhauser, R. (1979) 'Price Differences in Almost Competitive Markets', *Quarterly Journal of Economics*, 93(2), pp. 189–211.

Putterman, L. (1984) 'On Some Recent Explanations of Why Capital Hires Labour', *Economic Inquiry*, 12(2), pp. 171–87. Reprinted in Putterman (1986).

Putterman, L. (1986) *The Economic Nature of the Firm: A Reader* (Cambridge: Cambridge University Press).

Radner, R. (1968) 'Competitive Equilibrium Under Uncertainty', *Econometrica*, 36(1), pp. 31–58.

Radner, R. (1975a) 'A Behavioral Model of Cost Reduction', *Bell Journal of Economics*, 6, pp. 196–214.

Radner, R. (1975b) 'Satisficing', *Journal of Mathematical Economics*, 2, pp. 253–62.

Radner, R. and Rothschild, M. (1975) 'On the Allocation of Effort', *Journal of Economic Theory*, 10 pp. 358–76.

Randall, A. (1978) 'Property, Institutions, and Economic Behavior', *Journal of Economic Issues*, 12(1), pp. 1–21.

Rapping, L. A. (1984) 'Bureaucracy, the Corporation, and Economic Policy', *Journal of Post Keynesian Economics*, 6(3), pp. 337–53.

Rawls, J. (1972) *A Theory of Justice* (Oxford: Oxford University Press).

Reynolds, R. L. (1984) 'The Regulatory Matrix and the Rigidity of the Economic System', *Journal of Economic Issues*, 18(2), pp. 627–31.

Reynolds, R. L. (1985) 'Institutionally Determined Property Claims', *Journal of Economic Issues*, 19(4), pp. 941–9.

Richardson, G. B. (1959) 'Equilibrium, Expectations and Information', *Economic Journal*, 69, pp. 223–37.

Richardson, G. B. (1960) *Information and Investment* (Oxford: Oxford University Press).

Richardson, G. B. (1972) 'The Organisation of Industry', *Economic Journal*, 82, pp. 883–96.

Robbins, L. (1937) *An Essay on the Nature and Significance of Economic Science* (London: Macmillan).

Roberts, B. and Holdren, R. (1972) *Theory of the Social Process: An Economic Analysis* (Ames, IA: Iowa State University Press).

Roberts, K. (1983) *Automation, Unemployment and the Distribution of Income* (Maastricht, Netherlands: European Centre for Work and Society).

Robinson, J. (1951) *Collected Economic Papers – Volume One* (Oxford: Basil Blackwell).

Robinson, J. (1964) *Economic Philosophy* (Harmondsworth: Pelican).

Robinson, J. (1971) *Economic Heresies* (London: Macmillan).

Robinson, J. (1973a) 'What Has Become of the Keynesian Revolution?', in Robinson (1973b, pp. 1–11).

Robinson, J. (ed.) (1973b) *After Keynes* (Oxford: Basil Blackwell).

Robinson, J. (1974) *History versus Equilibrium* (London: Thames Papers in Political Economy).

Robinson, J. (1979) *Collected Economic Papers – Volume Five* (Oxford: Basil Blackwell).

Roemer, J. E. (1981) *Analytical Foundations of Marxian Economic Theory* (Cambridge: Cambridge University Press).

Roemer, J. E. (1982) 'Methodological Individualism and Deductive Marxism', *Theory and Society*, 11, pp. 513–20.

Rose, S., Kamin, L. J. and Lewontin, R. C. (1984) *Not in Our Genes: Biology, Ideology and Human Nature* (Harmondsworth: Penguin).

Rosenberg, N. (1982a) *Inside the Black Box: Technology and Economics* (Cambridge: Cambridge University Press).

Rosenberg, N. (1982b) 'The International Transfer of Industrial Technology: Past and Present', in *North South Technology Transfers: The Adjustments Ahead* (Paris: OECD).

Rosenzweig, M. R. and Porter, L. W. (eds) (1977) *Annual Review of Psychology* (Palo Alto, CA: Annual Reviews).

Rothschild, K. W. (ed.) (1971) *Power in Economics* (Harmondsworth: Penguin).

Rotwein, E. (1973) 'Empiricism and Economic Method: Several Views Considered', *Journal of Economic Issues*, 7, pp. 554–75.

Routh, G. (1975) *The Origin of Economic Ideas* (London: Macmillan).

Rowse, A. L. (1936) *Mr Keynes and the Labour Movement* (London: Macmillan).

Rowthorn, R. E. (1974) 'Neo-Classicism, neo-Ricardianism, and Marxism', *New Left Review*, no. 86, pp. 63–87. Reprinted in Rowthorn (1980)

Rowthorn, R. E. (1980) *Capitalism, Conflict and Inflation* (London: Lawrence and Wishart).

Rudner, R. S. (1954) 'Philosophy and Social Science', *Philosophy of Science*, 21, pp. 164–8. Reprinted in O'Neill (1973).

Russell, T. and Thaler, R. (1985) 'The Relevance of Quasi Rationality in Competitive Markets', *American Economic Review*, 75(5), pp. 1071–82.

Rutherford, M. (1984a) 'Rational Expectations and Keynesian Uncertainty: A Critique', *Journal of Post Keynesian Economics*, 6(3), pp. 377–87.

Rutherford, M. (1984b) 'Thorstein Veblen and the Processes of Institutional Change', *History of Political Economy*, 16(3), pp. 331–49.

Sahlins, M. (1972) *Stone Age Economics* (London: Tavistock).

Samuels, W. J. (ed.) (1979) *The Economy as a System of Power. Vol. 1: Corporate Systems* (New Brunswick: Transaction).

Samuels, W. J. (ed.) (1984) *Research in the History of Economic Thought and Methodology* (Greenwich, CT: JAI Press).

Samuels, W. J. (1985) 'A Critique of *Capitalism, Socialism and Democracy*', in Coe and Wilber (1985, pp. 60–119).

Samuels, W. J. (1986) 'What Aspects of Keynes's Economic Theories Merit Continued or Renewed Interest? One Interpretation', *Journal of Post Keynesian Economics*, 9(1), pp. 3–16.

Samuelson, P. A. (1938) 'A Note on the Pure Theory of Consumer's Behaviour', *Economics*, 5, pp. 61–71.

Samuelson, P. A. (1962) 'Economists and the History of Ideas', *American Economic Review*, 52(1), pp. 1–18.

Samuelson, P. A. (1975) *Economics*, 10th edn (New York: McGraw-Hill).

Schefold, B. (1985) 'Ecological Problems as a Challenge to Classical and Keynesian Economics', *Metroeconomica*, 37(1), pp. 21–62.

Schelling, T. C. (1978) *Micromotives and Macrobehavior* (New York: Norton).

Scherer, F. M. (1970) *Industrial Market Structure and Economic Performance* (Chicago: Rand McNally).

Scherer, F. M. (1984) *Innovation and Growth: Schumpeterian Perspectives* (Cambridge, MA: MIT Press).

Schoemaker, P. J. (1980) *Experiments on Decisions Under Risk: The Expected Utility Hypothesis* (Den Haag: Nijhoff).

Schoemaker, P. J. (1982) 'The Expected Utility Model: Its Variants, Purposes, Evidence and Limitations', *Journal of Economic Literature*, 20(2), pp. 529–64.

Schotter, A. (1981) *The Economic Theory of Social Institutions* (Cambridge: Cambridge University Press).

Schotter, A. (1985) *Free Market Economics: A Critical Appraisal* (New York: St Martin's Press).

Schotter, A. (1986) 'The Evolution of Rules', in Langlois (1986b, pp. 117–33).

Schumacher, E. F. (1973) *Small is Beautiful: A Study of Economics as if People Mattered* (London: Blond and Briggs).

Schumpeter, J. A. (1928) 'The Instability of Capitalism', *Economic Journal*, 38, pp. 385–6.

Schumpeter, J. A. (1934) *The Theory of Economic Development* (Cambridge, MA: Harvard University Press).

Schumpeter, J. A. (1976) *Capitalism, Socialism and Democracy*, 5th Edn (London: George Allen and Unwin).

Scitovsky, T. (1977) *The Joyless Economy* (Oxford: Oxford University Press).

Scitovsky, T. (1980 'Can Capitalism Survive? – An Old Question in a New Setting', *American Economic Review, Papers and Proceedings*, 70, pp. 1–9.

Scitovsky, T. (1981) 'The Desire for Excitement in Modern Society', *Kyklos*, 34, pp. 3–13.

Seabury, S. (1861) *American Slavery Justified by the Law of Nature* (New York: Mason).

Searle, J. R. (1983) *Intentionality: An Essay in the Philosophy of Mind* (Cambridge: Cambridge University Press).

Searle, J. R. (1984) *Minds, Brains and Science* (London: British Broadcasting Corporation).

Sebba, G. (1953) 'The Development of the Concepts of Mechanism and Model in Physical Science and Economic Thought', *American Economic Review*, Papers and Proceedings, 43, pp. 259–68.

Seckler, D. (1975) *Thorstein Veblen and the Institutionalists* (London: Macmillan).

Seidman, R. B. (1979) 'Contract Law, the Free Market, and State Intervention: A Jurisprudential Perspective', in Samuels (1979, pp. 219–41).

Sen, A. K. (1973) 'Behaviour and the Concept of Preference', *Economica*, 40, pp. 241–59. Reprinted in Elster (1986).

Sen, A. K. (1976–7) 'Rational Fools: A Critique of the Behavioural Foundations of Economic Theory', *Philosophy and Public Affairs*, 6, pp. 317–44. Reprinted in Hahn and Hollis (1979).

Sen, A. K. (1983) 'The Profit Motive', *Lloyds Bank Review*, no 147, pp. 1–20.

Sen, A. K. and Williams, B. (eds) (1982) *Utilitarianism and Beyond* (Cambridge: Cambridge University Press).

Sensat Jr, J. and Constantine, G. (1975) 'A Critique of the Foundations of Utility Theory', *Science and Society*, 39(2), pp. 157–79.

Shackle, G. L. S. (1955) *Uncertainty in Economics* (London: Cambridge University Press).

Shackle, G. L. S. (1969) *Decision, Order and Time*, 2nd edn (Cambridge: Cambridge University Press).

Shackle, G. L. S. (1972) *Epistemics and Economics* (Cambridge: Cambridge University Press).

Shackle, G. L. S. (1974) *Keynesian Kaleidics* (Edinburgh: Edinburgh University Press).

Shackleton, J. R. and Locksley, G. (eds) (1981) *Twelve Contemporary Economists* (London: Macmillan).

Shand, A. H. (1984) *The Capitalist Alternative: An Introduction to Neo-Austrian Economics* (Brighton: Wheatsheaf).

Shepherd, D., Turk, J. and Silbertson, Z. A. (eds) (1983) *Microeconomic Efficiency and Macroeconomic Performance* (London: Philip Allan).

Shiller, R. J. (1978) 'Rational Expectations and the Dynamic Structure of Macroeconomic Models', *Journal of Monetary Economics*, 4, pp. 1–44.

Shone, R. M. (1975) *Microeconomics: A Modern Treatment* (London: Macmillan).

Shubik, M. (ed.) (1967) *Essays in Mathematical Economics, In Honor of Oskar Morgenstern* (Princeton NJ: Princeton University Press).

Simmel, G. (1978) *The Philosophy of Money*, translated by T. Bottomore and D. Frisby from the German edition of 1900 (London: Routledge and Kegan Paul).

Simon, H. A. (1951), 'A Formal Theory of the Employment Relationship', *Econometrica*, 19, pp. 293–305. Reprinted in Simon (1957a) and Putterman (1986).

Simon, H. A. (1955) 'A Behavioral Model of Rational Choice', *Quarterly Journal of Economics*, 69, pp. 99–118. Reprinted in Simon (1957a).

Simon, H. A. (1956) 'Rational Choice and the Structure of the Environment', *Psychological Review*, 63, pp. 129–38. Reprinted in Simon (1957a) and Emery (1981, vol. 2).

Simon, H. A. (1957a) *Models of Man: Social and Rational* (New York: Wiley).

Simon, H. A. (1957b) *Administrative Behavior: A Study of Decision-Making Processes in Administrative Organization*, 2nd edn (New York: Macmillan).

Simon, H. A. (1959) 'Theories of Decision-Making in Economic and Behavioral Sciences', *American Economic Review*, 49, pp. 253–83.

Simon, H. A. (1962) 'The Architecture of Complexity', *Proceedings of the American Philosophical Society*, 106, pp. 467–82. Reprinted in Simon (1968).

Simon, H. A. (1968) *The Sciences of the Artificial* (Cambridge MA: MIT Press).

Simon, H. A. (1976) 'From Substantive to Procedural Rationality', in S. Latsis (1976b, pp. 129–48). Reprinted in Hahn and Hollis (1979).

Simon, H. A. (1979) 'Rational Decision Making in Business Organizations', *American Economic Review*, 69, pp. 493–513.

Simon, H. A. (1983) *Reason in Human Affairs* (Oxford: Basil Blackwell).

Singh, A. (1975) 'Take-Overs, Economic "Natural Selection" and the Theory of the Firm: Evidence from the Postwar United Kingdom Experience', *Economic Journal*, 83(3), pp. 497–515, pp. 441–51.

Singh, H. (1987) 'Comment on "The Rationalist Conception of Action"', *Journal of Economic Issues*, 21(1).

Skott, P. (1985) *Vicious Circles and Cumulative Causation* (London: Thames Papers in Political Economy).

Skouras, A.(1981) 'The Economics of Joan Robinson', in Shackleton and Locksley (1981, pp. 199–218).

Skouras, A. and Kitromilides, J. (1979) 'On a Communication Aspect of the Relationship Between Economic Theory and Policy-Making', *Kyklos*, 32, pp. 606–10.

Slovic, P., Fischhoff, B. and Lichtenstein, S. (1977) 'Behavioral Decision Theory', in Rosenzweig and Porter (1977), pp. 1–39.

Slovic, P. and Lichtenstein, S. (1971) 'Comparison of Bayesian and Regression Approaches to the Study of Information Processing and Judgement', *Organizational Behavior and Human Performance*, 6, pp. 649–744.

Slovic, P. and Lichtenstein, S. (1974) 'Who Accepts Savages's Axiom?', *Behavioral Science*, 6, pp. 368–73.

Slovic, P. and Lichtenstein, S. (1983) 'Preference Reversals: A Broader Perspective', *American Economic Review*, 73(4), pp. 596–605.

Smelser, N. J. (1959) 'A Comparative View of Exchange Systems', *Economic Development and Cultural Change*, 7, pp. 173–82.

Smelser, N. J. (ed.) (1965) *Readings in Economic Sociology* (Englewood Cliffs, NJ: Prentice-Hall).

Smith, A. (1922) *An Inquiry into the Nature and Causes of the Wealth of Nations*, 2 vols, (1st ed 1776) edited by E. Cannan (London: Methuen).

Smith, A. (1976) *The Theory of Moral Sentiments* (1st edn 1759) edited by D. D. Raphael and A. L. Macfie (Oxford: Clarendon).

Sommerhoff, G. (1974) *Logic of the Living Brain* (London: Wiley).

Sonnenschein, H. F. (1971) 'Demand Theory Without Transitive Preferences, With Applications to the Theory of Competitive Equilibrium', in Chipman et al. (1971, pp. 215–23).

Sowell, T. (1967) 'The "Evolutionary" Economics of Thorstein Veblen', *Oxford Economic Papers*, 19(2), pp. 177–98.

Sowell, T. (1972) *Say's Law* (Princeton, NJ: Princeton University Press).

Sowell, T. (1980) *Knowledge and Decisions* (New York: Basic Books).

Spencer, H. (1899) *The Principles of Sociology* (New York: Appleton).

Spradley, J. P. (ed.) (1972) *Culture and Cognition: Rules, Maps and Plans* (San Francisco: Chandler Publishing).

Sraffa, P. (1960) *Production of Commodities by Means of Commodities: Prelude to a Critique of Economic Theory* (Cambridge: Cambridge University Press).

Stanfield, R. (1986) *The Economic Thought of Karl Polanyi* (London: Macmillan).

Steedman, I. (1980) 'Economic Theory and Intrinsically Non-Autonomous Preferences and Beliefs', *Quaderni Fondazione Feltrinelli*, no. 7/8, pp. 57–73.

Stegmuller, W., Balzer, W. and Spohn, W. (eds) (1982) *Philosophy and Economics* (Berlin: Springer-Verlag).

Steinbruner, J. D. (1974) *The Cybernetic Theory of Decision: New Dimensions of Political Analysis* (Princeton NJ: Princeton University Press).

Stepan, A. (1978) *The State and Society: Peru in Comparative Perspective* (Princeton, NJ: Princeton University Press).

Stephen, F. H. (ed.) (1982) *The Performance of Labour-Managed Firms* (London: Macmillan).

Stephen, F. H. (ed.) (1984) *Firms, Organization and Labour: Approaches to the Economics of Work Organization* (London: Macmillan).

Stewart, I. M. T. (1979) *Reasoning and Method in Economics: An Introduction to Economic Methodology* (London: McGraw-Hill).

Stigler, G. J. (1961) 'The Economics of Information', *Journal of Political Economy*, 69, pp. 213–25. Reprinted in Lamberton (1971).

Stigler, G. J. and Becker, G. S. (1977) 'De Gustibus Non Est Disputandum', *American Economic Review* 76(1), pp. 76–90.

Stohs, M. (1980) '"Uncertainty" in Keynes' *General Theory*', *History of Political Economy*, 12(3), 372–82.

Stohs, M. (1983) '"Uncertainty" in Keynes' *General Theory:* A Rejoinder', *History of Political Economy*, 15(1), pp. 87–91.

Streissler, E. (ed.) (1969) *Roads to Freedom: Essays in Honour of Friedrich A. von Hayek* (London: Routledge and Kegan Paul).

Strumpel, B., Morgan, J. N. and Zahn, E. (eds) (1972) *Human Behavior in Economic Affairs: Essays in Honour of George Katona* (Amsterdam: Elsevier).

Sugden, R. (1986) *The Economics of Rights, Co-operation and Welfare* (Oxford: Basil Blackwell).

Sutcliffe, R. (1977) 'Keynesianism and the Stabilisation of Capitalist Economies', in Green and Nore (1977), pp. 163–81.

Sweezy, P. M. (1946) 'John Maynard Keynes', *Science and Society,* 10. Reprinted in Lekachman (1964, pp. 297–314).

Sweezy, P. M. (1968) *The Theory of Capitalist Development: Principles of Marxian Political Economy* (New York: Modern Reader).

Sylos-Labini, P. (1969) *Oligopoly and Technical Progress*, rev. edn (Cambridge, MA: Harvard University Press).

Tarascio, V. J. and Caldwell, B. (1979) 'Theory Choice in Economics: Philosophy and Practice', *Journal of Economic Issues*, 13, pp. 983–1006.

Tedeschi, J. T. (1972) *The Social Influence Processes* (Chicago: Aldine-Atherton).

Thaler, R. H. and Shefrin, H. M. (1981) 'An Economic Theory of Self-Control', *Journal of Political Economy*, 89, pp. 392–406.

Thoben, H. (1982), 'Mechanistic and Organistic Analogies in Economics Reconsidered', *Kyklos*, 35, pp. 292–306.

Thompson, G. (1977) 'The Relationship Between the Financial and Industrial Sector in the United Kingdom Economy', *Economy and Society*, 6, pp. 235–83. Reprinted in Thompson (1986).

Thompson, G. (1982) 'The Firm as a "Dispersed" Social Agency', *Economy and Society*, 11(3), pp. 233–50. Reprinted in Thompson (1986).

Thompson, G. (ed.) (1986) *Economic Calculation and Policy Formation* (London: Routledge and Kegan Paul).

Thurow, L. C. (1983) *Dangerous Currents* (New York: Random House).

Tinbergen, J. (1952) *On the Theory of Economic Policy* (Amsterdam: North-Holland).

Tisdall, C. A. (1976) 'Rational Behaviour as a Basis for Economic Theories', in Benn and Mortimore (1976).

Titmuss, R. M. (1970) *The Gift Relationship: From Human Blood to Social Policy* (London: George Allen and Unwin).

Tobin, J. (1980) 'Are New Classical Models Plausible Enough to Guide Policy?', *Journal of Money, Credit and Banking*, 12, pp. 788–99.

Tomlinson, J. (1984) 'Economic and Sociological Theories of the Enterprise and Industrial Democracy', *British Journal of Sociology*, 35(4), pp. 591–605.

Tomlinson, J. (1986) 'Democracy Inside the Black Box? Neo-Classical Theories of the Firm and Industrial Democracy', *Economy and Society*, 15(2), pp. 220–50.

Tool, M. R. (1981) 'The Compulsive Shift to Institutional Analysis', *Journal of*

*Economic Issues*, 15(3), pp. 569–92.

Toulmin, S. (1973) *Human Understanding*, vol. 1 (Oxford: Clarendon Press).

Trakhtenbrot, B. A. (1963) *Algorithms and Automatic Computing Machines* (Boston: D. C. Heath).

Troub, R. M. (1982) 'A General Theory of Planning: The Evolution of Planning and the Planning of Evolution', *Journal of Economic Issues*, 16(2), pp. 381–90.

Troub, R. M. (1983) 'General Adjustment Theory and Institutional Adjustment Processes', *Journal of Economic Issues*, 17(2), pp. 315–24.

Tuchman, B. W. (1984) *The March of Folly: From Troy to Vietnam* (London: Michael Joseph).

Tucker, D. F. B. (1980) *Marxism and Individualism* (Oxford: Basil Blackwell).

Tugwell, R. G. (ed.) (1924) *The Trend of Economics* (New York: Alfred Knopf).

Tversky, A. (1969) 'Intransitivity of Preferences', *Psychological Review*, 76, pp. 31–48.

Tversky, A. and Kahneman, D. (1973) 'Availability: A Heuristic for Judging Frequency and Probability', *Cognitive Psychology*, 5, pp. 207–32. Reprinted in Kahneman et al. (1982).

Tversky, A. and Kahneman, D. (1974) 'Judgement under Uncertainty: Heuristics and Biases', *Science*, 185, pp. 1124–31. Reprinted in Kahneman et al. (1982).

Tversky, A. and Kahneman, D. (1981) 'The Framing of Decisions and the Psychology of Choice', *Science*, 211, pp. 453–8.

Ullman-Margalit, E. (1977) *The Emergence of Norms* (Oxford: Oxford University Press).

Ullman-Margalit, E. (1978) 'Invisible Hand Explanations', *Sythese*, 39, pp. 282–6.

Van Parijs, P. (1981a) *Evolutionary Explanation in the Social Sciences: An Emerging Paradigm* (London: Tavistock).

Van Parijs, P. (1981b) 'Sociology as General Economics', *Archives européennes de sociologie*, 22, pp. 299–324.

Vanek, J. (ed.) (1975) *Self-Management: Economic Liberation of Man* (Harmondsworth: Penguin).

Vaughn, K. I. (1980) 'Economic Calculation Under Socialism: The Austrian Contribution', *Economic Inquiry*, 18, pp. 535–54.

Vaughn, K. I. (1982) 'Subjectivism, Predictability, and Creativity: Comment of Buchanan', in Kirzner (1982, pp. 21–9).

Veblen, T. B. (1898) 'Why Is Economics Not an Evolutionary Science?', *Quarterly Journal of Economics* 12, pp. 373–97. Reprinted in Lerner (1948) and Veblen (1919).

Veblen, T. B. (1899) *The Theory of the Leisure Class: An Economic Study of Institutions* (New York: Macmillan).

Veblen, T. B. (1909) 'The Limitations of Marginal Utility', *Journal of Political Economy*, 17, pp. 235–45. Reprinted in Veblen (1936).

Veblen, T. B. (1919) *The Place of Science in Modern Civilisation and Other Essays* (New York: Huebsch).

Veblen, T. B. (1921) *The Engineers and the Price System* (New York: Harcourt Brace and World).

Veblen, T. B. (1936) *What Veblen Taught*, ed. W. C. Mitchell (New York: Augustus Kelly).

Veblen, T. B. (1954) *Essays in Our Changing Order*, ed. L. Ardzrooni (New York: The Viking Press).

Veblen, T. B. (1958) *The Theory of Business Enterprise* (New York: Mentor Books).

Veblen, T. B. (1964) *The Instinct of Workmanship* (New York: Augustus Kelley).

Vickers, D. (1978) *Financial Markets in the Capitalist Process* (Philadelphia: University of Pennsylvania Press).

Vickers, D. (1986) 'Time, Ignorance, Surprise, and Economic Decisions: A Comment Williams and Findlay's "Risk and the Role of Failed Expectations in an Uncertain World"', *Journal of Post Keynesian Economics*, 9(1), pp. 49–57.

Vroom, V. H. and Deci, E. L. (eds) (1970) *Management and Motivation* (Harmondsworth: Penguin).

Wallsten, T. S. (ed.) (1980) *Cognitive Processes in Choice and Decision Behavior* (Hillsdale, JN: Lawrence Erlbaum Associates).

Walras, L. (1954) *Elements of Pure Economics*, translated from the French edition of 1926 by W. Jaffe (New York: Kelley).

Walsh, V. C. (1970) *Introduction to Contemporary Microeconomics* (New York: McGraw-Hill).

Ward, B. (1972) *What's Wrong with Economics?* (London: Macmillan).

Weber, M. (1947) *The Theory of Social and Economic Organization*, translated by A. M. Henderson and T. Parsons, and edited with an introduction by T. Parsons (Oxford: Oxford University Press).

Weintraub, E. R. (1979) *Microfoundations* (Cambridge: Cambridge University Press).

Weisskopf, W. A. (1979) 'The Method is the Ideology: From a Newtonian to a Heisenbergian Paradigm in Economics', *Journal of Economic Issues*, 8(4), pp. 869–84.

Westergaard, J. and Resler, H. (1976) *Class in a Capitalist Society* (Harmondsworth: Penguin).

White, H. C. (1981) 'Where Do Markets Come From?', *American Journal of Sociology*, 87(3), pp. 517–47.

Wible, J. R. (1982) 'Friedman's Positive Economics and Philosophy of Science', *Southern Economic Journal*, 49, pp. 350–60.

Wible, J. R. (1982–3) 'The Rational Expectations Tautologies', *Journal of Post Keynesian Economics*, 5(2), pp. 199–207.

Wible, J. R. (1984–5) 'An Epistemic Critique of Rational Expectations and the Neoclassical Macroeconomics Research Program', *Journal of Post Keynesian Economics*, 7(2), pp. 269–81.

Wicksteed, P. H. (1910) *The Commonsense of Political Economy*, ed. L. Robbins (London: Routledge).

Wilber, C. K. (1979) 'Empirical Verification and Theory Selection: The

Monetarist–Keynesian Debate', *Journal of Economic Issues*, 13(4), pp. 973–82.

Wilber, C. K. and Harrison, R. S. (1978) 'The Methodological Basis of Institutional Economics: Pattern Model, Storytelling and Holism', *Journal of Economic Issues*, 7(1), pp. 61–89. Reprinted in Marr and Raj (1983).

Wilber, C. K. and Wisman, J. (1975) 'The Chicago School: Positivism or Ideal Type', *Journal of Economic Issues*, 9(4), pp. 665–79.

Wiles, P. and Routh, G. (eds) (1984) *Economics in Disarray* (Oxford: Basil Blackwell).

Willer, D. and Willer, J. (1973) *Systematic Empiricism: Critique of a Pseudo-Science* (Englewood Cliffs, NJ: Prentice-Hall).

Williams, E. E. and Findlay III, M. C., (1986) 'Risk and the Role of Failed Expectations in an Uncertain World', *Journal of Post Keynesian Economics*, 9(1), pp. 32–47.

Williams, K. (1975) 'Facing Reality – A Critique of Karl Popper's Empiricism', *Economy and Society*, 4(3), pp. 309–58.

Williamson, O. E. (1975) *Markets and Hierarchies: Analysis and Anti-Trust Implications: A Study in the Economics of Internal Organization* (New York: Free Press).

Williamson, O. E. (1979) 'Transactions-Cost Economics: The Governance of Contractual Relations', *Journal of Law and Economics*, 22, pp. 233–61.

Williamson, O. E. (1980) 'The Organization of Work: A Comparative Institutional Assessment', *Journal of Economic Behavior and Organization*, 1(1), pp. 5–38. Reprinted in Putterman (1986).

Williamson, O. E. (1981) 'The Modern Corporation: Origins, Evolution, Attributes', *Journal of Economic Literature*, 19, pp. 1537–68.

Williamson, O. E. (1983) 'Credible Commitments: Using Hostages to Support Exchange', *American Economic Review*, 73(4), pp. 519–40.

Williamson, O. E. (1984) 'Credible Commitments: Further Remarks', *American Economic Review*, 74(3), pp. 488–90.

Williamson, O. E. (1985) *The Economic Institutions of Capitalism: Firms, Markets, Relational Contracting* (London: Macmillan).

Williamson, O. E. (1986a) 'The Economics of Governance', in Langlois (1986, pp. 171–202).

Williamson, O. E. (1986b) *Economic Organisation: Firms, Markets and Policy Control* (Brighton: Wheatsheaf).

Williamson, O. E., Wachter, M. L. and Harris, J. E. (1975) 'Understanding the Employment Relation: the Analysis of Idiosyncratic Exchange', *Bell Journal of Economics*, 6(1), pp. 250–77. Reprinted in Putterman (1986).

Wilson, B. R. (ed.) (1970) *Rationality* (Oxford: Basil Blackwell).

Wilson, R. (1975) 'Informational Economies of Scale', *Bell Journal of Economics*, 6, pp. 184–95.

Wilson, T. and Andrews, P. W. S. (eds) (1951) *Oxford Studies in the Price Mechanism* (Oxford: Clarendon Press).

Winston, G. C. (1980) 'Addiction and Backsliding: A Theory of Compulsive Consumption', *Journal of Economic Behaviour and Organization*, 1, pp. 295–324.

Winter Jr, S. G. (1964) 'Economic "Natural Selection" and the Theory of the Firm', *Yale Economic Essays*, 4(1), pp. 225–72.

Wohlstetter, R. (1962) *Pearl Harbour, Warning and Decision* (Stanford: Stanford University Press).

Wohlwill, J. (1962) 'From Perception to Inference: A Dimension of Cognitive Development', *Society for Research in Child Development Monograph*, 27(2), pp. 87–107.

Wolff, K. H. (ed.) (1960) *Essays on Sociology and Philosophy* (New York: Harper and Row).

Wong, S. (1978) *The Foundations of Paul Samuelson's Revealed Preference Theory: A Study by the Method of Rational Reconstruction* (London: Routledge and Kegan Paul).

Wright, E. O. (1983) 'Giddens' Critique of Marxism', *New Left Review*, no. 138, pp. 11–35.

# Index of Names

Ackoff, Russell L., 11, 306
Adler, Patricia, 297, 306
Adler, Peter, 297, 306
Agassi, Joseph, 61, 62, 306
Aglietta, Michel, 306
Akerlof, George A., 96, 165, 295, 306
Alchian, Armen A., 76–7, 141, 151, 196–9, 204, 291, 306
Aldrich, J., 307
Allison, Graham T., 59, 286, 307
Althusser, Louis, 277, 292, 307
Amsden, Alice H., 307, 323
Anacharsis of Scythia, 172
Anderson, John R., 287, 307
Andrews, Philip W. S., 288–9, 307, 320, 345
Angyal, Andras, 69, 283, 307
Anshoff, H. I., 307
Aoki, Masahiko, 307
Ardzrooni, Leon, 344
Arrow, Kenneth J., 46, 70, 80, 81, 85–6, 163, 166, 190, 200, 283, 284, 285, 296, 297, 307
Artis, Michael J., 307, 317
Asch, Solomon E., 53, 122, 283, 307
Ashby, W. Ross, 168, 257–8, 261, 262, 276, 307
Aspromourgos, Anthony, 275, 307
Auerbach, Paul, 307
Axelrod, Robert, 77, 285, 286, 298, 308, 313
Ayres, Clarence E., 308
Azariadis, Costas, 292, 308

Bacon, Nathaniel, 313
Bailey, Richard E., xxi
Baily, Martin N., 292, 308
Baker, Wayne E., 185, 297, 308

Balibar, Etienne, 277, 307
Balzer, W., 334, 341
Barber, Bernard, 308
Barnes, Barry, 308
Barry, Brian M., 92, 308
Battalio, Raymond C., 113, 324
Baumol, William J., 308
Bausor, Randall, 233, 308
Beam, Robert D., 308
Bear, D. V. T., 34, 308
Becker, Gary S., 14, 15–16, 54, 96, 101–2, 111, 117–18, 175, 212, 308, 341
Beer, Stafford, 224, 257, 262, 308, 316
Begg, David K. H., 231, 232, 308
Behrens III, William W., 276, 331
Bell, Daniel, 308, 320, 325
Belshaw, C. S., 308
Benello, C. George, 308, 331
Benn, Stanley I., 92, 284, 309, 342
Bentham, Jeremy, 55, 196, 219, 247, 276, 309, 332
Berger, Peter L., 288, 309
Bermant, Gordon, 315
Bertalanffy, Ludwig von, 18, 309
Best, Michael H., 270, 271, 309
Bharadwaj, Krishna, 284, 309
Bhaskar, Roy, 277, 309
Blau, Peter M., 149, 309
Blauberg, Igor, 309
Blaug, Mark, 38, 43, 53, 281, 309
Block, Frederick L., 309
Blumberg, Paul, 265, 309
Boehm, Stephan, 121, 309
Bohm, David, 169, 309
Boland, Lawrence A., 33, 38, 62, 87–9, 134, 276, 277, 278, 279, 283, 285, 290, 304, 309–10

Boltho, Andrea, 235, 310
Bongiorno, A., 334
Bosanquet, Nicholas, 286, 310
Bottomore, Thomas, 340
Boulding, Kenneth E., 20–1, 79, 81, 86, 276, 280, 294–5, 310
Bowles, Samuel, 211, 273, 275, 276, 295, 299, 310
Boyne, Roy, xxi
Bradley, Ian, 310, 325
Brainard, William, xiii, xiv, 310
Brodbeck, May, 281, 307, 310
Bromley, D. W., 310
Brothwell, John F., 310
Brown, Peter G., 315
Brown-Collier, E. K., 310
Bruner, Jerome S., 119, 310
Brunner, Karl, 291, 310
Brus, Wlodzimierz, 302–3, 310
Buchanan, James M., 20, 91–2, 112, 276, 302, 310–11, 326
Buchler, J., 335
Buckley, Walter, 311
Buiter, Willem H., 232, 311
Burkhardt, R. J., 278, 311
Burman, Patrick, 71, 311
Burnett, Sarah A., 285, 323
Burton, John, 302, 311
Butler, R. J., 311
Buyze, J., 324

Caldwell, Bruce J., 33, 43, 44, 45, 71–2, 88, 276, 279, 285, 309, 311, 313, 328, 329, 331, 332, 342
Cannan, Edwin, 341
Canterbery, E. R., 278, 311
Capek, Milic, 169, 280, 311
Capra, Fritjof, 19, 169, 280, 311
Carabelli, Anna, 301–2, 311
Carling Alan, 311
Carnap, Rudolf, 40
Carroll, Lewis, 300
Carter, Sir Charles, 271, 311
Carvalho, Fernando, 237–8, 311
Casson, Mark C., xxi, 312
Chaffee, Steven H., 120, 288, 331
Chalmers, Alan F., 277, 312
Champernowne, David G., 217, 312
Chandler Jr., Alfred D., 262, 312
Chase, William G., 285, 312
Chasse, John D., 285, 312
Cheung, Steven N. S., 312

Chipman, John S., 75–6, 312, 341
Chomsky, Noam, 287–8, 312
Churchman, C. West, 312
Clark, L. H., 312, 317, 324
Clower, Robert W., 297, 312
Coase, Ronald H., 151, 179–81, 199–202, 205–10, 291, 292, 299, 301, 312
Coates, David, 312, 335
Coats, Alfred W., 280, 311, 313
Coddington, Alan, 33, 276–7, 302, 313
Coe, Richard D., 313, 338
Cohen, Gerald A., 313
Cohen, Michael D., 313
Cohn, M. D., 313
Collard, David, 284, 313
Collins, Hugh, 155, 313
Commons, John R., 20, 57, 148, 313, 334
Conlisk, John, 313
Constantine, George, 284, 339
Copernicus, Nicolas, 70, 90, 280
Copi, Irving M., 313
Corry, Bernard, 329, 335
Coser, Lewis, 315
Cournot, Antoine Augustin, 173, 313
Cowling, Keith, 271, 313
Crosland, C. Anthony R., 258–9, 261, 313
Cross, Rodney, 40, 278, 313
Crowder, R. G., 287, 313
Crusoe, Robinson, 148
Cunnison, I., 331
Cyert, Richard M., 79–80, 92–3, 313

Daems, Herman, 312
Dahlman, Carl J., 200–1, 203, 313
Darwin, Charles, 70, 141, 143, 289, 323
Davidson, Donald, 111, 314
Davidson, Paul, xix, 218, 233, 297, 314
Day, Richard H., 313, 314
De Alessi, Louis, 291, 314
De Groot, Morris H., 313
Debreu, Gerard, 81, 190, 283, 297, 314
Deci, E. L., 265, 344
Demsetz, Harold, 151–2, 196–9, 204, 291, 306, 314
Denison, Edward F., xiv
Desai, Meghnad, v. xxi, 314
Descartes, René, 168–9
Dickens, William T., 96, 306
Dietrich, Michael D., 263, 314
Dillard, Dudley, 314
Dingwall, R., 331
Dixon, Robert, 314

Doeringer, Peter B., 175–6, 295, 314
Dolan, Edwin G., 314, 325
Dopfer, Kurt, 276, 314, 333
Dore, Ronald, 209–10, 271–2, 314
Dorfman, J., 332
Douglas, Mary, 123, 285–6, 288, 314
Dow, Alexander, 297, 314
Dow, Sheila C., xxi, 284, 297, 314
Downs, Anthony, 15, 91–2, 111, 314
Doyal, Len, 246, 249–51, 314–15
Dudycha, Linda W., 285, 315
Duesenberry, James S., 129, 315
Dugger, William M., 293, 315
Duhem, Pierre, 40, 88–9, 278, 313
Dunlop, John T., 164, 315
Durkheim, Emile, 25, 157–60, 169, 294, 315, 335
Dworkin, Gerald, 315
Dyer, Alan W., 289, 315

Earl, Peter E., xxi, 75, 238, 284–5, 287, 298, 315
Eatwell, John, 297, 315
Ebenfield, Helene, 324, 327
Edwards, Daniel, xxi
Edwards, Ward, 285, 315
Eichner, Alfred, S., 27, 288–9, 311, 315
Einstein, Albert, 38, 90, 221, 278, 323
Eiser, J. Richard, 283, 315
Ekins, Paul, 276, 303, 315
Elbaum, Bernard, 272, 315–6
Eliot, George, 304, 316
Elliot, John E., 296, 316
Elster, Jon, 95, 282, 283, 286, 316, 339
Ely, Richard T., 293, 316
Emery, Fred E., 11, 69, 257, 306, 316, 340
Emmet, D., 316, 329
Engels, Frederick, 256, 291, 330–1
Espejo, Raul, 257, 303–4, 316
Espinosa, Juan G., 265, 266, 316
Estrin, Saul, 271, 316, 332
Evans, Peter B., 292, 316
Eysenck, Hans, 277

Fabian, Robert G., 316
Fama, Eugene F., 299, 316
Farmer, Mary K., 316
Fazzari, Steven M., 316
Feibelman, James K., 277, 316
Feigenbaum, Edward A., 316
Feiwel, George R., 316
Feldman, Julian, 84, 285, 316

Ferber, Robert, 129, 317
Festinger, Leon, 96, 317
Feyerabend, Paul K., 277, 280–1, 317
Findlay III, M. Chapman, 158, 344, 345
Fischer, Stanley, 200, 317
Fischhoff, Baruch, 340
Fishburn, Peter S., 284, 287, 317
Fisher, Irving, 319
FitzRoy, Felix R., 265, 317
Flanagan, Robert J., 292, 317
Flemming, John S., 317
Forbes, Ian, 317, 332
Foucault, Michel, 317
Fowkes, Benjamin, 330
Fox, Alan, 164–5, 169–70, 296, 317
Francis, Arthur, 311, 317
Frankel, S. Herbert, 166, 296, 317
Frantz, Roger S., 317
Freeman, Christopher, 213, 317
Freeman, Richard B., 317
Freud, Sigmund, 38, 106–7, 109, 110, 317
Frey, Bruno S., 186, 317
Friedman, Benjamin, 317
Friedman, Milton, xvi, 28–35, 38, 42, 44, 46, 48–50, 76–7, 88, 98–9, 260, 276–7, 291, 295, 309, 311, 313, 317, 344
Frisby, D., 340
Fritz, Judy M., 288, 318
Fritz, Richard G., 288, 318
Fuchs, V. R., 312, 318
Furnham, Adrian, 318
Furubotn, Eirik G., 53, 151, 318
Fusfeld, Daniel R., 318

Galanter, Marc, 154, 318
Galbraith, John Kenneth, 20, 318
Galileo (Galilei), 70, 280–1
Garfinkel, Harold, 107, 318
Garner, C. Alan, 233, 318
Georgescu-Roegen, Nicholas, 20, 75, 140, 242, 284, 287, 318
Geras, Norman, 303, 318
Geschwind, N., 287, 318
Gettys, Charles F., 285, 318
Gibson, James, 287, 318
Giddens, Anthony, xxi, 9–10, 71, 110, 126, 138, 283, 284, 318, 346
Gilmore, Grant, 282, 318
Gintis, Herbert, 276, 295, 299, 318–19
Glucksberg, S., 287, 319
Gödel, Kurt, 46–7, 333
Goldberg, Victor P., 319

Goldthorpe, John H., 322
Gomes, Gustavo M., 231, 319
Gordon, David M., 273, 275, 310
Gordon, Wendell C., 319
Gorman, William M., 319
Gough, Ian, 246, 249–51, 283, 314–15, 319
Gowdy, J. M., 319
Graaff, Johannes de Van, 319
Grahl, John, 268, 319
Granbois, Donald H., 107, 129, 334
Grandy, Richard, 277, 319
Granovetter, Mark, 319
Green, Francis, xxi, 30–1, 275, 319, 342
Green, H. A. John, 284, 319
Green, L., 113, 324
Greenlee, Douglas, 289, 319
Grether, David M., 319–20
Grinder W. E. 326
Groot, Adriaan D. de, 285, 320
Grossman, S. J., 320
Groves, Theodore, 313, 314
Gruchy, Allan G., 271, 320

Habermas, Jurgen, 320
Hagstrom, W. O., 160–1, 320
Hahn, Frank H., 296, 297, 307, 320, 339, 340
Hall, Robert, xvii
Hall, Robert L., 288–9, 320
Halls, W. D., 315
Haltiwanger, John, 236, 320
Hammond, P. J., 320
Handa, Jagdish, 320
Hanson, Norwood R., 277, 320
Harcourt, Geoffrey C., xxi, 275, 297, 320, 328
Hare, Paul, 271, 320
Hargreaves Heap, Shaun P., 320
Harris, Jeffrey E., 199, 345
Harris, Marvin, 320
Harrison, Robert S., 345
Harrison, Ross, 284, 321
Harrod, Sir Roy F., 316
Harsanyi, John C., 321
Harth, P., 330
Hasenkamp, G., 284, 326
Havighurst, Harold C., 321
Hawtrey, Ralph G., 321
Hayek, Friedrich A., 3, 14, 60–1, 63, 66–9, 78, 87, 113–15, 121, 137–8, 238, 245–6, 260, 276, 278, 286–7, 295–6, 302, 303, 321, 342

Heathfield, David, 307, 321, 335
Hegel, Georg W. F., 169, 283, 321
Heiner, Ronald A., 4, 82, 109, 287, 289–90, 321, 324
Heisenberg, Werner, 43, 280, 344
Hempel, Carl, 34
Henderson, A. M., 344
Hey, John D., 81, 321
Hicks, Sir John R., xv, 47, 59, 223, 321, 326
Hill, C. W. L., 322
Hillard, John, 312, 335
Hindess, Barry, xxi, 40–1, 43, 45, 98, 103, 112, 277, 284, 322
Hirsch, Frederick, 271, 322
Hirschman, Albert O., 171, 322
Hirshleifer, Jack, 276, 291, 322
Hirst, Paul Q., 61, 277, 322
Hitch, Charles J., 288–9, 320
Hobbes, Thomas, 154, 156–7, 310, 322, 329
Hogarth, Robin M., 285, 322
Holdren, Robert, 337
Hollis, Martin, 73, 94, 277, 284, 320, 322–3, 339, 340
Holmes, Peter, 271, 316
Holton, Gerald, 278, 323
Homans, George C., 165, 323
Horvat, Branko, 249, 302–3, 323
Houthakker, Hendriks S., 129, 323
Howard, Michael C., 310, 325
Howard, Nigel, 257, 303–4, 316
Howell, William C., 285, 323
Hozelitz, B. F., 331
Hughes, Alan, 271, 323
Hume, David, 42, 43
Humphries, Jane, 323
Hunt, E. K., 323, 334
Hurwicz, Leonid, 312, 341
Hutchinson, Terence W., 323

Inhelder, Barbel, 336
Isherwood, Baron, 285–6, 314

Jaffé, William, 323, 344
Jarvie, I. C., 281, 323
Jensen, Michael C., 299, 323
Jevons, William Stanley, 3, 173, 301, 323
Jones, Derek, C., 210, 323
Jones, E., 317
Jones, Lamar B., 289, 323
Jones, Stephen R. G., 288, 324

Jussawalla, Meheroo, 324, 327

Kaen, Fred R., 324
Kagel, John H., 113, 324
Kahneman, Daniel, 85, 184, 186, 284, 285, 315, 318, 324, 343
Kalecki, Michal, 316, 324
Kamenka, Eugene, 292, 324
Kamin, Leon J., 277, 337
Kanel, Donald, 324
Kant, Immanuel, 87, 324
Kapteyn, A., 324
Katona, George, 125, 129, 288, 324, 342
Katouzian, Homa, 324
Kay, Neil M., xv, 70, 204, 213, 214, 262, 263, 264, 276, 287, 298, 300, 301, 315, 324
Keegan, John, 136, 324
Kelly III, Clinton, 285, 318
Kelvin, Lord William T., 42, 279
Keynes, John Maynard, xvii, xix, 24, 78, 87, 89, 128–9, 140, 188, 190–1, 205–6, 208, 217–41, 297, 300, 301–2, 310, 311, 313, 314, 316, 318, 321, 322, 324–5, 327, 328, 332, 335, 337, 338, 339, 341, 342
Keynes, John Neville, 29, 325
Kilpatrick, Andrew, 224, 325
Kindleberger, Charles P., 268, 325, 332
King, John E., 277, 325
Kirzner, Israel M., 53, 59, 121, 309, 311, 325, 327, 343
Kitromilides, J., 340
Klamer, Arjo, 325
Klant, Johannes J., 325
Klein, Burton H., 325
Kleinmuntz, Benjamin, 315, 325
Knetsch, Jack, 186, 324, 325
Knight, Frank, H., xvii, 20, 66, 125, 132, 188, 191, 204, 279, 301, 310, 325–6
Koestler, Arthur, 69–70, 90, 109–10, 128, 281, 287, 326, 336
Koo, A. Y. C. 284, 326
Koopmans, Tjalling C., 291, 326
Kornai, Janos 80, 132, 134, 271, 276, 302–3, 326
Kraft, Kornelius, 265, 317
Kregel, Jan A., 4, 190, 218, 326
Krelle, W., 326
Kreps, David M., 298, 326
Krimerman, Leonard I., 281, 326
Kristol, Irving, 308, 320, 325

Kuhn, Thomas, 37, 48, 87, 277, 326
Kunreuther, Howard C., 85, 326
Kuznets, Simon, 273, 326

Laband, David N., 292, 326
Lachmann, Ludwig M., 63, 67, 309, 326
Laffargue, J. P., 325, 332
Lakatos, Imre, 43, 73, 87, 89, 277, 278–9, 280, 313, 327
Lamarck, Jean-Baptiste, 143
Lamberton, Donald M., 307, 314, 327, 341
Lange, Oskar, 245, 327
Langlois, Richard N., 17, 69, 136, 203–5, 214, 276, 290, 291, 301, 321, 327, 328, 338, 345
Latsis, Spiro, J., 276, 313, 327, 340
Laudan, Larry, 48, 280, 327
Lavoie, Donald, 260–1, 286–7, 302–3, 305, 327
Lawson, Antony, xxi, xxii, 4, 139, 205–6, 224, 231, 240, 284, 311, 314, 322, 325, 327
Lazonick, William, 134, 272, 315–16, 327–8
Lee, Frederick S., 288–9, 328
Leibenstein, Harvey, 79, 291, 328
Leijonhufvud, Axel, 213–14, 221, 232, 328
Lekachman, Robert, 312, 328, 342
Lenin, Vladimir Ilich, 307, 336
Leontief, Wassily W., xv
Lerner, Max, 343
Lewis, Alan, 318
Lewis, D., 328
Lewontin, R. C., 277, 337
Lichtenstein, Sarah, 84–5, 284, 285, 328, 340–1
Lilienfeld, Robert, 18, 328
Lipsey, Richard G., 173, 328
Little, Ian M. D., 75, 328
Littlechild, Stephen C., 53, 267, 328
Livingston, A., 334
Llewellyn, Karl N., 293, 328
Lloyd, Barbara B., 119, 328
Lloyd, Dennis, 328
Loasby, Brian J., 4, 10, 204, 218, 238, 284, 300–1, 328–9
Locke, John, 330
Locksley, Gareth, 339, 340
Lofthouse, Stephen, 329
Lovell, Michael C., 129, 329
Lowe, Adolph, 276, 329
Lowry, S. Todd, 174, 296–7, 329

Lucas Jr., Robert E., 16, 46, 231–2, 235–6, 329

Luckmann, Thomas, 288, 309

Luhmann, Niklas, 116, 166, 329

Lukes, Steven, 56, 62, 72, 284, 323, 329

Lutz, Mark A., 93–4, 247, 249, 329

Lux, Kenneth, 93–4, 247, 249, 329

Macaulay, Stewart, 165, 329

Macfie, A. L., 341

Machlup, Fritz, 28, 30, 88, 163, 281, 308, 311, 327, 329

MacIntyre, Alasdair, 316, 329

MacKay, Donald M., 329

Macneil, Ian R., 329–30

Macpherson, C. B., 292, 330

Maital, Shlomo, 330

Majumdar, Tapas, 284, 330

Malcomson, James M., 330

Mandeville, Bernard, 155, 330

Mansfield, Una, 308, 311, 327, 329

March, James G., 79–80, 92–3, 313

Marglin, Stephen A., 214–15, 330

Margolis, Howard, 284, 330

Marr, William L., 330, 345

Marris, Robin, 330

Marschak, Jacob, 81, 330

Marsden, David, 164, 175–6, 296–7, 330

Marshall, Alfred, 3, 46, 172–3, 208, 222, 224, 241, 247, 284, 285–6, 301, 312, 330

Marx, Karl, xvii, 19–20, 24, 38, 57, 89, 140, 148, 164, 167, 169–71, 186–7, 195–6, 198, 221, 232, 242, 256, 282, 283, 291, 293, 294, 295, 296, 297, 303, 313, 316, 318, 322, 323, 330–1, 335, 336, 337, 338, 342, 343

Maslow, Abraham, 246, 248–51, 331

Matthews, Robin C. O., 203, 331

Mauss, Marcel, 165, 331

May, K. O., 284, 331

Mayhew, A., 331

McCloskey, Donald N., 42, 276, 279–80, 331

McCloskey, M., 287, 319

McEwan, John D., 257, 263, 331

McFarland, Floyd B., 331

McGuinness, Anthony, 331

McLeod, Jack M., 120, 288, 331

McNally, Mary, 276, 331

Meade, James E., 190, 283, 331

Meadows, Dennis L., 276, 331

Meadows, Donella H. 276, 331

Meckling, William H., 299, 323

Medoff, James L., 317

Mendel, Gregor, 142–3

Menger, Carl, 3, 247, 286–7, 321, 323, 331

Mepham, John, 309, 331

Merriam, Thornton W., 132, 188, 326

Merton, Robert K., 331

Metcalfe, J. Stanley, 235, 331, 335

Metzler, Lloyd A., xv

Michelson, Albert A., 278, 323

Middleton, E., 331

Milgram, Stanley, 122–3, 135, 283, 331

Milgrom, Paul, 298, 326

Mill, John Stuart, 14–15, 55–6, 88, 247, 331–2

Miller, A. V., 321

Miller, D. C., 278

Miller, David, 332

Miller, James G., 287, 332

Miller, Marcus H., 307, 317

Mini, Piero V., 276, 332

Minkowski, Hermann, xv

Minsky, Hyman P., 218, 268, 297, 332

Mises, Ludwig von, 3, 56–60, 62–4, 103, 112–15, 148, 173, 245, 260, 284, 286–7, 294, 332

Mitchell, Wesley C., 57, 98, 101–2, 332, 344

Moe, Terry M., 332

Moggridge, Donald E., 227, 332

Moore Jr., Barrington, 332

Morgan, J. N., 342

Morgenbesser, Sidney, 61, 332

Morgenstern, Oskar, 340

Morley, Edward W., 278

Mortimore, G. W., 284, 309, 342

Mosak, Jacob L., xv

Moss, Scott J., 134, 173–4, 213–14, 296, 332

Mueller, Eva, 129, 324

Murrell, Peter, 302–3, 332

Musgrave, Alan, 32–3, 276, 327, 332

Myrdal, Gunnar, 20, 285, 332

Nagel, Ernest, 32, 46–7, 276, 333

Naylor, James C., 285, 315

Neale, R. S., 292, 324

Neale, W. C., 333

Neisser, Ulric, 108, 119, 333

Nell, Edward J., v, 3, 73, 94, 277, 323, 333

Nelson, Richard R., 4, 78, 131, 140–3, 208, 210, 213, 215, 224, 263, 270, 288, 289, 333
Newell, Allen, 284, 333
Newman, Geoffrey, 290, 310, 333
Newman, James R., 46–7, 333
Newman, Joseph W., 129, 333
Newton, Sir Isaac, 221, 344
Nicolaus, Martin, 330
Nisbett, Richard E., 285, 333
Nock, F. J., 331
Nolan, Peter, 309, 323, 333
Nore, Petter, 319, 342
North, Douglass C., 27, 333–4
Nove, Alexander, 271, 276, 302–3, 326, 334
Nozick, Robert, 64, 112–13, 334
Nuti, D. Mario, 291, 297–8, 326, 334
Nutzinger, Hans G., 154, 197, 298, 301, 334

O'Driscoll, Gerald P., 334
O'Neill, J., 281, 334, 338
Oakeshott, Michael, 9–10, 126, 246, 253, 259, 286, 334
Okun, Arthur M., 176, 334
Olsen, J. P., 313
Olshansky, Richard W., 107, 129, 334
Olson Jr., Mancur, 273, 334
Orr, Daniel, 34, 308
Ouchi, William G., 334

Page, A. N., 334
Paine, Suzanne, 309, 323, 333
Panzar, J. C., 308
Pareto, Vilfredo, 57, 101–2, 334
Parker, David, 334
Parrinello, Sergio, 276, 334
Parsons, Kenneth H., 334
Parsons, Talcott, 123–4, 159, 283, 285, 335, 344
Pashukanis, Evgeny B., 335
Pasinetti, Luigi, 335
Pateman, Carole, 252, 335
Pearce, Ivor F., 14, 335
Peel, David A., 235, 331, 335
Peirce, Charles S., 289, 319, 335
Pejovich, Steven, 53, 148, 151, 318, 335
Penrose, Edith T., 288, 291, 335
Perrow, Charles, 335
Perry, George, xiii, xiv, 310

Pesaran, M. Hashem, xxii, 129, 311, 314, 322, 327, 335
Peston, Maurice, 329, 335
Peterson, Cameron R., 285, 318, 335
Peterson, Wallace C.,
Petr, Jerry L., 335
Pheby, John, xxi
Phelps, Edmund S., 307, 335
Phelps Brown, Sir E. Henry, 272, 335
Phillips, Alban William H., 47, 336
Phillips, Ronnie J., 336
Piaget, Jean, 108, 336
Pigou, Arthur C., 292
Piore, Michael J., 175–6, 295, 314, 336
Plott, Charles R., 319–20
Polan, Anthony J., 292, 336
Polanyi, Karl, xvii, 152–3, 195, 253, 333, 336, 341
Polanyi, Michael, 9–10, 126, 259, 260, 277, 278, 286, 336
Pollak, Robert A., 212, 336
Popovsky, Mark, 277, 336
Popper, Sir Karl R., 29, 34, 37–41, 43, 44, 49, 61–2, 88–9, 277, 278, 279, 280, 335, 345
Porter, L. W., 337
Pratt, John W., 336
Ptolemy, Claudius, 89–90, 280
Putterman, Louis, 305, 306, 310, 312, 316, 319, 321, 323, 328, 330, 336, 340, 345

Quine, Willard van Orman, 40, 88–9, 278, 313

Rachlin, Howard, 113, 324
Radner, Roy, 81, 330, 336
Raj, Baldev, 330, 345
Randall, Alan, 292, 336
Randers, Jorgen, 276, 331
Raphael, D. D., 341
Rapping, Leonard A., 271, 337
Rawls, John, 337
Reagan, Ronald, 305
Reisman, G., 332
Resler, Henrietta, 117, 344
Reynolds, R. Larry, 293, 337
Ricardo, David, xv, 46, 186–7, 247, 297, 303
Richardson, G. B., 188–94, 209, 268–9, 298, 329, 337
Richter, M. K., 312, 341
Riley, John G., 276, 322

Riviere, J., 317
Rizzo, Mario J., 334
Robbins, Lord Lionel, 74, 284, 335, 337
Roberts, Blaine, 337
Roberts, John, 298, 303, 326
Roberts, K., 337
Robinson, Joan, xvii, xix, 183, 188, 218, 222, 234, 275, 278, 284, 297, 320, 337, 340
Roemer, John E., 275, 282, 337
Rose, Steven, 277, 337
Rosenberg, Nathan, 273, 337
Rosenman, Robert E., 324
Rosenzweig, M. R., 337
Ross, L., 285, 333
Rothschild, Kurt W., 337
Rothschild, Michael, 336
Rotwein, Eugene, 276, 337
Roussopoulos, Dimitrios, 308, 331
Routh, Guy, 330, 338, 345
Rowse, A. L., 228–9, 338
Rowthorn, Robert E., 298, 338
Ruben, David-Hillel, 309, 331
Rudner, R. S., 121, 338
Rueschemeyer, Dietrich, 292, 316
Russell, Bertrand, 3
Russell, Thomas, 338
Rutherford, Malcolm, 234, 282, 338

Sahlins, Marshall, 292, 338
Samuels, Warren J., 296, 329, 338, 339
Samuelson, Paul A., xv, 45, 46, 48, 74–5, 234, 309, 338, 346
Sawyer, Malcolm C., xxi
Say, Jean Baptiste, 232, 341
Schefold, Bertram, 276, 338
Schelling, Thomas C., 338
Scherer, Frederic M., 184, 338
Schoemaker, Paul J., 285, 338
Schotter, Andrew, 4, 133, 135, 136, 191–4, 290, 298, 302, 338
Schumacher, E. Fritz, 21, 338
Schumpeter, Joseph A., xvii, 56, 147, 169–71, 242, 296, 313, 316, 338, 339
Schwartz, Jesse G., 323, 334
Schwier, A. S., 334
Scitovsky, Tibor, 339
Seabury, Samuel, 151, 197, 292, 339
Searle, John R., 110, 115, 339
Sebba, G., 276, 339
Seckler, David, 282, 339
Seidman, Robert R., 339

Sen, Amartya K., 284, 339
Sensat Jr., Julius, 284, 339
Shackle, George L. S., xvii, 4, 78–9, 86–7, 140, 184, 188, 193, 218, 230–1, 233, 238, 276, 282, 284, 311, 315, 339
Shackleton, John R., 339, 340
Shakespeare, William, 296
Shand, Alexander H., 339
Shefrin, H. M., 111, 126, 342
Shepherd, D., 331
Shiller, R. J., 129, 233, 340
Shone, Sir Robert M., 284, 340
Shubik, Martin, 335, 340
Silbertson, Z. Aubrey, 331, 339
Simmel, Georg, 94, 296, 340
Simon, Herbert, A., xvii, 4, 5, 9, 79–81, 84, 86, 94, 100, 102, 106, 112, 115, 149 193, 233, 284, 285, 287, 289, 290, 291, 295, 299, 312, 333, 340
Sinden, J. A., 325
Singh, Ajit, 284, 340
Singh, Harinder, xxi, 340
Skinner, Burrhus F., 312
Skocpol, Theda, 292, 316
Skott, Peter, 340
Skouras, Anthanos, 183, 340
Slovic, Paul, 84–5, 184, 284, 285, 318, 324, 328, 340–1, 343
Smelser, Neil J., 161, 335, 341
Smith, Adam, xvi, 19, 46, 186–7, 247, 297, 303, 304–5, 341
Smythies, J. R., 287, 326, 336
Sommerhoff, G., 341
Sonnenschein, H. F., 75–6, 312, 341
Sowell, Thomas, 23, 232, 341
Spencer, Herbert, 341
Spohn, W., 334, 341
Spradley, James P., 108, 288, 341
Sraffa, Piero, xix, 186–7, 275, 297, 311, 320, 341
Staelin, Richard, 129, 333
Stanfield, R., 341
Steedman, Ian, v, xxi, 123, 276, 283, 341
Stegmuller, W., 334, 341
Steinbruner, John D., 59, 98, 109, 341
Stepan, Alfred, 153, 341
Stephen, Frank, H., 210, 319, 330, 341
Stewart, Ian M. T., 341
Stigler, George J., 54, 201–2, 341
Stiglitz, Joseph E., 292, 308, 320
Stohs, Mark, 219, 341–2
Streissler, Erich, 311, 326, 342

Strumpel, B., 342
Sugden, Robert, 4, 135–8, 342
Sutcliffe, Robert, 301, 342
Svejnar, Jan, 210, 323
Sweezy, Paul M., 291, 302
Sylos-Labini, Paulo, 288–9, 342

Tarascio, Vincent J., 342
Taylor, Frederick M., 245, 327
Taylor, Lester D., 129, 323
Tedeschi, James T., 331, 342
Thaler, R. H., 111, 126, 186, 324, 338, 342
Thatcher, Margaret H., 58, 253
Thoben, H., 276, 280, 342
Thompson, Grahame, 224, 225, 342
Thurow, Lester C., 342
Tinbergen, Jan, 257–8, 342
Tisdall, C. A., 80, 342
Titmuss, Richard M., 161–2, 169, 342
Tobin, James, 232, 342
Tomlinson, James, xxi, 203, 298–9, 342
Tool, Marc R., 342–3
Toulmin, Stephen, 277, 343
Trakhtenbrot, B. A., 82, 343
Troub, Roger M., 276, 343
Tuchman, Barbara W., 286, 343
Tucker, D. F. B., 282, 343
Tugwell, Rexford G., 325, 332, 343
Tullock, Gordon, 91–2, 311
Turk, Jeremy, 311, 317, 331, 339
Tversky, Amos, 75, 184, 284, 285, 287, 318, 324, 343
Twain, Mark, 4

Ullman-Margalit, Edna, 135–6, 214, 343

Van Parijs, Philippe, 343
Vanek, Jaroslav, 343
Vaughn, Karen I., 113, 302–3, 343
Veblen, Thorstein B., xvii, 9–10, 20, 22–3, 24, 57, 74, 101–2, 125, 131, 139–40, 208, 215, 242, 282, 289, 313, 328, 331, 338, 339, 341, 343–4
Vickers, Douglas, 344
Vint, John, 329
Vroom, Victor H., 265, 344

Wachter, Michael L. 199, 345
Wagner, Richard E., 302, 311
Waldman, Michael, 236, 320
Walker, Arthur, xxi

Wallsten, Thomas S., 344
Walras, Leon, 3, 46, 57, 176, 182, 310, 323, 344
Walsh, Vivian C., 284, 344
Wansbeck, T., 324
Ward, Benjamin, 344
Weber, Max, 122, 344
Weber, W., 321, 326
Wegener, Alfred, 90–1
Weintraub, E. Roy, 18, 344
Weisskopf, Thomas E., 273, 275, 310
Weisskopf, Walter, A., 276, 280, 344
Westergaard, John, 117, 344
White, Harrison C., 344
Wible, James R., 232, 344
Wicksteed, Philip H., 284, 344
Wilber, Charles K., 313, 338, 344–5
Wiles, Peter, 330, 345
Willer, David, 277, 345
Willer, Judith, 277, 345
Williams B., 339, 344, 345
Williams, Edward E., 158
Williams, Karel, 279, 345
Williamson, Oliver E., 4, 5, 23, 154–8, 180, 199–216, 291, 293–4, 299–300, 301, 315, 322, 345
Willig, R. D., 308
Willman, Paul, 311, 317
Wilson, Bryan R., 284, 345
Wilson, E. O., 277
Wilson, Robert, 202, 298, 326, 345
Wilson, T. D., 320, 345
Winston, Gordon C., 111, 126, 345
Winter Jr., Sidney G., 4, 77–8, 99, 131, 140–3, 208, 213, 215, 288, 289, 333, 346
Wise, David A., 336
Wisman, J., 345
Wohlstetter, Roberta, 285, 346
Wohlwill, Joachim, 114, 346
Wolff, Kurt H., 346
Wong, Stanley, 45, 284, 346
Woolley, Penny, 61, 277, 322
Wright, Erik O., 346
Wright, Grahame, xxi

Yellen, Janet L., 306

Zahn, E., 342
Zeckhauser, Richard J., 336
Zimbalist, Andrew S., 265, 266, 316

# Index of Subjects

academics, xvi, 160–1, 265, 273–4
action, as 'exchange', 148
  indeterminacy of, 11–12, 17, 63–4, 66, 68, 225–6, 258, 264–7, 304–5
  and institutions, xvi, 117–44, 177–9, 182–4, 188–94, 205–8, 223–5, 238–41, 244, 267, 270, 284, 285, 290, 319, 336, 342
  purposeful, 10–12, 53–4, 56–66, 71, 99–100, 110, 112–14, 115, 117, 125, 139, 150–1
  rationalist conception of, 25, 98–116, 217, 226–9, 232, 286, 301, 322, 334
  and uncertainty, 78–9, 85, 132–3, 144, 158
  unintended consequences of purposeful, 144, 291
altruism, 77, 138, 155, 162, 205, 284, 313, 330, 335
anthropology, xvii, 8, 118, 165, 247, 285–6, 295, 314
  and economics, 28, 122–3
Antiquity, Classical, 254–6
Asch experiments, 122
Ashby's law, 257–8, 261, 262
assumptions, realism of, 22–3, 24, 28–30, 39, 49, 332, 333
Austrian economics, 3, 4, 7–8, 11–13, 25, 26, 45, 56, 59–69, 78–80, 93, 100, 103, 106, 112–15, 118, 120, 121, 125, 133–4, 137–8, 148, 173, 217, 218, 236–9, 242, 245–7, 259–62, 267–8, 275, 276, 282, 283, 286–7, 291, 294, 302–3, 314, 321, 325, 327, 334, 339, 343
  purposeful individual in, 11, 56–7, 59–64, 106, 112–15
axiomatic method, limitations of, 46–7

basic income allowance, 303
Bayesian probability, 11, 76, 84, 85, 184
behaviouralist economics, xvii, 13, 79–81, 92–3, 100, 102, 106, 112, 115, 233, 238, 287, 289, 291, 313, 315, 324, 331, 336, 340
behaviourist psychology, 287, 312, 326
biology, 49, 70, 76–8, 98–9, 125, 141–4, 214–16, 277, 284, 289, 323, 335, 337, 340, 346
blood, donation of, 161–3
  markets for, 162
Britain, xiii, xv, 24, 45, 152–3, 225, 265, 272–3, 278, 305, 312, 313, 314, 315, 316, 320, 325, 327–8, 336
  relative decline of, xiii, 272–3, 312, 315–16, 325, 335

Cambridge, 320
capital theory, controversies over, xix, 46, 275, 320
capitalism, 214, 219, 270, 292, 313, 314, 316, 317, 319, 322, 324, 328, 338, 339, 342, 344, 345
  fate of, 167–71, 295
Cartesian dualism, 103, 115–16
Cartesian modes of thought, 168–9, 286
causation, cumulative, 138–40
centralization, 237, 251, 259, 269–71, 273
chess, game of, 82–3, 87, 109, 304–5, 312, 320
Chicago, 279, 345
Chile, 316
China, 255
choice
  the human need for, 251

lexicographic, 104–5, 284–5, 318
meaning of, 10–11, 57, 99, 112–14, 115,
  149, 311, 329
preconditions of, 248–50
class, social, 59, 224, 228, 259, 282, 323
Classical School, 45, 46, 186–7, 247, 297,
  303, 310, 338
cognition
  cultural and institutional influences on,
    xvi, 7–8, 54, 118–23, 133, 178–9, 205,
    223, 225, 238, 240, 244, 271, 290, 341
  cultural specificity of, 119–20
  divergences in, 119–21, 203, 227, 229,
    235, 239, 259
  process of, 6, 22, 83, 106–10, 118–23, 285
cognitive dissonance, 96, 229, 306, 317
cognitive theory, 6, 25, 83, 95–6, 114, 116,
    118–23, 287, 288, 289, 307, 312, 315,
    318, 322, 323, 328, 333, 344, 346
  epistemological consequences of, 6–7,
    22, 36, 83, 120, 121, 227, 336
competition, 253, 297, 320, 326, 329, 336
  impossibility of perfect, 187–94, 253
composition, fallacy of, 69, 233–4
compositive method, 66–71
consciousness, levels of, 9–10, 25, 100,
    104–16, 118, 126–8, 247–8, 287
  practical, 126–7
constraints, enabling function of, 131–7
  hard and soft, 134
consumer behaviour, 74–6, 78, 128–9,
    142–3, 220, 284, 285–6, 312, 314, 315,
    317, 319, 323, 324, 328, 333, 334, 338
consumption function, 31, 129
continental drift, 90–1
contract law, 149–56, 282, 293, 313, 318,
    321, 328, 329, 330, 339
contracting, relational, 177, 182, 209–11,
    264, 271, 319
contracts, 25, 58, 147–71, 174–5, 176, 210,
    294, 316, 317, 319
  employment, 149, 164–5, 195–9, 265,
    295, 299, 306, 319, 340, 345
  imperfectly specified, 157–60, 163–4,
    198, 201–8
  implicit, 150–1, 197–9, 292, 308, 317
  impossibility of pure, 157–71, 294, 296
  and purposefulness, 58, 150–1, 168–9,
    282–3
conventions, 26, 130–44, 159–67, 174,
    188–94, 205–6, 208, 219–20, 223, 226,
    240, 297, 300, 303, 328

cooperatives, 215–16, 255
cosmology, 70, 89–90, 91, 280–1, 326
cost mark up, 186, 288–9, 328
costs, transaction, 26, 79–80, 155, 180–1,
    187, 199–208, 212–13, 293, 297, 299,
    301, 314, 315, 330, 336, 345
crises, causes of, 139–40, 143–4, 169–71,
    218–21
cumulative causation, 138–40
cybernetics, 257–8, 307, 308, 331, 341
  *see also* systems theory

decentralization, 237, 259, 269–71, 273
demand, effective, 220–1, 233–4, 236, 268,
    269
democracy, 252, 308, 310, 313, 314, 322,
    330, 338, 339
  as an end, 252
  industrial, 210, 215–16, 249, 265–7, 294,
    301, 307, 309, 316, 321, 322, 323, 335,
    341, 342, 343
  participatory, 210, 215–16, 249, 252, 307,
    308, 316, 335
determinism, 10–12, 16–17, 43, 63, 68, 115,
    139, 221, 225, 239, 276, 301, 327
dictatorship, 243–5, 251
dominance, principle of, 168–70, 256
Duhem-Quine thesis, 40–1, 88–9, 278, 313

Eastern Bloc, 255
ecology, and the economy, 16–19, 21
econometrics, 41, 121
economic man, *see* rational economic man
economic stagnation, causes of, 272–3
economics, boundaries of, 12–17, 19, 58,
    60–1, 66, 71
  end of consensus within, 120–1
economics of politics, 15, 91–2, 111
effective demand, 220–1, 233–4, 236, 268,
    269
empiricism, 22–3, 24, 27, 36, 83, 120, 121,
    203, 226–7, 229, 234–5, 277, 301–2,
    316, 319, 336, 337, 345
  critique of, 35–7, 39–43
  and empirical work, 35–6
ends
  adaptive, 93–7
  affected by means, 93–5, 243, 285–6
  and means, 93–7, 124, 252, 285
  retrospective determination of, 94–5
entrepreneurs, 212–13, 221–5, 226, 237,
    242, 249, 267–9, 312

equilibrium theorizing, xviii, 5, 17, 18, 23, 80, 134, 140, 172, 183, 242–3, 267, 304, 326, 332, 337

event-matching experiment, 84, 93, 316

evidence, its role in theoretical development, 35–6, 47–8, 89–93, 128–9
  theory-bound character of, 34–7, 40–1, 47, 89, 302

evolution
  Darwinian, 70, 77–8, 98–9, 141–4, 214–16, 289, 323, 335
  economic, 5, 17–18, 49, 76–8, 131, 138–44, 208, 214–16, 286, 289, 306, 310, 333, 341, 343
  Lamarckian, 143

exchange, 25, 26, 147–51, 206, 208, 293, 294, 309
  definition of, 148–9
  and institutions, 147–51, 253
  and markets, 173–87
  'social' and 'economic', 149, 169

expectations, xvi, 3, 7, 8, 12, 16, 76, 84–5, 96, 129, 131, 132–3, 137–40, 183–94, 205, 217–41, 301, 303, 312, 317, 318, 322, 326, 331, 335, 337
  adaptive, 231, 235–6
  divergent, 233, 226, 235–9
  endogeneity of, 217, 223–6, 230–6, 240, 241
  Keynes' view of, 217–41, 327
  in 'Keynesian' theory, 231
  long-term, 218–19, 220, 222, 230
  moulding of, 217, 223–6, 230–1, 239, 241
  rational, xvi, 3, 8, 16, 96, 129, 217, 218, 231–7, 239, 308, 314, 316, 317, 319, 320, 321, 327, 329, 335, 338, 340

expectations trap, 235–6, 310

externalities, 151–2, 313

facts, as always concept or theory-bound, 34–7, 40–1, 47–8, 89, 227, 277

fallacy of composition, 69, 233–4

falsificationism, 38–41, 278, 279, 303–4
  naive and sophisticated, 39–41, 278

family *see* marriage; household

feminism, 97, 276
  *see also* women, subjugation of

feudalism, 254, 256, 324

financial markets, 85–6, 185, 188, 219, 220, 222, 223, 270, 308, 324, 325, 332, 344

financial sector, 225, 235, 268, 273, 306, 319, 342

firms
  as 'black boxes', xiv, 337
  distinguished from markets, 195–208
  diversification within, 263
  efficiency of, 199–216, 301, 331
  existence of, 199–216, 301
  hierarchy within, 262–3, 312, 330, 345
  mergers of, 263–4, 284, 340
  as non-unitary phenomena, 59, 68, 223–6, 237
  organization of, xiv, 197–216, 224–6, 262–7, 307, 318, 324, 331, 335, 345
  participatory, 210, 215–16, 249, 265–7, 294, 301, 307, 321, 323
  research and development in, 212–13, 324
  as social systems, 68, 223–6, 262–7, 334
  theory of, 4, 26, 76–8, 99, 130–1, 142, 175–6, 179, 180–2, 187, 195–216, 223–6, 262–7, 288, 293, 299, 307, 308, 312, 313, 316, 321, 323, 324, 328–9, 335, 336, 340, 342, 346
  vertical integration of, 263, 307

formalism, xiv, xv, xix–xx, 21, 42–3, 46–7, 172, 274, 281

France, 316

freedom, 243–5, 276, 281, 317, 326
  of choice, 10–12, 17, 63–4, 99, 178–9, 196, 276
  preconditions of, 248–50

Freudianism, 38, 106–7, 109–10, 117, 228

functionalism, 123, 283, 286, 294, 316, 321
  and methodological individualism, 283

futures markets, 85, 189, 193, 212, 270, 297, 320

game theory, xix, 4, 77, 82–3, 133, 134–7, 191–4, 282, 290, 298, 307, 316, 321
  limitations of, 193, 298

general equilibrium theory, 18, 86, 89, 190, 204, 242, 283, 296, 300, 320

genes, routines as, 78, 131, 141–3, 208, 215

Germany, 283

Germany, West, xiii

gift-giving, 150, 161–7, 198–9, 294–5, 306, 307, 331, 342
  *see also* altruism

Gödel's proof, 46–7, 333

government
  distinguished from the state, 153
  intervention of, 151–3, 220–1, 232, 251–4, 339

Greece, ancient, 254–6

habits, 9–10, 25, 31, 78, 99, 101, 110–11,
    113, 116, 118, 124–44, 158, 162, 166–7,
    177, 183, 205–9, 213–14, 226, 236, 238,
    239, 240, 247, 259, 286–9, 291, 314,
    319, 336, 345
  acquisition of, 124–5, 127–8
  Austrian School's devaluation of,
    113–14, 125
  in business life, 125, 130, 288–9
  function of, 124–8, 130–3
  intellectual, 128
  neoclassical devaluation of, 125–6
health services, 160, 162
Heisenberg uncertainty principle, 43, 280,
    344
Hippocratic oath, 160
Historical School, the German, 45
holism, 17–19, 70, 286, 309
  definitions of, 17
  *see also* wholes and parts; systems theory
household, 254, 295
  economic theory of, 15–16, 68, 175, 212,
    307, 336
  as non-unitary phenomenon, 68
human nature, 61, 246, 277, 303, 318, 322,
    337
Hume's fork, 42–3
Hungary, 255

ideology, and orthodox economics, xiv, xv,
    16, 31, 97, 107, 216
impurity principle, 167–71, 254–62, 294,
    304
incomes policy, 272
incontinence, 111
indeterminacy, 11–12, 16–17, 43, 221,
    230–1, 236–8, 239, 258, 264, 267, 302,
    304–5
  of human action, 11–12, 17, 63–4, 66, 68
individual, as problematic concept, 69–71
  as a social entity, 53, 69–71, 119–23
individualism, 8, 16, 19, 59, 61, 66, 151–4,
    159, 177–9, 211, 224–5, 229, 236, 238,
    246, 251, 267, 294, 295, 295, 321, 329,
    334, 343
  institutional, 62, 306
  methodological, 25, 53–72, 135, 282,
    283, 284, 286, 291, 306, 316, 322, 326,
    329, 332, 337
  political, 53, 62, 251, 284, 330
  psychological, 62
induction, problem of, 38, 86–7, 128
industrial democracy, 210, 215–16, 249,
    265–7, 294, 301, 307, 309, 316, 321,
    322, 323, 335, 341, 342, 343
industrial policy, 271, 273, 313, 320, 323
industrial relations, 164–5, 265–6, 271–3,
    314, 315
industrial revolution, 214–15
infinite regress, problem of, 64–6, 102
inflation, 47, 235, 295, 297, 317, 320, 321,
    322, 328, 336, 338
  difficulties created by, 297
information
  cost of, 79, 163, 198, 201–8, 221, 306, 341
  decentralized and centralized, 237, 259,
    269–70, 345
  distinguished from knowledge, 6–7, 83,
    108–9
  distinguished from sense data, 6–8, 34–6,
    83, 108–9, 112, 113–14, 119–20, 202–3,
    227
  and gift-giving, 161–7
  lack of, 78–83, 111–14, 135, 201–8,
    218–20, 233, 263, 300, 329
  markets for, 163, 202
  overload, 9, 75, 79, 80–3, 87, 108–9,
    111–14, 126, 129, 131, 205, 233, 321
  problems of, xviii, 4–7, 9, 17, 75, 78–83,
    87, 108–9, 113–14, 126, 129, 131–40,
    163–4, 180–1, 198, 200–8, 244–5, 252,
    259, 298, 314, 320, 321, 322, 324, 327,
    329, 337
  significance in modern economy, 163,
    329
  supply of and demand for, 163, 202
informational reductionism, 201, 214, 287,
    297
innovation, 19–20, 23, 131–2, 212–13,
    262–74, 317, 333, 338
Institutional School, xvii, 20, 21–4, 44, 45,
    57, 98, 101, 102, 148, 289, 293, 313,
    314, 315, 319, 320, 323, 324, 328, 331,
    333, 334, 335, 338, 339, 342–3, 345
  empiricist bias in, 20, 22
  and human purposefulness, 57, 98, 101–2
  methodology of, 23
institutions
  definitions of, 10, 125
  functions of, xvi, 7–8, 26, 54, 62–6,
    116–44, 151, 158–9, 166, 174, 176,
    178–9, 184–94, 205–8, 223, 225,
    238–41, 267–72, 290, 338

information and, 124, 131–44, 182–94, 205–8, 269–70, 290, 309, 333
instrumentalism, 33–4, 276–7, 311
  and Friedman's methodology, 33–5, 276–7
  ideological, 34, 277
insufficient variety, law of, 257–8, 262–7, 303–4

Japan, xiii, 210, 225, 265, 314
Jewish people, the, 267–8

Kelvin's dictum, 42, 279
Keynesian economics, xvii, xix, 4, 13, 22–4, 27, 30, 44–8, 89, 140, 158, 188–91, 205, 217–41, 253–4, 268, 278, 284, 291, 301–2, 310, 313, 314, 318, 320, 321, 322, 324–5, 327, 328, 332, 335, 337, 338, 339, 341, 342, 344, 345
  devaluation of, xix, 217, 226, 240–1, 253–4
  formalistic versions of, xx
  imperfectionist interpretation of, 240
Keynesian policies, 217, 220–1, 233–4, 236, 268, 273
knowledge
  in future is unpredictable, 43, 212–13
  not directly given, 6–8, 34–6, 83, 108–9, 112, 113–14, 119–20, 227
  practical, 10, 126–7, 260, 288
  tacit, 6, 126, 259, 286–7, 336
  unteachable, 142, 288
Kuhnian 'normal science', 37
Kuhnian scientific revolution, 4, 326

labour
  distinguished from labour power, 164, 198, 295
  division of, 157, 173, 195, 237, 315
labour markets, xiii, 130, 164–5, 195, 233–4, 295, 296–7, 319, 330
  internal, 175–6, 314
  rigidities in, xiii, 130
labour process, xiv, 14–15, 19, 164–5, 196–9, 224, 237, 275
labour theory of value, 65–6, 283, 322
Lakatosian methodology, 74, 278–9
language, 36, 56, 119, 123, 227, 287–8, 290–1, 318
law
  contract, 149–56, 282, 293, 313, 318, 321, 328, 329, 330, 339
  and custom, 130, 149–50, 155–6, 158–60, 164, 168, 174
  employment, 164–5
  individualistic conceptions of, 151–4, 155, 293
  respect for the, 122, 136–7, 161, 288
  statutory component of, 149–50, 151–4, 253, 293, 318
legal centralism, 154–5, 293
legitimation, concept of, 122–4, 137, 156, 187, 206, 320
lexicographic model of choice, 104–5, 284–5
liberalism, 57, 156, 251, 269, 281, 292, 303, 310
  classical, xvi, 16, 21, 25, 55, 107, 127, 147, 152–9, 169, 179, 228, 243, 244, 251–2, 286–7, 290–1, 303
  *see also* New Right

macroeconomics and microeconomics, 53–4, 67–71, 233, 234, 241, 312, 320, 328, 338, 339, 344
malfeasance, 197, 211
market
  definition of the, 172–9, 296
  distinguished from firm, 195–208
  limits to growth of, 181–2
markets, 26, 162, 171, 172–94, 238, 252, 290, 297, 306, 315, 317, 322, 326, 328, 330, 332, 333, 334, 345
  assumption that they clear, 46, 182, 232
  auction, 176, 182–3
  black, 176–7
  customer, 176
  establishment of, 152–3, 173–82, 207, 253
  and exchange, 173–87, 206
  existence of, 179–82, 208–11
  extension of, xv–xvi, 53, 178, 217, 236, 240, 242, 253, 260–2, 273, 281, 287, 338, 339
  financial, 85–6, 185, 188, 219, 220, 222, 223, 270, 308, 324, 325, 332, 344
  function of rigidities in, xiii, 130, 133–44, 179, 188–94, 240
  futures, 85, 189, 193, 212, 270, 297, 320
  impossibility of pure, 167, 187–94, 240, 252–6, 259–62, 281, 294, 320
  inadequately defined by orthodoxy, 172–3, 177–9
  individualistic view of, 177–9, 182

information in, 174, 178–9, 183, 184–6
as institutions, 133, 172–94, 195, 206, 253, 296–7
internal labour, 175–6, 314
labour, xiii, 130, 164–5, 195, 233–4, 295, 296–7, 319, 330
limitations of, 5, 178, 187–94, 195–216, 219–21, 254–6, 269, 271–2
naturalistic view of, 177–9
and planning, 254–6, 259–62, 269, 271, 307
as 'state of nature', 177–9, 182, 206
stock, 185, 188, 219, 220, 222, 223
marriage, 175, 179, 198
*see also* household
Marxian economics, 4, 21, 24, 30, 44, 45, 57, 89, 164, 195–7, 221, 232, 273, 275, 283, 291, 295, 301, 310, 323, 330, 336, 337
human purposefulness in, 57
Marxism, 38, 59, 169, 170, 228, 256, 259, 282, 283, 286, 292, 294, 295, 303, 311, 316, 318, 331, 335, 338, 343, 436
formalistic developments in, xix–xx
maximization hypothesis, xviii, 5, 17, 25, 30, 48–50, 59, 73–100, 133, 142, 147, 180, 191–2, 232, 284, 289, 290, 304, 309, 310, 311
as either assumption or theory, 48–50xå
empirical critiques of, 83–93, 304
theoretical critiques of, 77–83, 86–8
maximizing behaviour, habits and, 111, 126
methodological
dogmatism, 45
nihilism, 44–5, 280–1, 317
methodological individualism, 25, 53–72, 135, 282, 283, 284, 286, 291, 306, 316, 322, 326, 329, 332, 337
definition of, 56, 282
and functionalism, 283, 286
and political individualism, 53, 62, 70–2
methodology, 24–50, 73–4, 280, 309, 310, 313, 316, 318, 322, 324, 325, 326, 327, 330
modernist, 42–3, 279
Popperian, 29, 37–42, 49, 88–9, 91, 277–8, 279
remaining scope for, 44–7, 279–80, 285
search for a prescriptive, 28, 43–4, 279
microeconomics and macroeconomics, 53–4, 67–71, 233, 234, 241, 312, 320, 328, 338, 339, 344

Milgram experiments, 122–3, 135, 283, 331
mixed economy, 245, 253, 258–61, 271, 294, 328
monetarism, 3, 40, 41, 45–6, 47–8, 89, 235, 314, 344–5
money, 195, 232, 290–1, 295–6, 312, 314, 317, 320, 328, 329, 330, 332, 340
as an end and a means, 94
hypothesis of stable demand for, 40
state monopoly of, 295–6, 321
trust or confidence in, 165–6, 295–6
natural environment, 16–19, 21, 261, 338
natural selection, 49, 76–8, 98–9, 125, 214–16, 284, 340, 346
needs, 243–52, 271, 303, 314, 315
distinguished from wants, 246–7
hierarchy of, 246–52
material, 248
physiological, 248
social, 248, 250–2, 271, 303
neoclassical economics
definition of, xviii, 275
determinism of, 17, 57, 97, 99
divisions within, 3, 46, 323
equilibrium theorizing in, xviii, 5, 17, 18, 23, 80, 134, 140, 172, 182–3, 207, 208, 242–3, 267, 276, 304, 326, 337
exogenous preferences and technology in, 13–18, 21, 54
formalism of, xiv, xv, 21, 42–3
hard core ideas of, xviii, xix, 4, 13, 73–4, 284, 339
human purposefulness in, 57, 98–102, 115
and ideology, xiv–xv, 16, 31, 97, 107, 216, 243, 332
lack of serious information problems in, xviii, 5, 201–2
market bias of, xiv, 18, 177–9, 194
methodological defence of, 24–5, 27–35, 39, 278, 279, 317
notion of exchange in, 148–9, 154
origins and use of the term, 275, 307
realism of, 22–3, 27–35, 285
scientific credentials of, 27–8
Sraffian criticisms of, xix, 275
its view of institutions, 134, 177–9, 192
view of market in, 26, 133–4, 172–3, 176–9, 182–94
New Right, xv–xvi, 57, 169–70, 192, 228, 244–6, 251, 259–62, 284, 305, 333

*see also* liberalism
norms
  behavioural, 130–44, 303
  emergence of, 134–8, 343
  function of, 26, 132–44, 159–67, 182–7, 190–1, 206–7
  price, 172, 174, 182–7, 190, 191, 206–7, 208, 297
Nuremburg, 283

open systems, theory of, 18
opportunism, 155, 205, 210–12, 299
order
  problem of, 157, 237–8
  spontaneous, 137–8, 238
ownership
  common, xiv, 215–16, 252, 254, 255, 268, 310, 311, 334
  private, xiv, xv, xvi, 242, 243, 254, 255, 268, 334

participatory democracy, 210, 215–16, 249, 252, 265–7, 294, 301, 307, 308, 316, 322, 323, 335
  as an end, 252
patents, 163
Pearl Harbour, 285, 346
perception, *see* cognition
Peru, 341
Phillips Curve, 47
physics, 19, 38, 43, 70, 89–90, 91, 169, 187, 221, 278, 280–1, 311, 323, 326, 339, 344
plannability, 271
planning, 251–2, 255, 260, 268–73, 302–3, 309, 313, 316, 320, 321, 327, 336, 343
  combination of markets with, 254–6, 260–2, 269, 271, 273
  indicative, 271, 273, 316, 320, 331
  versus market allocation, xiv, 113–14, 168, 243, 245, 252–3, 259–62, 302–3, 307
pluralism
  economic, 254–62, 271, 273, 294
  political, 271
political science, xvii, 102
  and economics, 28
politics, economics of, 15, 91–2, 111
pollution, 151–2
Popperian methodology, 29, 37–42, 49, 88–9, 91, 277–8, 279, 303–4, 345
  critique of, 39–42, 88–9, 91

residual empiricism in, 40–1
positivism, 29, 127, 203, 277, 279, 311, 317
  critique of, 35–43
Post-Keynesian economics, xvii, xix, 22, 23–4, 27, 158, 190–1, 218, 239–41, 278, 284, 320
  *see also* Keynesian economics
poverty, xv, 248–9, 274
power, 118, 122–4, 196, 198, 213–16, 229, 248, 266, 309, 317, 329, 330, 332, 337, 338
practical knowledge or consciousness, 10, 126–7
prediction
  economics and, 12, 43, 48–9, 237–8
  as goal of science, 34, 42–3
  as a methodological criterion, 29–35
  and self-fulfilling prophecy, 43
preference, theory of revealed, 45, 74–6, 284, 326, 346
preference reversals, 84–5, 319–20, 328, 341
preferences
  adaptive, 95–7, 133, 334, 335
  assumption of exogenous, 13–16, 46, 62–3, 97, 117, 135, 138, 211, 242, 244, 265, 286, 341
  counter-adaptive, 95
  endogeneity of, 13–21, 25, 26, 54, 62–6, 97, 135–8, 211, 243–5, 265, 284, 285, 319, 320, 334, 341
  intransitive, 75–6, 84–5, 312, 331, 341, 343
  moulding of, 54–5, 61–6, 93–7, 124, 133–9, 178–9
price norms, 172, 174, 182–7, 190, 191, 206–7, 208, 297
  moral dimension of, 186
prices, 176, 180, 182–7, 190, 192, 197, 199–200, 206, 207, 234, 297, 317, 320, 334, 336, 345
  of production, 186
prisoner's dilemma, 77, 298, 308, 326, 328
privatization, xiv, 242
  *see also* ownership
production
  as 'exchange with nature', 148–9
  relations of, 15, 224, 299, 314, 319, 340
  as social process, 14–15, 213–14, 224
production function, xix, 30, 323
productivity, variable character of, 15, 322
productivity growth,

determinants of, xiii–xiv, 210, 224, 265, 273, 333

failure of orthodox theory to explain, xiii–xiv, 15

property, 147, 151–4, 168, 292, 293, 316, 336, 337

individualistic conceptions of, 151–4, 253

property rights, 25, 148–54, 174, 314, 318, 328, 331, 334

Property Rights School, 23, 53, 148, 151–4, 157, 159, 298, 335

prophecy, self-fulfilling, 43

prostitution, 175, 251

psychologism, 61–2, 217, 222–5, 228, 238, 239, 249, 250, 332

psychology, xvii, xx, 8, 14, 25, 60–2, 101, 102, 105–10, 118, 246, 248–51, 317, 321, 324, 337

behaviourist, 287, 312

cognitive, 6, 25, 106–10, 114, 118–20, 307, 312, 315, 318, 333, 343

and economics, xx, 14, 28, 60–2, 96, 114–16, 123, 222–3, 249, 307, 313, 324

experimental evidence from, 83–7, 122, 135

social, 121–3, 135, 223, 307, 318

public choice, economics of, 15, 91–2, 111

public expenditure, 253–4, 268

cuts in, xv, 233, 235

purposefulness, 10–12, 53–4, 56–66, 71, 112–15, 117, 125, 129, 139, 150–1, 267, 282–3, 291, 306, 339

causality and, 59–60

and collectives, 58–9

and contract law, 58, 149–51, 157–60

psychological explanations of, 60–2

rational calculation, limits of, 9–10, 75, 78–83, 87, 98–116, 118–19, 126, 129, 135, 158–9, 161, 167, 188, 190, 193, 202–3, 206, 207, 211–12, 219–20, 224, 225, 259, 262, 300, 332

rational economic man, 24–5, 73–116, 123–4, 133, 147, 155–6, 161, 180, 192, 249, 284, 286, 288, 293–4, 300, 316, 323, 328, 329, 330

rational expectations hypothesis, xvi, 3, 8, 16, 96, 129, 217, 218, 231–7, 239, 308, 314, 316, 317, 319, 320, 321, 327, 329, 335, 338, 340

and academic promotion, xvi

rationalism, philosophical, 226, 301

rationalist conception of action, 25, 98–116, 217, 226–9, 232, 286, 301, 322, 334

defined, 98

rationality, xx, 5, 9, 17, 73–116, 246, 259, 270, 275, 303, 309, 314, 316, 321, 323, 327, 330, 338, 340, 342, 345

bounded, 9, 79–83, 100, 106, 109, 112, 190, 193, 211–12, 289, 300

neoclassical view of, xvii, xviii, 48–116

realist philosophy, 37, 277, 309

relational contracting, 177, 182, 209–11, 264, 271, 319

relativity, theory of, 38, 278, 323

Renaissance, the 267–8

requisite variety, law of, 168, 257–8, 276, 316

research and development, 212–13, 270–1, 307, 324

revealed preference theory, 45, 74–6, 284, 326, 346

Roman Empire, 254–6

routines, as genes, 78, 131, 141–3, 208, 215

*see also* habits

routinization, 10, 25, 78, 80, 116, 117–18, 124–44, 239, 259, 262–3, 288, 289

*see also* habits

Rubic's Cube, 82–3, 87, 109, 289

satisficing, 79–80, 92–3, 324, 336

as cost-minimizing behaviour, 79–80

*see also* rationality, bounded; behaviouralist economics

saving, paradox of, 233

Say's law, 232, 341

science, 34, 36, 38, 160–1, 280–1, 296, 311, 312, 315, 321, 336

and modern culture, 122

neoclassical economics as a, 27

Popperian definition of, 38–9

positive and normative, 29, 42–3

as a social activity, 36, 48

scientists, 160–1

Scottish Enlightenment, 267–8

self-interest, 77, 138, 155, 156–7, 168, 170, 180, 205, 210–11, 228–30, 284, 286, 294, 299–300, 330

and social cohesion, 156–7

as socially-formed phenomenon, 124

skills, 6, 127–8, 130–1, 142–4, 208, 262–6, 288, 296–7

transferable, 264–6

slavery, 151, 254–6, 276, 292, 297
social psychology, 121–3, 135, 223, 307, 318
social sciences, compartmentalization of, xvii, 154, 169, 308
socialism, 259, 294, 313, 314, 317, 326, 327, 332, 333, 334, 338, 339, 343
society, cohesion of, 156–7
sociobiology, 277
sociology, xvii, 8, 14, 101, 102, 118, 123, 165, 288, 295, 297, 308, 316, 318, 322, 331, 336, 341, 343, 346
  and economics, 28, 123, 156, 165
  neoclassical distrust of, xvii, 117–18
solipsism, 115
sovereign, Hobbesian, 154, 156–7
Soviet Union, 255, 277, 292, 334, 336
spontaneous order, 137–8, 238, 290–1
Sraffian economics, xx, 21, 89, 275, 320
state, the, 147, 151–6, 159, 164, 217, 220, 228, 243–5, 251–2, 268, 270, 281, 290–1, 292, 293, 295–6, 302, 303, 310, 316, 319, 322, 334, 341
  distinguished from government, 153
  intervention of, 151–3, 220–1, 232, 251–4, 339
  liberal view of, 147, 152–6, 159, 228–9, 290–1, 292
  its relation to society, 152–6, 159, 292, 293
statism, 251, 259, 269
stock markets, 185, 188, 219, 220, 222, 223
subjectivism, 7–8, 36–7, 54, 115, 121–3, 133, 177, 178, 205–6, 237, 239, 246–7, 250–1, 267, 269, 301, 303, 325, 343
symbolism, 119, 123, 133, 166, 227, 296
systems, informal, 263
systems theory, 11, 12–21, 69, 110, 167–8, 224, 257–8, 276, 306, 307, 308, 309, 310, 312, 316, 327, 328, 332, 335
  false hopes in, 18

tacit knowledge, 6, 126, 259, 286–7, 336
tastes, *see* preferences
technology
  endogeneity of, 13–21, 243, 265, 337
  and skills, 127–8, 131, 142–4
  as a socio-physical phenomenon, 14–15, 213–14, 333
  transformation of, 19–20, 23, 131–2, 209, 212–13, 242, 262, 316, 317, 342
Tinbergen's rule, 257–8

Toronto, 186
trade unions, 233–4, 240, 253, 265, 317
transaction costs, 26, 79–80, 155, 180–1, 187, 199–208, 212–13, 293, 297, 299, 301, 314, 315, 330, 336, 345
  lack of definition of, 200, 299
treason, 161
Troy, 343
trust, 116, 130, 160–2, 164–7, 170, 209–11, 213, 271–2, 295–6, 308, 317, 329

UK, *see* Britain,
uncertainty, xviii, 4, 5, 10, 17, 24, 43, 78–9, 83–4, 85, 132–3, 135, 144, 158–60, 167, 184, 190, 193, 198–208, 212–13, 217–20, 221, 225, 226, 229–30, 233, 238, 240, 245, 263, 275, 289–90, 295, 301, 306, 314, 318, 320, 321, 322, 323, 324, 325, 326, 327, 336, 338, 341, 342, 343, 344, 345
  distinguished from risk, 188, 204, 218–19, 233, 301
unemployment, xv, 47, 220–1, 233–4, 257, 265, 274, 292, 295, 303, 306, 308, 315, 317, 325, 336, 337
USA, xiii, xv, 45, 129, 162, 163, 270, 275, 294, 305, 312, 323, 339
  productivity growth in, xiii–xiv, 273, 275
USSR, 255, 277, 292, 334, 336
utilitarianism, 25, 55, 93–7, 136, 147, 157–9, 166–7, 211–12, 213, 243, 247–8, 285, 286, 293–4, 339
utility, 59, 67, 74–6, 94, 112, 117, 247, 295, 303, 312, 313, 317, 326, 330, 331, 335, 338, 339
  *see also* preferences
utility functions, interdependent, 67

value, labour theory of, 65–6, 283, 293, 322, 325
values, normative, 42–3, 97, 243, 315
variety, agent, 258, 264–7
  environmental, 257–8, 262–5
  insufficient, 257–8, 262–7, 303–4
  requisite, 168, 257–8, 276, 316
Versailles, 227
Vienna School, 38
Vietnam, 343
voting, paradox of, 92, 93

wages, xiii xiv, 149, 150, 175, 233–4, 272, 292, 306, 308, 317, 336

rigidity of, 150, 240
and unemployment, xiii, xiv, 233–4, 292, 308
wants
  distinguished from needs, 246–7
  moulded by activities, 94, 312
  unlimited, 292
war, 135–6, 324
water-diamonds paradox, 303
welfare economics, 26, 53, 135, 151–2, 242–52, 292, 318, 319, 342

wholes and parts, 66–71, 261, 327
  *see also* systems theory
women, subjugation of, 136
  *see also* feminism
worker cooperatives, 215–16, 323, 341
worker participation, 210, 215–16, 249, 265–7, 294, 301, 307, 309, 316, 321, 322, 323, 335, 341, 342, 343

X-efficiency, 79, 291, 314, 317, 328